# Stop and Go

Publication Series of the Academy of Fine Arts Vienna
Eva Blimlinger, Andrea B. Braidt, Karin Riegler (Series Eds.)
Volume 23

# Stop and Go
Nodes of Transformation and Transition
Michael Hieslmair
and Michael Zinganel
(Eds.)

Sternberg Press

On the Publication Series

We are pleased to present the latest volume in the Academy of Fine Arts Vienna's publication series. The series, published in cooperation with our highly committed partner Sternberg Press, is devoted to central themes of contemporary thought about art practices and theories. The volumes comprise contributions on subjects that form the focus of discourse in art theory, cultural studies, art history, and research at the Academy of Fine Arts Vienna and represent the quintessence of international study and discussion taking place in the respective fields. Each volume is published in the form of an anthology, edited by staff members of the academy. Authors of high international repute are invited to make contributions that deal with the respective areas of emphasis. Research activities such as international conferences, lecture series, institute-specific research focuses, or research projects serve as points of departure for the individual volumes.

All books in the series undergo a single blind peer review. International reviewers, whose identities are not disclosed to the editors of the volumes, give an in-depth analysis and evaluation for each essay. The editors then rework the texts, taking into consideration the suggestions and feedback of the reviewers who, in a second step, make further comments on the revised essays. The editors—and authors—thus receive what is so rare in academia and also in art universities: committed, informed, and hopefully impartial critical feedback that can be used for finishing the work.

We would like to thank the editors of this volume, Michael Hieslmair and Michael Zinganel, for proposing this volume. It is the outcome of a research project funded by the FWF, the Austrian Science Fund, within the program of development of the arts (PEEK). Hieslmair and Zinganel are both leading figures in the field of artistic research in Europe and their methodology of employing artistic practices within sociological questioning has for many years been "best practice" in the field. We are happy that they brought together artists and theoreticians for the timely topic of location studies and the highly charged places of interlocution on the rhizomatic space we call "Europe." We would like to thank Michael Hieslmair and Michael Zinganel for their excellent work and their commitment to the Academy of Fine Arts Vienna, as well as the authors for their contributions. As always, we are grateful to all the partners contributing to the book, especially Sternberg Press.

The Rectorate of the Academy of Fine Arts Vienna Eva Blimlinger,
Andrea B. Braidt, Karin Riegler

This is a peer-reviewed publication. We thank the anonymous reviewers for their in-depth comments and advice.

Editors: Michael Hieslmair and Michael Zinganel
Editorial Coordinator: Iris Weißenböck
English translation and copyediting: Peter Blakeney and Christine Schöffler, Jill Denton, Michael Haagensen, Peter Merriman, Tim Sharp, and the authors
Proofreader: Claire Cahm
Cover image: Michael Hieslmair and Michael Zinganel
Design: Anna Landskron, Surface, Frankfurt am Main/Berlin
Printing: Holzhausen Druck GmbH, Wolkersdorf
Binding: Buchbinderei Papyrus, Vienna

This book is a result of the project "Stop and Go: Nodes of Transformation and Transition," which was supported by the WWTF—Vienna Science and Technology Fund. https://tracingspaces.net

ISBN 978-3-95679-495-7

© 2019 Akademie der bildenden Künste Wien, Sternberg Press
All rights reserved, including the right of reproduction in whole or in part in any form.

Sternberg Press
Caroline Schneider
Karl-Marx-Allee 78
D-10243 Berlin
www.sternberg-press.com

# Contents

**Placeholder/Substitution
Artist Insert**
Sonia Leimer    10

**Road Map of Research:
Introduction**
Michael Zinganel    14

## Interrelated Networks: Material and Social Infrastructure between the Former East and West of Europe

**Networking Eurasia:
Bulgarian International Truck Drivers and SOMAT in the Cold War Era**
Emiliya Karaboeva    40

**Memoryscapes and the Legacy of SOMAT Networks and Nodes Today:
Reflections on the Applied Methodology**
Michael Zinganel, Michael Hieslmair, and Emiliya Karaboeva    68

## Corridors into Vienna and Beyond: The Bus, the Terminal, the Border—Infrastructural Publics and Politics

Gates to the City: Transformations and Encounters at Vienna's
International Coach Terminals
Michael Hieslmair                                                                 88

Check Point Nickelsdorf, 2015: Reactivation of a Border
for the Mobilization of Forced Migration
Michael Zinganel and Michael Hieslmair                                            120

## Tallinn Harbor: Rhythms of a Road to Sea Bottleneck and the Effects on the City

A Speaking Passenger Network Diagram:
Reflections on the Applied Methodology
Michael Zinganel, Michael Hieslmair, and Tarmo Pikner                            144

Harbors and Practiced Lines:
Evolving Mobilities between Tallinn and Helsinki
Tarmo Pikner                                                                      156

## Corridors Rerouted and the Choice of Vehicles

Secondhand Car Markets and Mobilization in Eastern Europe
Michael Zinganel                                                                  184

From Guangdong to Wólka Kosowska: Migrants' Transnational Trade
Katarzyna Osiecka and Tatjana Vukosavljević                                       200

The Last European: A Romanian Driver Navigates the Soul of the EU
Juan Moreno                                                                       224

Retraveling and Reknotting Ideas and Interim Findings of Our Project:
Summary
Michael Zinganel                                                                  236

**Modernize or Die!**
**Artist Insert**
Johanna Kandl                                                          244

**Appendix**

**Image Credits**                                                      248

**Biographies**                                                        252

# Placeholder Substitution Artist Insert

Sonia Leimer

Sonia Leimer's artworks are situated between real spaces and imaginary contexts: Her "cut-outs," pieces of street asphalt, were extracted during construction work from the context of their functional use in real places as the surface of Viennese streets and carefully stored. These pure material appropriations, literally "registering" the traces of their use, are combined with steel and plastic elements, which refer to construction site barriers or (sub-constructions for) traffic signs and their visual language; these isolated fragments are open to multiple interpretations on archaeological, psychoanalytical, political, and poetic levels. (Michael Hieslmair and Michael Zinganel)

Sonia Leimer

Figs. 1–3
Sonia Leimer, *Untitled*, 2015–16

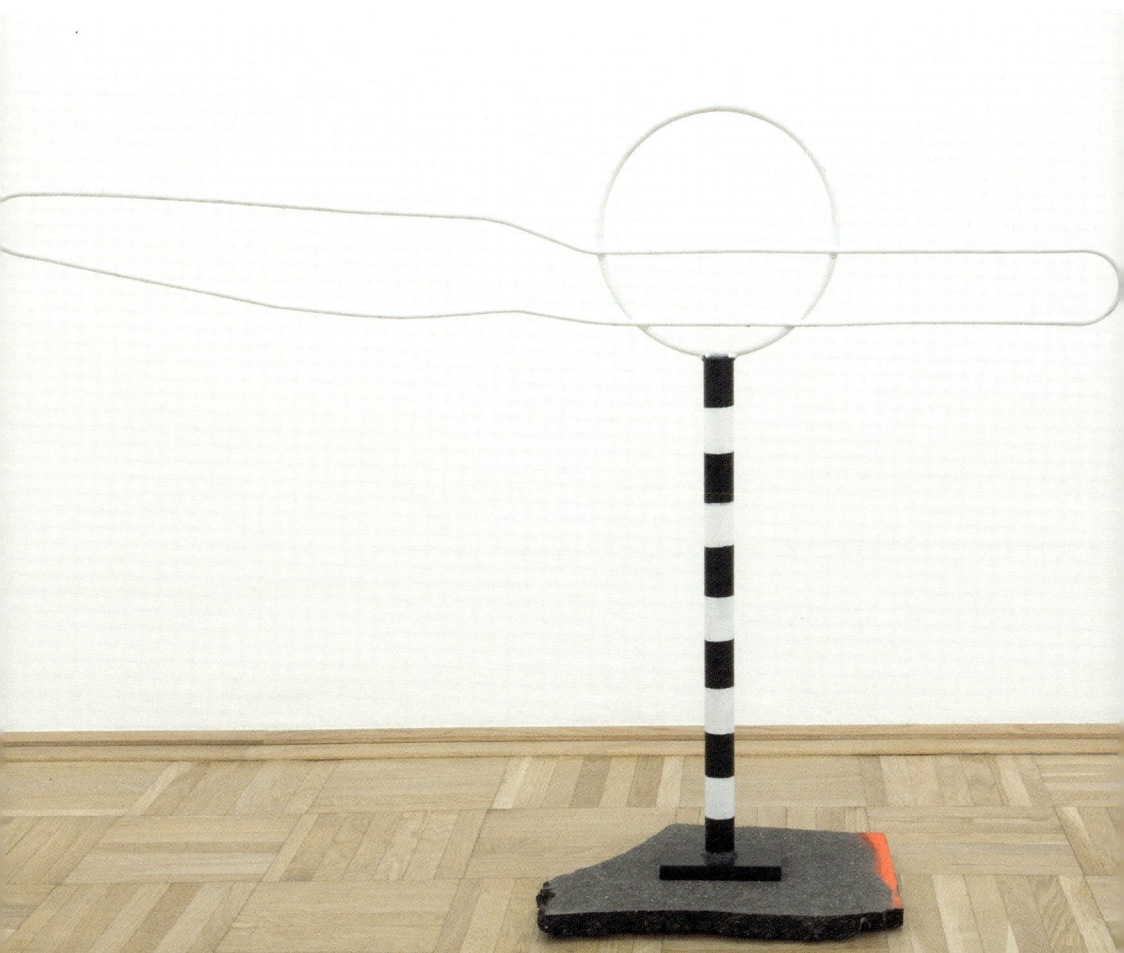

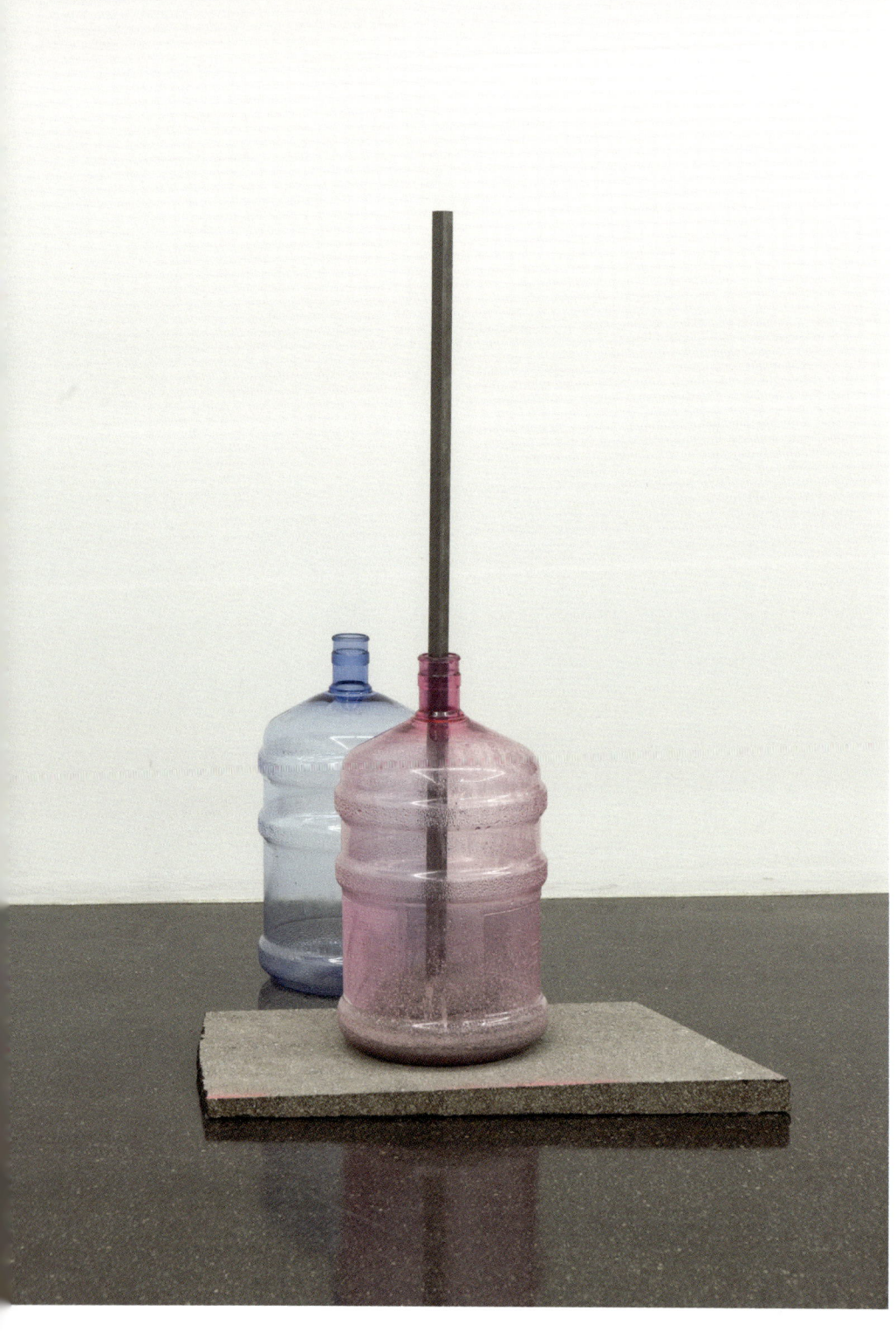

Sonia Leimer

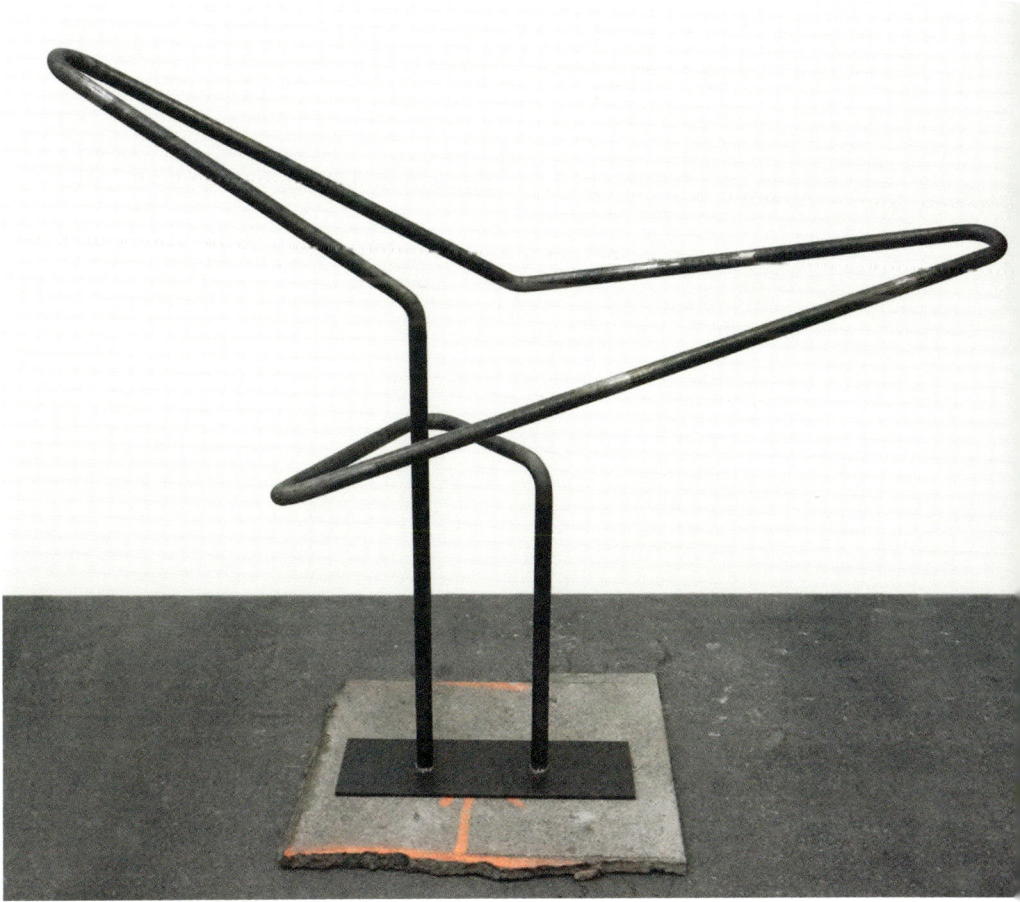

# Road Map of Research
# Introduction

Michael Zinganel

When increasing numbers of people are obliged to spend increasing amounts of time in transit, then routes, corridors, vehicles, and stopping points become operationalized as important public places for dwelling-in-transit (rather than as generic nonplaces). Here trade might happen, rituals and routines are developed, contacts initiated with regions of origin or target. This is also where those who were mobile before engage in cultivating and maintaining on-the-spot, fragmented communities. Here we can observe a "vernacular cosmopolitanism"[1] and "doing with space" becomes a kind of "knotting":[2] a multi and trans-local mobile culture of integration specific alongside these road corridors. The alternative models of urbanism that ensue from the paradigmatic shift at these spaces are shaped by polyrhythmic densifications and the continual performance of difference such as also increasingly inform our everyday lives. These nodes and knots are perfect places to investigate not only the strategies of (supra-)national institutions to control mobilities but also to examine how this "knotting" is practiced on site in a widely mobile/mobilized life and what kind of publics are already articulated.

After the fall of the Iron Curtain, "leaking eddies of small-scale traders" began to spread along the road corridors between what was the East and the West. According to Karl Schlögel, these were responsible for furthering the unification of Europe from below well before EU financing resulted in the development of the infrastructure and likewise before the large-scale logistics companies built their huge hubs and trading centers.[3] But the implementation of new modern traffic infrastructure went hand in hand with the expansion of the EU, albeit with different delays, speeds, and qualities. New highways might improve accessibility and accelerate connections between some places but will eventually also disrupt access between others by interrupting old paths or by bypassing entire regions. On new highways, the flow of traffic becomes increasingly organized and monitored, and there is hardly any place left for traders who attempt to earn a living by doing business by the side of the road, like those alongside the old low-speed corridors that pass through villages and towns, and especially close to major crossroads or border stations.

---

1  Homi Bhabha, "Unsatisfied: Notes on Vernacular Cosmopolitanism," in *Text and Nation*, ed. Laura Garcia-Morena and Peter C. Pfeifer (London: Camden House, 2001), 191–207.

2  See Michel Lussault and Mathis Stock, "Doing with Space: Towards a Pragmatics of Space," *Social Geography* 5, no. 1 (2010): 12; Sarah Green, "Anthropological Knots," *Hau: Journal of Ethnographic Theory* 4, no. 3 (2014): 1–21; and Tim Ingold, *The Life of Lines* (New York: Routledge, 2015).

3  Karl Schlögel, "Die Ameisenhändler vom Bahnhof Zoo: Über Geschichte im Abseits und vergessene Europäer," *Osteuropa* 11 (2009): 53–60.

The central questions of this project are: How have formal and informal nodes and knots of transnational mobilities alongside the major road corridors in the triangle between Vienna, Tallinn, and the Turkish-Bulgarian border been redeveloped and transformed since the fall of the Iron Curtain and the expansion of the European Union? What is this transformation doing to people and how are these nodes and knots being appropriated and transformed here into anchors in the everyday lives of their multi-local existence? Our perspective: the city of Vienna, a capital of the "former West," but once the center of a multi-national European empire and an important meeting point between the East and West during the Cold War, has been crisscrossed by traffic corridors connecting the East and West of Europe. By examining the changes in transnational mobility patterns starting from and arriving here, the post-socialist transformation of the wider geopolitical sphere—the former East of Europe—can easily be investigated. Transnational routes lead to the north- and south-east, for instance to Tallinn and the Bulgarian-Turkish border region, both located in the "former East" of Europe, at the two opposite ends of an important north-south axis (within the East), characterized by quite different geopolitical constellations and tensions, both historically and in contemporary political transitions and urban transformations. This post-socialist transformation, understood as "a process of decolonizing and disclosing the Cold War European mind and its spaces," "arrived with intense commitments to market reform, liberalization and internationalization of the economy, as well as to fast capitalism and primitive accumulation," "producing new class formations and deepening divisions between the winners and losers."[4] The regions we investigated (including Vienna) differ significantly in terms of state regulation, graduations between formal and informal economy and governance,[5] the discrimination of minorities, (de-)mobilization, the increase of transit and labor migration, and even the quantity and quality of the design of roads and roadside infrastructure.

The chapters of this book are based on fieldwork conducted during the research project "Stop and Go—Nodes of Transformation and Transition" (2014–16), hosted by the Academy of Fine Arts in Vienna and funded by the WWTF—Vienna Science and Technology Fund under the 2013 call *Public Spaces in Transition*. Principal investigators were the Vienna-based cultural historian Michael Zinganel and the architect and artist Michael Hieslmair, supported by international research partners at each research destination: for Bulgaria, the anthropologist Emiliya Karaboeva, from Eindhoven and Plovdiv Universities, and for Estonia and the Baltic, the geographer Tarmo Pikner, researcher at the Center of Cultural Studies of the Estonian Institute of Humanities, Tallinn University.

## Infrastructure, Power, and the Everyday Life on the Road

Since the discourse on globalization has denounced the restrictive mandate underpinning the "container theory" of space and its "methodological nationalism" as historical fiction,[6] mobility is discussed in the context of a "mobility continuum" that extends from one extreme form, tourism, to the other, migration.[7] These two forms of mobility are no longer perceived as dichotomies however. Instead, the focus has now shifted to their common and interchangeable features, indeed, even to their contingency on one another, which is also true for the logistics of transporting goods and refugee aid.

With the announcement of a general "mobilities turn" in humanities,[8] now infrastructure and logistics also seem to be a hot issue: Anna Tsing, for instance, theorized supply chain capitalism as a model for understanding both the continent-crossing scale and the constitutive diversity of contemporary global capitalism. In contrast with theories of growing capitalist homogeneity, her analysis points to the structural role of difference in the mobilization of capital, labor, and resources.[9] Deborah Cowen's book *The Deadly Life of Logistics: Mapping Violence in Global Trade* made it an even hotter issue: although the object of corporate and governmental logistical efforts is commodity supply, she demonstrates that they are deeply political—and, when considered in the context of the long history of logistics, deeply indebted to the practice of war (and colonialism).[10]

But what has been missing in critical Marxist and postcolonial critique of global capitalism and the spatial and functional analyses of logistic landscapes is the logistic landscape as a place of everyday encounter and experience. Ole B. Jensen, for instance, argues that "critical mobility thinking" should also "[re-concep-

4  John Pickles, "'New Cartographies' and the Decolonization of European Geographies," *Area* 37, no. 4 (December 2005): 359.
5  See e.g.: Jeremy Morris and Abel Polese, eds., *The Informal Post-socialist Economy: Embedded Practices and Livelihoods* (London: Routledge, 2014); Martin Demant Frederiksen and Ida Harboe Knudsen, eds., *Ethnographies of Grey Zones in Eastern Europe: Relations, Borders and Invisibilities* (London: Anthem Press, 2015); and many more mentioned later in this publication.
6  Helmuth Berking, "Raumtheoretische Paradoxien im Globalisierungsdiskurs," in *Die Macht des Lokalen in einer Welt ohne Grenzen*, ed. Helmuth Berking (Frankfurt am Main: Campus Verlag, 2006), 7–22.
7  See Zygmunt Bauman, *Liquid Modernity* (Cambridge: Polity Press, 2000); and Michael Hall and Alan M. Williams, eds., *Tourism and Migration: New Relationships between Production and Consumption* (London: Kluwer Academic Publishing, 2002).
8  E.g., John Urry, *Mobilities* (Cambridge: Polity Press, 2007); Tim Cresswell, "Towards a Politics of Mobility," *Environment and Planning D: Society and Space* 28, no. 1 (2010): 17–31; and Tim Cresswell and Peter Merriman, eds., *Geographies of Mobilities: Practices, Spaces, Subjects* (Farnham and Burlington, VT: Ashgate, 2011); among others.
9  Anna Tsing, "Supply Chains and the Human Condition," *Rethinking Marxism* 21, no. 2 (April 2009): 148–76.
10 Deborah Cowen, "A Geography of Logistics: Market Authority and the Security of Supply Chains," *Annals of the Association of American Geographers* 100, no. 3 (2010): 600–20.

tualize] mobility and infrastructures as sites of (potential) meaningful interaction, pleasure, and cultural production," where people engage in "negotiation in motion" and "mobile sense making"; and also to respect the material and affective dimensions of everyday social life en route or on hold.[11]

Another very different but equally productive approach, spreading around the humanities, is to discuss the relations of publics and infrastructures: Penny Harvey and Hannah Knox and Collier in "Publics Infrastructures/Infrastructural Public" analyze with reference to John Dewey how technical infrastructure projects induce or support the constitution of certain temporary publics, e.g., organizing against the construction, or in favor of the construction, and how specific communication and transport infrastructures enable the continuity of trans-local publics.[12]

Lyubomir Pozharliev, for instance, describes the effects of the construction of the Highway of Brotherhood and Unity in the 1940s and 1950s in socialist Yugoslavia, which was originally intended to support the formation of a trans-ethnic collective but through choice of route in fact contributed to reestablishing and reenforcing uneven economic developments in the federation and furthering the "peripheralization" of underprivileged regions.[13] Besides this, it was also used for purposes it was not planned for: foreign tourist transit, transcontinental cargo transport and labor migration. In two brilliant comprehensive anthropologies of roads, Penny Harvey and Hannah Knox reflected on both the conflicts caused *by* and the enchantment people attribute *to* a Peruvian road while under planning and (re-)construction,[14] while Dimitris Dalakoglou investigated a road between Albania and Greece, scaling up and down from the intimate interactions in a small Albanian town, to the political ambitions of the state, and to the cross-border migrations that structure Albania today. Roads, for Dalakoglou, are also anxious technologies, promising gifts but also bringing dangers: smuggling, drugs, human trafficking, and money laundering.[15] Here infrastructures like roads and road corridors are perceived as technical networks—representing tools of governance and governmentality. But simultaneously they are also perceived as "aesthetic networks," which support the circulation of people, goods, and capital, but also images, imaginaries and desires.[16]

## Pan-European Road Corridors

Pan-European transport-corridor(s) is the term used to describe the transport connections between the former Eastern European countries and Western Europe, intended to network Europe in vital ways. The ten corridors (fig. 4) were already defined at the second Pan-European Transport Conference in Crete, in March 1994, at the height of hostilities between the states that made up former Yugoslavia, and a year before Austria, Sweden, and Finland joined the EU, and even many more years before the former Eastern European nations followed. Additions were made at the third conference in Helsinki in 1997, regarding which routes in Central and Eastern Europe required major investment over the next fifteen years.[17]

Despite also producing unintended side effects for many regions, the implementation and upgrading of traffic corridors is the unquestioned core project of EU infrastructural planning.[18] We are dealing here with monuments to the modernization of both state and multi-state organizations, exceptional technical achievements and financial investments, which while being planned, built, and extended, are facing conflicting ideas even from inside the planning consortium and its experts and political and economic pressure from outside (including, for instance, protests against expropriation and ecological counter-arguments).[19] Since they are often contested they are subject to strict controls or at least a marked will toward the imposition of order and control. At the same time, however, they also stand for a great reserve of imagination and imaginaries to which individuals and institutions attach a great number of dreams (and nightmares).[20]

11  Ole B. Jensen, "Negotiation in Motion: Unpacking a Geography of Mobility," *Space and Culture* 13, no. 4 (2010): 389–402; Ole B. Jensen, *Staging Mobilities* (London: Routledge, 2013). For research about and by means of journeys with different kinds of vehicles see, for example, Tim Edensor, "M6 Junction 19–16: Defamiliarising the Mundane Landscape," *Space and Culture* 6, no. 2 (2003): 151–68; David Bissell, "Passenger Mobilities: Affective Atmospheres and the Sociality of Public Transport," *Environment and Planning D: Society and Space* 28, no. 2 (2010): 270–89; Eric Laurier et al., "Driving and 'Passengering': Notes on the Ordinary Organization of Car Travel," *Mobilities* 3, no. 1 (2008): 1–23; Eric Laurier and Hayden Lorimer, "Other Ways: Landscapes of commuting," *Landscape Research*, 37, 2 (2012): 207–24; Alan Latham and Peter Woods, "Inhabiting Infrastructure: Exploring the Interactional Spaces of Urban Cycling," *Environment and Planning A* 47 (2015): 300–19; Phillip Vannini, "The Techne of Making a Ferry: A Non-representational Approach to Passengers' Gathering Taskscapes," *Journal of Transport Geography* 19, no. 5 (2011): 1031–36.
12  Penny Harvey and Hannah Knox, *Roads: An Anthropology of Infrastructure and Expertise* (Ithaca, NY: Cornell University Press, 2015); Stephen J. Collier, James Christopher Mizes, and Antina von Schnitzler, eds., "Public Infrastructures/Infrastructural Publics," *Limn* 7 (2017); and John Dewey, *The Public and Its Problems* (Athens, Ohio: Ohio University Press, 1927).
13  Lyubomir Pozharliev, "Collectivity vs. Connectivity: Highway Peripheralization in Former Yugoslavia (1940s–1980s)," *The Journal of Transport History* 37, no. 2 (2016): 194–213.
14  Harvey and Knox, *Roads*.
15  Dimitris Dalakoglou, *The Road: An Ethnography of (Im)mobility, Space, and Cross border Infrastructures in the Balkans* (Manchester: Manchester University Press, 2017), 11 and 13.
16  Brian Larkin, "The Politics and Poetics of Infrastructure," *Annual Review of Anthropology* 42 (2013): 327–43.
17  Therefore, these corridors are sometimes referred to as the "Crete corridors" or "Helsinki corridors," regardless of their geographical locations. These development corridors had been distinct from the Trans-European transport networks, which include all major established routes within the European Union. There are proposals to combine the two systems, since most of the involved countries are now members of the EU.
18  Tim Richardson, "Making European Spaces: New Corridors in Eastern Europe," in *Transiträume: Transit Spaces*, ed. Regina Bittner, Wilfried Hackenbroich, and Kai Vöckler, Edition Bauhaus, vol. 19 (Berlin: Jovis Verlag, 2006), 50–73.
19  Harvey and Knox, *Roads*.
20  Michel Foucault, "Of Other Spaces," trans. Jay Miskowiec, *Diacritics* 16, no. 1 (1986): 22–27.

These range from anticipated economic growth and transnational reconciliation to troop deployment capabilities (on the part of the government), from motorized escapes away from petit bourgeois parental homes or anything alienating one's daily routine into the freedom of holidays to even labor migration and the mass exodus of refugees from war-torn regions.

Hence, "any given road or highway is socio-culturally many highways at the same time. [...] The meanings of a road as a product are open to [those who build it and] those who use it, experience its existence, [...] or even just expect it, or its rhythmic flows."[21] In fact, while being built and in operation these corridors function as magnets,[22] attracting both things and individuals that move into their orbit or accumulate around them.[23] These experiences are registered and reflected in construction records, official monitoring body statistics, mass media news clips, stories of the daily lives of road users and residents, popular songs, artworks, and research reports like ours.

## Investigating and Driving Nodes and Knots of Transnational Mobilities

In our research project we expanded the focus on a variety of mobile actors and the places where, for various reasons, the flow of traffic stops or is interrupted—bus terminals, ferry ports, parking spaces for international lorry drivers, TIR stops (named after the transnational transport organization TIR[24]), motorway service stations, logistics centers, formal and informal markets, or border crossing stations along the corridors. The strategies of both the government (and supragovernmental) institutions and large-scale concerns can be discerned from how they control the flows of mobility. This applies to the different routes as well as the motives and mobility biographies of the passing actors, "doing with" or "performing" space in various ways.[25] Sometimes, during the process, these anthropological non-places[26]—where, at best, objects communicate with each other—undergo transmutation into intimate anchor points in the daily routines of the multi-local existences of highly mobile subjects. They become places where trade might happen and where rituals and routines of relaxation are developed, contacts initiated with regions in which their destinations, origins, or targets lie, but these places are also where they engage in cultivating and maintaining the on-the-spot, fragmented communities. They are places to be inhabited for short periods of a break, overnight or sometimes even for weekends.

By describing driving as a social practice and the motorway as a place always in a state of becoming, Peter Merriman brilliantly deconstructed Marc Augè's notion of non-places,[27] still largely prevalent in the field of art and architecture. Samuel Austin juxtaposes Augè's negative perception, with similar ideas of highway stations as decentered, interrelated places of process, blurring the distinctions of local and global, place and non-place.[28] During pauses in truck drivers' auto-motion, Nicki Gregson argues, the space of the cab, made economic through driving the logistic network of supply chain capitalism, is morphed into a cozy and habitable space for dwelling in transit, a home-from-home.[29]

This continuous transformation *of* and *at* these transit spaces generates the development of a dynamic polycentric model of a multi-local (sub-)urbanity or post-urbanity comprising interconnected archipelagos whereby each represents only a single station on a route taken by individuals or objects in their vehicles.[30] They are not, however, permanent and may become obsolete or fall into disrepair to be replaced by new nodes (elsewhere). Alternatively, informal nodes may tend to become formalized and controlled so that new informal nodes pop up in other places.

Marxist thinkers in general, especially Michel de Certeau and Henry Lefebvre,[31] harshly criticized transnational streetscapes as both symbols *of* and vehicles *for* the expansion of global capitalism. And, although they juxtapose driving roads with their own rather romantic perception of face-to-face interaction when walking the city, they offered a perfect basis for also analyzing peoples' tactics for selecting, approaching and inhabiting such nodes and for appropriating and coproducing social space there. Following Michel de Certeau's distinction between "strategies" (of those in power) and "tactics" (of tricksters) we propose to introduce the notions of "nodes" and "knots," where nodes are constituted by strategies of powerful institutions within logistic networks and the network of road corridors, whereas

21 Dalakoglou, *The Road*, 11, 13.
22 Kathleen Stewart, "Road Registers," *Cultural Geographies* 21, no. 4 (2014): 552.
23 E.g., the enormous demand for labor force needed for the construction and expansion of such large-scale projects also caused and will cause waves of labor migration.
24 TIR stands for "Transports Internationaux Routiers," a multilateral organization established soon after the end of Second World War to simplify and harmonize the administrative formalities of international road transport.
25 Michel Lussault and Mathis Stock, "Doing with Space: Towards a Pragmatics of Space," *Social Geography* 5, no. 1 (2010): 12.
26 Mark Augè, *Non-places: Introduction to an Anthropology of Supermodernity* (New York: Verso Books, 1995).
27 Peter Merriman, *Driving Spaces: A Cultural-historical Geography of England's M1 Motorway* (Oxford: Blackwell Publishing, 2007).
28 Samuel Austin, "Travels in Lounge Space: Placing the Contemporary British Motorway Service Area," PhD thesis at the Welsh School of Architecture, Cardiff University, 2011.
29 Nicky Gregson, "Mobilities, Mobile Work and Habitation: Truck Drivers and the Crisis in Occupational Auto-mobility in the UK," *Mobilities* (2018).
30 See also Regina Bittner, Wilfried Hackenbroich, and Kai Vöckler, eds., *Transiträume: Transit Spaces*, Edition Bauhaus, vol. 19 (Berlin: Jovis Verlag, 2006); and Susanne Hauser, "Die Ästhetik der Agglomeration," in *B1/A40: The Beauty of the Grand Road*, ed. MAPS Markus Ambach Projekte et al. (Berlin: Jovis Verlag, 2010), 202–13.
31 Henri Lefebvre, *The Production of Space* (Oxford: Blackwell, 1991); and Michel De Certeau, *The Practice of Everyday Life* (Berkeley: University of California Press, 1984).

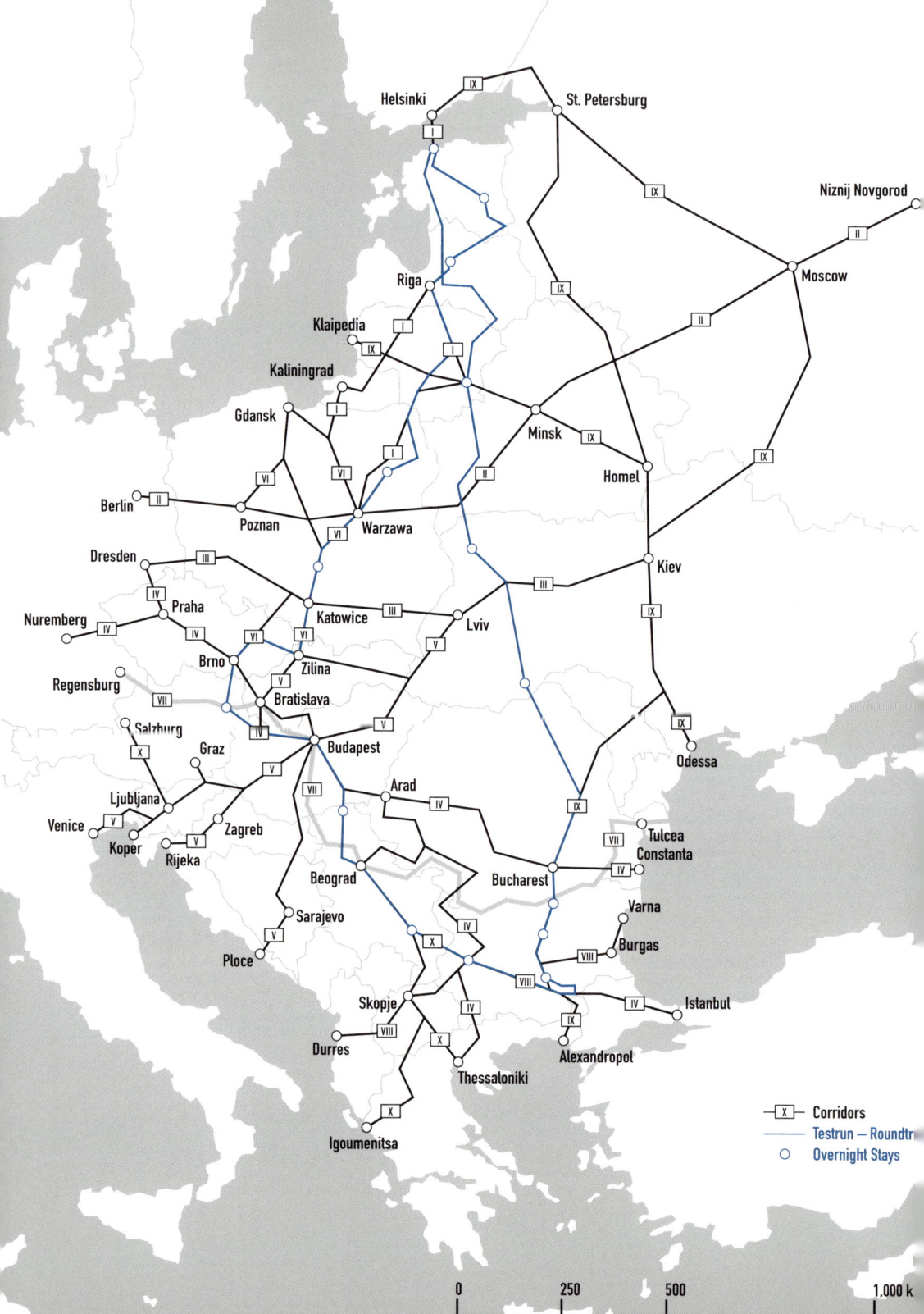

Fig. 4
Hieslmair and Zinganel, 2018
Map of the ten so-called Pan-European traffic corridors, defined in 1994 and 1997 and intended to interconnect the former communist East and capitalist West of Europe; the roads driven and investigated by the research team are marked in blue.

knots are established by the tactics of individuals to fulfil their everyday needs in transit. Nodes and knots can be independent from one another, but they are not always distinct, they often overlap, when existing nodes are used for the individuals' practice of knotting. With reference to Lefebvre's "Rhythmanalyses," these nodes and knots represent "polyrhythmic" ensembles of (post-)urban architecture, mobile objects, and individuals that are dependent on rhythmic flows of traffic that fluctuate on a daily, weekly, or seasonal basis, only to contract again, challenging the traditional notion of public space.[32]

## Mobilizing Ourselves by the Mobile Lab

Investigations of such places, constituted by polyrhythmic flows of people and vehicles, obviously also mean driving these routes and following the fluid characters from one stop to the next. In response to the call from Mobilities Studies protagonists for "mobile methods,"[33] we proposed a mobile ethnography enabling us to become physically immersed in mobile activities while simultaneously working on material and visual representations of networked mobilities.

The core elements of investigation were to be intensive research trips along the geographic triangle of Vienna, Tallinn, and the Bulgarian-Turkish border (fig. 4). Hence, we wanted to rent a small van to pull a trailer that could be used both as a mobile toolbox and a fold-out display for producing large-scale mapping exercises in our projected field of research. However, we came to learn that there was no chance of renting any vehicle to drive to high-risk areas like the Baltic states, Romania, Serbia, or Bulgaria due to potential car theft. So we needed to purchase a secondhand vehicle ourselves. But after a desperate search we could not find any smaller car for a reasonable price, outside of a large Ford Transit transporter van (fig. 5).

32 Henri Lefebvre, *Rhythmanalysis: Space, Time and Everyday Life* (London: Bloomsbury Academic, 2013). See also Michael Crang, "Rhythms of the City: Temporalised Space and Motion," in *Timespace: Geographies of Temporality*, ed. Jon May and Nigel Thrift (London: Routledge, 2001), 187–207; Tim Edensor, "Introduction: Thinking about Rhythm and Space," in *Geographies of Rhythm: Nature, Place, Mobilities and Bodies*, ed. Tim Edensor (London: Ashgate, 2010), 1–20.

33 Monica Büscher and John Urry, "Mobile Methods and the Empirical," *European Journal of Social Theory* 12 (February 2009): 99–116.

The van also helped us to assimilate into the field of research: it looked like so many other vans driving the very same routes. And when waiting at one of the nodes, nothing helps you strike up a little conversation more easily than talking about your own experience with the vehicle itself, the items loaded, the workload of the driver, the route, the rhythm, the trouble with police and border controls, or the transport business in general. Transporter vans like ours are an attractive choice for professionals to escape the strict regulations and control mechanisms imposed on drivers of full-size trucks. They offer the opportunity to drive seven days a week around the clock and bypass the long waiting queues of border controls for heavy trucks to transport goods and people—with or without proper papers. Transporter vans of this type are the favorite vehicles for fitters and market vendors. Thus, we eventually decided to follow their routes from wholesale markets to open-air markets and vice versa.

But actually, we were also stopped to purchase road tax discs close to each border station, to refill our gas tank every 650 kilometers at reliable-looking gas stations, to go to toilet, or to eat and drink what we considered "authentic" local or truck drivers' food. We had some areas in mind where to stay overnight—but we wanted to keep the freedom of choice where exactly to stop. So each day when the sun started to set we would go in search of cheap motels with parking lots, large enough to park our 14-meter-long van and trailer combination. The more LGV trucks and vans like ours, the safer we felt protected against car theft and street robbery. But unlike truck drivers, we decided not to sleep in our van. Checking into motels, having a beer at night and breakfast in the morning seemed more promising for triggering additional chances for conversations and interactions with experts working at these nodes of transnational mobilities! To anticipate potential stops, we traced our route on printed maps beforehand, attentively observed street side building types and signs, and stopped at gas stations with Wi-Fi access to google overnight accommodation we could reach before it got too dark. And—in case of emergency—we even asked a driver of another van with a regional number plate for advice, who personally guided us to the motel of a friend or cousin.

Of special interest to us had been the variety of highway service stations, and especially TIR stops, parking lots and service facilities specialized in HGV trucks and their drivers. While at newly constructed highway intersections national or private operator companies and professional gas stations are used to offering modern and well-serviced parking facilities for HGV trucks at a predefined distance to each other, along the many other roads which are not yet modernized, the quality of built infrastructure and services, the social status of operators and visitors—but also the visual language, communicating toward the road—differs radically: we stopped at super modern TIR stops with huge illuminated displays visible from a long distance, and with all kinds of facilities such as toilets, showers, laundry machines, special lounges for drivers, separated parking for small trucks,

Michael Zinganel

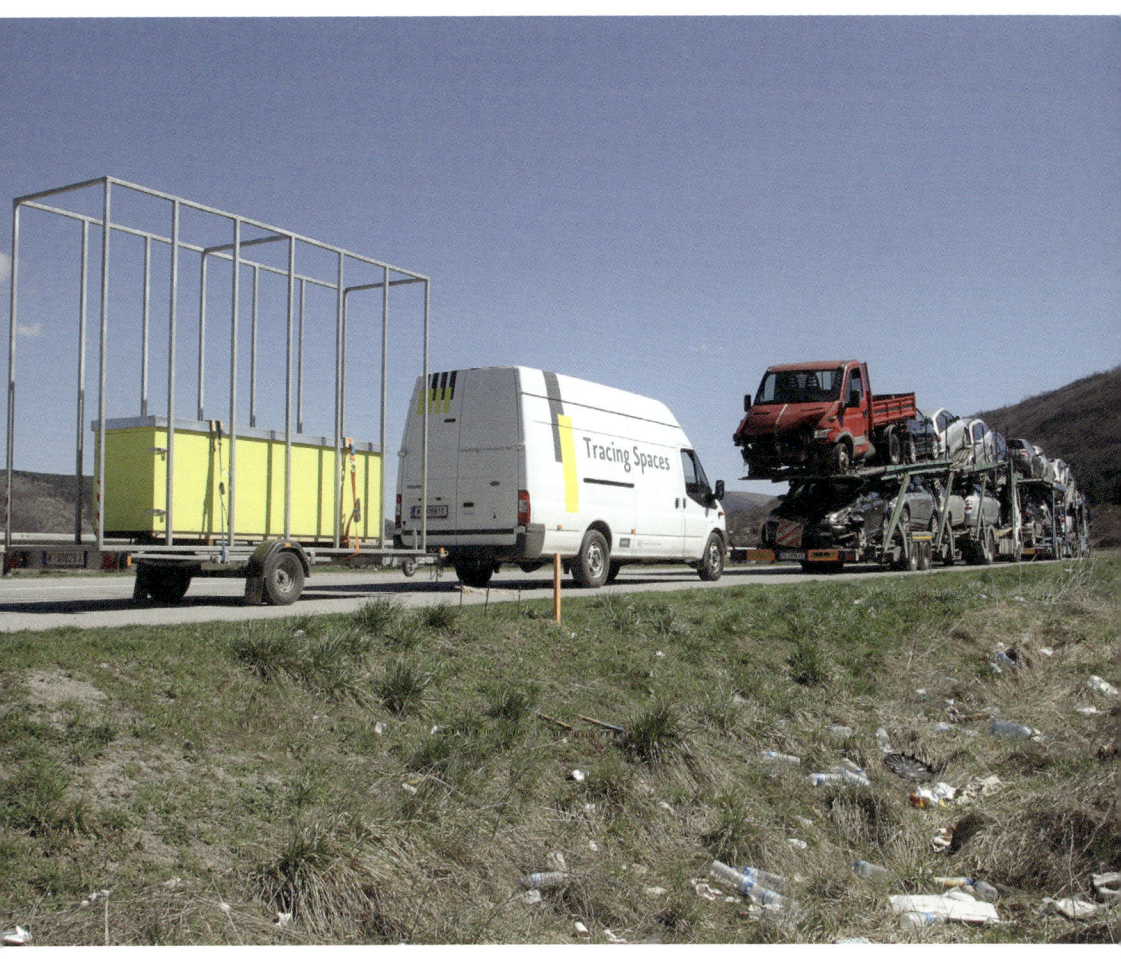

Fig. 5
Hieslmair and Zinganel, 2014
A Ford Transit transporter and a trailer equipped with tools for performing and documenting live mapping exercises, setting up on-site interventions, collecting and exhibiting material to trigger feedback on site, and heading for nodes and knots in a triangle between Vienna, Tallinn, and the Bulgarian-Turkish border; here queuing up at the Serbian border to Bulgaria.

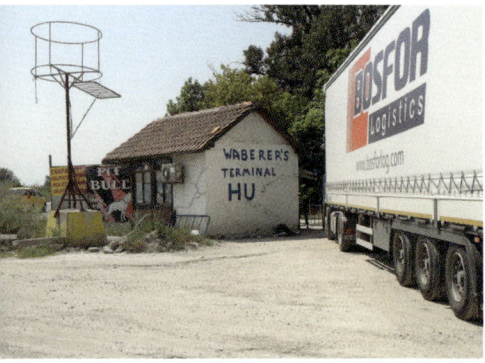
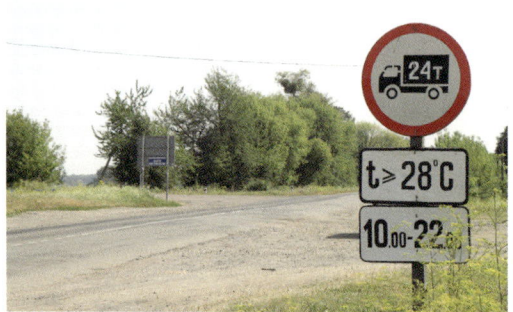
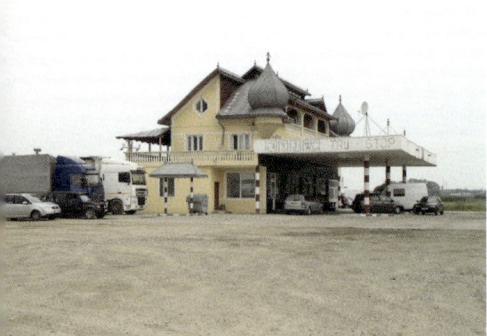
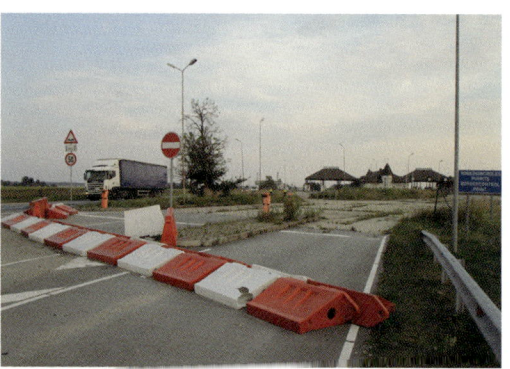
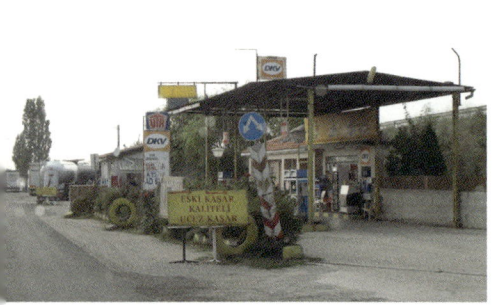
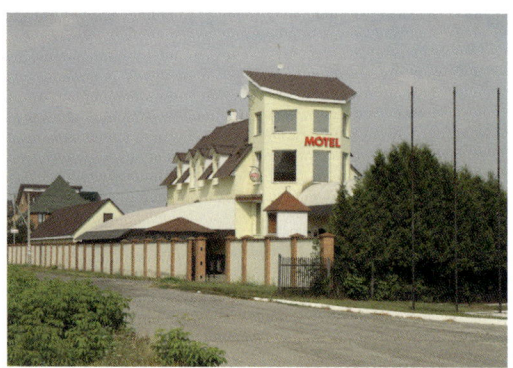
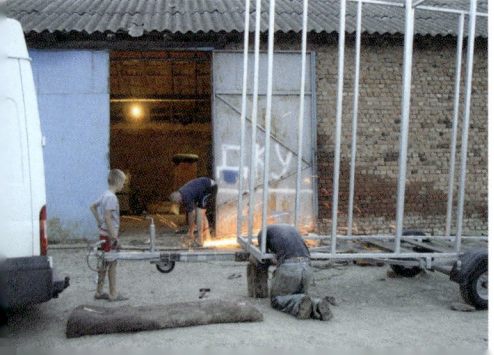
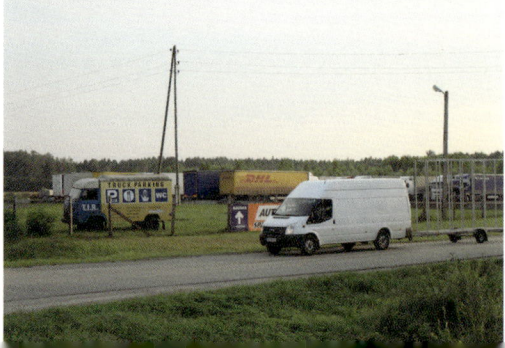

Figs. 6–13
Hieslmair and Zinganel, 2014
The many shades of gray at highway service stations
we passed on our way

Left column:
Corridor 7/E 45 in Bulgaria: basic truck parking, explicitly aimed at Hungarian drivers
Corridor 9/E 85 in Romania: an old gas station kiosk from communist times transformed into a generic rustic inn by a Roma family
Corridor 4/8 border crossing at Kapitan Andreewo-Kapıkule between Bulgaria and Turkey: informal border economy on the old road now in decline since being bypassed by the new freeway A 80
E 85/M 19 in northern Ukraine: repairing the trailer at a former kolkhoz (collective farm) after our tow bar snapped due to poor road conditions

Right column:
E 85/M 19 between Ternopil und Czernowitz, Ukraine: Road signs warning of a driving ban for trucks on hot summer days due to road surface issues
Corridor 1/E 67 border station between Latvia and Lithuania: opened in 1989, closed in 2007
E 85/M 19 between Ternopil and Czernowitz, Ukraine: brand-new basic motel facilities, typically fortified by a (prefab) wall and a little guardhouse
Corridor 1/E 67 north of Bauska, Latvia: A fenced-off piece of grassland with a container-toilet, -office, -bar, and -brothel, representing the most basic TIR stop in the Baltic region

standard HGV trucks, and refrigerated vehicles, even offering power supply jacks for their cooling units, because otherwise these vehicles have their engines running throughout the night. Many of these modern stations, built or modernized with European Union infrastructure funds, might at first sight match Marc Augè's perception of anthropological non-places, a-historic and highly regulated by predefined paths, regulations and barriers, and plenty of signs and billboards, control and surveillance technologies.

But by driving the roads and stopping at nodes, we at least attributed specific meanings to these places in the context of this travelogue. And depending on the time spent there and the interest we showed, they were transformed into spaces of aesthetic, gastronomic or social experience. Here we either observed, directly encountered, or recorded the individual experience of others, owning these spaces, working there or passing by. By means of participant observation, conversations—and the method of live mapping—or online research for gaining further information, what had been non-places before for others, soon became deeply loaded with history and histories to us.

And although the combination of the geopolitical sphere, the specific landscape, the many signs and billboards, and the design of buildings and vehicles, and the service advertised there, are far from being neutral, these elements constitute an emotional semiotic appeal. And to be frank, we often enjoyed stopping out of pure aesthetic interest and anthropological curiosity, triggered by the attraction of this visual language (figs. 6–13). For instance, we encountered such picturesque attractions as an old low-bed truck parked by the road carrying an even older municipal bus with signs on the windows advertising the services of a rather informal looking TIR stop on a vacant derelict industrial estate beyond it (fig. 14). Or we visited a graveled site by the roadside, where a local farmer was trying to

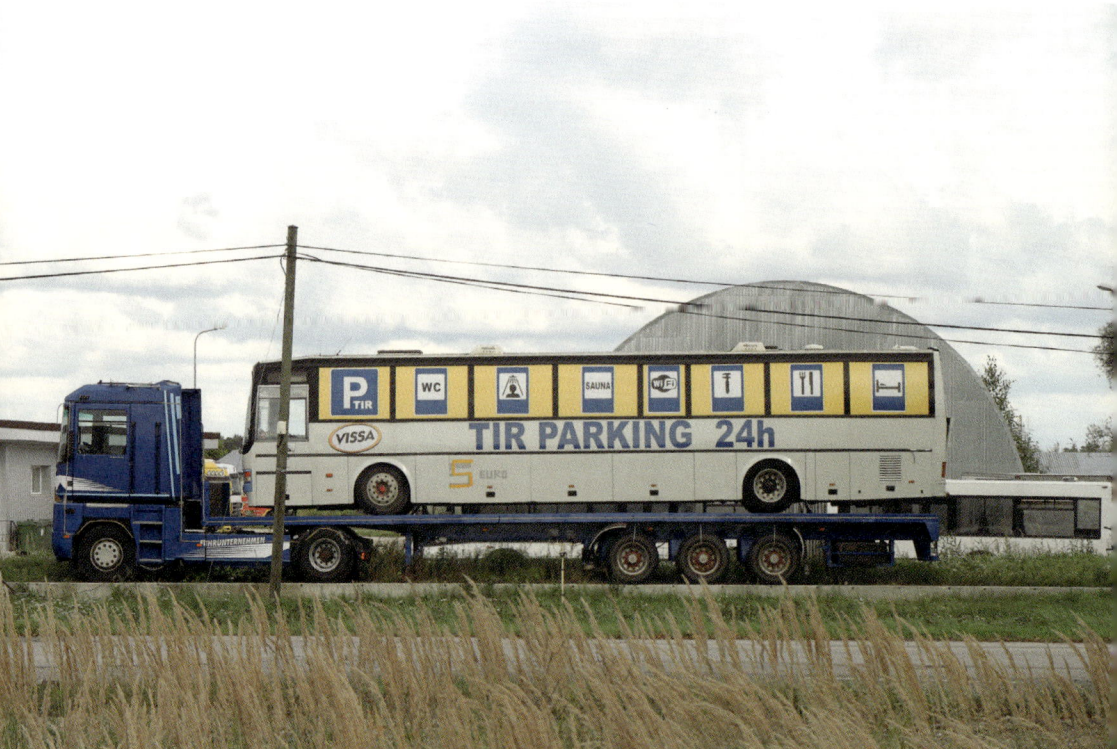

Fig. 14
Hieslmair and Zinganel, 2014
Corridor 1/E 67 Ādaži, Latvia: An old low-bed truck parked by the roadside carrying an even older municipal bus with large signs on the windows advertising the services of a rather informal-looking TIR truck drivers' stop on a vacant, derelict industrial estate

capitalize on his piece of land, simply with a mobile toilet and three small containers for the security guard, a bar, and a prostitute offering her services. Prostitution had been present almost everywhere, mostly offered by ethnic minorities, while watchdogs and guards, went about their job of controlling each of the TIR stops and motels, some motorized and wearing up-to-date professional uniforms, others looking scary in their paramilitary combat dress—and baseball bats.

## Mapping, Collecting, and Exhibiting as Forms of Participative Knowledge Transfer

At these nodes and knots, it seems, human forms of mobility are inseparably linked with nonhuman and immaterial forms, and cartographic techniques seem to provide the most appropriate tools for the analysis and representation of such multilayered, dynamic networks and hierarchies, as Gilles Deleuze and Felix Guattari and Bruno Latour have argued.[34]

We are, of course, aware that maps have had a hard time in the context of Marxist, poststructuralist, and postcolonial critique. David Harvey's analysis examined the role of global images in the expansion of European colonial powers.[35] Denis Wood employed semiotics to persuasively argue that the power of maps lies in the interests they represent. Mapping in this light always has a political purpose, and this "interest" often leads to people being pushed "off the map."[36] However, the very same arguments empowered the strategy of counter-mapping in critical geography, arts, political, and urban activism, making visible who and what had been underrepresented thus far or entirely repressed from representation and revealing the networks of established power structures. While the world has been increasingly redefined in terms of dynamic and complex networks of mobilized and demobilized people, objects, and capital, "mapping has become a way of making sense."[37]

Following Deleuze and Guattari's and Bruno Latour's enthusiasm for the capacities of mapping, we argue to view maps (the noun) not only as an appropriate device for the representation of mobility patterns, but moreover live mapping (the verbal noun or action) as a great relational tool for stimulating interaction

---

34 Gilles Deleuze and Felix Guattari, *A Thousand Plateaus: Capitalism and Schizophrenia* (Minneapolis: University of Minnesota Press, 1987); Bruno Latour, *Reassembling the Social: An Introduction to Actor-Network-Theory* (Oxford: Oxford University Press, 2005).

35 David Harvey, *The Condition of Postmodernity* (London: Blackwell, 1989).

36 Denis Wood, *The Power of Maps* (New York: Guilford Press, 1992).

37 Janet Abrams and Peter Hall, eds., *Else/Where: Mapping. New Cartographies of Networks and Territories* (Minneapolis: University of Minnesota Press, 2006), 12.

with mobile actors en route and for the evaluation of research findings. These attempts are explained in detail in our contribution to JAR 14.[38]

Purchasing a van had a strong impact on the design of the study. This meant we were not only able to drive more often and be much more flexible according to the routes and rhythms of our trips, but because of its large size we were able to transport building material for artistic interventions on site, much larger pre-produced maps, and indeed also collect significant everyday life objects during our trips, additional "actants," with reference to Latour's actor-network theory[39] and even art pieces—items we found relevant to combine with the materials from interviews, observations, and the artistic representations. Therefore, in addition to the combination of the immersive mobile method, being on the ground and witnessing what is going on there, and the method of live mapping on route, "collecting" and hence "exhibiting" (the actions rather than the nouns) became core strategies for disseminating, rearranging, and reevaluating interim research findings.

For this purpose, we rented a stationary project-space in an old warehouse at Vienna Nordwestbahnhof (Vienna's northwest station), a former railway station close to the city center. This huge compound is still in operation today as a road-to-rail cargo terminal run by the national railway company, a logistic hub for many smaller hauling companies and a parking lot for coaches of a major bus company also operating transnationally. Therefore, this site was a perfect location with practical connections to the subject matter along with a special aesthetic quality, "authentic" atmosphere and a great deal of mobility expertise. After testing relational assemblages of research material in the field of research, at smaller workshops and exhibitions in Tallinn, Sofia, and in our project space in Vienna beforehand, we opened a comprehensive exhibition at the large exhibition halls of the Academy of Fine Arts in Vienna in September 2016. Like all other exhibitions, this show was intended for the dissemination of research methods and findings, here in the growing community of arts-based research and research-based art at our host institution—and for successfully communicating the project to a wider audience in Vienna, but also to reevaluate the vast material we had accumulated, before selecting photos and redrawing diagrams and maps and writing up the papers for this book. For the title of this exhibition we appropriated the notion of Road*Registers from Kathleen Stewart,[40] which we considered both a perfect title and a more open and inclusive framework for an exhibition, combining our own research with the referential work of other scholars and artists.[41]

## Signposts throughout the Book Chapters and Visual Essays

As shown in the various exhibitions that we organized throughout this research project, the aesthetics of roads, vehicles, and roadside infrastructure has inspired many visual artists in a variety of ways. To "frame" this publication we selected works from two of the involved artists: The photos of art installations by Sonia Leimer at the very beginning of this book show "cutouts" of asphalt road surfaces, which literally "register" the traces of their use (figs. 1–3). These pure material appropriations are combined with steel elements, which refer to construction site barriers; both isolated fragments are open to multiple interpretations on archaeological, psychoanalytic, political, and poetic levels. At the very end of the book we present another artist's approach: Johanna Kandl's contrastingly descriptive "travelogue," reflecting upon her own travel experiences in Eastern Europe, critically juxtaposes handwritten neoliberal slogans with paintings of the everyday life at nodes of transnational transit such as gas stations, bus-stops, and open-air (car) markets (figs. 69–71). It also introduces the types of vehicles that are key "actants" driving these corridors and thereby interconnecting the very nodes and knots with different velocities and rhythms.

The main case studies in this publication not only represent the effects of the transformation of nodes and knots in different geographic and geopolitical locations and different push-and-pull factors driving mobilities and migration, they also illustrate different scales of investigations, ranging from distanced views of transcontinental networks to close-ups of very specific nodes, while in each case study the methods we applied were adapted to the specific needs and opportunities.

We start back in the history of the Cold War and with the largest geographic scope of road networks, crossing not only the borders of a nation and/or the permeable Iron Curtain, but also the borders of the European continent. In the 1960s and 1970s the volume of overland cargo transport in transit between Western Europe, COMECON countries such as Bulgaria, and the developing countries of the Middle East region, the Arabian Peninsula, and North Africa—most notably Iraq, Iran, Jordan, and Libya—increased significantly.[42] The state monopolist of cross-border heavy goods traffic in socialist Bulgaria, SOMAT (International Road

---

38 Michael Zinganel and Michael Hieslmair, "Stop and Go," *JAR Journal of Artistic Research*, no. 14 (2017), https://www.researchcatalogue.net/view/330596/330597 (accessed January 15, 2018).

39 Bruno Latour, *Reassembling the Social: An Introduction to Actor-Network-Theory* (Oxford: Oxford University Press, 2005).

40 Kathleen Stewart, "Road Registers," *Cultural Geographies* 21, no. 4 (2014): 549–63.

41 The exhibition had a total of 3,400 visitors. Michael Zinganel and Michael Hieslmair, *Road*Registers: Logbook of Mobile Worlds*, exhibition catalogue (Vienna: Academy of Fine Arts, 2017).

42 Also featured in Western European specialist truck driving literature, e.g., Ashley Coghill, *The Long Haul Pioneers: A Celebration of Astran, Leaders in Overland Transport to the Middle East over 45 Years* (Ipswich: Old Pond Publishing, 2010).

Transport Corporation), took on critical importance: Thousands of heavy trucks driving for the communist state enterprise had been crossing the borders of the Iron Curtain.

Emiliya Karaboeva investigates the overlapping interdependent networks established first by transnational transport organizations TIR, then by the former monopolist for transnational transport in Bulgaria SOMAT, and by the individual truck drivers working for the state-owned company during the times of Cold War, who had largely benefited from all kinds of legal and illegal side business during their extensive tours. Thanks to the Bulgarian photographer Nikola Mihov, we were able to find a vast array of visual material in the SOMAT archive, which enabled us to set up a workshop and exhibition in the "social condenser" of the truck drivers' canteen at SOMAT's former headquarters in Sofia. These events successfully triggered feedback from local experts, which supported us in expanding the scope of research from the communist history of SOMAT to the legacy of SOMAT service stations today.

In the second case study, the geographic scope of the network is smaller, but the focus on specific nodes is more intense and the zoom-in more detailed: Michael Hieslmair analyzes the history and legacy of Vienna International Busterminal. The traffic network of transnational bus routes that start or intersect here reflects the interconnections of destination and departure regions of tourists, former guest workers from Yugoslavia and Turkey (since the 1960s) and their relatives, commuters, and legal and illegal labor migrants from Eastern Europe (since the fall of the Iron Curtain). The bus terminal has suffered from an unfavorable reputation, being primarily associated with the influx of Eastern European migrants, and has therefore fallen victim to urban gentrification and displacement—with the result that today the current station, hidden under a motorway bridge, resembles one of the many gray infrastructural spaces usually associated with the former East of Europe.

In order to investigate the routes and nodes of the buses, driving with our van and exploring the terminals during our trips did not seem to be the appropriate means: instead, we visited the Vienna bus terminal several times and at different seasons, days of the week, and times of the day. We organized public excursions and also joined a bus trip on one of the most popular bus lines connecting Vienna and Sofia. But in fall 2015, at the midpoint of our research project, the perception of this route changed drastically: During the "wave of refugees" the Austria-Hungary border station of Nickelsdorf was reactivated as a key site for the management of the massive flows of migration, and buses became the preferred means for their mobilization. We expanded and adapted our research to include the new nodes and modes of mobilization.

For the third case study, we chose the special example of two interconnected harbor towns, which are penetrated by major road corridors: Today between Tallinn in Estonia (part of the Soviet Union prior to the fall of the Iron Curtain) and Helsinki in Finland (part of the capitalist West) a continuation of the Pan-European road corridor(s) is in place in the form of a highly efficient, regular ferry connection. The driving force for the enormous volume of passengers between Tallinn and Helsinki is the radical difference in wages and the price of services and consumer goods in both countries. While 15 percent of the Estonian population try to make their fortune as labor migrants in Finland, groups of Finns travel as tourists to Tallinn to consume and shop cheaply—above all, for alcohol. Pedestrians, cars, buses, and lorries are transported across the Baltic Sea in huge ships that leave every three hours. In both cities three major highways arrive at large terminal complexes, which represent bottlenecks that narrow traffic to the limited capacities and decelerated speed of the vessels. The vehicles are delivered over to the harbor on the opposite side of the Baltic, where they are redirected to the road corridors once again.

As a means of disseminating our interim research findings and gaining further feedback for our research, we realized a large network diagram in the public space in front of Tallinn's Ferry Terminal D. The installation also contained audio tracks, which told of the experiences of individuals, of the variety of routes and the motives of passengers, Finnish tourists and Estonian labor migrants alike, or the staff of the ferry line itself. The chapter begins with these transcribed audio tracks based on a series of interviews conducted on site at the port and on board the ferries. Then Tarmo Pikner consciously takes the linear path of a typical ferry passenger, traveling from the Port of Helsinki to Tallinn, following the beaten paths of tourists through Tallinn, so as to structure his memories and descriptions of urban transformation—from the communist period up to today—and show how the rhythm and capacities of this ferry line affects the city.[43]

The very choice of our research vehicle—a Ford Transit—inspired three smaller case studies: transporter vans like ours are the favorite vehicles for fitters and market vendors, so we decided to follow their routes from wholesale bazaars to open-air markets and vice versa. At the first open-air market we visited in Tallinn we learned from Russian vendors that they usually purchased their goods at Wólka Kosowska on the southern outskirts of Warsaw, today the largest Asian wholesale and retail market in Eastern Europe. When passing by Warsaw on our next trip, we took the opportunity to visit this market. Katarzyna Osiecka and Tatjana Vukosavljević investigate the market's history going from a single wholesale hub for Chinese vendors to a multiethnic village structure representing a constitutive part of a transnational trade network.

[43] Research conducted for this chapter was also supported by the Estonian Research Agency grant IUT3-2: Culturescapes in transition.

The van also shifted our interest toward a specific kind of market. The availability of transporter vans like ours is a precondition for the development of small and medium-scale trade. As purchasing power had been rather low during the period of transition, huge markets for secondhand cars imported from the West emerged all over Eastern Europe, like the one in Marijampolė, Lithuania, famously described by Karl Schlögel in support of his thesis of a European East-West integration starting from below.[44] In my essay I compare the transformation of the structure of the Marijampolė market with that of Dimitrovgrad, Bulgaria, as I do their different rhythms and "staged informalities."

And while driving or stopping on our trips we encountered so many minivans transporting migrant workers between the East and West of Europe—predominantly women whose modestly paid work facilitates the above-average quality of everyday life for Western Europe's middle class in the first place. We felt that these vehicles, their rhythm and mode of transport, and the people driving and being transported should not be missed in this publication. For this reason, we added an excellent reportage by the journalist Juan Moreno, who celebrates a Romanian minibus driver as a hero of European integration.

[44] Karl Schlögel, *Marjampole oder Europas Wiederkehr aus dem Geist der Städte* (Munich: Hanser, 2005).

Literature

Abrams, Janet, and Peter Hall, eds. *Else/Where: Mapping; New Cartographies of Networks and Territories*. Minneapolis: University of Minnesota Press, 2006.

Augè, Mark. *Non-places: Introduction to an Anthropology of Supermodernity*. New York: Verso Books, 1995.

Austin, Samuel. "Travels in Lounge Space: Placing the Contemporary British Motorway Service Area." PhD thesis, Welsh School of Architecture, Cardiff University, 2011.

Bauman, Zygmunt. *Liquid Modernity*. Cambridge: Polity Press, 2000.

Berking, Helmuth. "Raumtheoretische Paradoxien im Globalisierungsdiskurs." In *Die Macht des Lokalen in einer Welt ohne Grenzen*, edited by Helmuth Berking, 7–22. Frankfurt am Main: Campus Verlag, 2006.

Bhabha, Homi. "Unsatisfied: Notes on Vernacular Cosmopolitanism." In *Text and Nation*, edited by Laura Garcia-Morena and Peter C. Pfeifer, 191–207. London: Camden House, 2001.

Bissell, David. "Passenger Mobilities: Affective Atmospheres and the Sociality of Public Transport." *Environment and Planning D: Society and Space* 28, no. 2 (2010): 270–89.

Bittner, Regina, Wilfried Hackenbroich, and Kai Vöckler, eds. *Transiträume: Transit Spaces*. Edition Bauhaus, vol. 19. Berlin: Jovis Verlag, 2006.

Brown, Barry, Eric Laurier, Hayden Lorimer, Owain Jones, Oskar Juhlin, Allyson Noble, Mark Perry, Daniele Pica, Philippe Sormani, Ignaz Strebel, Laurel Swan, Alex S. Taylor, Laura Watts, and Alexandra Weilenmann. "Driving and 'Passengering': Notes on the Ordinary Organization of Car Travel." *Mobilities* 3, no. 1 (2008): 1–23.

Büscher, Monica, and John Urry. "Mobile Methods and the Empirical." *European Journal of Social Theory* 12 (February 2009): 99–116.

Coghill, Ashley. *The Long Haul Pioneers: A Celebration of Astran, Leaders in Overland Transport to the Middle East over 45 Years*. Ipswich: Old Pond Publishing, 2010.

Collier, Stephen J., James Christopher Mizes, and Antina von Schnitzler, eds. "Public Infrastructures/Infrastructural Publics." *Limn* 7 (2017).

Cowen, Deborah. "A Geography of Logistics: Market Authority and the Security of Supply Chains." *Annals of the Association of American Geographers* 100, no. 3 (2010): 600–20.

Crang, Michael. "Rhythms of the City: Temporalised Space and Motion." In *Timespace. Geographies of Temporality*, edited by Jon May and Nigel Thrift, 187–207. London: Routledge, 2001.

Dalakoglou, Dimitris. *The Road: An Ethnography of (Im)mobility, Space, and Cross-Border Infrastructures in the Balkans*. Manchester: Manchester University Press, 2017.

De Certeau, Michel. *The Practice of Everyday Life*. Berkeley: University of California Press, 1984.

Deleuze, Gilles, and Felix Guattari. *A Thousand Plateaus: Capitalism and Schizophrenia*. Minneapolis: University of Minnesota Press, 1987.

Dewey, John. *The Public and Its Problems*. Athens, Ohio: Ohio University Press, 1927.

Edensor, Tim. "M6 Junction 19–16: Defamiliarizing the Mundane Roadscape." *Space and Culture* 6, no. 2 (2003): 151–68.

———. "Introduction: Thinking about Rhythm and Space." In *Geographies of Rhythm: Nature, Place, Mobilities and Bodies*, edited by Tim Edensor, 1–20. London: Ashgate, 2010.

Foucault, Michel. "Of Other Spaces." Translated by Jay Miskowiec. *Diacritics* 16, no. 1 (1986): 22–27.

Frederiksen Demant, Martin, and Ida Harboe Knudsen. "What Is a Grey Zone and Why Is Eastern Europe One?" In *Ethnographies of Grey Zones in Eastern Europe: Relations, Borders and Invisibilities*, edited by Ida Harboe Knudsen and Martin Demant Frederiksen, 1–22. London: Anthem Press, 2015.

Green, Sarah. "Anthropological Knots." *Hau: Journal of Ethnographic Theory* 4, no. 3 (2014): 1–21.

Gregson, Nicky. "Mobilities, Mobile Work and Habitation: Truck Drivers and the Crisis of Occupational Automobility in the UK." *Mobilities* 13, no. 3 (2018): 291–307.

Hall, Michael, and Alan M. Williams, eds. *Tourism and Migration: New Relationships between Production and Consumption*. London: Kluwer Academic Publishing, 2002.

Harvey, David. *The Condition of Postmodernity*. London: Blackwell, 1989.

Harvey, Penny, and Hannah Knox. *Roads: An Anthropology of Infrastructure and Expertise*. Ithaca, NY: Cornell University Press, 2015.

Hauser, Susanne. "Die Ästhetik der Agglomeration." *B1/A40: The Beauty of the Grand Road*, edited by MAP Markus Ambach Projekte and StadtBauKultur NRW e.v., 202–13. Berlin: Jovis Verlag, 2010.

Ingold, Tim. *Lines: A Brief History*. New York: Routledge, 2007.

Jensen, Ole B., "Negotiation in Motion: Unpacking a Geography of Mobility." *Space and Culture* 13, no. 4 (2010): 389–402.

———. *Staging Mobilities*. London: Routledge, 2013.

Larkin, Brian. "The Politics and Poetics of Infrastructure." *Annual Review of Anthropology* 42 (2013): 327–43.

Latham, Alan, and Peter Woods. "Inhabiting Infrastructure: Exploring the Interactional Spaces of Urban Cycling." *Environment and Planning A* 47 (2015): 300–19.

Latour, Bruno. *Reassembling the Social: An Introduction to Actor-Network-Theory*. Oxford: Oxford University Press, 2005.

Laurier, Eric, and Hayden Lorimer. "Other ways: Landscapes of Commuting." *Landscape Research*, 37, no. 2 (2012): 207–24.

Lefebvre, Henri. *Rhythmanalysis: Space, Time and Everyday Life*. London: Bloomsbury Academic, 2013.

———. *The Production of Space*. Oxford: Blackwell, 1991.

Lussault, Michel, and Mathis Stock. "Doing with Space: Towards a Pragmatics of Space." *Social Geography* 5, no. 1 (2010): 11–19.

Merriman, Peter. *Driving Spaces: A Cultural-Historical Geography of England's M1 Motorway*. Oxford: Blackwell Publishing, 2007.

Morris, Jeremy, and Abel Polese, eds. *The Informal Post-socialist Economy: Embedded Practices and Livelihoods*. London and New York: Routledge, 2014.

Pickles John. "'New Cartographies' and the Decolonization of European Geographies." *Area* 37, no. 4 (2005): 355–64.

Pozharliev, Lyubomir. "Collectivity vs. Connectivity: Highway Peripheralization in Former Yugoslavia (1940s–1980s)." *Journal of Transport History* 37, no. 2 (2016): 194–213.

Richardson, Tim. "Making European Spaces: New Corridors in Eastern Europe." In *Transiträume: Transit Spaces*. Edition Bauhaus, vol. 19, edited by Regina Bittner, Wilfried Hackenbroich and Kai Vöckler, 50–73. Berlin: Jovis Verlag, 2006.

Schlögel, Karl. "Die Ameisenhändler vom Bahnhof Zoo: Geschichte im Abseits und vergessene Europäer." *Osteuropa* 11 (2009): 53–60.

Schlögel, Karl. *Marjampole oder Europas Wiederkehr aus dem Geist der Städte*. Munich: Hanser, 2005.

Sheller, Mimi. "Mobility." *Sociopedia.isa*, 2011, http://www.sagepub.net/isa/resources/pdf/mobility.pdf (accessed January 12, 2016).

Stewart, Kathleen. "Road Registers." *Cultural Geographies* 21, no. 4 (2014): 549–63.

Tsing, Anna. "Supply Chains and the Human Condition." *Rethinking Marxism* 21, no. 2 (April 2009): 148–76.

Vannini, Phillip. "The Techne of Making a Ferry: A Non-representational Approach to Passengers' Gathering Taskscapes." *Journal of Transport Geography* 19, no. 5 (2011): 1031–36.

Von Schnitzler, Antina. "Traveling Technologies: Infrastructure, Ethical Regimes, and the Materiality of Politics in South Africa." *Cultural Anthropology* 28, no. 4 (2013): 670–93.

Wilson, Helen. "Passing Propinquities in the Multicultural City: The Everyday Encounters of Bus Passengering." *Environment and Planning* A 43, no. 3 (2011): 634–49.

Zinganel, Michael, and Michael Hieslmair. "Stop and Go." *JAR Journal of Artistic Research*, no. 14 (2017), https://www.researchcatalogue.net/view/330596/330597 (accessed January 15, 2018).

Zinganel, Michael, and Michael Hieslmair. *Road*Registers: Logbook of Mobile Worlds*. Exhibition catalogue. Vienna: Academy of Fine Arts, 2017.

# Interrelated Networks
Material and Social Infrastructure between the Former East and West of Europe

# Networking Eurasia
## Bulgarian International Truck Drivers and SOMAT in the Cold War Era

Emiliya Karaboeva

Fig. 15
SOMAT Archive, 1984
Poster representing the geographic scope of SOMAT, the Bulgarian state-owned company's transnational transport activities; used as teaser for workshops and exhibitions, for instance at Red House Sofia and in the SOMAT canteen in April 2015 as well as at the final exhibition in Vienna in 2016

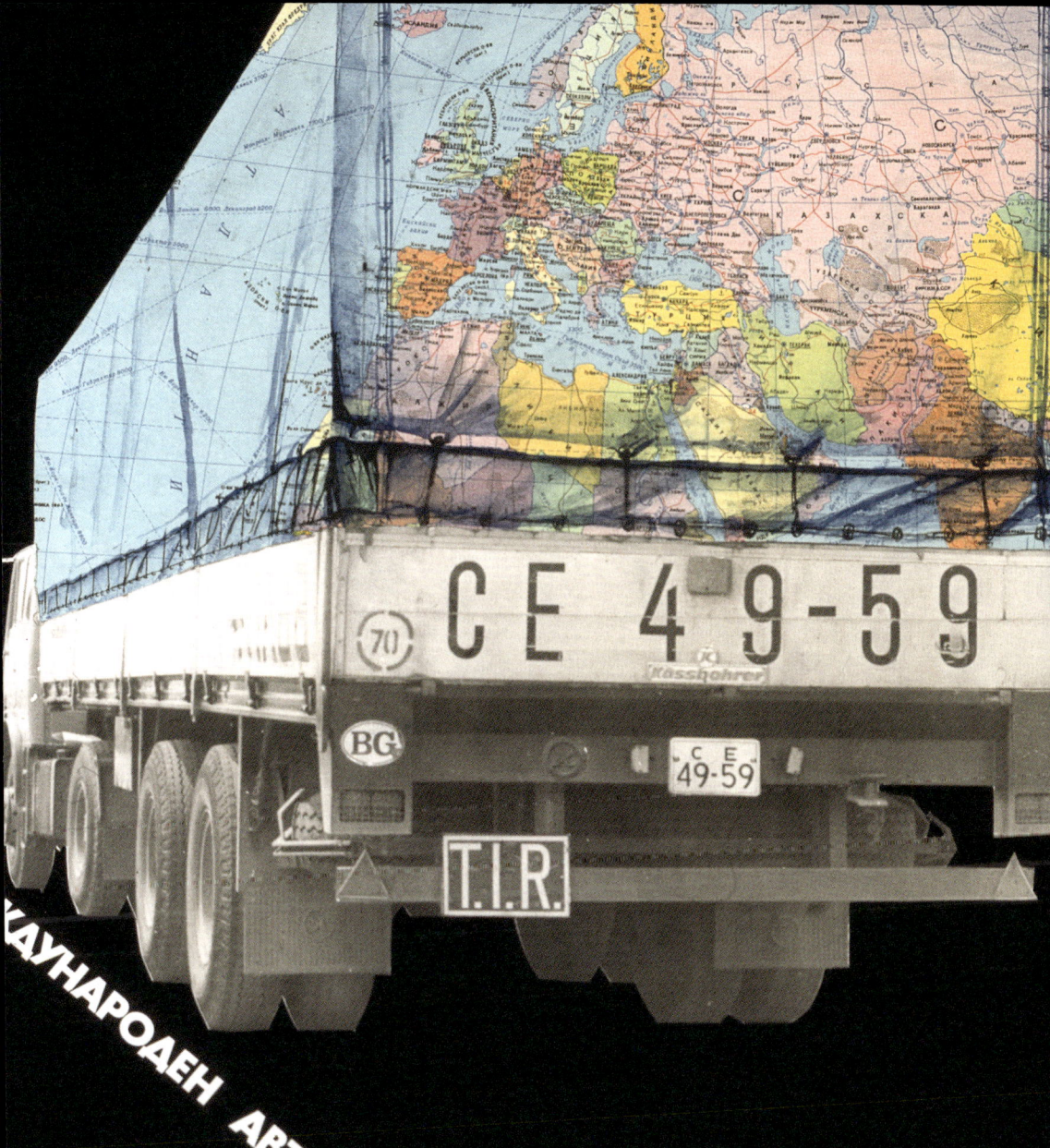

After the fall of the Berlin Wall both the nature of the Cold War and conventional Cold War studies started being questioned by researchers. Many authors, for example, avoiding the agenda of high-policy, diplomatic and governmental history, emphasize the importance of the Cold War for such ambivalent processes as Americanization and globalization.[1] It is important to note, however, that there is a long way to go for the "other" side of the Iron Curtain to be involved in the picture.[2] It seems to be taken for granted that Cold War processes were predominantly aimed at ruining Communism and therefore can only be analyzed by emphasizing the Western, capitalistic context, policy, or values. But if we consider the very Cold War not as a seclusion (according to traditional views), but rather as an intensive process of interaction, affecting all levels of social life on both sides of the Curtain, we will see that the socialist part of the world was equally involved in the process of globalization.

Aiming to construct a more complex picture of the interactions across the Iron Curtain, this project focuses on the rather elaborate and complex transcontinental network created by Bulgarian international truck drivers who worked during the Cold War era for SOMAT—Bulgaria's "International Automobile Transport Business Association."[3] My thesis is twofold. Firstly, I argue that this network drew on elements from several intertwined and interdependent networks, the most important of which under discussion here are the TIR system (in French: Transports Internationaux Routiers/International Road Transport),[4] the SOMAT network itself, and the aggregated personal transnational networks of the Bulgarian international truck drivers. This latter informal network not only straddled the Iron Curtain and the so-called First, Second, and Third Worlds, but also served to interlink all the aforementioned networks in a single heterogeneous entity. Secondly, I contend that each one of these networks was designed with a certain purpose, but the outcome of their work in some cases significantly deviated from the original purpose.

Contrary to the still dominant view of European infrastructural integration as the outcome of various national players' interactions, I follow, in turn, the Dutch and Swedish historians of technology Erik van der Vleuten and Arne Kaijser in propounding the concept of a "transnational network" comprised of "human made, materially integrated structures that cross national boundaries"[5] and encompass the entire sociotechnical configuration of people, institutions, and technology. By *network* here I also mean the "link that connects the supply side and the demand side, the structure and resources, and opportunity and individual characteristics at different levels"[6] and across spatial distance[7]—the macro level of the international and national policy in the global Cold War context; the mezzo level of the international transport companies' interests and strategies; and the micro level of the individuals, in this case the international truck drivers and their transnational activities. The dynamic interplay between these network levels and between structures, actors, and resources, will be seen through the lens of the trucker's official and private business, which is considered a junction where all flows, interests, and relations are crossed. The paper also adopts the concept of the structured flows (of information, capital, goods, etc.) as embedded networks in particular geographic, political, or institutional contexts.[8] This approach emphasizes the impact and the importance of real space.

The research for this chapter draws on state archival documents consulted in the Bulgarian Central State Archive, the State Archive in Rousse, the Archive of the Committee for Disclosing the Documents and Announcing Affiliation of Bulgarian Citizens to the State Security and Intelligence Services of the Bulgarian National Army (ACDDAABCSSISBNA), the Archive of the Bulgarian Prosecutor's Office, personal interviews with former Bulgarian international truck drivers and SOMAT officials, and memoirs. The interviews for this chapter were conducted in Sofia, Rousse, and Chepelare between the end of 2007 and

1  Christopher Endy, *Cold War Holidays: American Tourism in France* (Chapel Hill: University of North Carolina Press, 2004); D. Morley and K. Robins, *Spaces of Identity: Global Media, Electronic Landscapes and Cultural Boundaries* (London: Routledge, 1995); Arjun Appadurai, *Modernity at Large* (Minneapolis: University of Minnesota Press, 1996).
2  Rana Mitter and Patrick Major, *Across the Blocs: Cold War Cultural and Social History* (London: Frank Cass, 2004), 2.
3  SOMAT (created in 1960) stands for *Стопанско обединение международен автомобилен транспорт* (Business association of international automobile transport). It was a state-owned transnational corporation, and the only company for international automobile cargo transport in Bulgaria working with capitalist countries under socialism. Officially, the state automobile company for international haulages (initially known as DAP MP) was created in 1960 by a Council of Ministers' order N 1576/05 September 1960: Sofia State Archive, Fonds 1587, Record. 1, file 1, 25.
4  The Transports Internationaux Routiers/International Road Transport system was developed soon after the Second World War for encouraging the European postwar economies. The first TIR Convention was established in 1959 ("Status of Multilateral Conventions in Respect of Which the Secretary-General Acts as Depositary 1959–1963," ed. United Nations (New York: United Nations, 1959), XI.A-66. The Second TIR Convention was signed on December 14, 1975, and Bulgaria was among its founding members: "Multilateral Treaties in Respect of Which the Secretary-General Performs Depositary Functions. Annex: Final Clauses," ed. United Nations (New York: United Nations, 1976), XI.A-37; "TIR Handbook: Customs Convention on the International Transport of Goods under Cover of TIR Carnets (TIR Convention, 1975)," ed. United Nations Economic Commission for Europe (New York and Geneva: United Nations, 2013), 259.
5  Erik van der Vleuten and Arne Kaijser, "Prologue and Introduction: Transnational Network and the Shaping of Contemporary Europe," in *Networking Europe. Transnational Infrastructures and the Shaping of Europe, 1850–2000*, ed. Erik van der Vleuten and Arne Kaijser (Sagamore Beach: Science History Publication, 2006), 6.
6  Wenhong Chen and Justin Tan Chen, "Understanding Transnational Entrepreneurship through a Network Lens: Theoretical and Methodological Considerations," *Entrepreneurship Theory and Practice* 33, no. 5 (2009): 1081.
7  Jennifer Bair, "Analyzing Global Economic Organizations: Embedded Networks and Global Chain Compared," *Economy and Society* 37, no. 3 (2008): 339–64.
8  Bair.

the summer of 2016. During the summer of 2016, within the framework of the "Stop and Go" project I had regular weekly meetings with a group of former international truck drivers, who gathered weekly for lunch at the SOMAT canteen. The information was gathered through personal and group interviews with them, as well as with former or current employees, in situ. In the same time period a regular annual meeting of SOMAT drivers took place. There I had the opportunity to meet a large group (more than seventy people) of former drivers and officials.

My choice of respondents was influenced by the concept of targeted sampling developed by John K. Watters and Patrick Biernacki for a population or a group that is hard to access,[9] or is invisible and hidden,[10] as is the case with the group of former international truck drivers outside the official documentation of SOMAT's institutional framework. Such sampling, which combines theoretical sampling techniques, snowball sampling, and word of mouth, allowed for a broad variety of perspectives and information, a necessary condition for this study.[11] Given the sensitivity of some of the questions, I refer to the individual interviewees by first name or first name and initials in order to maintain their anonymity.

I used semi-structured, open-ended interviews, with detailed questions (different for each group of interviewees) for every respondent. In this manner, I sought to shed light on some aspects of the everyday and "unofficial" aspects of Cold War interactions across the Iron Curtain, as well as issues related to truckers' identity and their perceptions about the world beyond the Wall. All interviewees were also asked standard demographic questions about age, education, marital status, current occupation, and why and how long they had worked for SOMAT. I juxtaposed personal accounts with unpublished state documents regarding international transport and the truck drivers (issued by the Politburo, the Cabinet, the Ministry of Interior, the Ministry of Transport, and SOMAT) and State Security Services documents—the main archival sources consulted for combining different official (public and classified) information about border regime and practices, the institutional history of international truck transportation, as well as the official and illicit activities of the international truck drivers. Other sources helped contextualize the Bulgarian state's propaganda concerning the image of international truckers and the official, state image of the world beyond the Iron Curtain. These materials include published collections of interviews with international truckers, articles from the most popular newspapers and magazines in Bulgaria, and transport industry journals.

This paper accordingly first briefly presents both the TIR system, which is the foundation of contemporary international road transport, and the history and structural development of SOMAT, then it discusses the truck drivers' own informal network and how this related to TIR and SOMAT respectively. The last part discusses the unintended consequences of the networks' interplay within the context of the Cold War.

## TIR—The Large Framework

International road transport—also known as road haulage—is governed by European legislation. During the Cold War, there were several international conventions regulating international haulage. Bulgaria and most other socialist countries were signatories to them and also helped draw them up, in cooperation with the Economic Commission of Europe (ECE). The rules defined by those conventions were then and still are binding for all parties.

The most important of them regarding road haulage was the TIR: the UNECE's "Convention on International Transport of Goods under Cover of TIR Carnets."[12] This served to simplify, standardize and coordinate all customs formalities in a way that allowed haulage trucks to be sealed at their point of departure and then cross European borders without further inspection. The TIR system did not entirely rule out cargo controls at border crossings but stipulated that they should be carried out only in exceptional cases, such as when signs of tampering or other irregularities raised suspicion of contraband. The main goals of the convention were to standardize customs procedures, facilitate an international customs transit system and trade and, last but not least, reduce the scope for contraband activities.

The TIR system also replaced previously existing national customs regulations and guarantees by introducing the TIR Carnet, a single, internationally recognized guarantee document for road transport or transit. This facilitated the flow of goods in Europe and beyond and also served as a bridge between the transport systems then in existence on either side of the Iron Curtain: that of the European Union in the West and of the COMECON in the East. Although important enough on paper, it was over the course of their implementation on the road and in real economic and political contexts that the conventions became truly powerful. The various national haulage companies responsible for international transport were the most important players in this arena—and the Bulgarian SOMAT numbered among them.

9   John K. Watters and Patrick Biernacki, "Targeted Sampling: Options for the Study of Hidden Populations," *Social Problems* 36, no. 4 (1989).
10  Watters and Biernacki, 417.
11  Watters and Biernacki, 201.
12  TIR carnet is a "Customs transit document permitting facilitation of international trade and international road transport, under cover of which transport of goods from (a) Customs office(s) of departure to (a) Customs office(s) of destination is carried out under the procedure called "TIR procedure" laid down in the TIR Convention": Sorin Maier, *Transport & Logistic Glossary* (Constanta: Athos, 2009).

## SOMAT—The Network Company

SOMAT was officially established in 1960,[13] initially to serve the needs of Bulgaria's foreign trade. Later, its remit was revised: SOMAT launched transit transportation operations between Western Europe and Asia almost exclusively to earn precious hard currency, of which Bulgaria was much in need.[14] SOMAT statistics for 1980 show that Bulgarian import/export already accounted for 23 percent of all the company's transport runs while transit haulage, mainly between Western Europe and the Middle East, accounted for 77 percent.[15]

Following the logic of typical network development, SOMAT's own transcontinental network was an outcome of different exogenous factors,[16] among which the most important was the need to optimize its haulage capacity. At the time also, one of the most popular ways to overcome the obstacles to trade with the world beyond the Iron Curtain—not least the CoCom embargo imposed on the socialist countries[17] from shortly after the Second World War until 1994[18]—was to establish a chain of joint stock companies (JSCs) abroad, with foreign capital. This was common practice for all of the socialist countries and many of their state-run companies. SOMAT, too, founded more than twenty such companies abroad,[19] the most notable of which were Demand and Vienna Transport in Austria,[20] IBTC in Iran, Libutco in Libya,[21] MAT-Betz in Germany and Medlink in the United Kingdom. Relatively small groups of SOMAT employees (between fifty and five hundred drivers each) were settled in different countries, in Austria and Kuwait, for example, to oversee transnational and domestic haulage there.[22]

SOMAT also created a string of agencies and terminals in almost all major cities of Europe and the Middle East, as well as offices at the relevant border crossings. An intermodal transport system was established too, comprised of several sea and river ferry lines and roll-on roll-off boats, likewise owned by SOMAT.[23] The first such line was designed for transportation of auto transport trailers for Iraq, Syria, Jordan, Lebanon, Kuwait, and the United Arab Emirates.[24] Close cooperation was also established between the socialist international transport companies and various forwarding companies abroad, both from capitalist and socialist countries. For example, SOMAT worked with Militzer & Münch,[25] Schenker,[26] Danzas & Co,[27] Willi Betz, and many others.[28]

According to the scarce information available, the development of international truck transportation in the other socialist countries was similar.[29] All the socialist road haulage companies were almost identical in structure, with branches in various regions of the country, joint stock companies with foreign capital in several countries, border and sales offices, and terminals. However, due to the particular geopolitical position of Bulgaria and the state transportation policies, SOMAT gradually became the largest European company for international automobile cargo transport—most evident after 1969. According to Dimitar R., former Chief Executive Officer of SOMAT, one of the main reasons the Bulgarian company was able to become the European leader in international haulage was its truck drivers' willingness to accept a low salary that was disproportionate to the difficulties and complexity of their job.[30] They were mainly attracted by the opportunity to start a parallel business of their own: the job of truck driver was, after all, a passport to the world beyond the Iron Curtain and, hence, also to considerable opportunities for making money on the side. Another major reason SOMAT and all the socialist transport companies were so successful on the transport market was their low cost at the time—and their competitive rates were in turn possible thanks in part to the critically low salary of the drivers, who were nonetheless willing to work under very difficult conditions and to take risks because of their own private agendas. Thus, even if the socialist companies did not actively encourage their drivers' smuggling activities, they certainly turned a blind eye to them. Accordingly, drivers had an incentive to work hard for their companies because a bigger and better company meant more opportunities and greater scope for their own business initiatives. In the 1980s,

13 Sofia State Archive, Fonds 1587, Record. 1, file 1, 25.
14 Марин Георгиев, *Развитието на транспорта в България и международното разделение на труда* (София: Наука и изкуство, 1970) [Marin Georgiev, The development of the Bulgarian transport and the international divison of labor (Sofia: Nauka and Izkustvo, 1970)].
15 Decision N 1/16 March 1981 of the Currency Committee of Politburo: Central State Archive, Fonds 1B. Record 93, file 18, 39.
16 Ranjay Gulati and Martin Gargiulo, "Where Do Interorganizational Networks Come From?," *American Journal of Sociology* 104, no. 5 (1999): 1440.
17 Sumner Benson, "How National Security Considerations Affect Technology Transfer," *Journal of Technology Transfer* 13, no. 1 (1988).
18 Benson, "How National Security Considerations Affect Technology Transfer."
19 Борис Димитров, съст. *История на международния автомобилен транспорт в България* (София: Българско транспортно издателство, 2004) [Boris Dimitrov, ed. *History of the Bulgarian International Automobile Transport* (Sofia: Bulgarian Transport Publishing, 2004), 55].
20 Central State Archive, Fonds 1B, Record 88, file 119, 13.
21 Central State Archive, Fonds 259, Record 45, file 245, 113.
22 Central State Archive, Fonds 1B, Record 88, file 30, 1.
23 Central State Archive, Fonds 1B, Record. 93, file 18, 25-26; Fonds 1B, Record 88, file 198, 4; file 211, 2; file 204, 15.
24 Central State Archive, Fonds 1B, Record 93, file 18, 25-26.
25 Sofia State Archive, Fonds 1587, Record 1, file 4, 7; Central State Archive, Fonds 493, Record 1, file 14, 53.
26 Sofia State Archive, Fonds 1587, Record 2, file 40, 828; Central State Archive, Fonds 493, Record 1, file 22, 52-60; file 23.
27 Central State Archive, Fonds 493, Record 1, file 17, 51-60.
28 Sofia State Archive, Fonds 1587, Record 2, file 40, 828.
29 Jaroslav Blaha, Michèle Kahn, and Michel Vale, "Transportation in the East: The Key to Trade between the Two Europes," *Eastern European Economics* 29, no. 2 (1990-1991).
30 D. Raychev, former Deputy Main Director of SOMAT, interview by the author, Sofia, January 16, 2008.

SOMAT operated with more than 4,500 heavy trucks and 7,000 drivers,[31] carried out haulage to thirty-five countries, and cooperated with more than sixty foreign international transport companies. By comparison, the Soviet company for international transport Sovtransavto, operated at the peak of its activity only 3,500 vehicles;[32] and it is not clear from the data provided how many of these actually served international transport. The largest fleet ever run by Hungarocamion, another major competitor in Europe at the time, numbered only about 1,900 trucks in 1989.[33]

Launched in 1960, SOMAT existed until the end of the communist regime and was then gradually bought out by a former cooperation partner, the German businessman Willy Betz.

## The Drivers—Moving between the Legal and Illegal

Being a vital part of the SOMAT network, from the 1960s to the early '90s, drivers had more than thirty years to develop their own networks. Some truckers worked for the company for this entire period before founding their own haulage or forwarding business after the fall of Communism in Eastern Europe. One of my respondents, former deputy Chief Operating Officer at SOMAT, called the socialist international truck drivers "walking CORECOMS,"[34] which is a rather ingenious description of the truckers' easy access to the kind of Western goods available at the time only in Bulgaria's eponymous and expensive hard currency stores. However, the drivers were also far more than that. The special permission given them to regularly cross the border facilitated frequent and extensive contacts throughout Europe and the Middle East. Such contacts were used to develop a relatively stable transnational network of people and places for smuggling and trade, which assured a parallel unofficial market and the steady circulation of goods between Western Europe, the Eastern bloc and the Middle East.

On the subject of contraband in Bulgaria, numerous and diverse data (reports, records and analyses)[35] compiled by the former Bulgarian state security services between the late 1950s and late 1980s show that non-state contraband (along with state-run contraband named "hidden transit" in the Bulgarian State Security Services' documents[36]) flourished on the whole thanks to the TIR system. In terms of the frequency and the scale of smuggling and the volumes of contraband moved, international transport workers—mainly sailors and truck drivers—were by and large the most important group. Smugglers exploited the advantages of international haulage: regular schedules, plus untold opportunities to devise hiding places, contact a broad range of people in different countries, and thus establish contraband channels for consumer goods, arms, gold, drugs, and works of art.[37] This unofficial activity of truck drivers was highly valued also by ordinary people in the Eastern bloc. Not only did international truck drivers return from their trips with consumer goods emblematic of life beyond the border—for example, blue jeans, fashionable clothes, candies, canned drinks, and small technological devices, especially music recorders, cameras, etc.—but also with something even more important, namely, images, information and stories about the West and the Western way of life.

Hence, not only did state-run companies and the official international trade figures benefit from international transit workers but also ordinary people. Transport workers were able to bridge various consumer environments and market standards, and partially satisfy demand for alternative types of goods both in the Eastern bloc and beyond the Curtain.

31 "Top Secret Report by the First Main Directorate of the State Security Services (Intelligence) on Ensuring the Safety of the Bulgarian Institutions and Citizens Abroad Who Are in Short or Long Business Trips in Capitalist and Developing Countries" (1979): ACDDAABCSSISBNA Fonds 9, Record 4, file 250P, 48.
32 Ольга Павук, "Сначала было „Совтрансавто," Латвийское авто, декабри 14, 2006 [Olga Pavuk, "The Beginning was set by Sovtransavto," *Latvian Auto*, December 14, 2006].
33 My thanks for these statistics to Atilla Szabo, archivist at the National Archive of Hungary, IV Department of Business Archives. See also: Hammer who claims that "in its heyday 3,000 drivers drove 1,200 trucks to every country in Western and Eastern Europe, North Africa and the Arab countries": Ferenc Hammer, "A Gasoline Scented Sindbad: The Truck Driver as a Popular Hero in Socialist Hungary," *Cultural Studies* 16, no. 1 (2002): 87.
34 Peycho P., former director and representative of SOMAT, interview by the author, Sofia, April 1, 2015. CORECOM is a sophisticated name, composed of the first syllables of the French term COMPTOIR DE REPRESENTATION COMMERCIALE = bureau for trade agency. CORECOM was a chain of shops in Bulgaria where all kinds of Western goods were sold for hard currency. Such shops existed in all socialist countries (*Intershop* in the GDR, *Beriozka* in the USSR, *CORECOM* in Bulgaria): Jonathan Zatlin, "Making and Unmaking Money: Economic Planning and the Collapse of East Germany," *Occasional Papers*, 14–15, https://escholarship.org/uc/item/44h5r8sz (accessed January 15, 2018); Central State Archive, Fond 541, Record 1, file 22; Rossitza Guentcheva, "Mobile Objects: Corecom and the Selling of Western Goods in Socialist Bulgaria," *Études Balkaniques* XLV, no. 1 (2009): 8.
35 ACDDAABCSSISBNA Fonds 2, Record 4, file 34 M, 9, 12. 92, 102, 107; file 66 M, 9,117, 104, 196; file 93 M, 72; file 121 M, 40, 51–52; Fonds 2, Record 3, file 305 M, 48; file 368, 71–72; Fonds 32, Record 2, file 102 M, 3–4; Fonds VI Record Л, file 970, 57, 91, 131.
36 The term "скрит транзит" (hidden transit) was coined by the communists in the 1970s to indicate the state contraband carried out under the control of the State Security Services: Archive of the Bulgarian Prosecutor's Office, case N4/1990, Volume 42, page 23, 84 and Volume 529, page 88. See also: Христо Христов, Империята на задграничните фирми (София: Сиела, 2009) [Hristo Hristov, *The Empire of the Foreign-Trade Companies Settled Abroad* (Sofia: Siela, 2009)], 11.
37 ACDDAABCSSISBNA Fonds 2, Record 4, file 22 M, 14.

Fig. 16
SOMAT Archive, 1984
Water towers of Bagdad: Photos of LGV trucks in front of landmarks abroad became trophies of success for the company and its drivers. The original caption handwritten by a driver says: "Passing the 'cups' of Baghdad, between the brick factory, where we loaded 200 liters of fuel, Abu Ghraib, and the customs office at the terminal. We saw the same type of 'cups' on our trip to Kuwait in Basra and Safwan."

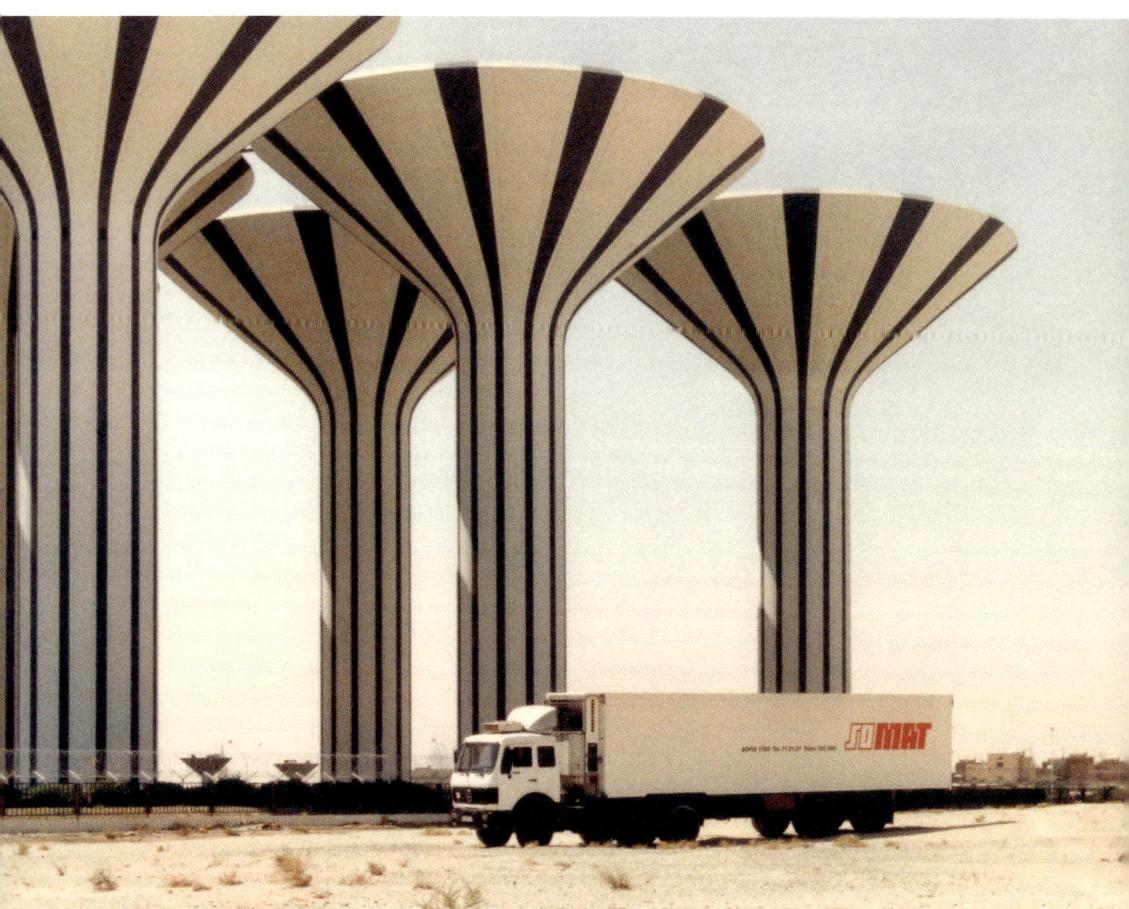

## Network upon Network

To a certain extent, Bulgarian drivers' extensive networks and access to various kinds of scarce products and services in their own country were a result of the privileges they enjoyed as a professional group within the framework of the socialist planned economy and the restrictive Cold War–era border regime.[38] Above and beyond that, they were able to exploit their privileged occupational status abroad, and thereby develop far more elaborate and lucrative networks that even the best *blat* connections at home would not allow.[39]

As employees in international road transport, the drivers became part of at least two intertwined and heterogeneous transnational networks: TIR and SOMAT.

I argue here that the TIR system is not just a set of rules for standardizing and coordinating the machines used in road transport along with all the attendant details of documentation, legislation, rates, insurance policies, and containerization policy, etc., but should also be considered a network in its own right. For when one considers that TIR consists of various interconnected elements and actors, such as road infrastructure and the International Road Transport Union (IRU), it does evidently qualify as a heterogeneous and complex network. IRU is the institution that issues TIR carnets and administers secure payments and all signatories to the TIR system are therefore automatically IRU members. Border checkpoints and customs systems can likewise be seen as nodes in this network of intersecting flows, for that is where TIR procedures and rules are carried out and monitored. These heterogeneous elements compose a complex infrastructural network, the legislative and material basis upon which subsequent transport networks were built.

The TIR system is also a device for European governance that "takes place through a process of negotiations in network settings that link public and private actors of different levels (regional, national and European) and dimensions (legislature, judiciary and executive) of government. In such contexts, political power is exercised by sharing and pooling resources through the establishment of networks."[40] The TIR system created favorable conditions for intensifying the trade and other contacts, and for the transportation needed

---

38 Emiliya Karaboeva, "Borders and Go-Betweens: Bulgarian International Truck Drivers during the Cold War," *East Central Europe* 41, nos. 2–3 (2014).

39 Alena Ledeneva, *Russia's Economy of Favours: Blat, Networking and Informal Exchange* (Cambridge: Cambridge University Press, 1998).

40 Karen Heard-Laureote, "Transnational Networks Informal Governance in the European Political Space," in *Transnational European Union Towards a Common Political Space*, ed. Wolfram Kaiser and Peter Starie (London: Routledge, 2005), 37.

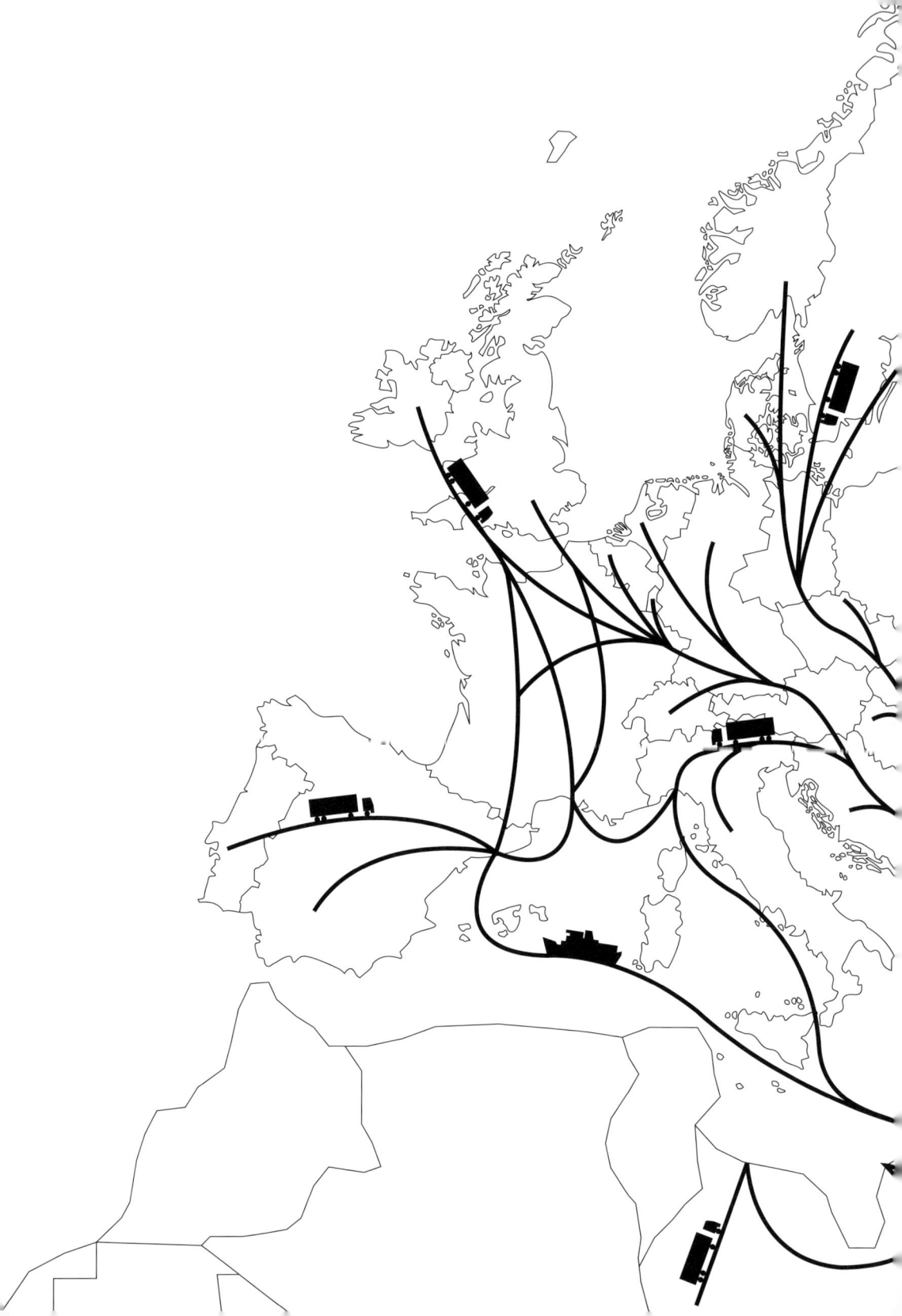

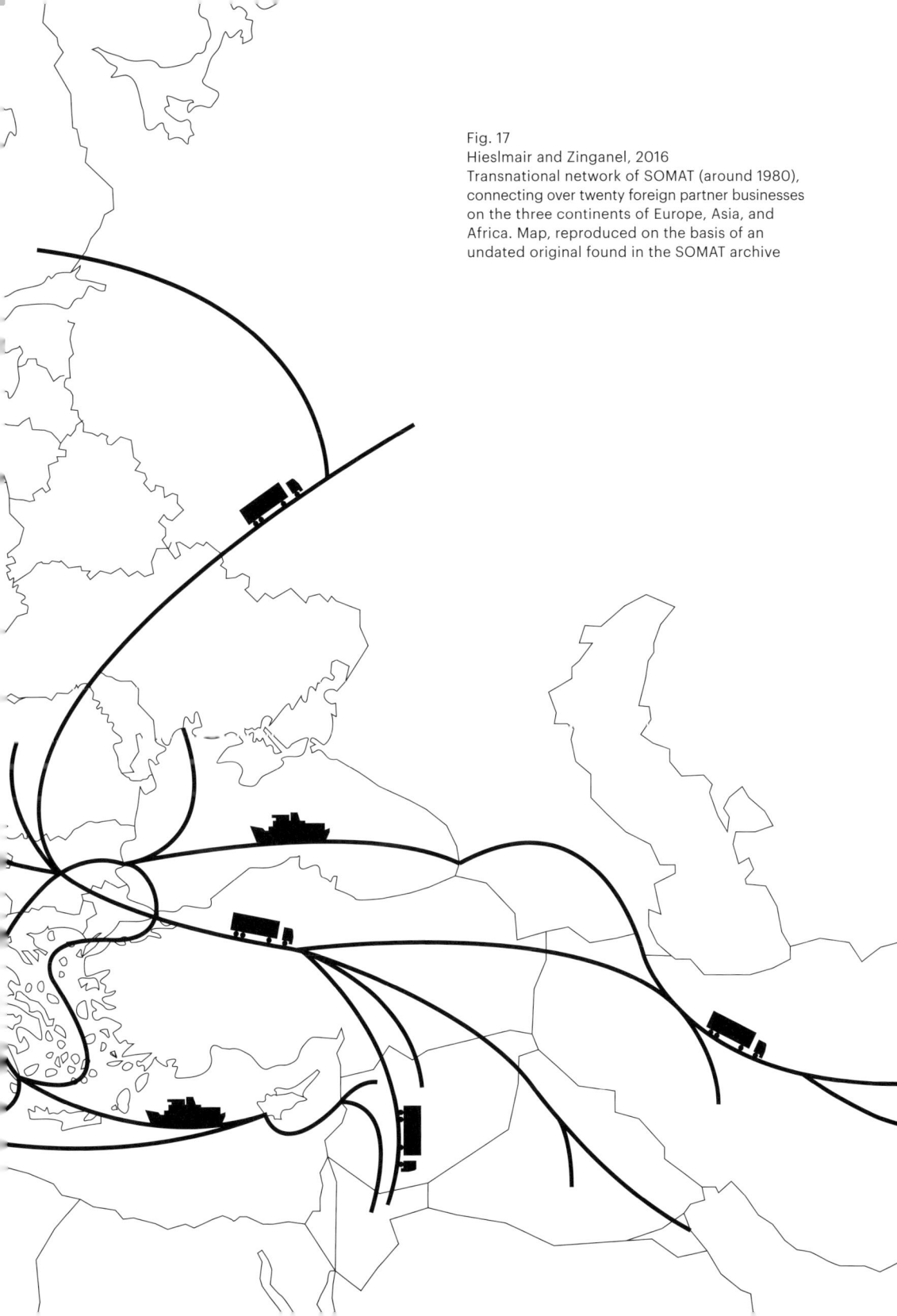

Fig. 17
Hieslmair and Zinganel, 2016
Transnational network of SOMAT (around 1980), connecting over twenty foreign partner businesses on the three continents of Europe, Asia, and Africa. Map, reproduced on the basis of an undated original found in the SOMAT archive

for them, by standardizing the procedures and documentation, and by facilitating the border crossing. Actually, at the level of the international organizations and the transnational trade/contraband, intensive contacts existed, many of which remained invisible due to their secrecy or illegality. One could even argue that the very Cold War, by means of prohibition, regulation and separation, (which caused an extensive wave of avoidance and violation of these restrictions) and by means of the active "war" policy against the rivals, turned out to be a generator of intensifying connections and collaborations in many directions and with different, sometimes contradicting goals and consequences. Officials and institutions, involved in this process, as well as secret agents and contrabandists, built a sophisticated multi-level network, via which flows of people, goods, images, ideas, and information moved in all possible directions. The cardiovascular system of this transnational, transpolitical, transcontinental, and trans-ideological (actually global) network was transportation and as one of the largest carriers at that time, SOMAT held a prominent place in this process.

SOMAT, for its part, was also a network comprised of agencies, parking lots, terminals, joint stock companies with foreign capital, representative offices, truck drivers, and other employees spread across almost all the major cities in Europe and the Middle East as well as at relevant border crossings that was built upon the TIR network. The nodes of this rather complex and heterogeneous system partly overlapped with the TIR nodes, but were mainly a result of various economic, geopolitical, and practical factors. Vienna, for example, was one such important node with three major joint-stock companies—Demand, the coordination center for European operations, was launched in 1970, Vienna Transport in 1981 and Rokomat in 1989. It also maintained a representative office there, a terminal with a garage for sixty trucks and a hotel with sixty beds.[41] The importance of Vienna for Bulgarian international transport and, more generally, for European transnational transport and trade hinged on several geopolitical factors: the Central European city of Vienna lies close to the former Iron Curtain border, at the intersection of several major European transit routes connecting different parts of the continent; it is also linked with Western and Eastern Europe by the River Danube and by rail, and it can thus offer intermodal transport (shipping and rail freight);[42] and, finally, Austria's neutral status appealed at the time to many of the socialist companies operating in Western Europe.[43] One of the specifics of this network is that the company itself was a network and its main purpose was to connect other economic or political entities using the TIR legislative system and the road network.

Though the TIR network was created mainly for preventing illicit flows and contraband, the abundant use of the TIR convention precisely for contraband activities was one of its unintended consequences. During the Cold War such transnational networks encompassed all aspects of the conflict both officially and unofficially via the TIR network. They performed official haulages both between the socialist countries, capitalist and socialist countries, socialist countries and Third World countries and finally, between capitalist and Third World countries. The same applied to the illegal transportation of goods and their re-export, where all kinds of politically "separated" actors worked together and built a global network, which partly served the policy of the Cold War, but mainly profited from it. SOMAT's structure also enabled a large number of employees to operate relatively independently, free of centralized control. The employees evolved over time. Most notable among them were the truck drivers.

## The Hidden Flows

The truck drivers' network was actually modeled on the official SOMAT network. Accordingly, their own flows, were different from those of SOMAT, but nonetheless prestructured by these. The nodes in the drivers' network, at which they obtained or distributed goods, were usually the company's own network nodes, i.e., border or sales offices, terminals, ports, or petrol stations. However, the drivers' network also included elements distinct from the SOMAT structure, such as scrap yards, shops, or metropolitan markets. Thus, Mexico Platz in Vienna[44] and the Kapaliçarşi (Grand Bazaar)[45] in Istanbul were important points in the truckers' unofficial network, as were parking lots in Turkey, on the road to Iran and Iraq.[46]

An imaginary generic journey of a typical truck driver traveling from Bulgaria to Western Europe, then via Bulgaria to the Middle East, and then back to Bulgaria would reveal that the flow of goods obtained and distributed by truck drivers was more complex and elaborate than SOMAT's own flow. While, as a

41 Petar P., former representative of SOMAT, interview by the author, Vienna, December 7, 2015.

42 Combined transport—transport of goods where at least for a part of the operation a different means of transport is used rather than the one initially utilized, e.g., by road, rail, air, waterways, sea, etc., or a combination of these, e.g., roll-on roll-off.

43 Gunter Bischof, "Of Dwarfs and Giants: From Cold War Mediator to Bad Boy of Europe—Austria and the U.S. in the Transatlantic Arena (1990-2013)," in *Austria's International Position after the End of the Cold War*, ed. Gunter Bischof and Ferdinand Karlhofer (New Orleans: University of New Orleans, 2013), 13.

44 "Top Secret Report by the Second Main Directorate (01/17/1976) about the Counter-intelligence Activities Performed by the 4th Department of the Directorate for 1985": ACDDAABCSSISBNA, Fonds 2, Record 4, file 102M, 102.

45 "Top Secret Report by the Second Main Directorate (01/17/1976) about the Counter-intelligence Activities Performed by the 4th Department of the Directorate for 1985": ACDDAABCSSISBNA, Fonds 2, Record 4, file 102M, 135-39.

46 Stefan B., Todor Ch., and Georgi B., former international truck drivers, interviews by the author, Sofia, August 19, 2016.

rule, one official trip served to transport only one type of goods from one point to another, the drivers on that same trip would use it to obtain, smuggle and sell various types of goods at various destinations and for various purposes. A considerable proportion of the goods bought from Western Europe or (mainly) from Turkey and the Middle East were destined for Bulgaria, for distribution among drivers' local networks of relatives, friends, customers, or officials. Other goods went to other socialist countries, especially if the truckers traveled via Romania. Such goods then served not only for barter and bribing, but also as an unofficial means of alleviating local shortages and amending the uneven distribution of goods among the socialist countries. One last percentage of goods was destined for the Middle East or the USSR. For example, the German home shopping catalogue Neckermann or soft drinks such as Schweppes were extremely popular in the USSR while alcohol and porn magazines enjoyed significant interest in the Middle East.[47] These types of goods were mostly used to bribe customs officials and traffic police, but also as gifts for key players within the drivers' trade network. A fair amount of the purchased or smuggled goods went to various administrative bodies, likewise in the form of bribes. One of my respondents, truck driver Ivan Ch., explained in his interview that he had stable "connections" at the German, Polish, and Soviet borders and that his "friends" there expected him to hand them a certain amount of money at the border, in exchange for their cooperation. International truck drivers also developed specific connections and networks with customs officials, as well as skills in negotiating border regulations, i.e., in finding loopholes in certain restrictions.[48] Bribes or "gifts" served to "grease palms" and thus make both private and official business operations smooth and unproblematic.

The trade in petrol had its own trajectory and was very important, especially when crossing Eastern bloc borders. In the USSR, Bulgarian drivers almost never paid for fuel with money, but with alcohol. Later, after bribing customs officials at each border to issue fraudulent documents regarding the quantity of petrol in the tank, they would sell some fuel in Poland or elsewhere. Basically, local supply and demand was the main factor determining the flow and types of goods. Drivers therefore had to know these specifics in order to successfully adapt their official trips to their own interests. As a whole, the success of the international truck drivers' private business was due mainly to the different economic standards across the Iron Curtain and the inequality of goods distribution between the socialist states.[49]

Truckers in the rest of the Eastern bloc pursued similar strategies: for example, the *dalnoboyshiki* (Soviet international truck drivers) mainly exported alcohol to Scandinavian countries and gold and precious stones to Poland while their top imports were Scandinavian cigarettes, Polish leather goods, Yugoslav shoes, East German toys, and luxury items from the West.[50]

It is often emphasized that transnational networks differ from policy networks because they are not confined to national policy or sector.[51] However, it is also important to stress that a transnational network does not mean that the actors do not depend on the particular geographical or cultural space. The nodes of the truck drivers' networks (as well as the other transnational networks explored here), are situated in different economic, cultural or social environments or contexts. Thus, one could argue that the networks are simultaneously transnational (in respect of the links and flows) and multifocal (in respect of the nodes). Following the people and objects,[52] we see that the truck drivers are (predominantly) embedded in this complex multidimensional network and their behavior depends heavily on the particular place or the contractor they deal with.[53] Although the driver is also the network builder of his own informal network, he needs to adapt in every separate case or point. Accordingly, the goods he buys or distributes vary considerably not only in type, but also in the way they are used—some of them being used for trade, others for bartering, and others as bribes or gifts.

The network itself exists simultaneously in different contexts and the drivers' movement in space between the different nodes could be seen also as trans-contextual. This characteristic of trucker networking is specific both in the context of the SOMAT network and in the context of the individual private networks. Both of them are networks of intermediaries and hence, their main purpose is to link different individuals, companies, economics, and even political blocs within the framework of the Cold War.

Finally, the individual networks of the drivers could be seen as parasitic entities as far as they emerged spontaneously, given that they used and adapted for their own goals other networks (one can also list here the networks of the socialist emigrants, the network of the state security services, blat), they were pervasive and hard to control, but they were also fully dependent on the Cold War's physical and mental topography of separation.[54]

47 Petar R. and Sasho S., former international truck drivers, interviews by the authors, Chepelare, August 20, 2010, and Ivan Ch., former international truck driver, interview by the author, Sofia, January 4, 2010.
48 Ivan Ch., former international truck driver, interview by the author, Sofia, January 4, 2010; Stayko T., former international truck driver, interview by the author, Lopyan, April 13, 2009.
49 Peter Jackson, Philip Crang, and Claire Dwyer, "Introduction: The Spaces of Transnationality," in *Transnational Spaces*, ed. Peter Jackson, Philip Crang, and Claire Dwyer (London, New York: Routledge, 2004), 5.
50 Дмитрий Васильев, *Фарцовщики. Как делались состояния. Исповедь людей "из тени"* (СПб: Вектор, 2007) [Dmitri Vasiliev, Black marketeers: How the fortunes have been made; A confession by the shady people (St. Petersburg: Vektor, 2007)].
51 Heard-Laureote, "Transnational Networks Informal Governance in the European Political Space," 47.
52 Jackson, "Introduction: The Spaces of Transnationality," 10.
53 Bair, "Analysing Global Economic Organizations."
54 Karaboeva, "Borders and Go-betweens."

## Stitching (or: Knitting/Knotting) Eurasia Networks

Thus, in view of the truck drivers' official and unofficial activities, the aforementioned networks should be seen as a complex constellation of people, institutions and technology, a three-dimensional one, as the drivers' network was modeled on SOMAT's elaborate network and SOMAT's on the TIR network. Therefore, the TIR network should be considered as the primary factor in this constellation (although, theoretically speaking, it is a second-order technical system based on the road network[55]), SOMAT as the secondary factor, and the drivers' network as the tertiary factor.

The three networks were intertwined and embedded in each other—they were interdependent and had common nodes (border checkpoints for all three of them; terminals, offices and parking lots for SOMAT and the drivers). SOMAT's transcontinental network could not have been established without the TIR network, the drivers could not have built their system for distributing goods without the SOMAT framework and the access it assured them to foreign travel as company employees; and, finally, SOMAT and even such a large system as TIR's could not have survived without the truck drivers, major players who literally and figuratively drove the system.

Hence, the drivers should be seen as the link between the three systems. Accordingly, their network has two dimensions—horizontal and vertical. The horizontal one encompasses a huge territory—Europe, the Middle East and North Africa. It also not only extends across national state borders but also, more importantly, across the Iron Curtain, at the time a border between two ways of life and two rival value systems; and across the borders of what were known in the Cold War era as the "First," "Second," and "Third" Worlds. The local national network, which itself had both—vertical and horizontal dimensions, should be regarded as a part of the drivers' largest network since it was provided with some of the goods and services brought from abroad. This is also a network that connects different kinds of people from different countries, with different occupations, political systems, cultures, religions, etc.

The vertical network consists of nodes that are actually parts of other networks. The truck drivers connect them and thus merge them in one complex entity. The drivers communicate with elements of the other networks—with customs officials, SOMAT representatives, employees—and by connecting and using them for official or personal purposes, they make them part of their own network. Simultaneously, the drivers themselves are important players in the TIR and SOMAT networks. Although we will limit the discussion here to only these three networks, it is important to add that the truckers communicate with other networks, and thus also become a part of them: like those of Bulgarian and Turkish emigrants in Western Europe and Turkey, or of Bulgarian or, in certain cases, even of foreign intelligence networks (the Turkish one, for instance).[56] Relations between the nodes varied. They depended on kinship and friendship, on the transfer of goods, money, or information, or on official obligations. Drivers, however, predominantly connected nodes by physically moving from one to the other, as well as by using other types of node (facilities or people) to further their own agenda, regardless of the company's goals.

Although I refer here to the drivers' network as one single network, every driver actually developed a network of his own, and every truck figured therein as a coordination center or mobile office. The aggregate drivers' network consisted of thousands of overlapping networks that followed the logic of official trade channels. Every relation meant a different sequence of nodes and, accordingly, each driver followed specific algorithms that described his own goals, perceptions and activities. All these overlapping networks multiplied and established a common model of connections and behavior, but they were not identical. Rather, they were dynamic, flexible and easily adaptable to the changing sets of groups, individuals, and tasks specific to every relation and trip.

The Bulgarian international truck drivers' behavior, functions and roles were designed in accordance with the agenda of efficiency and control—both of the business operations and of the truckers themselves. Thus, the drivers' practice and image were constructed on three different levels—technical, organizational, and ideological. On the technical level they were perceived as operators of the vehicles, as mere drivers. On the organizational level however, the truckers received more responsibilities than just driving a vehicle and were seen as agents. They had to deal with the goods and truck documentation, know the border regulations and procedures and the local transport regulations, and be able to deal efficiently with unexpected situations on the road.[57] On the ideological level—the driver was constructed as a messenger of the

55 Erik van der Vleuten, "In Search of the Networked Nation: Transforming Technology, Society and Nature in the Netherlands during the Twentieth Century," *European Review of History* 10, no. 1 (2003): 67.

56 There is a considerable body of documents from the State Security Services on the agents and collaborators in international automobile transport, especially for the counterintelligence (for the period from 1960 to 1989). For example, in 1985, a Second Main Directorate's (counter-intelligence) report reveals that two agents—drivers, working for SOMAT, became double agents recruited by MIT (the Turkish National Intelligence Organization): "Top Secret Report by the Second Main Directorate (01/17/1976) about the Counter-intelligence Activities Performed by the 4th Department of the Directorate for 1985," ACDDAABCSSISBNA, Fonds 2, Record 4, file 102M, 102.

57 Dimitar Raychev, former Deputy Chief Director, interview by the author, Sofia, January 16, 2008. Petar G, working as a SOMAT driver and representative for more than thirty-two years, also underlined in his stories that a good driver should be able to control transportation, loading and delivery, know what documentation to be aware of, respect local attitudes and customs, and act appropriately in any given situation. Interview by the author, Sofia, February 7, 2008.

socialist way of life or as soldier of Communism. In line with the overall ideology that asserted the superiority of socialist people, the truck drivers (as strangers in a hostile territory) were portrayed as heroes by the authorities. Especially at the end of the 1980s,[58] the image of the trucker-hero was deliberately popularized by the socialist authorities in order to eliminate the power of the unofficial, but common image of the truckers as greedy and rich smugglers and to publicly refute any claims that the drivers violated the core values of the socialist moral code. Official propaganda suggested that everything that the truckers had earned, including privileges or extra income from their jobs, was well-deserved because of the hostile environment they had to fight constantly—horrible weather, road bandits, the locals' strange customs, war, etc.[59]

Truckers themselves internalized this socialist hero image. Their travel stories echoed the official representations of their difficult daily life and the constant battle with the hostile natural and cultural environment but were also preconditioned by the very nature of truckers' quasi-nomadic life, reenacting archaic patterns of man's travel adventures in an unknown world.[60] Accordingly, based on their special status, their official and unofficial functions, and their privileged perspective, the socialist international truck drivers built a dynamic and contextual identity, comprising various features and layers. They perceived themselves first as professionals,[61] then as virile,[62] and finally as Bulgarians.[63] But in order to fulfil their various professional and ideological tasks, they also had to be businessmen, accountants, cashiers, diplomats, soldiers, and ambassadors. At home however, these drivers officially portrayed as ambassadors of the socialist life, became unofficial ambassadors of the capitalist lifestyle, trading in Western goods and spreading stories about the West.

Precisely this side of their identity and their unofficial practices deviated from the control and monitoring of the state and the company. In this respect the authorities faced some very important unexpected ideological consequences due to the discrepancy between the theoretical visions of the company network builders and the drivers' practical use of the network. The relationship between design and practice could be seen metaphorically as the difference between narrative structure and actual experience. Illustrating this relationship, the members of the "Stop and Go" project built a large interactive map of the SOMAT network and displayed it in the SOMAT canteen during the summer of 2016. The drivers were encouraged to edit the map and to add their own nodes or links, but also to connect them with stories from their own real experience as drivers as well as to add photographs or material objects to the narrative. Thus, the abstract network was transformed into a mechanism of combining the abstract, the territorial, and the social dimensions of both SOMAT and the relatively autonomous drivers' networks before 1989.

# Dumping, Eye-Opening, and the Flip Side of the Cold War

The unintended consequences regarding mainly the drivers' activities could be observed in three major aspects: in the context of SOMAT's company success story; in the context of the socialist system *per se*; in the context of the global issues of the Cold War.

First, as already mentioned above, an important reason for the success of the Bulgarian international truck transport enterprise was the truck drivers' willingness to work for SOMAT for a critically low salary and therefore enhance the company's competitiveness on the international haulage market. In this regard the formal and informal networks existed in a form of economic mutualism, which forced the authorities to allow the drivers to conduct their private business. However, this rather fortunate circumstance was neither envisioned nor calculated by the company and state officials.

58 Кирил Янев, *Мъжка Участ* (София: Профиздат, 1988) [Kiril Yanev, Male destiny (Sofia: Profizdat, 1988)].

59 Георги Милчев, *Отличията задължават* (София: Профиздат, 1979) [Georgi Milchev, The distinctions oblige (Sofia: Profizdat, 1979)]; cf. Hammer, "A Gasoline Scented Sindbad," 100–1.

60 Kiril L. and Dragan. A., former international truck drivers, interview by the author, Sofia, December 20, 2007; Petar G., former SOMAT international truck driver and representative, interview by the author, Sofia, February 7, 2008; Sasho S., and Petar R., former international truck drivers, interview by the author, Chepelare, August 20, 2010.

61 All the interviewed truck drivers emphasized their self-confidence as being not only professionals but "the best" international truck drivers in the Eurasian world. The repeated formulas were: "We were the best"; "The Western Europeans almost did not travel, our transport was the biggest one [...] because they were not able to endure the heavy conditions on the roads downwards" (i.e., in the Middle East and Anatolia); "We taught the Hungarians"; "All [i.e., Hungarians, Turkish] learned from us".

62 This is another aspect all the drivers were unanimous about: "This is not a job for women"; "Women have no place on the road"; "It is too heavy/dangerous for women"; "It is a male occupation." There were, however, by way of exception, some women employed as international truck drivers, but they did not stay long. In the interviews the drivers recalled two such women, and another two were listed among the drivers in the Rousse branch of SOMAT, who stayed for one and two years respectively: State Archive Rousse, Fonds 1031, Record 1, file 24, 21, 26; file 25, 13; file 26.

63 The emphasis on their Bulgarian identity draws on two main sources—the first is the natural focus on their Bulgarian nationality being constantly in a foreign environment. The second is the attitude of the authorities toward them, emphasizing their status as "ambassadors" of the Bulgarian and socialist way of life (see, for example, "Report on the State of the Working Discipline in the DAP MP Rousse [the local branch of SOMAT] for the First Nine Months of 1972," State Archive Rousse, Fonds 1031, Record 1, file 6, page 25, where it is argued that "Two Bulgarians, representatives of socialist Bulgaria [...] show the foreigners on a small scale the image of our working people, running towards the construction of socialism and Communism." Most of the drivers appropriated this official image. The respondents emphasized that they were widely respected both in the East and in the West. Kiril L. also added that in many places and cases when he was able to contact some locals, it was clear that the only Bulgarians known at these places were the international truck drivers, so that people created an image of Bulgaria based on the behavior and appearance of the drivers.

Second, the socialist heroes' widespread practices of goods distribution contributed to people's changing image of the world beyond the Iron Curtain and cracked the monolithic system of the monopolistic communist redistribution system of goods and information. The truckers became vehicles of the "Western" ideological influence upon Eastern European people during the Cold War (consumerism, free market, individualism), on a basic tangible level. The large-scale Cold War battle of values, institutions, technologies, symbolic systems, ethics, or, generally—different lifestyle, was conducted on the basic level of smuggled clothes (especially blue jeans), shoes, cosmetics, technological gadgets, chocolate products, chewing gum, alcohol and Western cigarettes, magazines, and records.[64] The basic and negligible objects undermined the bigger ideological narratives.

Finally, the informal and interpersonal drivers' networks are not just a perspective on the Cold War "from below". Paradoxically, the socialist, semi-official, state contraband schemes and the neglected and invisible non-institutional actors' networks provide a lens through which the very contradictory and multidimensional nature of the Cold War becomes visible. The described pervasive networks and speculative practices were also facilitated by the Cold War's highly ambivalent relations between the two antagonistic blocs. The intense, cross-bloc interaction was possible through the active participation of capitalist companies and individuals from the three worlds, which were also interested in profiting from the embargo conditions. However, only a limited and privileged number of state representatives were aware of, and participated actively in, this sophisticated process of exchange, cooperation, and collaboration with the political opponents. After the fall of the Iron Curtain, the international truck drivers were among the first individuals in Bulgaria who were ready for the considerable economic and cultural changes, and started their own businesses.[65] In the framework of the Stop and Go project, I was able to conduct an interview in Rousse with Bojidar A., who was the founder of the "first private automobile (bus) line" in Bulgaria after 1989.[66] Soon afterwards, he built two gas stations, and today he also owns a cardboard tubes factory for the spinning and weaving industry, and a small hotel. The former driver claimed in the interview that his knowledge of economics was acquired via his economic experience as a driver and smuggler, but mainly "because he had been traveling the world" able to observe, compare, and understand the political processes and tendencies and prepare for the changes. By his accounts, he had actually started a semi-legal private business even before the fall of the Wall. Another group of former SOMAT drivers and officials founded a successful company for international forwarding, logistics, and transport in 1992.

The drivers were agents of communication between the two worlds on a very basic material and individual level. It could be also argued that they were in fact agents of European integration. This aspect of their activities is even more visible considering that after the fall of the Berlin Wall, they became among the first people to be actively involved in the new economic system as entrepreneurs, being familiar with the rules of the capitalist economy, but also having already established contacts across Europe and the Middle East. Thus, some of the private and individual networks of the truck drivers before 1989 were transformed into successful business networks. Therefore, the proposed three-dimensional scheme of transnational networks comprised of international, state, and individual actors. It shows that international truck transport, once further developed and coordinated by international conventions, evolved into a well-developed network extending across Eurasia and North Africa and therefore facilitated smooth flows between East and West under the conditions of Cold War stalemate and political rivalry. This three-dimensional scheme was also the primary link between producers and consumers in all of these regions. International transport connections fostered encounters between Western and Eastern Europe and between Europe and the "Third World": encounters that culminated in coordinated regulations, notions, documents and even objects; in trade, political and economic exchange, and social interaction; and, ultimately, in the everyday experience of countless ordinary people, as represented here by the experience of international truck drivers.

64 See also Hammer, "A Gasoline Scented Sindbad," 113–14. An important line of the semi-legal trade of Bulgarian international truck drivers were vinyl records and music magazines. Many Bulgarians touched Western mass culture for the first time through the contraband of the international truck drivers.

65 Petar R., former international truck driver, interview by the author, Chepelare, August 20, 2010.

66 Bojidar A., former international truck driver, interview by the author, Rousse, August 9, 2014.

## Archival Documents

### Central State Archive (CSA)
Fonds 1B
Record 45, file 245
Record 88, file 30, 119, 198, 204, 211
Record 93, file 18, 39
Fonds 493
Record 1, file 14, 17, 22, 23
Fonds 541
Record 1, file 22

### Sofia State Archive
Fonds 1587
Record 1, file 1, 4
Record 2, file 40

### Archive of the Committee for disclosing the documents and announcing affiliation of Bulgarian citizens to the State Security and Intelligence services of the Bulgarian National Army (ACDDAABCSSISBNA)
Fonds V
Record Л, file 970M
Fond 2
Record 3, file 305M, 368
Record 4, file 22M, 34M, 66M, 93M, 102M, 121M
Fonds 9
Record 4, file 250P
Fonds 32
Record 2, file 102M

### Archive of the Bulgarian Prosecutor's Office
Case 4/1990, vol. 42, 529 (Case for the Culprits of the Economic Catastrophe)

### State Archive Rousse
Fonds 1031
Record 1, file 6

## Interviews

Interviews with former and current Bulgarian international truck drivers and former SOMAT officials taken by the author:
Bojidar B., Rousse, August 9, 2014
Dimitar Raychev, Sofia, January 16, 2008
Dragan A., Sofia, December 20, 2007
Georgi B., Sofia, August 19, 2016
Georgi D., Chepelare, July 17, 2013
Ivan Ch., Sofia, January 4, 2010
Kiril L., Sofia, December 20, 2007
Petar G., Sofia, February 7, 2008
Petar P., Vienna, December 7, 2015
Petar R., Chepelare, August 20, 2010
Peycho P., Sofia, April 1, 2015
Sasho S., Chepelare, August 20, 2010
Stayko T., Lopian, April 13, 2009
Stefan B., Sofia, August 19, 2016
Todor Ch., Sofia, August 19, 2016

## Literature

Appadurai, Arjun. *Modernity at Large*. Minneapolis: University of Minnesota Press, 1996.

Bair, Jeniffer. "Analysing Global Economic Organizations: Embedded Networks and Global Chain Compared." *Economy and Society* 37, no. 3 (2008): 339–64.

Benson, Sumner. "How National Security Considerations Affect Technology Transfer." *Journal of Technology Transfer* 13, no. 1 (1988): 34–41.

Bischof, Gunter. "Of Dwarfs and Giants: From Cold War Mediator to Bad Boy of Europe—Austria and the U.S. In the Transatlantic Arena (1990–2013)." In *Austria's International Position after the End of the Cold War*, edited by Gunter Bischof and Ferdinand Karlhoper, 13–52. New Orleans: University of New Orleans, 2013.

Blaha, Jaroslav, Michèle Kahn, and Michel Vale. "Transportation in the East: The Key to Trade between the Two Europes." *Eastern European Economics* 29, no. 2 (1990–91): 29–63.

Chen, Wenhong and Justin Tan. "Understanding Transnational Entrepreneurship through a Network Lens: Theoretical and Methodological Considerations." *Entrepreneurship Theory and Practice* 33, no. 5 (2009): 1079–91.

Endy, Christopher. *Cold War Holidays: American Tourism in France*. Chapel Hill: University of North Carolina Press, 2004.

Guentcheva, Rossitza. "Mobile Objects: Corecom and the Selling of Western Goods in Socialist Bulgaria." [In English]. *Études Balkaniques* XLV, no. 1 (2009): 3–28.

Gulati, Ranjay, and Martin Gargiulo. "Where Do Interorganizational Networks Come From?" *American Journal of Sociology* 104, no. 5 (1999): 1439–93.

Hammer, Ferenc. "A Gasoline Scented Sindbad: The Truck Driver as a Popular Hero in Socialist Hungary." *Cultural Studies* 16, no. 1 (2002): 80–126.

Heard-Laureote, Karen. "Transnational Networks Informal Governance in the European Political Space." In *Transnational European Union Towards a Common Political Space*, edited by Wolfram Kaiser and Peter Starie, 36–60. London: Routledge, 2005.

Jackson, Peter, Philip Crang, and Claire Dwyer. "Introduction: The Spaces of Transnationality." In *Transnational Spaces*, edited by Peter Jackson, Philip Crang and Claire Dwyer, 1–23. London: Routledge, 2004.

Karaboeva, Emiliya. "Borders and Go-Betweens: Bulgarian International Truck Drivers During the Cold War." *East Central Europe* 41, nos. 2–3 (2014): 223–53.

Ledeneva, Alena. *Russia's Economy of Favours. Blat, Networking and Informal Exchange*. Cambridge: Cambridge University Press, 1998.

Maier, Sorin. *Transport and Logistic Glossary*. Constanta: Athos, 2009.

Mitter, Rana, and Patrick Major. *Across the Blocs: Cold War Cultural and Social History*. London: Frank Cass, 2004.

Morley, D., and K. Robins. *Spaces of Identity: Global Media, Electronic Landscapes and Cultural Boundaries*. London: Routledge, 1995.

"Multilateral Treaties in Respect of Which the Secretary-General Performs Depositary Functions. Annex: Final Clauses." Edited by United Nations. New York: United Nations, 1976.

"Status of Multilateral Conventions in Respect of Which the Secretary-General Acts as Depositary 1959–1963." Edited by United Nations. New York: United Nations, 1959.

"TIR Handbook. Customs Convention on the International Transport of Goods under Cover of TIR Carnets (TIR Convention, 1975)." Edited by United Nations Economic Commission for Europe. New York and Geneva: United Nations, 2013.

Vleuten, Erik van der. "In Search of the Networked Nation: Transforming Technology, Society and Nature in the Netherlands during the Twentieth Century." *European Review of History* 10, no. 1 (2003): 59–78.

Vleuten, Erik van der, and Arne Kaijser. "Prologue and Introduction: Transnational Network and the Shaping of Contemporary Europe." In *Networking Europe: Transnational Infrastructures and the Shaping of Europe, 1850–2000*, edited by Erik van der Vleuten and Arne Kaijser, 1–22. Sagamore Beach: Science History Publication, 2006.

Watters, John K., and Patrick Biernacki. "Targeted Sampling: Options for the Study of Hidden Populations." *Social Problems* 36, no. 4 (1989): 416–30.

Zatlin, Jonathan. "Making and Unmaking Money: Economic Planning and the Collapse of East Germany." *Occasional Papers*: 1–28. Published electronically April 28, 2007. http://repositories.cdlib.org/ies/070428 (accessed January 15, 2018).

Васильев, Дмитрий *Фарцовщики. Как делались состояния. Исповедь людей « тени»*. СПб: Вектор, 2007 [Vasiliev, Dmitri. Black marketeers. How the fortunes have been made; A confession by the shady people. St. Petersburg: Vektor, 2007].

Георгиев, Марин. *Развитието на транспорта в България и международното разделение на труда*. София: Наука и изкуство, 1970 [Georgiev, Marin. The development of the Bulgarian transport and the international divison of labor. Sofia: Nauka i Izkustvo, 1970].

Димитров, Борис, съст. *История на международния автомобилен транспорт в България*. София: Българско транспортно издателство, 2004 [Dimitrov, Boris, ed. History of the bulgarian international automobile transport. Sofia: Bulgarian Transport Publishing, 2004].

Милчев, Георги. *Отличията задължават*. София: Профиздат, 1979 [Milchev, Georgi. The distinctions oblige. Sofia: Profizdat, 1979].

Павук, Ольга. "Сначала было 'Совтрансавто'." *Латвийское авто, декември* 12, 2006 [Pavuk, Olga. "The beginning was set by 'Sovtransavto.'" *Latvian auto*, December 12, 2006].

Христов, Христо. *Империята на задграничните фирми*. София: Сиела, 2009 [Hristov, Hristo. The empire of the foreign-trade companies settled abroad. Sofia: Siela, 2009].

Янев, Кирил. *Мъжка участ*. София: Профиздат, 1988 [Yanev, Kiril. Male destiny. Sofia: Profizdat, 1988].

# Memoryscapes and the Legacy of SOMAT Networks and Nodes Today
## Reflections on the Applied Methodology

Michael Zinganel, Michael Hieslmair, and Emiliya Karaboeva

Today, Bulgaria is considered a typical outsourcing destination for Western European enterprises, especially for logistics industries, which register subsidiaries in the low-tax country and exploit badly paid drivers. That was different in the past: during the Cold War the Bulgarian government was able to establish SOMAT as a strong economic player with a high degree of expertise in contested geopolitical areas, "reaching far beyond 50 percent of the transit market share between Europe and the Middle East."[1] By the mid-1980s (and by their own accounts) SOMAT was the largest transport company in Europe with 4,500 modern lorries, a fleet of cargo ships, and a correspondingly far-flung transnational network.

International truck drivers were considered the ambassadors of Bulgaria abroad. When leaving Bulgaria signboards at border control stations reminded them to behave well to preserve the reputation of their homeland (fig. 31). But although the communist propaganda celebrated international Bulgarian truck drivers as "heroes of work" shaping the new socialist society, these drivers simultaneously acted as mediators between the East and West, who, by importing consumer articles and lifestyles, revealed the scarcity of the praised political system and thereby contributed to its erosion.[2]

The official wages of the drivers were modest, but compared to the majority of Bulgarian citizens they were privileged in that they were able to travel abroad. Traveling long-distance transnational routes in all directions, they could earn considerable income with black market activities and by smuggling goods of all kinds. Consumer goods brought from abroad also significantly increased their personal social status at home and that of their families. But also for Bulgarian hitchhikers, not permitted to travel to the West of Europe, SOMAT trucks often offered a lift to other communist nations, attractive for more generous leisure time possibilities compared to Bulgaria: for instance, to rock festivals in Budapest or nudist beaches on the Baltic Sea in the GDR.[3]

The development of SOMAT was thus a crucial element in Bulgaria's national identity and thoroughly embedded in the everyday life of its citizens. For this reason, the successive reorganization of SOMAT following the fall of the Iron Curtain in 1989 and the company's privatization with the majority of shares sold to the German freight forwarding company Willi Betz in 1994, were experienced by many as a painful loss. But even after the omnipresent symbols of the power of SOMAT had disappeared and thousands of trucks had been

---

1 Helmuth Trischler, "Geteilte Welt? Verkehr in Europa im Zeichen des Kalten Krieges," in *Neue Wege in ein neues Europa: Geschichte und Verkehr im 20. Jahrhundert*, ed. Ralf Roth and Karl Schlögel (Frankfurt am Main: Campus Verlag, 2009), 168–69.

2 Trischler, "Geteilte Welt?," 168.
3 Velislav Altanov, paper presented at the "Stop and Go" workshop at SOMAT canteen (Sofia, April 4, 2016).

rebranded with the Willi Betz logo, the company SOMAT did not yet disappear from the Bulgarian trade register: SOMAT still is the largest haulage company in Bulgaria, and its special expertise in the Middle East and Central Asia is still in high demand. For example, in 2010 SOMAT was commissioned by the US forces to exclusively supply US troops in Afghanistan.[4]

In the West of Europe, the company became widely known when the new German owner of SOMAT was involved in a big scandal: Thomas Betz, the son of the company founder and managing director, was accused of bribing authorities and underpaying illegally-employed, Bulgarian long-distance drivers. In March 2003 there were police raids at the headquarters in Reutlingen and company branches across Europe. In 2005 Thomas Betz was arrested for the first time; in September 2006 the lawsuit began in Stuttgart. In 2008 he was convicted of bribery, social security fraud, and forgery of documents in Germany. The regional court in Stuttgart deemed it proven that Betz illegally deployed Eastern European truck drivers on journeys within the EU between 1999 and 2002. He did not register the Bulgarian drivers for social security and evaded 9.6 million euros in payments—in order for the drivers to work for him, the forwarding agent fraudulently obtained more than 1,000 visas from the Immigration Service with the help of his proxy. And through bribery in the millions Betz obtained approximately 2,700 permits for cross-border freight transport.[5]

Against the backdrop of this scandal, Rimini Protokoll, a Swiss-German theater and performance collective, which has attained international acclaim for their works with "experts of the everyday," developed the idea for a mobile performance. It was based on interviews with Bulgarian truck drivers of the Bulgarian branch of Willi Betz and investigations into the network of transnational chains of goods transported by this company. For this purpose, they hired real Bulgarian truck drivers as the main actors to offer insights into their everyday life and how all of us rely on their smooth operation to fulfil our demands for daily provisions.[6] *Cargo Sofia-X: A Bulgarian Truck-Ride through European Cities* debuted in Basel in 2006 and has toured more than thirty cities in Europe—including our research destinations Sofia, Vienna, and Tallinn—and the Middle East, and since 2009 also in parts of Asia. For us, this piece served as an incentive to expand our immersed mobile research methods and the application of (artistic and non-artistic) visual material in our fieldwork.[7]

## The Current Condition of SOMAT Service Stations as Indicators of Transition

SOMAT had a network of service stations all over Bulgaria—in the capital Sofia, near the crossroads of the most important corridors, close to border crossings—but also at a number of chosen sites abroad, at nodes on the road network. They were fenced-off complexes with huge parking areas and a number of buildings: a gatehouse with a boom barrier, a weighbridge, a company fuel station, a large workshop with a lorry wash, a modernist tower accommodating offices with a safe for trips requiring foreign currency, freight documents and customs declarations, a company canteen, toilets, and for the drivers, showers, lodgings, and a surgery for medical examinations.

In keeping with our mobile research design, we also applied the method of driving road corridors used by SOMAT (and Willi Betz) truck drivers and visiting the nodes and knots of their network—at least on Bulgarian soil. We considered the current condition of SOMAT service stations as perfect physical indicators of the post-socialist transition of this company and the road transport business in Bulgaria. Furthermore, we also expected to meet "experts of the everyday" at these very places, who could offer more insights into the routines and rituals on the road and at these nodes.

For the investigation of the recent transformation of these nodes, we took the opportunity to visit as many of these service stations as possible during our research trips: for example, the station in the Bulgarian-Romanian border city of Russe, in Kapikule close to the Bulgarian-Turkish border, in Pazardzhik in the very heart of Bulgaria (fig. 18), and in the capital Sofia, which is located in the very west of the nation close to the border with Serbia. On these visits we

4   Herbert Schadewald, "Somat versorgt die US-Streitkräfte," *DVZ Deutsche Verkehrszeitung*, November 18, 2013, https://www.dvz.de/rubriken/region/laender/osteuropa/single-view/nachricht/somat-versorgt-die-us-streitkraefte.html (accessed May 24, 2017).

5   On "System Betz" see Uli Röhm and Wilfried Voigt, *Tatort Autobahn – Kriminelle Machenschaften im Speditionswesen* (Frankfurt am Main: Campus Verlag, 2006); Karsten Weber, "Unterwegs im gewerkschaftlichen Niemandsland. Auseinandersetzungen in der Speditionsbranche," *express-Zeitung für sozialistische Betriebs- und Gewerkschaftsarbeit* 12 (2016): 10–11.

6   Annika Wehrle, *Passagenräume. Grenzverläufe alltäglicher und performativer Praxis im Theater der Gegenwart* (Bielefeld: transcript, 2015), 179–80.

7   We presented *Cargo Sofia-X* during the pre-research phase to encourage our research partners to work with visual material and narrations more intensively, and a video documentation of *Cargo Sofia-X* had also been part of the exhibitions in the framework of the project. See: Michael Zinganel and Michael Hieslmair, *Road*Registers: Logbook of Mobile Worlds*, exhibition catalogue (Vienna: Academy of Fine Arts, 2017).

learned that after privatization, the new owner did not have any use for so many service stations. Only Russe and Sofia are still partly in use by Willi Betz today. In most of the stations, spaces are rented out to a range of other logistic companies; many spaces are left vacant and at least one was entirely up for sale, the station in Kapikule, which is now bypassed by a new highway.

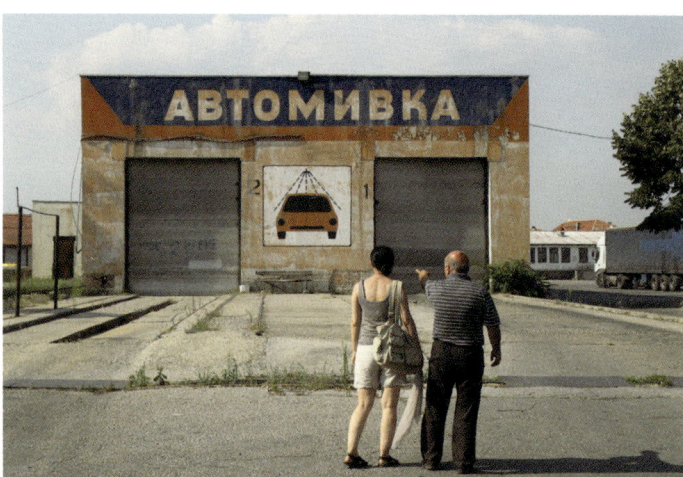

Fig. 18
Hieslmair and Zinganel, 2015
On tour visiting former SOMAT service stations all over Bulgaria: here in Pazardzhik in front of the former lorry wash station, with a doorman guiding the research team around the site which is partly abandoned today and partly used by other companies

We consciously chose to drive the old road from Svilongrad toward the Bulgarian-Turkish border to see the current status of the infrastructure of border economies at the old border station. On our way we coincidentally also noticed a late modernist tower with the lettering "Hotel SOMAT," a landmark located on a hillside along the street (fig. 19). The old border station turned out to be entirely closed off; the road was one way only to redirect the traffic to a few kilometers of highway that was recently built to access the many new checkpoints of a modern, EU-funded border control station. Hence, we found the many stalls, kiosks, and workshops close to the border station vacant and derelict. When driving back we stopped at Hotel SOMAT.

While curiously gazing over the closed gate we noticed a bored guard who then approached us. He spoke surprisingly good English and invited to us to visit the compound that had once been managed by his mother, he said. He told us about his childhood memories while walking around the site, and he opened every door also giving us a look into the interior of the compound:[8] The parking lots of the complex had been able to accommodate 160 trucks, there was a car wash for lorries and a hall for repair, crowned by huge illuminated letters offering "Service." The modernist style hotel housed fifty to sixty persons in double rooms (figs. 19–20) with bathroom and toilet, and even one apartment with two rooms. In the vacant lobby of the hotel we even found a simple architectural model of the compound protected in a glass display case, clearly indicating the importance the place might have had. Another building offered bathrooms, toilets, and changing rooms for truck drivers, who used to spend the nights in their own trucks. There had been a canteen, which, according to him, had never worked because the restaurant in the adjacent building offered an attractive terrace where you could sit outside. The complex was finished before 1989. Originally, access was limited to SOMAT drivers, but in the period of transition it gradually opened up to drivers from international partner companies, then to all transnational traffic passing through here or getting stuck in the endless traffic jam at the borders checks—and finally, to all kinds of other businesses: slot machines were installed inside and prostitutes also offered their services here.

His stories were intriguing and interesting yet anecdotal and limited to this very station. But they stirred our curiosity and encouraged us to look for a place that is visited by many more people, who would tell us their memories from the trucker milieu.

## Exhibition and Workshops at the Social Condenser of a Truck Drivers' Canteen

During our research period the surviving privatized branches of SOMAT were still operating from SOMAT's former logistics base in the neighborhood of Gorublyane in the south-east of Sofia, close to a major highway intersection. But the Bulgarian branch of Willi Betz did not own the estate but merely rented space for offices and handling cargo, like many other transport and service companies from the logistics field (fig. 21).

We discovered that the canteen in the center of this compound still offered several dishes at lunchtime. It therefore seemed to be a promising informal social network node for truck drivers and other people working in the logistics business, and indeed, many of them had been former employees of SOMAT—or at least had relatives who had worked for SOMAT in the past. We considered this place an ideal social condenser,[9] to set up an exhibition that automatically finds its own audience without any PR work necessary.

8   Mr. Bekiarov, interview by the authors (Kapikule, August 9, 2014).
9   We have borrowed this specialist term from architectural history to describe how certain spaces traverse social boundaries because they serve as channeling points for the circulations of diverse groups. Michał Murawski: "Introduction: Crystallising the Social Condenser," *Journal of Architecture* 22, no. 3 (2017): 372–86.

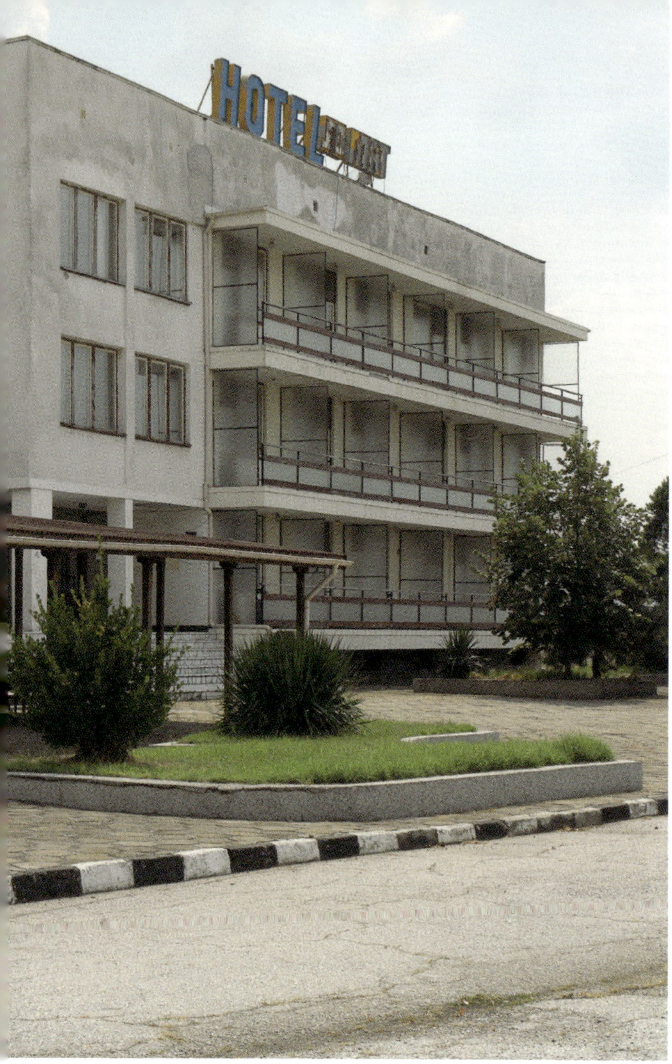

Figs. 19–20
Hieslmair and Zinganel, 2015
Vacant service station once operated by SOMAT with hotel, canteen, gas station, workshop, and lorry wash station located close to the Bulgarian-Turkish border. Due to the construction of a new section of motorway as part of new border control infrastructure it had been cut off from Pan-European Corridor IV.

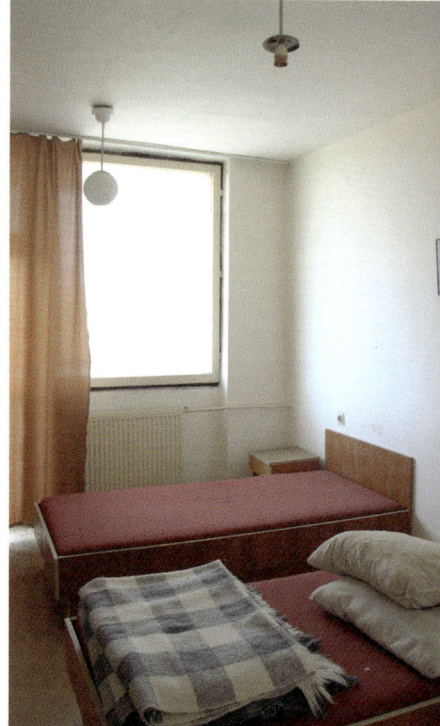

We had found documents, photos, and films in the company's archive beforehand, therefore we were able to present an assemblage of visual material, documenting parts of SOMATs history: we, for instance, showed an old poster (fig. 15) and a rather pathetic public relations film about SOMAT from 1982, praising the competence of the company's wide-ranging network; we re-made a map of this network as a large-scale installation on the back wall of the canteen; directly on the dining tables we showed beautiful photos of SOMAT's service stations with their modern workshops, canteens, offices, and training facilities at the various locations in Bulgaria, taken by a professional photographer in 1984 on the occasion of the twentieth anniversary of SOMAT (figs. 23–31). In display cases we showed awards *for* and gifts *to* the company's best drivers, such as a handmade Arabic brass plate for a trip to Libya, and even a collection of small-scale goods, cigarettes, pop records, jewelry, and henna, smuggled in the good old days (fig. 22). We also displayed the architectural model transported from Kapikule and our own photographs of this station's current partly derelict and vacant status.[10]

We also hosted an academic workshop in the framework of this exhibition. But the main intention of our intervention was to trigger further feedback from the many people with logistics and mobilities expertise whom we expected to meet here. And indeed, the exhibition seemed to be appreciated by staff and regular visitors of the canteen from the very start: we created a memoryscape,[11] where visitors felt both familiar with, and intrigued by, the material displayed. The chef of the canteen invited us to drink a bottle of his homemade spirit We observed several people enjoying a look at the items smuggled by drivers back in the good old days exhibited in the display case, while chatting with each other with a smile. But lacking the necessary linguistic skills we were not able to speak to all of them. When we saw a man, who according to his habitus, dress code, and hairstyle obviously belonged to a higher social rank at one of the companies located at this site, we actively approached him. It turned out he spoke English very well and even a bit of German.

Georgi Dimitrov became one of our major sources: he invited us to his workspace on site and provided us with an overview of his own work. But moreover, he instructed us—from his point of view—about the history of SOMAT, its

10 The same material was later shown in a truck drivers' canteen next to our Vienna project space and as a central piece in the exhibition at the Academy of Fine Arts in 2016. See Zinganel and Hieslmair, *Road\*Registers*.

11 In addition to Appadurai's exploration of the various "scapes," the notion of "memoryscapes" connotes the real and tangible, but often nostalgic and idealized, recollections of places, landscapes, and people remembered from the distant past, or from more recent experiences of visits. Arjun Appadurai, "Disjuncture and Difference in the Global Cultural Economy," *Theory Culture Society* 7, no. 2 (1990): 230–38; Kendall R. Phillips and G. Mitchell Reyes, eds., *Global Memoryscapes: Contesting Remembrance in a Transnational Age* (Alabama: University of Alabama Press, 2011).

1 Guard house with turnpike/road barrier
2 Seminar rooms [vacant]
3 Customs services [offices of various companies]
4 Office building and medical check [offices of various companies]
5 Canteen
6 Hairdresser/rooms for drivers [vacant]
7 Warehouse [used by various companies]
8 Warehouse [TV studio]
9 Warehouse [distribution center for express courier service]
10 Truck repair workshop of Balkanstar, service for Mercedes Benz trucks
11 Truck wash
12 Oil change [truck repair shop]
13 Truck repair shop
14 Gas station
15 Weigh station
16 Guarded TIR parking for trucks of other companies

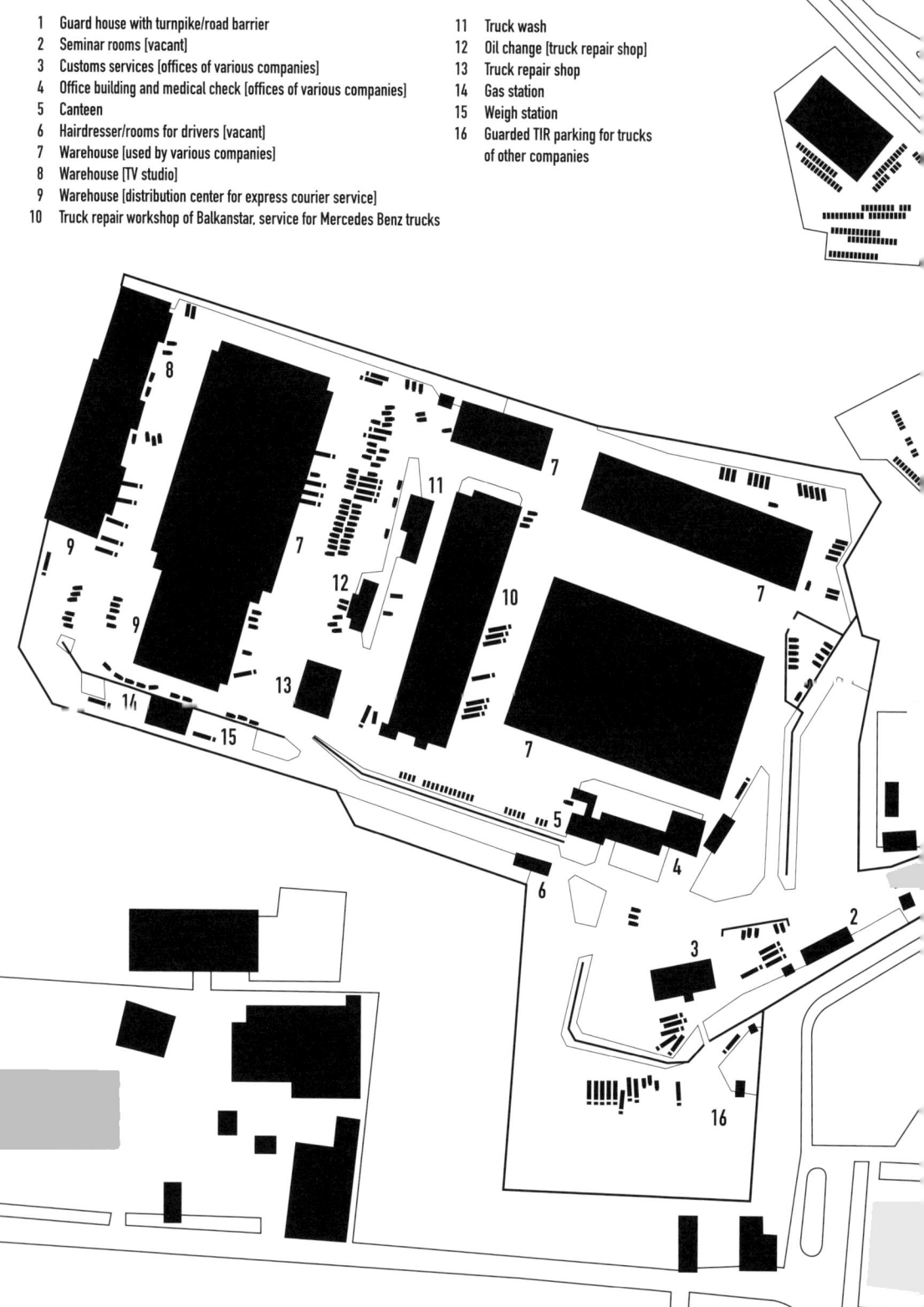

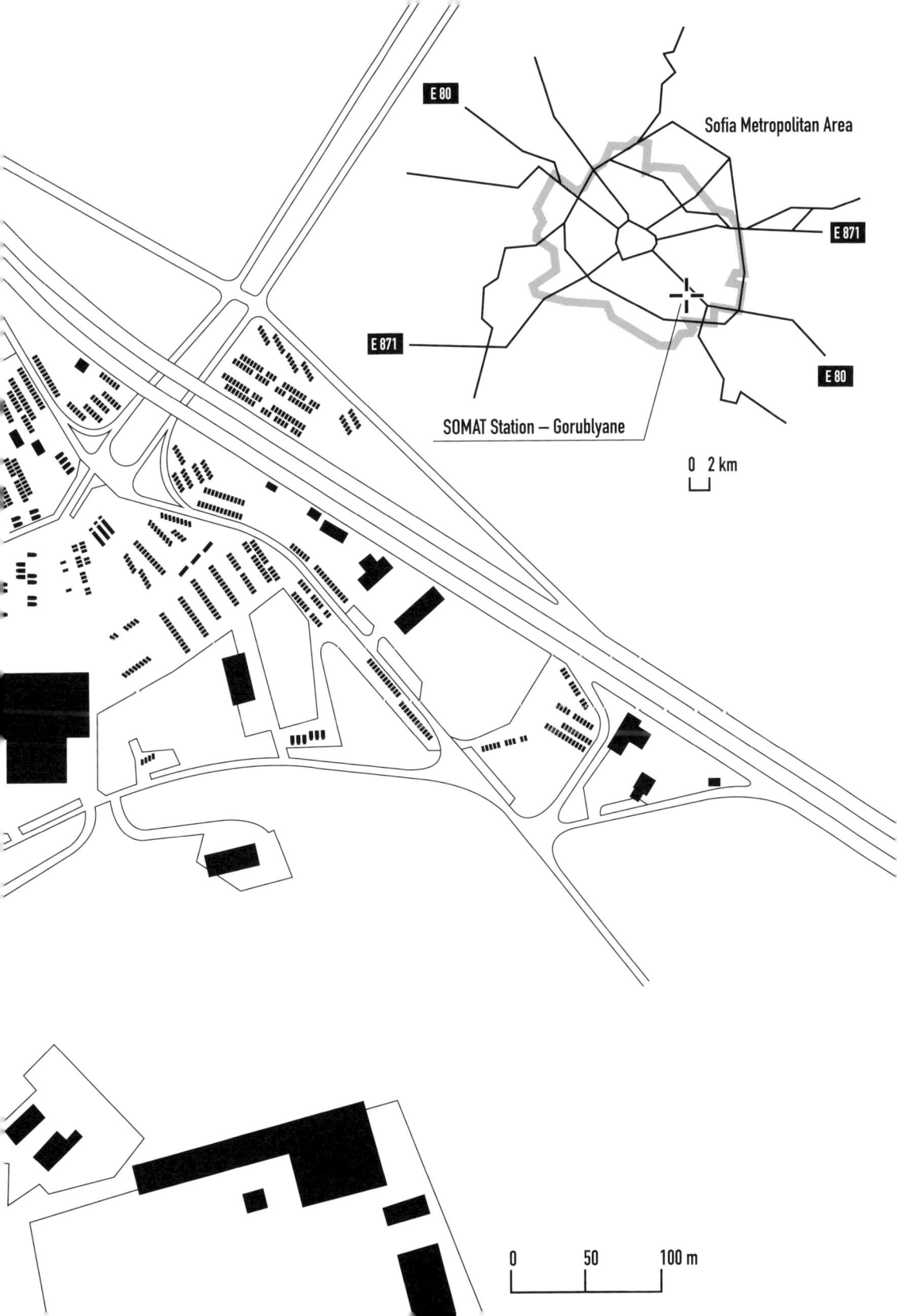

Fig. 21
Hieslmair and Zinganel, 2018
SOMAT's former headquarters in Gorublyane, on the outskirts of Sofia as used in 1984 (and repurposed in 2014)

current German owner, and the reasons for the decline of the company (as touched upon above).[12] At the time he was the manager of Balkanstar repair and service workshop, specializing exclusively in Mercedes Benz trucks, and in charge of a huge workshop space at the former SOMAT compound (fig. 21). In communist times Balkanstar was a sub-branch of SOMAT and imported Mercedes trucks to Bulgaria in cooperation with Willi Betz, who also operated a small transport company in Germany. This collaboration is one of the reasons behind the rather paradoxical situation that a state-owned company in a relatively poor communist state had a fleet of thousands of Mercedes Benz trucks, symbols of the superiority of Western capitalist technological.[13] But the Bulgarian truck drivers, in turn, argued proudly that they had significantly contributed to the technical development of Mercedes trucks by test-driving them both in cold winters and hot summers in the hardest possible conditions of Asian mountains ranges and deserts.

During the later liberalization and privatization phase, both the government and the management board at SOMAT considered Willi Betz an appropriate partner to purchase the majority of SOMAT shares. However, many Bulgarians made Willi Betz responsible for the decline of the company. While the business still flourished during the time of Soviet occupation in Afghanistan (since 1978) and the Iran-Iraq war (1980–88), the process of decline accelerated already in 1991 with the UN sanctions against Iraq and the wars and insurgencies in connection with the disintegration of Yugoslavia, interrupting the major transport routes of SOMAT and causing a significant loss of business for the company. The new owner was also facing hard times with the general economic crisis in Bulgaria in 1996. After losing the state monopoly position on the market in the liberalization process, new co-competitors appeared, both international and national,[14] and Willi Betz needed to modernize and rationalize the management of the company and close down parts of the service stations and warehouses to capitalize at least the real estate value of the sites.[15]

The importance of the network of SOMAT service stations in Bulgaria and abroad declined in the new times of cashless payment, online paperwork, and GPS-controlled vehicles. Today, trucks are often just leased and drive primarily between outsourced warehouses and cargo hubs, and in the event of repair hire highly mobile service companies.

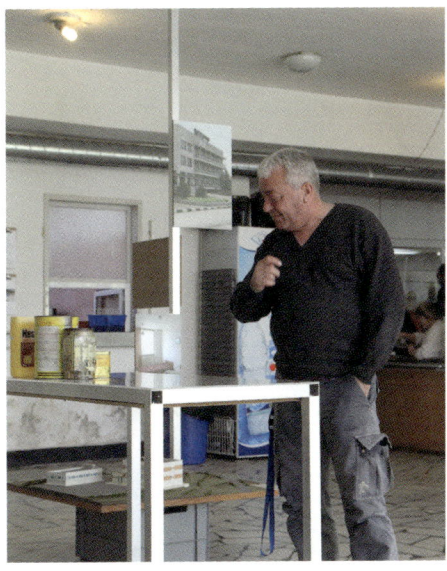

Fig. 22
Hieslmair and Zinganel, 2016
Exhibition in the canteen of SOMAT's former headquarters in Sofia-Gorublyane aimed at triggering the mutual exchange of knowledge, featuring a map of SOMAT's transcontinental network, photographs, and a PR film from the company's archive, but also a display case showcasing old smugglers' goods—that successfully attracted truck drivers, evoked memories, and sparked conversations

In the old days driving trucks was a dangerous enterprise for numerous reasons: high-value vehicles and load—often machinery parts or even weapons were exported—needed to be protected from street robbery or theft. But communications devices were limited in range. Hence, the drivers generally grouped into convoys traveling from one safe node to the next —and preferably without any stops in dangerous regions. Safety was often better guaranteed by tribal chiefs than by official police forces. Medical checks of drivers were necessary both when leaving Bulgaria for visa requirements and when returning to prevent importing diseases from abroad. Workshop spaces were needed to repair vehicles, sometimes to prepare hideouts for smuggling goods—extra hidden gasoline tanks had been a popular device—complicated paperwork had to be prepared and cash stored in bank vaults, necessary for loading goods or bribing customs officers abroad.

12 Georgi Dimitrov, interview by the authors (Sofia, April 14, 2016).
13 Originally, they started out using French trucks and then changed to the Swedish brand Volvo.
14 In 2004 the number of smaller transport companies in Bulgaria had reached 4,290 owning altogether 15,563 trucks. The number of companies owning one or two trucks was 2,372. Most of them had been uncompetitive in the free market, engaging instead in risky or outright smuggling operations. Center for the Study of Democracy, eds., *Transportation, Smuggling, and Organized Crime* (Sofia, Center for the Study of Democracy, 2004), 8.
15 In Sofia, for example, the huge property had been sold to a firm named Vienna Real Estate. And in 2016 Speedy Group, the parent company of the express delivery firm Speedy, also running a large modern distribution center on site, purchased the majority of shares.

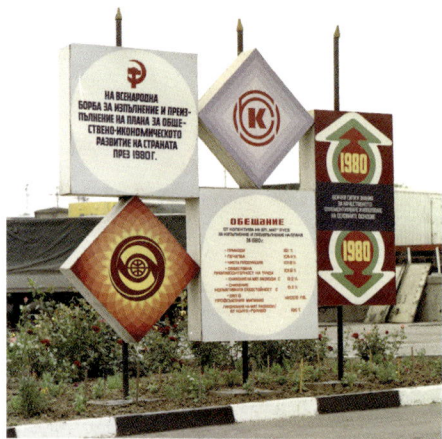
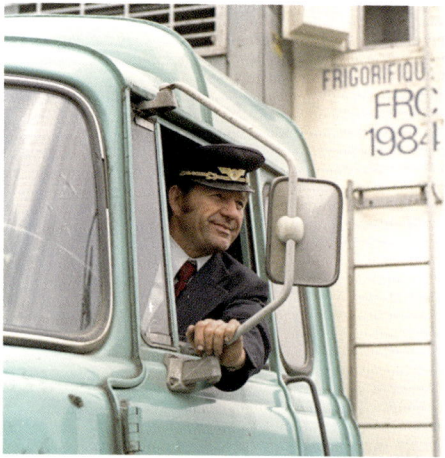
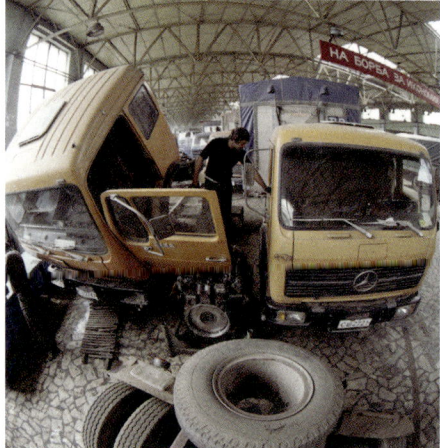
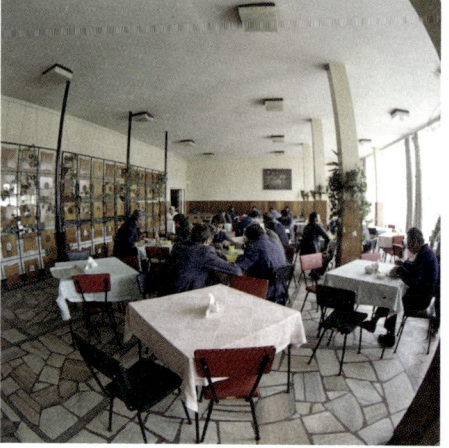

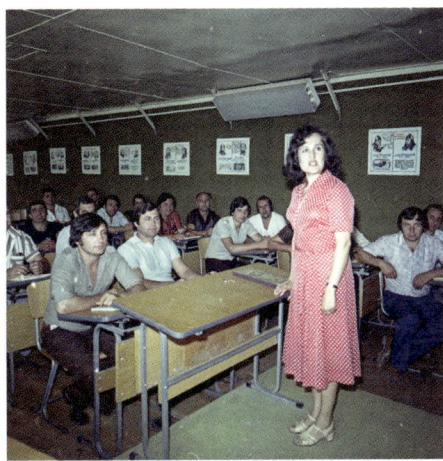
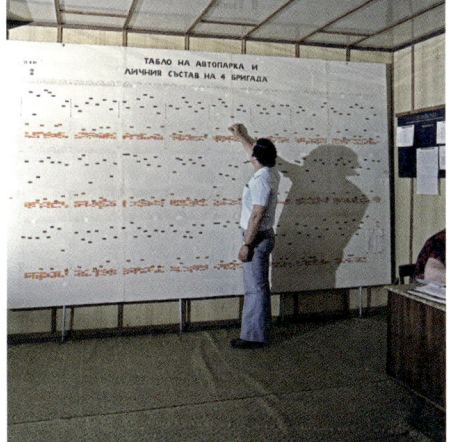
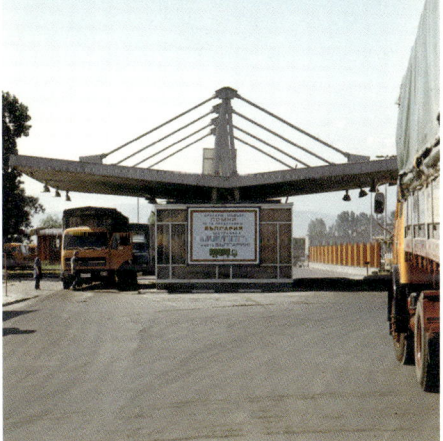
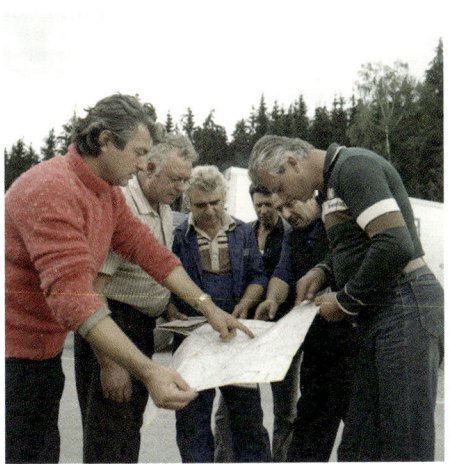

Figs. 23–30
SOMAT Archive, 1984
The life and times of the world of SOMAT: photos taken by a professional photographer on the occasion of the company's twentieth anniversary at SOMAT service stations—which featured modern repair workshops, canteens, offices, and training facilities at various locations across Bulgaria

Dimitrov also told us about his early days, when he worked at the SOMAT service station in Vienna, close to the city's Danube port and the black market at Mexiko Platz, which was initiated and managed by Jews who had emigrated to Vienna from Georgia in the 1970s. At the height of the Cold War Vienna represented a kind of paradise for Bulgarian truck drivers: For them, Vienna was the first metropolitan city on the other side of the Iron Curtain, a relatively safe place to stay, enjoy the nightlife, and take home Western brand consumer goods.

Fig. 31
SOMAT Archive, 1984
Sign addressing Bulgarian truck drivers at a border station before leaving Bulgaria: Comrades, drivers, please remember: Keep the name of Bulgaria clean and spotless on the three continents beyond the borders of Bulgaria!

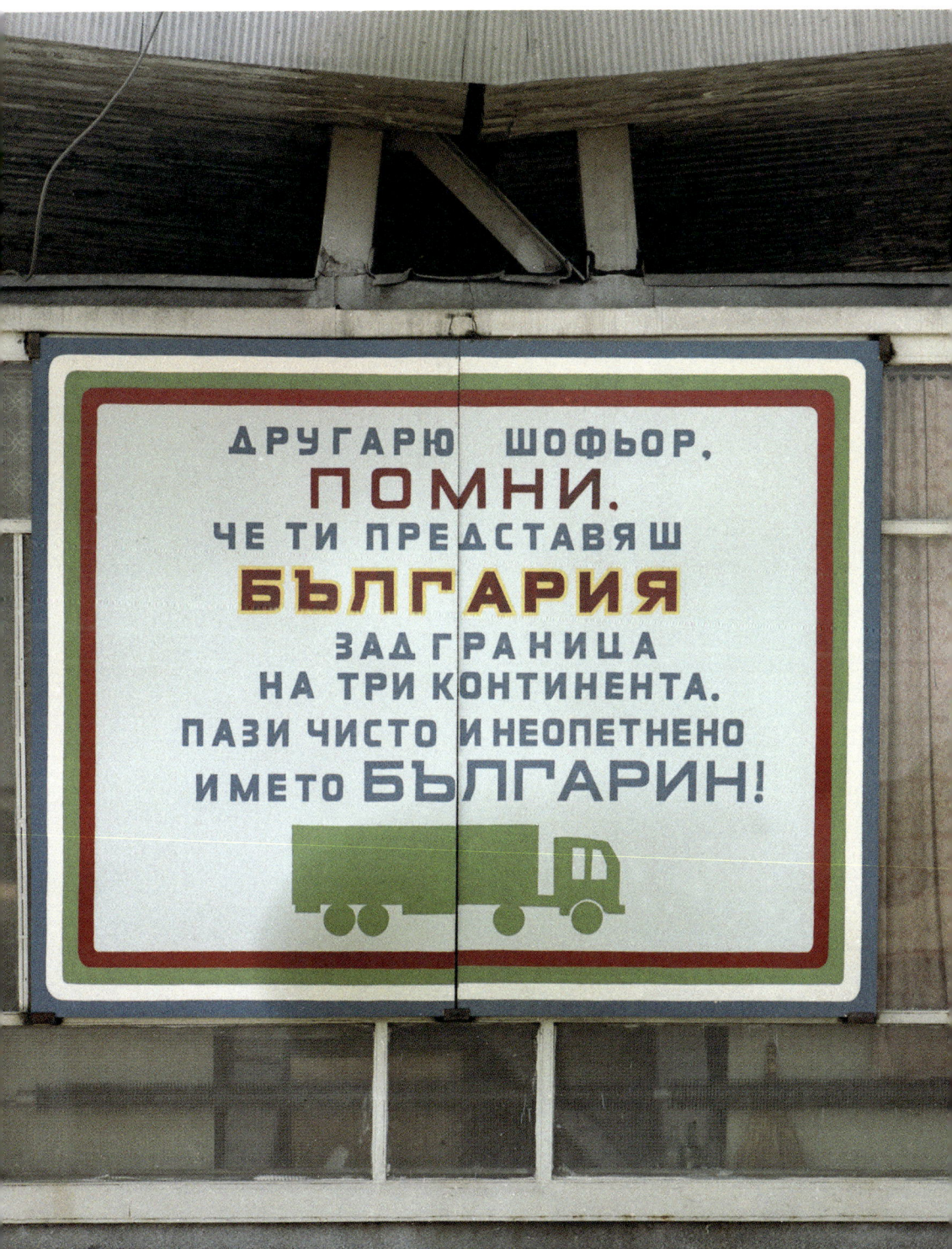

Literature

Altanov, Velislav. Paper presented at the "Stop and Go" workshop at SOMAT canteen (Sofia, April 4, 2016).

Appadurai, Arjun. "Disjuncture and Difference in the Global Cultural Economy." *Theory Culture Society* 7, no. 2 (1990): 230–38.

Bekiarov, interview by the authors, Kapikule, August 9, 2014.

Center for the Study of Democracy, ed. *Transportation, Smuggling, and Organized Crime*. Sofia, 2004.

Dimitrov, Georgi, interview by the authors, Sofia, April 14, 2016.

Murawski, Michał. "Introduction: Crystallising the Social Condenser." *Journal of Architecture* 22, no. 3 (2017): 372–86.

Phillips, Kendall R., and G. Mitchell Reyes, eds. *Global Memoryscapes: Contesting Remembrance in a Transnational Age*. Alabama: University of Alabama Press, 2011.

Röhm, Uli, and Wilfried Voigt. *Tatort Autobahn–Kriminelle Machenschaften im Speditionswesen*. Frankfurt am Main: Campus Verlag, 2006.

Schadewald, Herbert. "Somat versorgt die US-Streitkräfte." *DVZ Deutsche Verkehrszeitung*, November 18, 2013, https://www.dvz.de/rubriken/region/laender/osteuropa/single-view/nachricht/somat-versorgt-die-us-streitkraefte.html (accessed May 24, 2017).

Trischler, Helmuth. "Geteilte Welt? Verkehr in Europa im Zeichen des Kalten Krieges." In *Neue Wege in ein neues Europa: Geschichte und Verkehr im 20. Jahrhundert*, edited by Ralf Roth and Karl Schlögel, 168–69. Frankfurt am Main: Campus Verlag, 2009.

Weber, Karsten. "Unterwegs im gewerkschaftlichen Niemandsland: Auseinandersetzungen in der Speditionsbranche." *express—Zeitung für sozialistische Betriebs- und Gewerkschaftsarbeit* 12 (2016): 10–11.

Wehrle, Annika. *Passagenräume: Grenzverläufe alltäglicher und performativer Praxis im Theater der Gegenwart*. Bielefeld: transcript, 2015.

Zinganel, Michael, and Michael Hieslmair. *Road*Registers: Logbook of Mobile Worlds*. Exhibition catalogue. Vienna: Academy of Fine Arts, 2017.

# Corridors into Vienna and Beyond
## The Bus, the Terminal, the Border
### Infrastructural Publics and Politics

# Gates to the City
## Transformations and Encounters at Vienna's International Coach Terminals

Michael Hieslmair

Michael Hieslmair

## A Prehistory of International Coach Terminals in Vienna

When, in the 1920s, horse-drawn omnibuses were finally replaced by motor driven ones, the prestige of bus travel was, to some extent, naturally due to the newness of the technology. At that point in time new travel agencies sprang up in city-center locations especially along Vienna's Ringstrasse, that splendid boulevard of the bourgeoisie. Buses arrived and departed from there. The state-owned Österreichisches Verkehrsbüro (Austrian travel agency), for example, was opened in 1923 in an almost palatial Art Deco building opposite the Vienna Secession, one of the most important exhibition spaces for contemporary visual arts. However, the catastrophic economic situation of the interwar years imposed limits on these developments and the civil branch of long-distance bus travel was provisionally brought to an end when, in preparation for war, the National Socialists confiscated all serviceable vehicles. This revived only with the economic boom at the end of the Second World War. Naturally, in the 1960s buses were still regarded as a genuinely modern means of transport now available to a broader sector of the population. In many places especially designed coach terminals were placed close to the city center at strategically connected sites. This was not only in recognition of the increase in traffic volume but also due to the need to stage this form of travel in an appropriate manner.[1] And so it was with Vienna. In 1962 the Vienna Landstrasse bus terminal was opened at a site on top of the urban railway station Wien Mitte where today there is a shopping center. This is a perfect example that allows us to follow how an urban site develops in parallel with the various phases of modernization of means of transport, models of investment and, consumer culture: a site that goes from being an inland harbor for cargo vessels to a railway goods station then a passenger station, undergoes a conversion into a bus terminal and into its current incarnation as a mixed-use development with a huge shopping center that hopes to profit from the high volume of transit passengers at the major junction of underground, urban, and suburban railways.

The glacis in front of the former Stuben Gate, part of the old city fortification, had developed into a "central market complex for retail and wholesale business" and thus an important traffic node and transhipment point for supplying Vienna.[2] The origins lie in the excavation of the harbor basin in 1803

---

1   In terms of design, an example of an exceptional building is the George Washington Bridge Bus Station located at the east end of the George Washington Bridge in Manhattan, New York, designed by the famous Italian architect and engineer Pier Luigi Nervi in 1963.

2   Renate Wagner-Rieger, ed., *Die Ringstraße: Bild einer Epoche: Die Erweiterung der Inneren Stadt Wien unter Kaiser Franz Joseph*, vol. 11 (Wiesbaden: Steiner, 1969–1981), 209ff. Unless otherwise noted, all translations are my own.

as part of the Wiener Neustädter canal[3] and the central customs office[4] close by which, with its associated warehouses, began operations in 1844. However, shipping goods by canal soon became uneconomic when faced with competition from railways. Between 1847 and 1849 the harbor basin and the canal bed were adapted to house the connecting line between the Nordbahnhof (north railway station) and the Südbahnhof (south railway station). Finally, in 1899, during the construction of the urban railway and the work to regulate the Wien River, a new, subsurface railway station was opened.

After the Second World War, many of the warehouses and sales halls that had been built here were successively demolished and, in 1957, the railway tracks and station were covered over with a concrete slab. The Vienna property developers, Zwerenz & Krause,[5] then built the AEZ Ausstellungs- und Einkaufszentrum (exhibition and shopping center) from plans by architect Josef Wöhnhart in the international modern style. This was the first shopping center with integrated covered parking in Vienna and was attached to the new central bus terminal, Wien Landstrasse, to the north (fig. 36a). Opened in 1962, it had a number of winged-roof bays. Its interior provided a waiting room, a post office, newsagents and tobacconists, various kiosks, and shops with provisions for the journey. These were open till late in the evening and on weekends and holidays too at a time when Saturday opening ended at midday. Access was via the airy ground floor of the AEZ which comprised two blocks facing each other housing, amongst other things, a modern parking garage, a new market hall, exhibition spaces, and various businesses all connected by escalators—Hotel Zentrum, the Vindobona Travel agents, offices, event rooms, and a festival hall. It was here that the extremely popular radio program, *Autofahrer Unterwegs* (The motorist en route), was recorded live for broadcasting throughout Austria. A radio show open to the public, it featured live music, star guests, reporting on potential travel destinations, and practical tips and traffic information for motorists.[6] Because of its hybrid structure, a mixture of traffic node and prestigious consumer and entertainment temple, the centrally located building was a symbol of modernity, progress and (mass) mobility during the boom years of the 1950s. Its reputation was enhanced by the opening of the Hilton International Hotel in 1975 which was built opposite the main entrance to the railway station and replaced the former central market. The hotel also offered its own airport bus terminal, a booking hall for Trans World Airlines and shops aimed at exclusive customers in accordance with the social status of the international hotel's jet-set guests.[7]

With the opening to the east, however, the image of the railway station was radically transformed: it functioned as the gateway access for tourist shoppers and migrants from Eastern Europe, quickly becoming a hotspot for the downwardly mobile who sought refuge here by day and night. The profitability of the shops in the area declined to less than break-even. With increasing pressure from investors, the site, located as it is close to the city center, became too valuable to remain unchanged. The extensive vacant area of the bus terminal stood in the way of developing a new project with a greatly increased density. In 2002 Vienna's mayor, Michael Häupl, confronted with a possible postponement of the planning and realization of a new project, called the old terminal a "rats' nest" and a "blot on the landscape" that needed demolishing as soon as possible.[8] There was speculation at the time that Häupl's statement not only referred to the building complex, but also those who used it—in particular the coach terminal users. The project, backed by investors with close connections to the Vienna City administration and the ruling Social Democratic Party, was fought to a standstill not least because the planned high-rise development would call into question the city's UNESCO World Cultural Heritage status. A few years and a further architectural competition later, there was nothing left of the old coach terminal building and the terminal itself was moved. Instead, the site above the railway terminal underwent development as a massive shopping center and office block, a joint venture between property developers Zwerenz & Krause, who had taken a significant role in building the now demolished multifunctional building that stood there, Bank Austria Creditanstalt as financial investor, and

3  The plan envisaged a canal to the Adriatic Sea. The only section built was from Vienna to Wiener Neustadt linking the industrial area to the south of the city with the capital. Fritz Lange, *Von Wien zur Adria—Der Wiener Neustädter Kanal* (Erfurt: Sutton Verlag, 2003).
4  Renate Wagner-Rieger, *Wiens Architektur im 19. Jahrhundert* (Vienna: Österreichischer Bundesverlag, 1970), 87f.
5  The property development company Zwerenz & Krause was founded by Carl Maria Zwerenzost and Heribert Krause in Vienna in 1950 as a concert and event organization enterprise. Their experience in this area and the contacts they made enabled them to become active in the real estate business. The AEZ project, in cooperation with the Austrian National Railway and the Austrian Post Office was only their first large-scale project. Up to the present the successor company, BETHA Zwerenz & Krause, or the associated INVESTER United Benefits GmbH, is involved whenever property of the state-owned Austrian Railway company is to be developed. See http://www.betha-zwerenz-krause.com, http://www.invester.at (accessed March 26, 2018).

6  District Museum—Vienna's 3rd District. http://web.archive.org/web/20140106191737; http://www.dasmuseen.net/Wien/BezMus03/page.asp/1624.htm (accessed March 26, 2018).
7  In 1967, Hilton International Hotels was taken over by the US American airline TWA (Trans World Airlines). The Hotel Intercontinental, in the direct line of sight, was opened in 1964 and owned by the second-largest US airline, Pan Am. The engagement of the two American companies in such a central location in the city was part of a SOFT POWER strategy that was part of the competition for spheres of influence during the Cold War.
8  Statement by Michael Häupl, Vienna's incumbent mayor during the debate about the proposed high-rise project for this specific site: "I want this project to happen— And that this gateway to Vienna is appropriately attractive—what I certainly do not want is that this pigsty continues to be there." *Der Standard*, February 19, 2002, https://derstandard.at/862478/Haeupl-Sauhaufen-Wien-Mitte-muss-weg (accessed March 26, 2018).

Fig. 32
Gastarbeiter (guest workers): labor migrants waiting outside a Turkish travel agency offering round trips between places of work and family, between homelands old and new

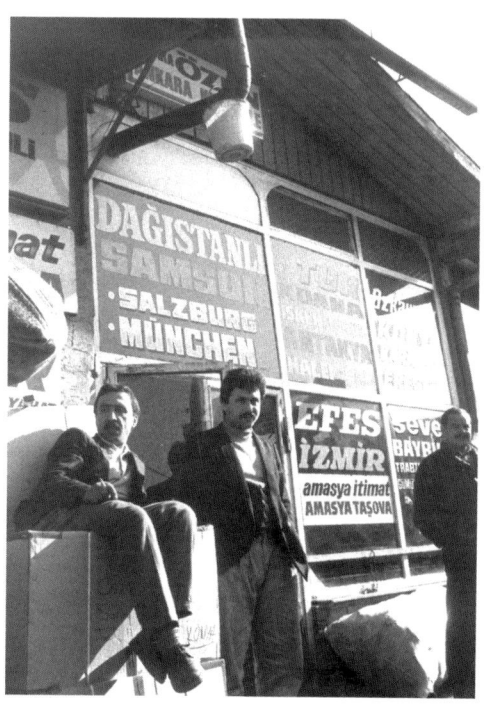

Fig. 34
Bus terminal in Vienna's Landstrasse district (rear left: the AEZ and tower of the Hilton International): while buses from the state-run monopoly conveyed commuters, private operators started to interconnect Vienna with its Eastern European neighbors

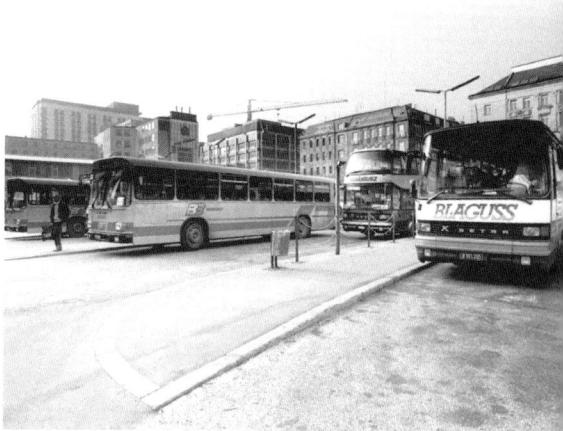

Fig. 33
Ostbusparkplatz (East Bus Terminal) at Handelskai: improvised parking lot for the masses of visitors arriving in Vienna from Eastern Europe after the fall of the Iron Curtain, where a black market soon established

the property developer, Bauträger Austria Immobilien GmbH.[9] It was completed and opened in 2012 and called The Mall.

## Bus Routes and Migration History in Vienna

During the Cold War, Vienna with its position just outside the Iron Curtain, was generally regarded as being effectively cut off from international transit traffic. However, in the case of goods traffic this was only partially true. In the main there was little change especially with the bustling Danube barge traffic and the numerous cooperation agreements between forwarding agents in Vienna, Eastern and Southeastern Europe.[10] In contrast, when it came to passenger services the Iron Curtain had only few holes which were controlled by strict visa regulations. It was only with the recruitment agreements with Turkey (1964) and Yugoslavia (1966) and the resulting inflow of guest workers that traffic flows once again began to reorient themselves to South-East Europe as they had been during the Habsburg monarchy. Between the signing of these agreements and 1974 around 265,000 people came to Austria. Most of these immigrants (approx. 78.5 percent) arrived from former Yugoslavia, a smaller number (around 11.8 percent) from Turkey.[11] The first guest workers from Turkey—almost all of them men—arrived in Vienna on a special train and were received at the South Station with appropriate media coverage. From there they were taken by bus to their new workplaces and dormitories (very often barracks) in the industrialized area south of Vienna.

Initially, the work contracts were fixed term and their stay was regarded as temporary. This meant that maintaining the connections to the regions from which the workers came was important. In order for these cyclical journeys

9   Bank Austria-Creditanstalt was the largest financial institute in Austria, formed in 1991 from a fusion of Zentralsparkasse and Länderbank, both state-owned, merging with Creditanstalt in 1996. Via shares of a private foundation the bank was controlled by the City of Vienna. In 2000 the majority of the shares were sold to the Hypovereinsbank München, which was taken over by the Italian Uni-Credit in in 2005. BAI, formerly Bank Austria Immobilien, today Bauträger Austria Immobilien, was put up for sale by Uni-Credit in 2016. In 2017 it was taken over by the SIGNA-Gruppe (Renè Benko) and the investor group, INVESTER United Benefits—owned in equal parts by the property investors Erwin Krause, Franz Kollitsch, Hannes Gruber, and Martin Huber, the former General Director of Austrian National Railways—as a fifty-fifty joint venture.

10  Evidence of this can be found in the network of the state-owned forwarding agents, SOMAT, which entered into cooperation with agents in Western Europe and Vienna in particular located in "neutral" Austria. More details can be found in the case study of Bulgaria.

11  Medienservicestelle, *Anwerbe-Abkommen mit Türkei—geschichlicher Hintergrund* (2014), http://medienservicestelle.at/migration_bewegt/2014/05/07/anwerbe-abkommen-mit-tuerkei-geschichtlicherhintergrund (accessed March 26, 2018).

home to be economically feasible a mode of transport was needed that was direct and flexible—the coach. It did not take long for coach lines to be established that connected Vienna with the relevant regions of origin in Yugoslavia and Turkey.[12] In the succeeding years the network was consolidated and increased in density. This network still had no official or particularly visible stops in Vienna. For example, instead of stopping at the central bus terminal in Vienna's 3rd district (Landstrasse) the first BOSFOR buses,[13] which provided a regular service between Vienna and Istanbul, stopped in Argentinierstrasse, in front of the travel agency of the same name in Vienna's 4th district. The buses had to start their motors a considerable time before departure so that the operating pressure necessary for their pneumatic brakes was achieved. This noise represented a serious disturbance for neighbors.[14] In addition, there were a large number of waiting passengers as well as family members who arrived before departures and arrivals. In a high-density residential district this was not welcome as even the normal procedure for travel groups (including Austrian travel groups) was to collect in front of travel agencies before leaving for holidays (fig. 32). So, during the 1980s, the bus stops that were scattered throughout the city slowly became concentrated around the South Railway Terminal.[15]

## A New Village Square—South Rail Terminal, East Rail Terminal, and the Schweizergarten

The second South Railway Terminal consisted of two termini and was the end of the line for the southern railway (to Trieste) and the eastern railway (to Budapest). It was constructed in 1873 right by Linienwall.[16] This outer ring of fortifications ran along what is now the multi-lane, heavily traveled Gürtel and, at the time, it represented the customs border between the city center and the suburbs.

Although damage to the railway terminals during the Second World War could have been easily repaired, it was decided to build a massive ticketing hall to serve both stations.[17] This came into service in stages between 1955 and 1961. The favorable location near to two major roads (to the east and south) and the connection with the rail lines almost predestined the site as a major stop for international coaches (fig. 36b). The ample and fixed open area on the east flank of the terminal building offered sufficient space. Further bus stops were to be found deep in the adjoining Schweizergarten, a park crisscrossed by traffic-bearing streets. These stops were marked with small unobtrusive signs. During the warmer part of the year, the open space and park benches were popular as a picnic zone and meeting place. The fact that the infrastructure in and around the railway terminal was available for use by coach passengers and their relations was a significant factor in making the site one of the most important meeting points:[18] a supermarket with extended opening hours for food for the journey, a railway restaurant, numerous stands and kiosks selling snacks etc., and extensive toilet facilities that were free. The railway terminal offered a large-scale covered area outside, a spacious ticketing hall with seating, a number of protected niches which, during the colder parts of the year were particularly important for both waiting and arriving passengers in equal measure: "Above all, the South Station became an almost mythical place for many—here began the first steps of an unknown future, later on many came here regularly to meet fellow countrymen and for news about what was going on at home."[19] During the early stages of guest worker recruitment, the South Station was also a popular destination for curious Austrians who came to see the workers arriving from foreign parts. The role of the railway terminal as a place where the foreign and foreigners were encountered is also visible in numerous photos that were published in the daily newspapers. Whereas initially the great numbers and presence of the necessary workforce was still proudly presented in the commentaries as evidence for the onset of economic growth, the mood later changed to that of increasing fear of too many foreign men.[20]

## International Networks and Partnerships in Transnational Coach Traffic

Right from the beginning, scheduled transnational coach service traffic was regulated and run as a monopoly under defined-term licensing. In order to inaugurate a route, the route itself, the total time taken, the timetable, and the scale of ticket costs had to be fixed, approved, and authorized by the appropriate ministry of transport beforehand. A further precondition was a partnership between local enterprises in each of the countries of departure and

12  Peter Peyer, *Gehen Sie an die Arbeit: Zur Geschichte der 'Gastarbeiter' in Wien 1964–1989*, Wiener Geschichtsblätter 1 (2004): 1–19.
13  Bosfor-Turizm was founded in 1963 in Istanbul and later, in 1992, taken over by Deniz Gönül, the long time manager of the Vienna branch. Deniz Gönül, CEO of BOSFOR, interview by the authors, Vienna, November 10, 2015.
14  Gönül, interview.
15  Gönül, interview.
16  Extending the railway network had the effect of greatly increasing rail traffic. The private Südbahn Gesellschaft built the "first South Station." This went into service in 1841 but was replaced only thirty-two years later by a much bigger and more impressive terminal building. Wolfgang Kos, ed., *Grosser Bahnhof: Wien und die weite Welt* (Vienna: Czernin Verlag, 2006), 228–31, 276–78.
17  Kos, *Grosser Bahnhof*, 380–85.
18  Peyer, *Gehen Sie an die Arbeit*, 8. Translated by Tim Sharp.
19  Peyer, 8. Translated by Tim Sharp.
20  Vida Bakondy, *Bahnhofs-Bilder: Historischer Ort und visuelles Chiffre der Arbeitsmigration nach Österreich*, paper presented at Zeitgeschichtetag Graz, June 8, 2016.

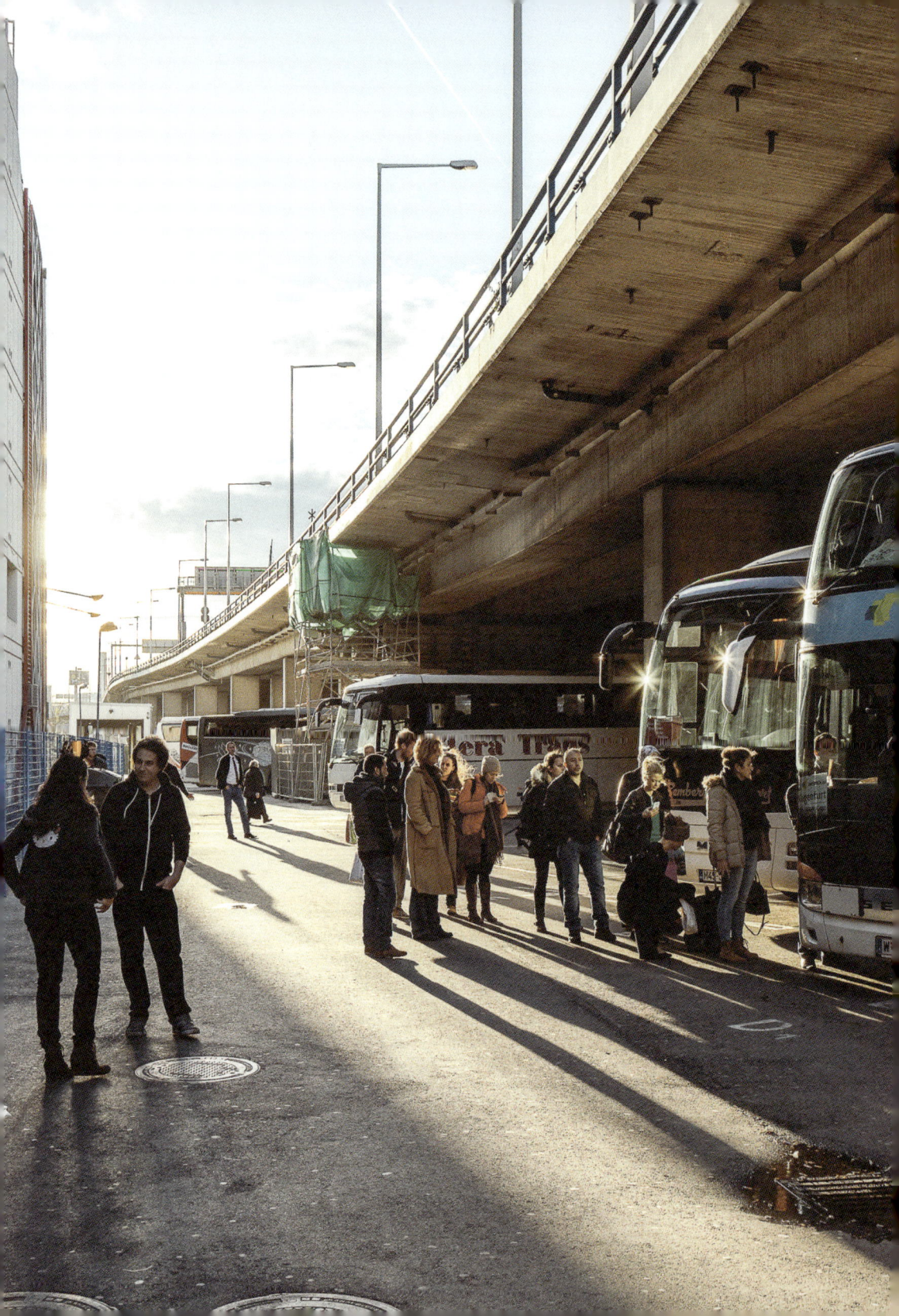

# Michael Hieslmair

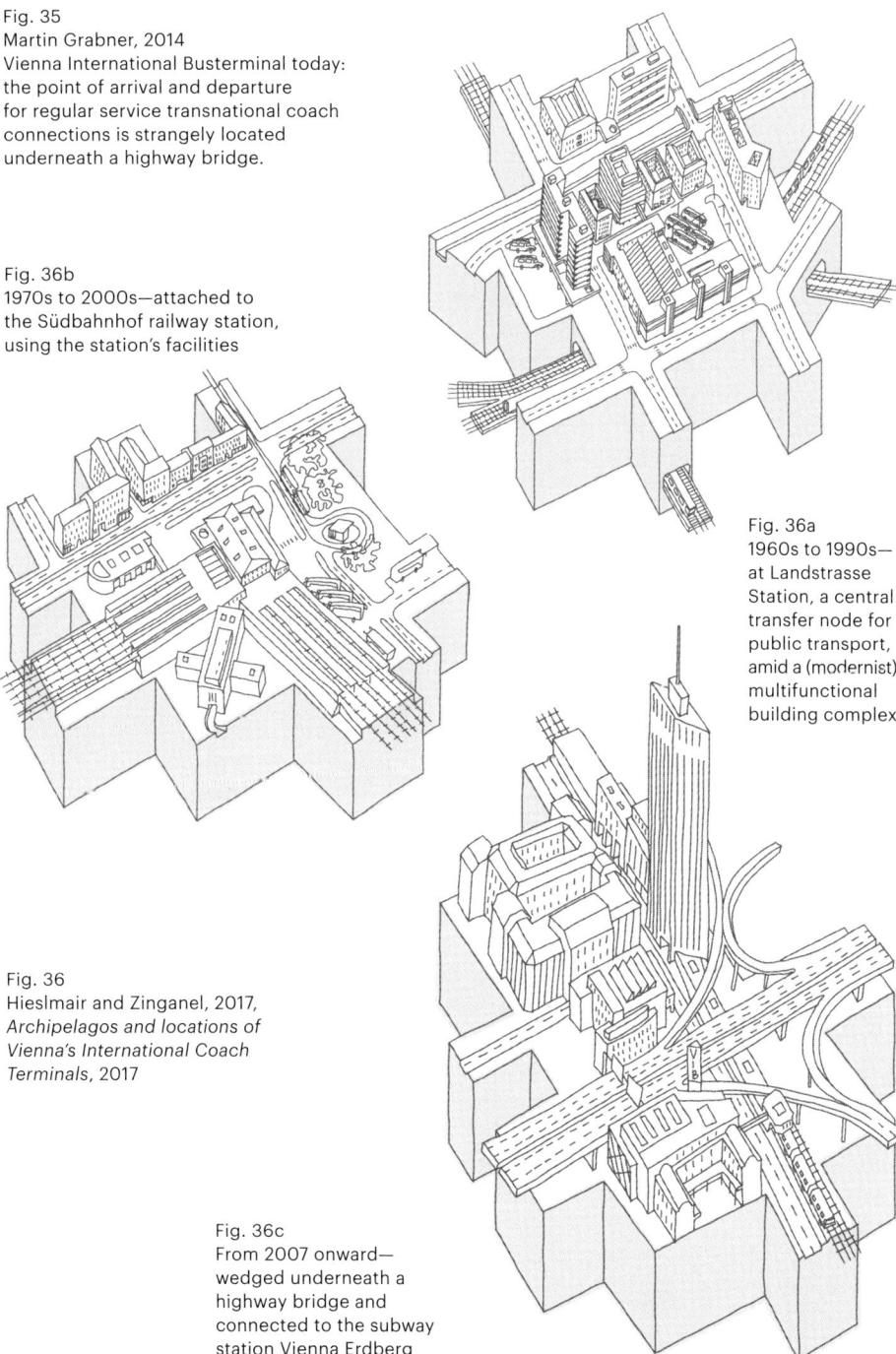

Fig. 35
Martin Grabner, 2014
Vienna International Busterminal today: the point of arrival and departure for regular service transnational coach connections is strangely located underneath a highway bridge.

Fig. 36b
1970s to 2000s—attached to the Südbahnhof railway station, using the station's facilities

Fig. 36a
1960s to 1990s—at Landstrasse Station, a central transfer node for public transport, amid a (modernist) multifunctional building complex

Fig. 36
Hieslmair and Zinganel, 2017, *Archipelagos and locations of Vienna's International Coach Terminals*, 2017

Fig. 36c
From 2007 onward—wedged underneath a highway bridge and connected to the subway station Vienna Erdberg

destination.²¹ It was not until relatively late, in 1978, that six Austrian coach companies from Vienna, Burgenland, and Eastern Styria got together to found the Austratrans Kraftfahrlinienbetriebs Ges.m.b.H.,²² which initially operated on eight of the so-called guest worker routes to Yugoslavia from Vienna's south terminal. There were also routes that led to Poland and Bulgaria. Parallel to this, an increasing number of smaller bus companies from East and Southeast Europe organized charter buses between east and west. However, because they were unlicensed, the journeys were often disguised as excursions. In the 1980s the international bus networks began a consolidation. In particular, the founding of the long-distance coach company Eurolines was a factor here. By 1985 it consisted of thirty-two private companies (incl. National Express from Great Britain, Deutsche Touring from Germany, and Lasta from Yugoslavia) with a head office in Brussels.²³ Suddenly, via national partnerships, there was a logical and bookable international scheduled coach service covering the whole of Europe. So, right from the beginning, there was a self-confident depiction of these scheduled coach services as part of a passenger transport network with offshoots that extended throughout Western Europe but also covered Eastern Europe too.

## The Year 1989 and the Consequences—The Post-socialist Transformation of the Nodes in the Vienna Area

The collapse of the so-called Eastern bloc in 1989, initiated a cross-border shopping tourism boom. Chartered coach tours in both directions became ubiquitous very quickly. Austrian coach companies offered inexpensive package rates or shopping trips that were mainly booked by bargain hunters. In the opposite direction, the first shopping tourists from Czechoslovakia, Poland, and Hungary arrived in Vienna. At that point, the majority of tourists came by coaches chartered in the country of destination. As a result, the already existing transportation nodes and markets (including the informal ones) spread out and other temporary ones became established. For example, an important transhipment point was Mexikoplatz (Mexico Square) situated between Handelskai—an important docking area for Danube barge traffic—and the goods yard of the northwest railway terminal with its small-scale trading enterprises that was long seen as a center of the black market. Another was Mariahilfer Strasse, a city center transport and shopping axis: because of the construction work for the underground, the U3 line, which lasted years, many of the old-established businesses temporarily moved away and rented the empty premises to small-scale traders for the duration of the underground project. These were specialized in providing consumer goods that were in demand from shopping tourists—especially electrical and electronic items, cosmetics, cheap clothing, coffee, and so forth.

The coach terminals in service at this time very quickly reached the limits of their capacity with the scheduled services and the first contingents of tourist charter coaches. Informal markets were immediately established at the terminals round Vienna Landstrasse and the South Rail Station. At the beginning of the 1990s, in order to be able to deal with the volume of coach traffic in the city, additional emergency and temporary coach parks were set up. A large one was to be found at the beginning of Mariahilfer Strasse, at Europaplatz, opposite the west station terminal, a site where two streams of traffic circled the Gürtel in opposite directions. Another, the Ostbusparkplatz (east bus terminal), lay far from the center, in an area between the Danube and a railway track in the Freudenau area (fig. 33). These spaces were not simply arrival and departure points because here, too, there was lively trading by small-scale retailers with goods from both sides of the border. On the gravel surface of these parking lots the luggage compartments of the buses were loaded and unloaded, goods were spread out on the ground or sold directly from car boots of vehicles that had been made in the Eastern bloc. In the short period between the opening to the east and the establishment of a functioning international trade network with a reach well beyond the fringe of the old Iron Curtain, numerous trading posts were to be found on the outskirts of Vienna but also in the city center.[24]

In addition, 1991 saw the beginning of the disintegration of Yugoslavia. The next ten years saw around 115,000 people fleeing former Yugoslavia (including some 90,000 inhabitants of Bosnia and Herzegovina) for Austria because of military action: the destruction and ethnic cleansing that took place. Initially,

21  A so-called reciprocal partnership had to be established if the destination lay somewhere in a third state i.e., there was no bilateral agreement in force regulating length of stay or customs issues. Paul Blachnik, Fachverband Autobus-, Luftfahrt- und Schifffahrtunternehmungen, Wirtschaftskammer Österreich, interview by the authors, February 24, 2016.
22  According to the articles of incorporation dated January 11, 1978, the following enterprises held shares in Austratrans Kraftfahrlinienbetriebs Ges.m.b.H—Austrobus Österreichische Autobusgesellschaft KG (today Dr. Richard): Blaguss Reisen GmbH, Autoreisen Schuch GmbH, Panorama Reisen Reisebüro GmbH, Euro Tours Klaushsecker GmbH & Co. KG, and Panorama Bus-Flug-Schiffsreisen GmbH. From the very beginning, Blaguss provided the largest share of the capital and at that point in time had 147 employees. *Commercial Register Report*, February 15, 2016.
23  Martin Schiefelbusch, *The Coach on the Leisure Travel Market: A Comparison between Britain and Germany* (Hamburg: Diplomica Verlag, 1998), 57. The association of companies under the name Eurolines Organization I.V.Z.W was an "international non-profit association" according to Belgian law. In Austria Blaguss company operated as the national partner of Eurolines, in Germany it was the long-distance coach market leader, Deutsche Touring. See https://de.wikipedia.org/wiki/Eurolines (accessed March 26, 2018).
24  At the time Vienna was regarded as the "first (Western) city in Eastern Europe," Friedrich Haberfellner, interview, Vienna, April 28, 2014.

buses were often used to flee.²⁵ Having arrived in Vienna, the refugees were housed in emergency quarters such as the Arsenal, an old barracks adjoining the South Railway Station and thus in the immediate vicinity of the bus station. Because the military action often abated and not all regions were affected to the same degree, a regular shuttle service developed between old homes and new. The refugees, together with the guest workers who had been living in the diaspora in the city for longer, caused an enormous rise in international coach traffic.

But while some sought refuge here, others who had been living in Austria for longer were also affected by war. Many men from ethnic groups on opposite sides felt under an obligation (or were pressurized) into fighting for their "homeland." During the week they went about their regular jobs in Austria and at the weekend they took "weekend warrior" buses to the front.²⁶ Often the different buses left from the same place at the same time—for example, directly from the construction site at which the men were employed, or from one of the Vienna bus terminals. In an interview for the Wirtschaftsblatt in 1999, Branimir Zebić, the office manager of the bus terminal stated: "Here in the bus terminal you feel nothing of the problems in the Balkans. It is almost a miracle that nothing happens here. At the front there are Croatians from Bosnia, alongside Moslems from Bosnia and behind them there are Serbs."²⁷ At times the men from the construction site, who had worked alongside each other or who had met while getting onto the bus, were to be on opposite sides at the front, as enemies, just a few hours later.

## Boom of the International Long-Distance Coach Traffic— Formalization of the Nodes in the City

In the allegedly liberalized West, specifically Germany and Austria, both the national and international coach services were under surprisingly strict regulation until 2013. In contrast, with the end of socialism in East and Southeast Europe a radical liberalization of the long-distance coach market took place as early as the 1990s. Monopolies were quickly abolished, and licenses were granted relatively "liberally." Buses were affordable and the road network much cheaper to maintain than the rail network. A number of bus companies from East and Southeast Europe began regular, direct international services that were capable of directly and flexibly connecting regions very far away from each other but also far from the Pan-European traffic corridors (fig. 34). This is still the case today and has given regular international coach services a significant advantage over rail travel and (cheap) flights. Up to the present day, many villages, cities, or even entire regions are partially dependent on direct connections provided by very small bus companies. These companies often go under the name of the family or village that operates them while the buses, acquired secondhand, continued their service with the liveries of their previous German and Austrian owners.

In the mid-1990s, around Vienna's South Railway Station, the most important inner-city node for international coach services, the coaches parked all over the gravel parking lot which lacked any systematically designated bays. The alternative was the parking lanes in the Schweizergarten. Chaos reigned here, especially at peak times around holidays such as Christmas, Easter, and the beginning of the school holidays. The situation was made even more critical because of all the cars driven by relatives who drove the passengers and their large amounts of luggage as close to the appropriate coach as possible to drop them off. With the formalization of the bus terminals in 1998 an attempt was made to bring some order into the situation which, at the time, was generally self-regulated. The measures introduced a simple guidance and booking system which, however, was restricted to coaches. The Blaguss company that had been a key player in the formation of the above-mentioned consortium of Austrian bus companies, Austratrans Kraftfahrlinienbetriebs Ges.m.b.H, was at that point the only Austrian partner in the long-distance coach network, Eurolines, when it took over the administration of the coach terminal.[28] In succeeding years, with the introduction of new labor agreements, special regulations, freedom of movement and work, quota regulations, entry into the EU, and the Schengen area regulations, there were new work commuters from East and Southeast Europe who sought work in Western Europe because of the great differential in salaries and wages. In addition, there were cyclical increases in traffic to the nodes as a result of the new Austrian citizens living in the diaspora. There were also tourists and commuters from Poland, the successor states to Yugoslavia, Bulgaria, Romania, and Kosovo, and so on. When, in the mid-2000s, plans became more concrete for building a new central railway terminal to replace both the South Station and East Station, the new concept involved the whole area but made no provision for an international coach terminal with sufficient capacity to deal with the amount of traffic. It was apparent that the mainly East and Southeast European clientele

25 In Croatia, because of the dearth of tourists caused by the war, the travel agency infrastructure and services, including their buses, were employed in the logistics of refugee distribution and accommodation in the hotels on the coast. Following 1991, the next few years saw 80 percent of the hotels on the Croatian Adriatic coast being used as refugee camps. Elke Beyer, Anke Hagemann, and Michael Zinganel, eds., *Holidays after the Fall: Seaside Architecture and Urbanism in Bulgaria and Croatia* (Berlin: Jovis Verlag, 2013).

26 Tyma Kraitt and Anna Thalhammer, "Die Wochenendkrieger," *Almanah, Jahrbuch für Integration in Wirtschaft, Politik und Gesellschaft* 15 (2014): 14–17.

27 Silvana Gemma, "Im Autobus Richtung Balkan fährt immer der Friede mit," *Wirtschaftsblatt*, July 24, 1999.

28 Friedrich Haberfellner, Blaguss, manager and coordinator of Vienna International Busterminal Erdberg, interview by the authors, Vienna, April 28, 2014.

of the bus terminal did not fit into the picture of a prestige project that the developers and the city administration had in mind.

## The New "Vienna International Busterminal"

With the demolition plans for the South Railway Station (and, simultaneously, Wien Mitte) announced, the operators of the international coach terminal, the Blaguss company, were forced to look for a suitable alternative site. Here it was clear that the chosen site should be a long-term solution and not one where gentrification of the area would lead to a renewed search a short time later. Thus, the new location should be potentially unimportant for the city's branding plans and as unattractive as possible from the point of view of the profit expectations of the real estate owners. On the other hand, the parcel of land should be located as closely as possible to the international road network and have good connections to the city's public transport network. The solution found for the VIB—Vienna International Busterminal—can be characterized as almost radical in its practicality (fig. 36c). The company located a parcel of land on the eastern periphery of the city that did not have a particularly good reputation—the area had always been associated with supplying the city's needs and disposing of its waste: old industry and business premises, warehouses and customs depots, gas works, slaughterhouses, refrigeration units, sewage treatment plants etc.

Immediately next to the Erdberg underground station and a Park-and-Ride terminal there is an elongated rectangular parcel of 8,000 square meters that lies directly under the Südost-Tangente (fig. 35), a multilane bypass that at this point runs over a ten-lane bridge, with a motorway that carries 170,000 vehicles a day.[29] The parcel belongs to the ASFINAG, the Motorway and Dual Carriageway Finance Company which is 100 percent owned by the Austrian state. The City of Vienna has little influence here. Furthermore, for developers the parcel is of no interest because no "permanent buildings" may be constructed either above or below a roadway. The dark area under the massive bridgework with its reinforced concrete underside and weighty columns, which crudely structure the space, also provide a free roof that covers almost the whole parcel of land. Today, the coach terminal in Erdberg handles around 60 percent of the international coach traffic to and from Vienna.[30] That amounts to around 425 scheduled service coaches a week (around 22,000 per annum), that is, about 2,000 passengers a day, as of the middle of 2015. Since summer 2015 the cooperation with Flixbus, a new company from Germany, has come into operation and brings a further six hundred people a day. At peak times like Christmas and Easter, the traffic increases to between 3,000 and 4,000 per day.[31] Yet despite all this the bus terminal does not even appear on most of the city maps.

Generally speaking, it is scheduled coach services and charter coaches operated by many different companies that use Vienna International Busterminal (VIB). They pay the operator, Blaguss, a service fee to do so. The parking bays are connected by a one-way system. The coach entrance is far down at the southern end of the area (fig. 39, pos. 9). Here the drivers announce their arrival to the terminal manager and have a bay allocated to them. The result of the liberalization of the international coach market in Germany in 2013 was a long-distance coach boom in Austria too. It began in 2015.[32] With this additional increase in traffic, the terminal in Erdberg has just reached full capacity.[33] For this reason, the coaches have to navigate precisely to the allocated bays and, depending on how busy it is, may only park for a short time. However, drivers must conform to legally fixed break times, which means the vehicle may have to remain stationary for a longer period. That is only conditionally possible here and, in any case, only in the parking lane at the back of the area. In addition, coaches that travel very long distances require a minimum maintenance service procedure for which the driver is responsible. This eventuality is covered by service facilities—an automatic coach wash as well as a number of refuse containers and a large collection point to allow the toilets on board to be emptied. These extras have to be paid for. After his break the driver can drive the freshly cleaned and serviced coach to its allocated bay.

Passenger access is from the north end of the terminal (fig. 39, pos. 1), parallel to the arrival and departure area of the coaches, in a gap between the terminal building and the urban motorway. At right angles there are 16 parking bays for the coaches, marked and delineated by posts on which there are numbers. Here there is no difference between bus stop and parking space. This makes boarding and exiting the coaches easier than in a solid-design bus terminal. At the entrance to the access area there is a steel guiding rail on which there are unobtrusive advertising posters for translation services. In between there are large refuse bins alongside which there is a huge ashtray which, during peak periods, is surrounded by groups of people. To the rear of the terminal building, and thus outside the covered area, is a small

29 Autobahnen- und Schnellstraßen-Finanzierungs-Aktiengesellschaft, ed., *Das Autobahnnetz in Österreich* (Vienna: ASFINAG, 2012).
30 The remaining 40 percent of the international coach traffic make stops at various other places where there is a consolidation of bus traffic, such as along the side of the Stadioncenter shopping center, near the main railway terminal, or at smaller stops scattered throughout the entire city.
31 Friedrich Haberfellner, interview, Vienna, April 28, 2014.
32 In Austria, however, the market is still strictly regulated by national laws related to road traffic services (Kraftfahrlinien-gesetz), Blaguss, Dr. Richard, and Gschwindl participate in the transborder coach business by means of cooperation. The Austrian National Railways (ÖBB) made a cameo appearance with their own Hello service in 2016 but gave up the business again in 2017.
33 Friedrich Haberfellner, interview, Vienna, April 28, 2014.

waiting room, the only place offering protection from the wind—during normal opening hours.

It is interesting to note that in a place with such a high volume of traffic as the Vienna International Busterminal VIB there is virtually no security. In contrast, in the capitals of Southeast Europe, for example at the international coach terminals in Belgrade and Sofia security personnel are omnipresent. Their presence is even advertised there, and emphasis laid on the fact that all areas are under video surveillance. The atmosphere created is in no way inviting. On the contrary, the Vienna terminal gives the impression of being an informal, stop-gap solution.

The front of the terminal along Erdbergstrasse is defined by a high wall of advertising hoardings which is broken only where the coaches exit and ends just a few meters away from the entrance area for people. Generally speaking, the whole area is fenced in and only accessible by vehicles through two secured gates. Frequently, passengers departing from here are either brought by friends or family members by car or come by taxi, especially if they have a lot of luggage. However, most arrive by underground. For many, despite being close to an underground station, the way to the coach terminal is difficult to find, especially for first time arrivals and departures. From the platform in the underground a stairway or lift takes you to the mezzanine level of the station building. An enclosed, glassed-in bridge leads from there over Erdbergstrasse to the main access level of a huge, run-down, mixed-use development built in the 1980s. One of the access thoroughfares to a multistory park and ride terminal is also located here.[34] Very self-deprecating, almost imperceptible signs indicate the way to the coach terminal. At times this may be via the emergency stairs or the lift of the multistory car park. Where routes intersect, it is not unusual to encounter disoriented passengers who ask directions and are desperately looking for the way to the coach terminal or the underground station while at the same time they are hindered by their multiple large and unwieldy pieces of luggage. Having reached ground level, the route is then in the open air. Here, the wind hits you as if you had just stepped into a wind tunnel. Because of the booming sound of speeding traffic, it is quickly clear that you are standing under a heavily used urban motorway. A few meters further on, at right angles to the street, in a narrow gap between the bridge of the Südost Tangente motorway and the neighboring multistory car park, is the bleak, functional terminal building made of prefabricated parts painted blue. The main entrance to the building leading to the tiny ticket office is accentuated by large-format writing. At this point, the official routes intersect with an informal pathway that connects the terminal directly by running obliquely over the street to the underground station. Frequent travelers acquainted with the situation cross the street rapidly, coming directly out of the underground station and looking neither right nor left. This is where those who came or are being picked up by cars or taxis leave or enter the site. The parking lane that runs parallel to the street alongside the coach station is used in peak hours as a terminal extension—as additional coach stops—or, in contravention of the general no-stopping rule in effect here, as a drop-off point. It is not unusual to see coaches being held up at the coach exit by hurrying people—by a young woman, for example, dressed in casual sports clothing on a fashionable vintage racing bike who, with wild gesticulation, brings the coach to a halt. The driver opens the door. She jumps from the bike and quickly hands over a small parcel, contents unknown. The coach then continues on its way. Here, between street space and the coach terminal compound, the pulse of the nodal point is particularly clear. The spectrum runs from time spans when the coach terminal appears to be almost empty to those when so much is happening that traffic on Erdbergstrasse is impeded and grinds to halt. The number and frequency of coaches arriving and departing is very much determined by the transitions between work and leisure. Peak periods are before and after weekends—every Friday from late afternoon till around 9 p.m. and the following Mondays from early morning till midday. The increasing frequency is particularly noticeable before and after holidays. This does not just apply to Christian holidays, but to Christian Orthodox ones too. Because of the special circumstances whereby under the bridge structures of the urban motorway no "permanent buildings" can be erected, the two-story terminal building lies, in part, in the only possible place—the small strip between the urban motorway and the multistory car park. Accordingly, there is only space for the most essential functions. The roof supports a high advertising pylon that can be seen from afar and acts as a landmark, towering above the edge of the road surface of the ten-lane urban motorway. The main entrance leads to a long, narrow waiting room that can be overseen at a glance and is provided with seating and a number of conventional, flat-panel displays that serve to announce upcoming arrivals and departures. This room is flanked by four ticket counters oriented both toward the interior of the building as well as outwards to the coach parking area. These are manned by staff, all of whom have a migratory background and Austrian citizenship. Their regions of origin (or those of their parents or grandparents) are often ethnically very diverse. Accordingly, in addition to conventional foreign languages such as English, French and Spanish, they speak languages of the most popular coach destinations: Bratislava, Kosice, Budapest, Zagreb, Belgrade, Leskovac, Sarajevo, Banja Luka, Sofia, Timisoara, Brasov, Bucharest Kiev, Warsaw, etc.

34 The building complex administered by the ARWAG as part of Wien Holding contains a number of shop spaces at ground level most of which are empty today. These are oriented on a large, terraced, interior courtyard. Located above these are the administrative offices of the Vienna Public Transport System, a few small catering businesses, and a car hire agency that benefit from the coach terminal traffic frequency as well as a gym with a large-scale sports complex on the top floor of the multistory car park.

First-time visitors to the coach terminal intuitively enter the waiting room first. Most of them are directed to the counters at the side of the bus parking where tickets to the popular destination in successor states to Yugoslavia, and Bulgaria and Romania are issued. The position of these counters in the open air is less about discriminating those routes and more to do with the frequency of departures and arrivals. It is not often that a long discussion is necessary and the ticket buying rituals are correspondingly precise and well-practiced.[35] Immediately alongside there is a display cabinet with its collection of A4 timetables, an attempt to convey an overview of the multiplicity of scheduled connections covering all the coach companies. Only regular passengers who know the layout are able to get an overview with any speed. In the interior of the waiting room, at the far end, there are snack and drinks machines and a few lockers. The toilet facilities with a service fee of fifty cents—with or without a bus ticket—are even further back and only accessible from outside. There is a stairway from the extension of the toilet access area that leads to the upper floor, to the administrative center of the coach terminal. This is where the coordinators sit with their monitors and can also oversee what is happening in the parking area through the window. Down below, in the parking bays that are laid out at an angle to the terminal building, coaches from various lines and companies, types, years, and sizes stand alongside each other in an order that reflects the schedule. This almost random order leads to passengers of differing social milieus having close encounters with one another.

When the coach of the South Serbian company, Zoran Reisen, arrives at its allocated bay at 8:30 p.m. there is already a crowd of people waiting there. It comes to a halt between a Semberija Transport coach and a Dragic one, both of which are headed for Zvornik in Bosnia. Alongside there is an Atlas Sib coach headed for Suceava in Romania. The coach, as with all coaches, is met in the parking space by the duty coordinator in person. Part of the ritual includes a short exchange about events on the route, complications at the borders but also about private matters because the two have known each other for a considerable time. Slowly the passengers alight, most of them in casual clothing such as jogging pants but some dressed elegantly. They are laden with bags, rucksacks, plastic bags, neck pillows, jackets, and bottles of water. The experienced crowd collects a short distance from the coach. The travelers who were awaited, are greeted, hugged, kissed, some quickly light up a cigarette. The bus driver opens up the luggage compartment, pulls out one piece of luggage after another, exchanging them for the luggage checks—suitcases, sacks, boxes, bulky parcels with intriguing contents, usually gifts intended for friends and relations. They include homemade foods, schnapps and cigarettes. Packages like this assume impressive dimensions. Even when the actual passengers have long left the terminal, the driver is still handing out packages and envelopes to people who were waiting for the bus.

Right on schedule, a brand new, bright green Flixbus in corporate identity livery arrives from Berlin. Only the number plate and the discreet company address on the front door indicates the origins and legal status of the franchise partner. These companies often have their head offices in Eastern Europe or Eastern Germany. Blaguss itself is a Flixbus partner via its Slovakian subsidiary. One after another the passengers stumble out of the bus, form a small crowd and wait for their luggage to be handed out. Almost all of them are very young, dressed in the hip alternative style though all very chic. A mustachioed knife salesman in a leather jacket and pointed shoes poses with an open briefcase in which his goods are displayed—taking advantage of the wait to try his luck. Right next to him is a coach clad in a slightly torn Eurolines adhesive banner, its motor running. You can really see the many thousands of kilometers it has under its belt. Number plate and the destination sign jammed against the windscreen fit together—Sarajevo. A group of people cluster around a large ashtray. A good third of them are smoking among a whole slew of luggage: rucksacks, older trolley cases, large checked bags, and a number of bundles of plastic carrier bags.

At peak times, the huge coaches standing next to each other form small ravines between high walls toward the back. It only has gaps for a short time, dependent on the rhythm of the arrivals. It also happens that smaller buses stop here—a sixteen-seater Mercedes Sprinter, for example, that serves a noticeably less frequented route to Doboj in Bosnia. It is dealt with in exactly the same way as its bigger brothers. Behind this wall of coaches there are further, but clearly longer, coach lane markings. An Atlas Sib coach, the Romanian company that has its own postal license, is parked here. A queue of people has formed in front of the open trailer attached to the coach. The people in the queue are holding parcels, envelopes, or collection vouchers printed on A4 paper.

A refreshment stand has a small customer garden with a beer table and benches diagonally opposite, facing the main entrance and under the overhead bridge. The VIB Imbiss (refreshment stand) is housed in a standard blue office container and is open during the terminal's normal operating hours. A lady with a Hungarian accent offers a wide range of simple dishes through a half-open sliding window: meatloaf, grilled sausages, coffee-to-go, nonalcoholic drinks in cans or plastic bottles, beer in cans, and even Slivovitz (plum schnapps). In the area in front of the container there are a couple of benches. Waiting passengers sit here sipping coffee, eating hotdogs and staring into their cellphones. Surprisingly there is no Wi-Fi service here. But whenever a recent model coach arrives with an onboard router, many guests take this opportunity

35 Sybille Hamann, "Willkommen, sagt das Schmuddelkind: Der Busbahnhof in Erdberg," *Falter*, Europa-Heft, March 3, 2015.

to go online. During the warm part of the year, there are high tables directly in front of the stand and these are very popular with the bus drivers. According to current laws, they have to take clearly defined breaks which they use here to swap information and gossip or to talk to former driver colleagues who often come here for exactly that purpose.

In addition to its role as the site of coach-related activities such as the purchase of tickets, the handing in and out of parcels, money, presents, and smuggled goods, bus terminals (in all locations and states of development) are always points of contact for many different people. Here, translation services and work are offered, apartments advertised etc. Coach terminals have a central place in the lives of many migrants living in the diaspora and have always provided identity-generating anchor points as well as being sites of transfer and communication in the city they just arrived in. The cyclical journeys and the personal encounters produce close ties that have made coach terminals an important part of the infrastructure of emigration. Over the years, they have become thresholds between old and new homelands, continuing to structure the multi-local lives of emigrants and their cyclical journeys even today. The cultural area designated in the vernacular as "the Balkans" begins in numerous places in the city of Vienna,[36] along specific streets, in cafés with an ethnic flavor but, at the very latest, at the Erdberg coach terminal—the "gateway to the Balkans"—when the luggage is entrusted to the driver, a few words are exchanged and, on boarding, the destination is announced.

## The Coach Driver as Multi-optional Key Figure

The pattern of the coaches follows the fixed rhythm of the timetables. The vehicle itself is a container for passengers, luggage, goods but also the site of human interaction (fig. 38). The coach driver has a special role here. For regular passengers he is a person of trust who maintains trans-local, socio-economic relationships and brings the most recent news and gossip from home. He sells and checks tickets and passports, stows the numerous pieces of luggage in the vehicle's trunk. Buses, coaches, and their operating companies have always been important for goods transport and thus also involved in providing an international network of reliable courier services. The spectrum here goes from enterprises such as the Rumanian Atlas Sib that has an official postal and parcel license, to the informal arrangements made by individual drivers. The latter have always been responsible for transferring cash, a fact that underlines their position as persons of trust. Recently, consignments in connection with online transactions have greatly increased because in many Southeast European countries it is risky to shop on Amazon—book parcels look as if they contain valuables and are therefore often misappropriated. For this reason, they are delivered to an Austrian address and then sent on by coach.[37] Generally speaking, the driver is also responsible for estimating how much luggage can be transported in his coach and the tolerance limits of the customs officers on the route with whom he also keeps in contact. So smuggling can still pay, even today![38] Between Vienna and East and Southeast European destinations there are, in both directions, particular goods with enormous price differentials. A small profit can be made with cartons of cigarettes, alcohol, etc.[39]—at least enough to cover the cost of the coach journey. Regulations pertaining to the allowable per head amounts are discreetly avoided by self-organized temporary distribution strategies (cartons of cigarettes) carried out just before a border crossing and then recollected by their owners from the passengers afterwards.

Although with the system of timetabled coaches, schedule and stops are clearly determined and optimized, and the exact position of the bus can be determined by GPS at any point in time, the driver still has a certain amount of leeway. This increases noticeably when a border crossing is imminent. Because the border process is dependent on many factors and may take a long time—caused by stricter controls or a reactivated EU interior border, the volume of traffic, the directives and mood of the customs officers—a sufficient time buffer has been built in. When controls at the border do not exhaust it, drivers make use of it for doing favors or business on the side. It is a distinct possibility that the coach will stop in the middle of the night in an area next to a roadside restaurant and that two men will hurry up to it to unload illegally exported bicycles packed in plastic bags. Or, for a few euros, the driver clearly deviates from the predetermined route to drop off a few older ladies and their luggage (which they would never have been able to carry on their own) right in front of their house in a small village. Or, at a smartened up ÖMV gas station just before an important holiday, a couple of bags of semi-grilled suckling pig destined for illegal import into Vienna are shoved into the belly of the coach. It may also occur that the fully laden bus comes to a stop in front of a single-family house into which the driver disappears only to continue the journey a few minutes later.

36 As in the saying attributed to Chancellor Metternich: the Balkans begin on Rennweg (a major street leading from the center of Vienna outwards).
37 Hamann, "Willkommen, sagt das Schmuddelkind."
38 E.g., described in a report based on the experiences of the author Milan Milanski, "Schmuggel, Schmiergeld, Spanferkel: Auf Balkan-Busreisen lernst du fürs Leben," *VICE Magazine*, October 22, 2017, https://www.vice.com/de_ch/article/pa3ypm/schmuggel-schmiergeld-spanferkel-auf-balkan-busreisen-lernst-du-furs-leben (accessed March 26, 2018).

39 In addition to the obvious economic motives of smuggling there are certainly some that are cultural. For example, it is almost customary that entire suckling pigs are smuggled in coaches coming from Serbia in the period immediately preceding important public holidays. Should there be a border control it is completely up to the customs officers as to whether the large family waiting at home will have to find an emergency substitute meal for their celebration.

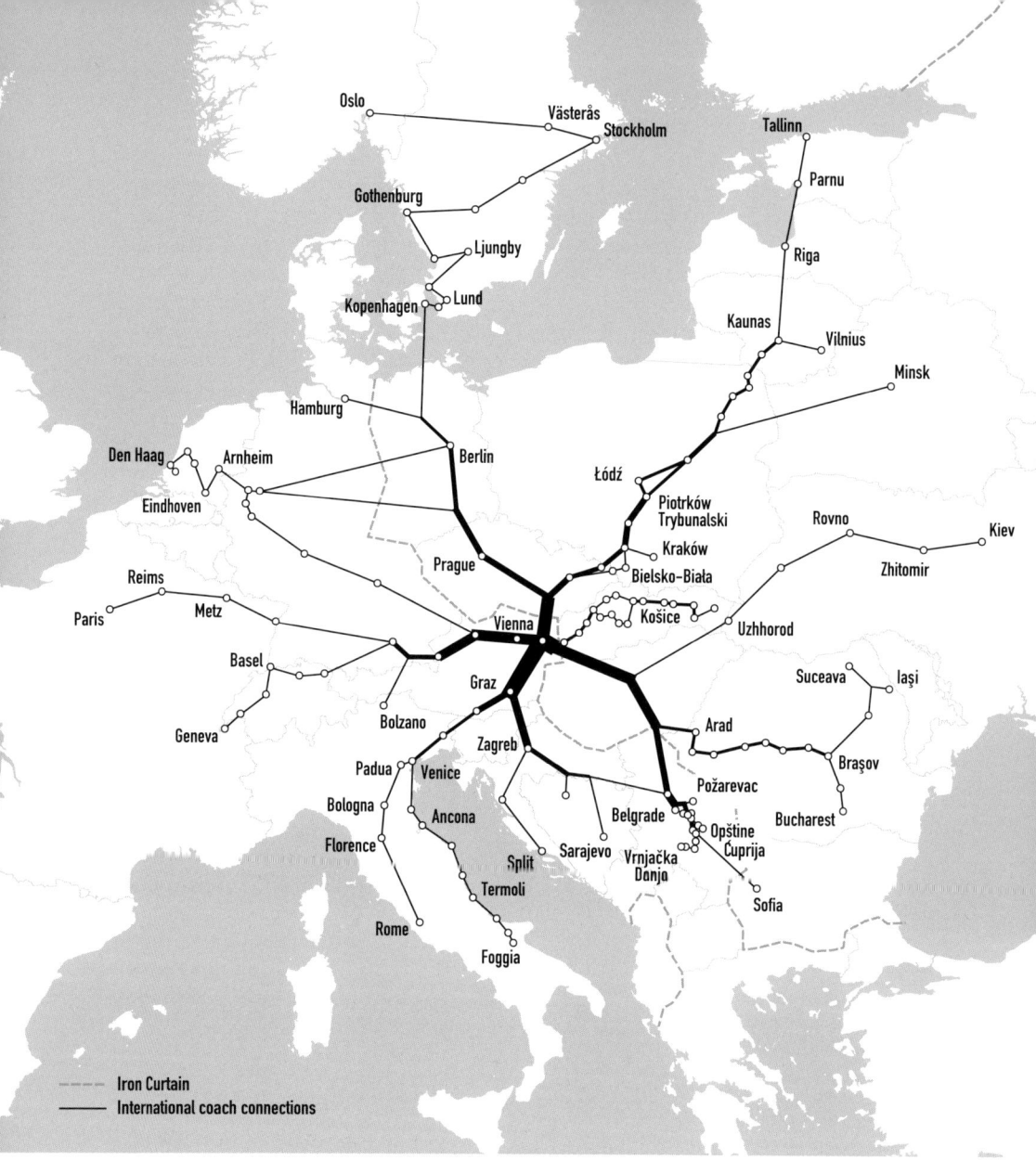

Fig. 37
Hieslmair and Zinganel, 2016
Vienna at the center of a network of international bus connections. Most notable are the many stops in Eastern and Southeastern Europe. The map is redrawn from the timetable data on bus connections and estimated passenger numbers provided by the management of Vienna International Busterminal; however, many smaller bus lines depart from, and arrive at, other often quite informal coach stops around the city.

Although legally speaking the coach terminal is a private enterprise, it possesses essential qualities of a public space too. Time windows during which the wide expanses of traffic space remain bare stand in contrast to the peak periods when a wide social spectrum of passengers transform the terminal and its immediate surroundings into an extremely busy and bustling urban space. Here, networks are formed and those that already exist are maintained. So in this sense neighborhoods are not generated out of the immediate surroundings of the area where people live but extend over great distances. They are transborder entities, between migrants' regions of origin and the regions that are their destinations. Regular and affordable coach service connections link individuals and family members and in that way enable the multi-local life of many in the first place.

## Mutual Existence—A Terminal Never Stands Alone

International coach terminals are nodes at which transnational routes cross and form a network. A coach terminal never stands alone. Forming the basis for its existence are close and regular connections between partner-terminals. Each single coach terminal takes center stage in its respective radial route-network (fig. 37). The importance of a route connection is depicted in the timetable, which indicates the number and frequency of coaches traveling a specific route. At the interchange stations the network re-centers itself and results in a sequence of meshing sub-networks, which, overall, form a theoretically endlessly branching spatiotemporal network. Between the main coach terminals, the formal core nodal points, there are also subsidiary nodal points, stopovers which lie on the routes and serve as transfer points, providing for rest periods for the drivers or facilitating their on-the-side business. These will be visited or omitted from the route depending on momentary needs. The only way to experience this social/spatial nodes/routes continuum and thus to make contact with the social actors involved with it, is to take a coach journey. For our purposes we chose one of the most popular routes to and from Southeast Europe. It is more or less congruent with the route to our southeastern research destinations: the scheduled daily service of the Bulgarian enterprise, Air Kona, between Sofia and Vienna.[40]

In comparison with Vienna International Busterminal, the Sofia coach terminal is situated in a prominent location in the city. It is sited immediately next to the monumental main railway terminal building that was constructed in 1974 during the communist era in a brutalist, late-modernist style. After a long

[40] According to a self-description, AIR KONA GmbH was founded in 1991, and in the same year entered into an international transport agreement with the Austrian bus company, Blaguss, which among other things operates Vienna International Busterminal in Erdberg and has an interest in Austratrans Kraftfahrlinienbetriebs Ges.m.b.H. AIR KONA owns more than 20 coaches, its own garages, and workshop. See http://www.airkona.com/about-us_en.html (accessed March 26, 2018).

phase of neglect and non-investment it was renovated in recent years using EU funds. Half of it has been transformed into a consumer zone while the locomotives and rolling stock still await modernization.

The Sofia coach terminal actually consists of two terminals located next to each other, one for national and the other for international routes. A multilane boulevard leads from the city center directly to the terminal site and then bends off the northwest, parallel to the railway lines. The entrance to both terminals lies exactly at the point where it changes direction. The original bus terminal, the Centralna Avtogara,⁴¹ clearly distanced from the railway terminal is mainly used by scheduled national coach services going to Plovdiv, Bansko, Varna, Burgas, Haskovo, Rouse, and Pleven, etc., and has an area that is approximately four times the size of the international coach terminal. It is similar in outline and plan to an airport terminal. A multistory block separates the site from the main road. A large area for parking coaches sits alongside it. On the roof of this mixed-use development with its post-modern appearance is a sign that can be seen from afar—Centralna Avtogara—in Cyrillic and Latin letters. The side facing the street has a lane for private cars with a drop-off zone and a lane for waiting taxis. On the concave rear of the block there is a roofed-in extension of tinted glass. It covers about half of the bus bays and gives direct access to the waiting hall. An open-winged roof on stilts that stretches across two stories links the building with further bus bays on the opposite side. Arriving and departing coaches are guided round the central building by a one-way system. This takes them past the two guard posts with barriers which are manned by security personnel. On the ground floor of the terminal there is a spacious, high-ceilinged waiting hall with about forty ticket counters, car hire company stands, a first aid center, the branch office of a bank as well as substantial toilet facilities one floor lower. Located behind a balustrade on the top floor (visible from the waiting hall) is a restaurant, a coffee shop, a room with slot and game machines, and a book shop. All of this is open 24/7, is air conditioned and checked by security personnel as well as being under surveillance by 130 video cameras.

Immediately beside this and closer to the rail terminal is the terminal for the international coach lines and services, Serdika Station, also known by the name of Traffic Market Square. The terminal shares its entrance—separated by barriers—with the entrance to a secured parking area used by the so-called *mashrutkas*—informally organized minibuses of which the most popular is the Mercedes Sprinter—as boarding and arrivals area. The entrance is flanked by two spiral but unused ramps, remnants of the socialist era. In the basement, in the eye of one of the ramps, there is an ancient public pay toilet. Two two-story terminal buildings face each other and define the space. They are built of standardized cheap hall elements with large glass facades and automatic sliding doors on the side nearest the bus boarding bays. Ticket counters of the various operators and coach companies—including that of Air Kona—are

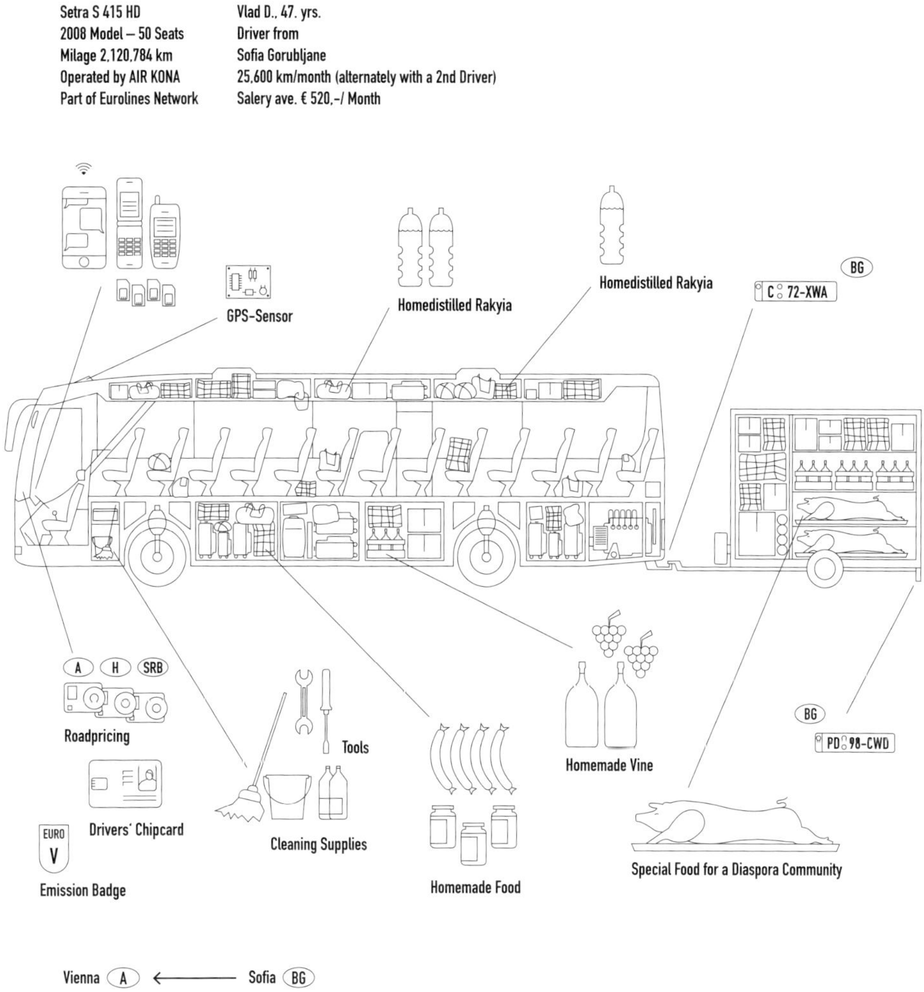

Michael Hieslmair

Setra S 415 HD
2008 Model — 50 Seats
Milage 2,120,784 km
Operated by AIR KONA
Part of Eurolines Network

Vlad D., 47. yrs.
Driver from
Sofia Gorubljane
25,600 km/month (alternately with a 2nd Driver)
Salery ave. € 520,-/ Month

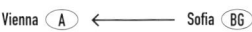

Fig. 38
Hieslmair and Zinganel, 2016
Cross-sectional diagram of a tour coach operated by the Bulgarian company Air Kona connecting Vienna and Sofia: For many, buses are the preferred means of transport, not only because of the reasonable ticket prices but moreover because a bus can take them much closer to their source and target destinations. Buses are also able to transport goods of significant size—which is important for small suitcase traders and those wishing to send gifts to family and friends.

41 Self-reported: http://www.centralnaavtogara.bg/index.php#b (accessed March 26, 2018).

42 The starting point for the boom was the liberalization of the monopoly under defined-term licensing in Germany in 2013.

to be found on the ground floor level of the interiors of both buildings. At the ends of the buildings there are small refreshment stands and mini-shops with a few standing tables in the open-air. The second story contains offices, some of which belong to the bus lines. Immediately next to that, in the former rail terminal forecourt, there are a host of small single-story kiosks that give the impression of being almost structural in nature, These form a labyrinth, an open-air, miniature shopping mall with extended business hours. Planned and executed as a package, the individual units, mostly very small, have direct access to the exterior. In the interstitial spaces there is seating, potted plants, rubbish bins, street lights—all situated according to a grid plan. Where the pathways cross there are small, intimate "squares" accentuated by street furniture. In addition, some of the interstitial spaces between the units are covered by tinted glass roofs. The windows and walls of the kiosks are covered in signs and advertising displays including international travel agents, refreshment stands, small grill restaurants, and coffee shops with seating in the open air, shops for travel provisions, currency exchange and money transfer offices (such as Western Union)—an ideal place to wait or to acquire enough provisions from the kiosk labyrinth to last a very long journey.

## Vienna International Busterminal—From Eyesore to Grubby Urchin and Finally the Citygate in a Welcoming Setting

How long the coaches will continue to arrive at and depart from the terminal in Erdberg is not yet clear: since the delayed (and only partial) liberalization of the long-distance coach services in Western Europe the most profitable routes have seen a real boom caused by user-friendly online booking platforms with extremely low and competitive prices along with new coaches equipped with Wi-Fi.[42] In just a few short years, the German Flixbus has managed to become the market leader—as early as 2014 the daily service between Vienna and Berlin ran four times a day. Neither the well-established network cooperations such as Eurolines nor new platforms which attempted to gain a foothold in the promising business showing high growth rates have been able to compete.[43] In order to counteract the competition with rail travel, even the state-owned Austrian Railways (ÖBB) made an attempt to break into the long-distance coach business. They formed a subsidiary company to run the coaches with the brand name Hello as a joint venture with the mid-sized, privately owned Austrian bus company, Gschwindl. Affiliation with the ÖBB meant that Hello had access to extremely central locations for their stops immediately adjacent to all Austrian railway stations. Despite this major competitive advantage, it was not possible to run the enterprise anywhere near break-even point. In a final attempt to save the venture, a cooperation with Flixbus was agreed even using its online booking platform—but to no avail. After only one year, Hello had withdrawn from the market. Meanwhile, Flixbus, run as a franchise, continued to expand and gained steadily in customers of various types. The self-confident market presence—as in the case of the cheap airlines—the expanded services on offer and the low ticket prices eliminate the old misgivings about bus travel. Increasingly, the new cool coach lines are creating currents of chic and affluent tourists from Western Europe into the city of Vienna.

As early as July 2014, the volume of coaches arriving at Vienna International Busterminal had grown so great that Norbert Kettner, head of Wien Tourismus Werbung (Vienna tourism marketing), demanded the immediate construction of a new coach terminal.[44] In contrast to the terminal in Erdberg in Vienna, which has been criticized, the replacement should take into account the high volume of passengers and be a correspondingly representational arrival point, a gateway to the city.[45] As a result, the Planning Department of Vienna City Council carried out a feasibility study and came to the conclusion that the new coach terminal would pay for itself from the projected revenue and, in particular, bearing in mind the affiliated consumer zone.[46] The Österreichische Wirtschaftskammer (Austrian Chamber of Commerce), as lobbyist for the business community, sounded out potential new locations. In February 2018 a representative presented a realistic rendering of a design for a terminal with a connection to the underground as well as a node for national and international coach line services. It includes a shopping area.[47] The preferred location was the large traffic roundabout in the Favoriten district of Vienna with its direct connection to the Südost-Tangente (urban motorway with connections to the south and east). That places it just five kilometers north of Vienna International Busterminal in Erdberg.

43 One of the most important partners within the Eurolines Network, Deutsche Touring, became insolvent in 2017 and was later bought up by Croatia Bus. Manfred Köhler, "Deutsche Touring kann weiter fahren," *FAZ.net*, August 8, 2017. http://www.faz.net/aktuell/rhein-main/wirtschaft/omnibus-betreiber-deutsche-touring-kann-weiter-fahren-15151441.html (accessed March 26, 2018).

44 Simone Hoepke, "Bus-Terminal dringend gesucht," *Kurier*, July 19, 2014, https://kurier.at/wirtschaft/bus-terminal-dringend-gesucht/75.525.429 (accessed March 26, 2018).

45 It did not take long before the operator Blaguss started an offensive to prettify the terminal. Colorful subjects printed on tarpaulin and attached to the fence which surrounds the area, were to create a more friendly atmosphere. These depict tourist landmarks of Vienna in combination with an advertisement for the Vienna Pass, a bonus card for sightseeing-packages as part of the firm's own business empire.

46 Josef Gebhard, "Großer Busbahnhof für Wien geplant," *Kurier*, August 8, 2014, https://kurier.at/chronik/wien/grosser-busbahnhof-fuer-wien-geplant/79.260.116 (accessed March 26, 2018).

47 Gabriele Kolar, "Fernbusterminal muss bald gebaut werden," *Wiener Wirtschaft* 7, February 15, 2018.

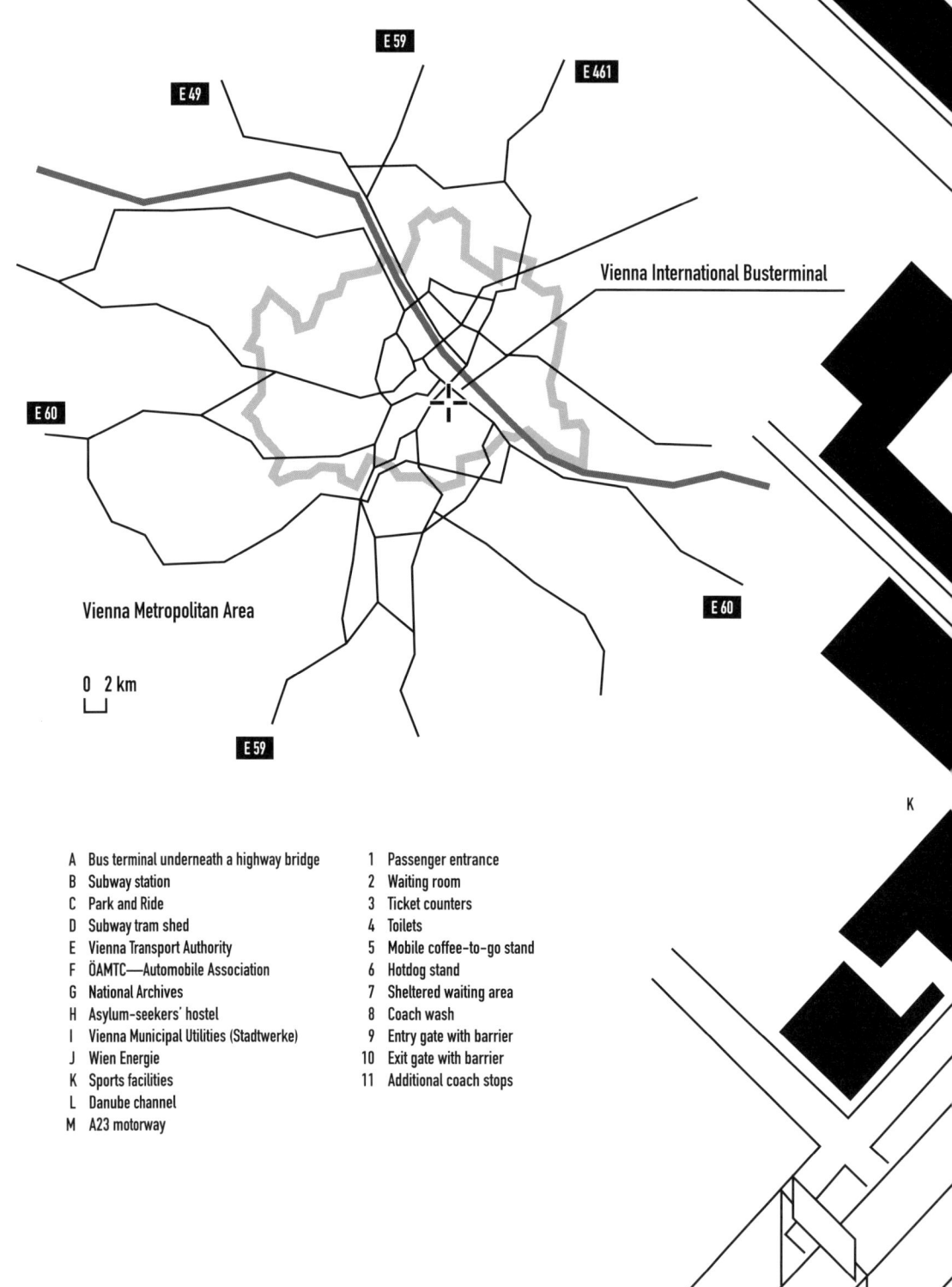

**Vienna International Busterminal**

**Vienna Metropolitan Area**

0  2 km

A  Bus terminal underneath a highway bridge
B  Subway station
C  Park and Ride
D  Subway tram shed
E  Vienna Transport Authority
F  ÖAMTC—Automobile Association
G  National Archives
H  Asylum-seekers' hostel
I  Vienna Municipal Utilities (Stadtwerke)
J  Wien Energie
K  Sports facilities
L  Danube channel
M  A23 motorway

1  Passenger entrance
2  Waiting room
3  Ticket counters
4  Toilets
5  Mobile coffee-to-go stand
6  Hotdog stand
7  Sheltered waiting area
8  Coach wash
9  Entry gate with barrier
10  Exit gate with barrier
11  Additional coach stops

0  50 m

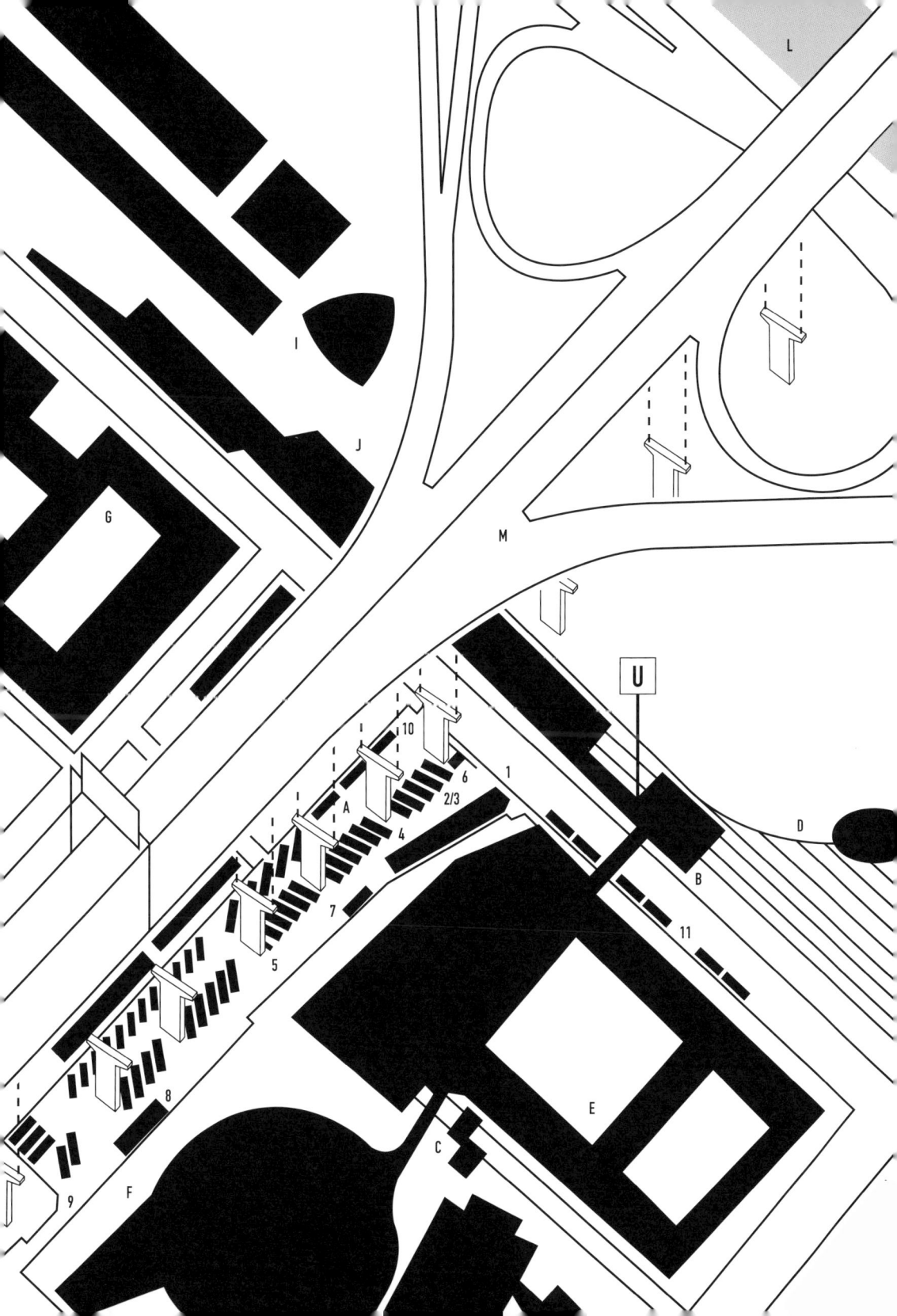

Fig. 39
Hieslmair and Zinganel, 2018
Location and surroundings of Vienna International
Busterminal, wedged under a highway bridge,
initiated and operated by the private, Austria-based
company Blaguss

## Literature

Autobahnen- und Schnellstraßen-Finanzierungs-Aktiengesellschaft, ed. *Das Autobahnnetz in Österreich: 30 Jahre ASFINAG*. Vienna: ASFINAG, 2012.

Bakondy, Vida. "Bahnhofs-Bilder: Historischer Ort und visuelles Chiffre der Arbeitsmigration nach Österreich." Paper presented at the Zeitgeschichtetag Graz, June 8, 2016.

Beyer, Elke, Anke Hagemann, and Michael Zinganel. "Holidays after the Fall: Seaside Architecture and Urbanism in Bulgaria and Croatia." Berlin: Jovis Verlag, 2013.

*Commercial Register Report*, February 15, 2016.

Gebhard, Josef. "Großer Busbahnhof für Wien geplant." *Kurier*, August 8, 2014, https://kurier.at/chronik/wien/grosser-busbahnhof-fuer-wien-geplant/79.260.116. (accessed March 26, 2018).

Gemma, Silvana. "Im Autobus Richtung Balkan fährt immer der Friede mit." *Wirtschaftsblatt*, July 24, 1999, http://wirtschaftsblatt.at/archiv/wirtschaft/970578/index (accessed March 26, 2018).

Hamann, Sybille. "Willkommen, sagt das Schmuddelkind: Der Busbahnhof in Erdberg." *Falter*, Europa-Heft, March 3, 2015.

Hoepke, Simone. "Bus-Terminal dringend gesucht." *Kurier*, July 19, 2014, https://kurier.at/wirtschaft/bus-terminal-dringend-gesucht/75.525.429 (accessed March 26, 2018).

Köhler, Manfred. "Deutsche Touring kann weiter fahren." *FAZ.net*, August 8, 2017. http://www.faz.net/aktuell/rhein-main/wirtschaft/omnibus-betreiber-deutsche-touring-kann-weiter-fahren-15151441.html (accessed March 26, 2018).

Kolar, Gabriele. "Fernbusterminal muss bald gebaut werden." *Wiener Wirtschaft* 7, February 15, 2018: 7.

Kos, Wolfgang, ed. *Grosser Bahnhof. Wien und die weite Welt*. Vienna: Czernin Verlag, 2006.

Kraitt, Tyma, and Anna Thalhammer. "Die Wochenendkrieger." *Almanah, Jahrbuch für Integration in Wirtschaft, Politik und Gesellschaft*, 15 (2014): 14–17.

Lange, Fritz. *Von Wien zur Adria: Der Wiener Neustädter Kanal*. Erfurt: Sutton Verlag, 2003.

Medienservicestelle, ed. *Anwerbe-Abkommen mit Türkei – geschichtlicher Hintergrund*, May 7, 2014, http://medienservicestelle.at/migration_bewegt/2014/05/07/anwerbe-abkommen-mit-tuerkei-geschichtlicherhintergrund (accessed March 26, 2018).

Peyer, Peter. "Gehen Sie an die Arbeit: Zur Geschichte der 'Gastarbeiter' in Wien 1964–1989." *Wiener Geschichtsblätter* 1 (2004): 1–19.

Schiefelbusch, Martin. *The Coach on the Leisure Travel Market: A Comparison between Britain and Germany*. Hamburg: Diplomica Verlag, 1998.

Wagner-Rieger, Renate, ed. *Die Wiener Ringstraße, Bild einer Epoche. Die Erweiterung der Inneren Stadt Wien unter Kaiser Franz Joseph*, vol. 11. Wiesbaden: Steiner, 1979.

———. *Wiens Architektur im 19. Jahrhundert*. Vienna: Österreichischer Bundesverlag, 1970.

# Check Point Nickelsdorf, 2015
## Reactivation of a Border for the Mobilization of Forced Migration

Michael Zinganel and Michael Hieslmair

The traffic network of transnational bus routes that start or intersect at Vienna International Busterminal represents the connections of destination and source regions of tourists, former guest workers and their relatives, commuters, and labor migrants. Currently, the most frequented strand leads via the A4 eastern highway to Hungary, either in the direction of Romania or via Serbia and on to Bosnia and Bulgaria. On these buses one can naturally also find persons who are regarded as unwelcome in Vienna's majority population: beggars, prostitutes, thieves, people with valid or with fake ID documents.[1] For the most part, however, these buses carry those service personnel whose modestly paid work facilitates the above-average quality of everyday life for Vienna's middle class in the first place—the invisible "human infrastructure" of the city.[2]

Irrespective of the refugee crisis, the transformation of the border crossing between Austria and Hungary and the history of the small border municipality of Nickelsdorf would in itself be worthy of research. The current road network had been gradually developed and improved, and the traffic volume shifted to this new A4 route. The old road led right through the village, past small old customs houses and the tollgate, then on to a street with pubs and stores bustling with activity.[3] But the new modern border crossing was constructed far outside the municipality and finally complemented with a fully-fledged highway in 1994.[4] While the former border village went silent, the new border crossing with its highway entrance and exit ramps on both sides of the border and its more modern control facilities evolved into what seems to be an arbitrarily densifying agglomeration of streets and building complexes—an urban archipelago typical of the modern mobility landscape. Several gas stations, hotels and motels, restaurants, and markets, some partly designed and branded as theme parks (Paprika Csarda), night clubs, brothels and betting shops, kiosks, and truck parks settled along the new route, touting for the best location and subjecting themselves—especially on the Hungarian side—to tough predatory

---

1   Although a valid passport is obligatory on all transnational bus routes—even inside the European Union—problems of trafficking occur frequently on regular international bus services, according to Gerald Tatzgern, head of the Central Service on Combating Alien Smuggling and Human Trafficking, Federal Ministry of the Interior, Federal Criminal Police Office, interview by the authors, Vienna, September 8, 2016.
2   AbdouMaliq Simone, "People as Infrastructure: Intersecting Fragments in Johannesburg," *Public Culture* 16, no. 3 (2004): 407–29.
3   During the time of the Iron Curtain the small road border crossing in the middle of the Nickelsdorf was relatively insignificant. The freight and customs station on the important Vienna–Budapest railway line, situated on Hungarian territory in Hegyeshalom, was far more important. Numerous railway workers from Nickelsdorf worked there shunting and conducting customs clearance, so they crossed the Iron Curtain on a daily basis in a rail bus on their way to work. Hans-Paul Limbeck, retired railroad worker, amateur historian and chairman of "Kulturverein Kugel," interview by the authors, June 3, 2014. Gerhard Zapfl, mayor of Nickelsdorf, interview by the authors, March 18, 2016.
4   ASFINAG, *Das Autobahnnetz in Österreich: 30 Jahre ASFINAG* (Vienna, 2012), 44.

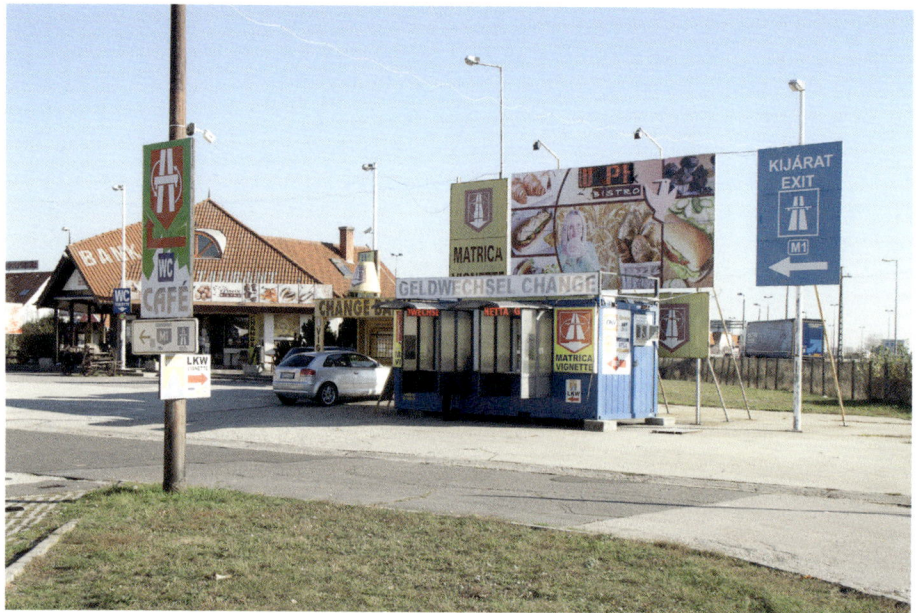

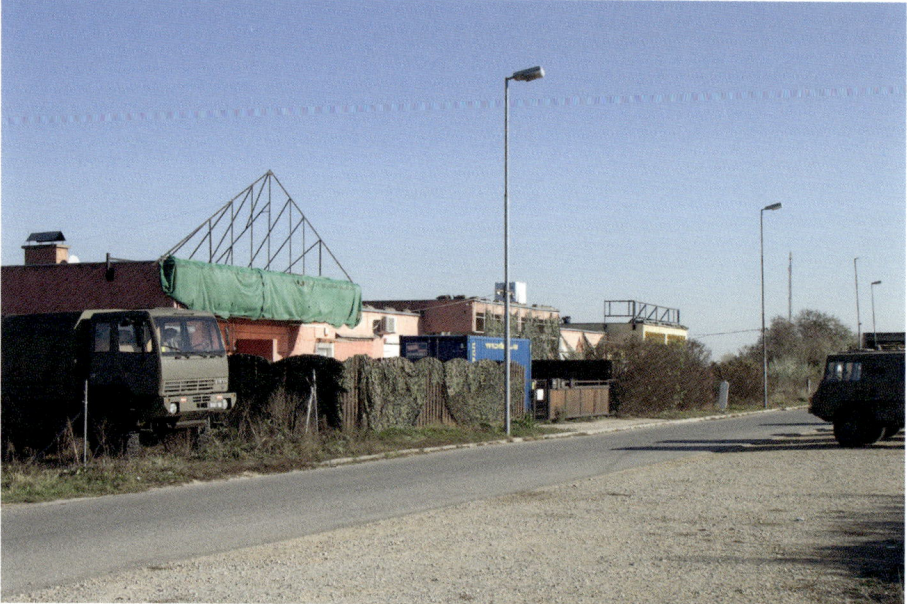

Figs. 40–41
Hieslmair and Zinganel, 2018
Vestiges of once-booming border economies at the border checkpoint of Nickelsdorf-Hegyeschalom between Austria and Hungary

competition. In our research project, however, we had initially stipulated different emphases, different case studies, and had found other border crossings along our routes more important, so for the time being we had no free capacities available.

The unforeseeable dimension of the wave of refugees and migrants in late summer and fall 2015 threatened to completely overshadow every discourse on mobility and migration—including our research project as well, which was now deemed particularly topical. We decided to incorporate the Nickelsdorf border crossing—which we had already passed through many times on our research trips—more strongly in our investigations.

## The Austria-Hungary Border Post and the "Wave of Refugees" in Fall 2015

To this end, we organized a one-day public-coach excursion in December 2015 as part of a workshop; the tour started at Vienna International Busterminal and visited other urban archipelagos and hubs of mobility and migration along the A4 eastern highway before arriving at the border crossing. To escape the danger of social voyeurism when gazing at masses of refugees and migrants at the border we consciously chose a time period when the wave was already over, the station entirely vacant, and only remnants of control and first aid infrastructure remained. Beforehand, we had contacted Hans-Paul Limbeck, a retired railway worker, amateur historian, and head of a local cultural association, who had already curated two exhibitions about historic waves of refugees in a vacant local pub. He introduced us to Gerhard Zapfl, mayor of the village of Nickelsdorf, who significantly contributed to the on-site coordination at that time. Both guided us to all the places in and around Nickelsdorf where just two months earlier the tremendous influx of refugees and migrants had to be handled without any preparation.

Up to this point, we had regarded the border crossings along the routes of our research trips—as with other stops—simply as thresholds in the mobility landscape. We had overlooked that, out of fear of the controls, there was expertise to be sold concerning evasion of the controls and that the differences between the availability and costs of goods and services produce booming border economies on both sides, which attract mobile actors and that are used by those in transit.[5]

---

5   Karl Schlögel, *Marjampole oder Europas Wiederkehr aus dem Geist der Städte* (Munich: Hanser, 2005); Yulian Konstantinov, "Patterns of Reinterpretation: Trader-Tourism in the Balkans (Bulgaria) as a Picaresque Metaphorical Enactment of Post-totalitarianism," *American Ethnologist* 23, no. 4 (1996): 762–82.

Initially, we scarcely realized that custom and border police were important employers in border regions. In almost every family in the border villages there was at least one member who had found work in this field or still worked there. A smuggler who doesn't personally know at least one of the border officers and their work roster and doesn't know the level of smuggled goods they will tolerate or the costs is incompetent. Hence, the reliability of these social networks influences the choice of smuggling routes to allow as many people as possible to have their share in the added value.

This applies to the smuggling not only of goods but also of people. During the so-called refugee crisis in late summer 2015, the majority of the refugees and migrants did not take, as one would expect, the regular and low-priced bus connections from Turkey to Bulgaria and then, within the EU, travel on to Vienna and further to Germany. Many were led along the much more dangerous route across the Mediterranean to Greece, and from there overland to Macedonia and Serbia. But most of those who made it to Bulgaria were again smuggled out of the EU into Serbia and then back in the EU via Hungary. This seemingly unnecessary crossing of two EU external borders cannot be explained alone by the fact that the border between the two neighboring EU states, Bulgaria and Romania,[6] is exceptionally well-controlled; rather, it also involves the networks that have been growing for many years along the Serbian-Bulgarian and Serbian-Hungarian borders, which had latterly gained key significance during the wars in Yugoslavia.

From Hungary the refugees and migrants passed the border crossing near Nickelsdorf. Since Hungary joined the EU in 2004, it has been an inner-EU border crossing, and since 2007 also a crossing between two Schengen states; hence, from Hungary on, borders toward the west of Europe had been essentially open and controls only carried out randomly in exceptional cases. Accordingly, the infrastructure for border controls has been gradually reduced to a minimum, and the vast parking lots for trucks became wastelands or were adapted for other purposes.

## Mobilization instead of Control

The humanitarian situation in the refugee camps in and around the crisis regions of the Middle East had gradually worsened since 2008 due to the growing influx and the continued cutbacks in the realm of development cooperation and refugee care. In 2011, following the peaceful protests known as the "Arab Spring," the Assad regime's attempt to regain power in Syria resulted in a civil war and a marked rise in the number of refugees. Many people had often been stuck in the camps for several years already without any chance of improvement. In summer 2015, when the massively underfunded World Food Program even had to curtail food coupons for Syrian refugees, many decided to set off.[7]

By this point in time, the steady influx of refugees and migrants was also recognized in Austria through reports about the deteriorating conditions in the overcrowded reception center Traiskirchen south of Vienna.[8] Already in July 2015 the ever-growing number of refugees and migrants seized at the Austrian-Hungarian border was indicative that the influx was about to increase: "Latest by July 2015 it is clear: […] For the first time, more migrants are coming via the Balkans than via the central Mediterranean route and Italy."[9] But the intensity changed radically in August 2015: Bernd Kasparek detailed what had happened alongside the route of refugees, beginning in Athens, following the "March of Hope," and how national governments and the EU reacted by first demobilizing and then remobilizing refugees in corridors, up to the day the wave arrived in Austria.[10]

The route out of the crisis regions led refugees and migrants first to Turkey where they did not require a visa at that time, and then, guided by smugglers, further to the Greek islands near the Turkish coast in overladen rubber dinghies. The Dublin Regulation II, generally applicable in EU countries, stipulates that the Member State responsible for processing an asylum application is the one where the asylum seeker first entered the EU. Hence, once registered, refugees and migrants can time and again be deported back to the respective country. Greece, however, has been excluded from this regulation since 2011. However, this makes the country, despite its poor provisions, an attractive stopover as refugees and migrants do not run the risk of getting stuck there after registration.[11] At this time detailed travel guides circulated—especially on social media—with tips and warnings tailored for refugees and

6 Despite their longstanding membership in the EU since 2007, Bulgaria and Romania are still not part of the Schengen Area. Accordingly, the highly controlled internal EU border is located in Hungary.

7 Ferry Maier and Julia Ortner, *Willkommen in Österreich: Was wir für Flüchtlinge leisten können und wo Österreich versagt hat* (Innsbruck: Verlagsanstalt Tyrolia, 2017), 22–23.

8 Politicians from the two coalition parties were shuffling the responsibility back and forth at that time in order to avoid protests in their own ranks and having to set up any more refugee reception centers in the provinces.

9 Colonel Gerald Tatzgern, head of the Central Service on Combating Alien Smuggling and Human Trafficking, Federal Ministry of the Interior, sounds the alarm in a press conference on July 1. By May 2015 more than 20,224 people had illegally crossed the Hungary-Austria border, more than double the amount in the year before." Rainer Nowak, Thomas Prior, and Christian Ultsch, eds., *Flucht: Wie der Staat die Kontrolle verlor* (Vienna: Molden Verlag, 2017), 19 (our translation).

10 Bernd Kasparek, "Routes, Corridors, and Spaces of Exception: Governing Migration and Europe," *Near Futures Online* 1, "Europe at a Crossroads," March 2016, 4, http://nearfuturesonline.org/routes-corridors-and-spaces-of-exception-governing-migration-and-europe/ (accessed March 21, 2018).

11 According to the 2011 judgement of the Court of Justice of the European Communities and the European Court of Human Rights, the regulation was entirely suspended due to the "systemic failure" of the Greek asylum system and not fulfilling human rights standards. Nowak, Prior, and Ultsch, *Flucht*, 28–29.

migrants. The onward travel from the Greek islands to Athens or Thessaloniki is straightforward with ferries. From here, they departed northward and made their way via Macedonia, Serbia, and Hungary to Austria, Germany, and Sweden. In Macedonia this situation was reinforced by a law passed on June 20, 2015 by its parliament, stating that anyone who entered the country had seventy-two hours to either apply for asylum or cross the country—a small risk for Macedonia as it was obvious that the majority was heading north anyway. This law enabled refugees and migrants to officially proceed on their travels by train and bus. As similar provisions were already set up in Serbia, smugglers were no longer needed to the Hungarian border. "The state-organized onward transport along the Balkan route had commenced."[12]

Shortly before, on June 17, news broke that the government in Budapest had decided to build a one-hundred-seventy-five-kilometer fence along the border to Serbia. "Chaos breaks out. The combination of open borders, waving through tactics, and last-minute panic after the announced closed-door policy triggers a huge dynamic on the Balkan route. A real race takes hold on the refugee route"[13] The beginnings of this development became more and more tangible, also in the border town of Nickelsdorf. Inhabitants increasingly sighted groups of refugees and migrants right in the town center. Already from July 2015, the large flying roof at the south of the border terminal was in use for the initial reception of refugees who had been dropped off there by the smugglers. Additionally, emergency shelters were set up close to the terminal at "Novarock Hall," a big barrel-shaped building that served as a VIP area and infrastructural hub during the eponymous rock festival.[14]

On August 25 a missent message went viral, soon as a tweet, and inflamed the already volatile situation: A working paper intended for internal purposes by the German Federal Office for Migration and Refugees (BAMF) leaked that there were thoughts about suspending the Dublin Regulation for Syrian asylum seekers—making Germany the number one destination country for migrants in Europe.[15] It is this message, which would later be cited as an invitation by many refugees and migrants as well as by critics of liberal asylum policies.

Just two days later on August 27 a refrigerated truck was found on the service lane of the A4, close to the Designer Outlet Parndorf shopping center, twenty-two kilometers from the Austria-Hungary border. Seventy-one dead refugees were found inside. They were brought for forensic examination and identification to a border crossing cooling hall, which had originally been set up to control imported food.[16]

The public worldwide is deeply moved by this event. At her annual summer conference on August 31, German chancellor Angela Merkel reacts with the momentous sentence: "Wir schaffen das! (We [i.e., Germany] will make it!)"[17]—

meaning that Germany will successfully handle the arrival and integration of the refugees and migrants. Already on the same day police forces suddenly withdrew from Keleti train station in Budapest, where countless refugees and migrants had ended up. The trains were stormed by hundreds of people. A few hours later 3,650 people arrived at Vienna West Station. For a brief moment, the "corridor" extended to Austrian territory.[18]

## Improvised Crisis Intervention—Bottom Up

Given the lack of provisions at Budapest Keleti train station, whether tolerated or consciously caused by Hungarian authorities, some of the refugees and migrants set out on a march toward the Austria-Hungary border on September 4, which soon became known under the hashtag #marchofhope. Just a few hours later the crowd reached the highway; it was getting dark. Deep into night people were picked up on the highway by buses. Together with those who had remained behind at Keleti station and been collected in buses as well, they were all brought to the Austria-Hungary border.[19] On that night Hungarian authorities sent, in their own words, 104 buses, including articulated buses, long-distance buses—everything the Budapest transport services and the state enterprise Volàn had to offer.[20] In order to avoid being accused of human smuggling, Hungarian bus drivers received the order to stop close to the border on Hungarian territory: the train station square in the Hungarian border town Hegyeshalom. From there the passengers once again had to walk further in the pouring rain. On September 5 the crowd of people slowly moved in clusters along the four-kilometer stretch of road to the highway border terminal on the Austrian side. On the way they passed the small old border checkpoint, where they were supplied with food and beverages by volunteers from Austria, Hungary, and Slovakia. Later on, volunteers from Nickelsdorf and a few police officers awaited them at the highway border terminal.

12 Nowak, Prior, and Ultsch, 17.
13 Nowak, Prior, and Ultsch, 16–17.
14 The hall was provided free of charge by the festival organiser Ewald Tatar. Zapfl, interview, March 18, 2016.
15 Kasparek, "Routes, Corridors, and Spaces of Exception," 4.
16 APA, "A4-Schlepperprozess," *Die Presse Online*, August 23, 2017, https://diepresse.com/home/ausland/welt/5273326/A4Schlepperprozess_Wind-blies-uns-Verwesungsgeruch-entgegen (accessed March 21, 2018).
17 Günter Bannas, "Merkel: 'Wir schaffen das,'" *FAZ Online*, August 31, 2015, http://www.faz.net/aktuell/politik/angela-merkels-sommerpressekonferenz-13778484.html (accessed March 21, 2018).
18 Nowak, Prior, and Ultsch, *Flucht*, 36.
19 Nowak, Prior, and Ultsch, 44.
20 Nowak, Prior, and Ultsch, 56–57.

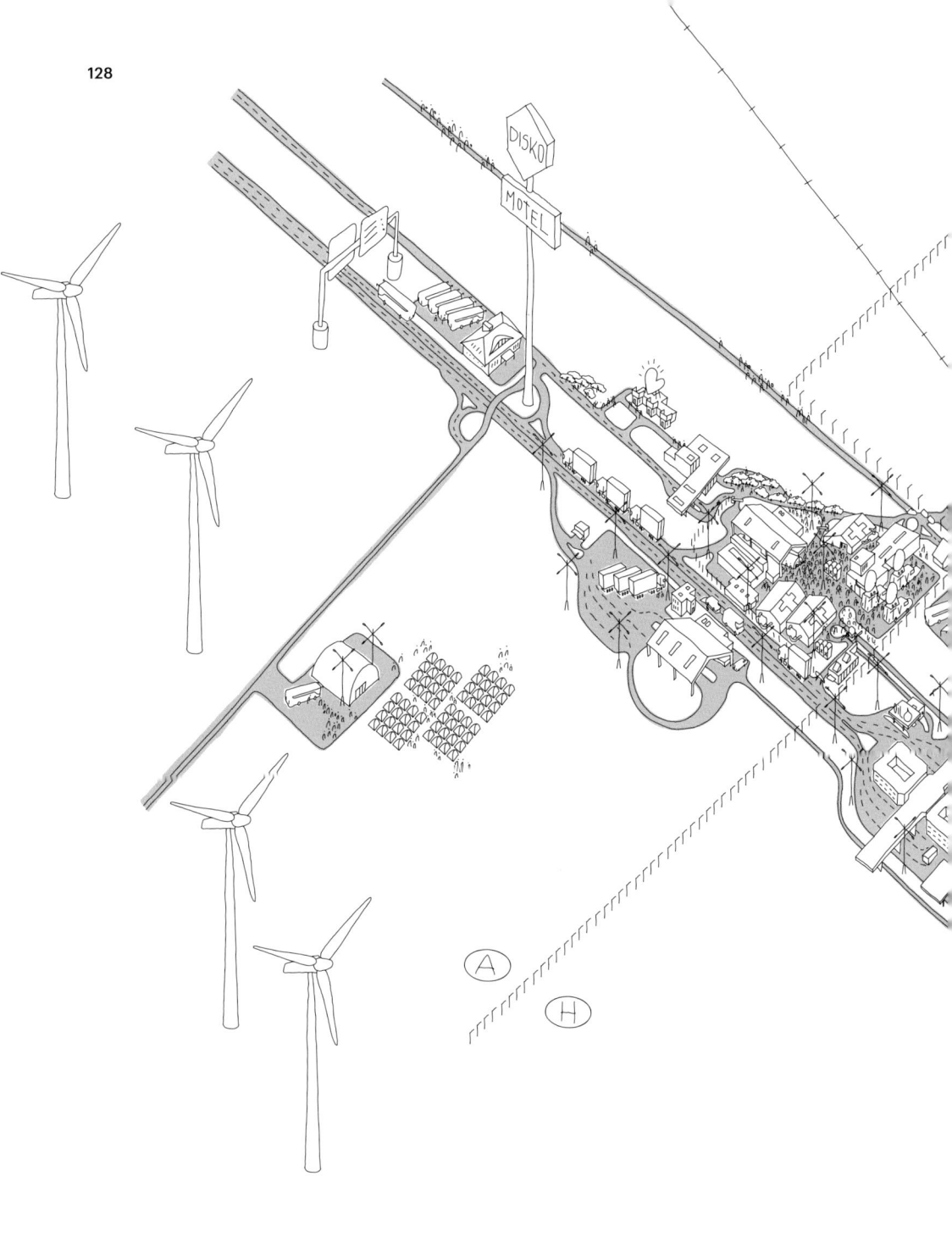

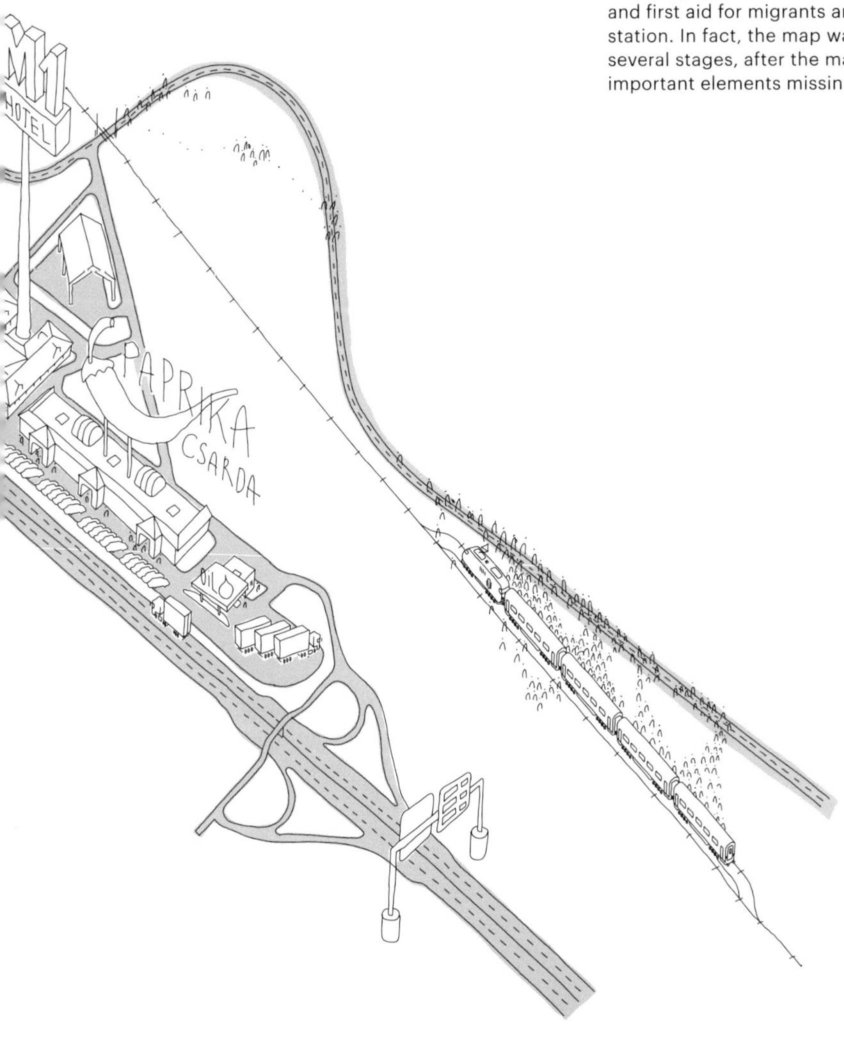

Fig. 42
Hieslmair and Zinganel, 2016
Reactivation of border infrastructure:
From July to October 2015 thousands of refugees a day had assembled at the Austria-Hungary border checkpoint of Nickelsdorf. Within a few hours auxiliary structures had been provided by emergency aid NGOs and event industries for first aid and onward transport coordination. The drawing is based on conversations with Gerhard Zapfl, mayor of the border village of Nickelsdorf, who was in charge of managing the flows of forced migration and first aid for migrants arriving at the station. In fact, the map was redrawn in several stages, after the mayor found important elements missing each time.

In order to be prepared for a potential increase of arriving people, representatives of the municipality and engaged citizens in coordination with the local police department began organizing aid measures on their own. It soon became obvious that the first aid provision and reception of a large number of people would require a sufficiently large and solid terrain.[21] The defunct border clearance terminal on Austrian territory proved to be ideal for this purpose.[22] The large-scale infrastructure with its spacious asphalt lots on both sides of the A4 eastern highway, for the most part covered by large flying roofs, represented an optimal structure for the quick set-up of temporary facilities for first aid measures: Amongst them, ephemeral architectures from the realms of crisis intervention and leisure events, such as tents in different sizes, mobile kitchens, toilets, and sanitary facilities, etc.

In the beginning there was chaos. In the first hours the volunteers from Nickelsdorf organized themselves until the arrival of the Red Cross. Then large crowds of helpers also flocked to the border crossing from Vienna, Hungary, and Slovakia. Together, under the "flying roof north" banner they provided the refugees and migrants with vital supplies—food, clothes, and blankets. Besides journalists—the first ones had already traveled on the buses from Budapest's Keleti train station—the momentous event attracted more and more media representatives, but also curious spectators. Gerhard Zapfl, nearly the only representative from the state who gave one interview after the other, said in retrospect: "The press was everywhere."[23]

## Instruments of (De-)mobilization—Top Down

Since the night of September 4, Austria's official authorities were eager to transport the refugees and migrants on to Germany as fast as possible. To avoid anyone being sent back pursuant to the Dublin II Regulation they were not registered in the first place. In this regard the Austrian authorities imitated their Hungarian counterparts—the difference being that they did not treat the people in a decidedly hostile but decidedly friendly way. This highly motivated onward transport was reasoned with Merkel's "invitation." Most of the refugees and migrants did not realize that they had already arrived in a very wealthy country with an outstanding social system.

Not to waste any time with this onward transport, before Germany could change its mind, buses were chosen as the best-suited means. However, the Austrian federal government does not own any buses, and its military has only twenty-eight units in use. At first, the railway operator's "Postbus GmbH"—the biggest bus company in Austria with strong ties to the state and a fleet of 2,200 buses—could not provide any vehicles as all of them were in use for local public transport. For short-term crisis situations the military does have basic agreements with private bus companies for transporting their soldiers but, like other entities of the federal government, it cannot place an order directly. An EU-wide tender would be required for such a large volume of buses. Moreover, this would constitute "organized people smuggling," representatives of the Federal Ministry of Internal Affairs argued.[24]

In the first hours of that night four buses were used which the Red Cross and Vienna Social Fund ordered at their own financial risk. Three more buses were organized by the Burgenland State Police Department. Just after midnight a telephone call reached Austria's second-biggest bus company "Dr. Richard"—"The Republic is calling." Shortly thereafter the company sent out several of their tour buses to the border, despite the unclear legal and financial situation.[25]

Already in the early morning of September 5, a first convoy of buses with hundreds of refugees and migrants departed from the truck parking lot on the border crossing and headed to Vienna West Station. As the new Vienna Main Station had commenced operations, it provided enough space to serve as a hub for the onward transport by rail to Germany. The regular trains were quickly overcrowded. "In the course of the morning Austrian Federal Railways installed a shuttle train connection between Nickelsdorf and Vienna West Station. Special trains now ran at two-hour intervals."[26] The special trains were full to capacity, resulting in multiple problems with the distribution of the arriving people and shortages of supplies. In order to transport even more people—but also as a buffer—buses still ran from the border to Vienna West Station. Suddenly, ten buses appeared at the station, which the coordinators did not know about. However, these so-called ghost buses, ordered by an unknown source, were

21 Dealing with the logistics of large gatherings of people is nothing new for the Municipality of Nickelsdorf. With the annual "Novarock" music festival, which took place between June 12 and 14 of the same year with seventy bands and 125,000 visitors, many operational procedures were already well-practiced and event equipment like mobile toilets are stored temporarily on municipal property and readily available. During the festival there is regular bus shuttle transportation provided between the local railway station and the festival grounds.
22 And fortunately so. Following an EU directive the border terminal buildings should have been long gone. In order to emphasize the idea of European unity, as many traces as possible indicating former borders should successively vanish.
23 Tatzgern, interview.
24 Wolfgang Mayerhofer, Logistics Command, Head of Traffic and Transport, Major in the Austrian Armed Forces, interview by the authors, Vienna, September 8, 2016.
25 The state only assumed responsibility several days later after a civil servant identified that a general agreement of the federal procurement institute already existed for such cases. Over the course of months Ludwig Richard sent fifty—on peak days up to one hundred—of his buses to the border towns Nickelsdorf and Spielfeld to transport refugees. Vehicles from Postbus and other private enterprises like Blaguss were soon also in use. Nowak et al., *Flucht*, 67.
26 Nowak, Prior, and Ultsch, 59–61.

rejected at the station as the additional number of people would have risked closure of the train station building by public authorities.[27] By this point it was clear that the onward transport of the refugees and migrants had reached full capacity also at the distribution points. In order to gain control over the waves of people, emergency shelters were quickly set up as a buffer: for example, at Vienna Main Station,[28] at the Ferry Dusika stadium, in the former customs school in the Erdberg district, and in a centrally located former tax office building on Marxergasse. The transport runs to these places took place with buses inconspicuously at night.

In Nickelsdorf the logistics for the onward transport required ever more space. This was further complicated at dawn with the many cars of the growing number of volunteers as well as the vehicles and equipment of the relief organizations and the temporary structures from the emergency aid and event sectors. To meet these demands more and more sections of the border area were approved for use. For instance, the gravel parking lot of a former roadhouse and disco on the regional highway served as a collection point and waiting zone for the arriving buses—at peak times forty buses were readily available. Many drivers were often waiting here for a long time for further instructions. Then they were sent off in small convoys to the large truck parking lot at the border terminal and into the heart of events. Crowd control barriers were mounted there to facilitate an orderly boarding of the buses, and long queues started to form.[29]

Many of the refugees and migrants who did not make it onto the buses were taken to Vienna West Station or Main Station by volunteers in private vehicles. A growing number of taxis—primarily with Viennese license plates—began appearing along the edge of the truck parking lot. The drivers, often poorly paid migrants with Austrian citizenship, saw the lucrative opportunity and asked exorbitant prices for the ride to Vienna. In the following days Mayor Zapfl counted up to 150 taxis at peak times on the specially created taxi parking lane, which ran along a row of bordello houses on the border.[30]

On September 5, just before midday on the border crossing at Hegyeshalom, Hungary's government speaker Zoltan Kovacs announced that his country would not be organizing any more bus journeys to the Austrian border. But that had no effect on the stream of people: In the meanwhile, the refugees and migrants had begun organizing rides on their own to the Austria-Hungary border.[31] Over the course of the following days, the first aid and transportation for the refugees and migrants from Nickelsdorf to the Austria-Germany border was working out well. To this end, a crisis management committee was established, which was stationed at the coordination center of Austrian Federal Railways at Vienna Main Station. It provided precise and overarching coordination in the background.[32]

The refugees and migrants continued on their journey either on regular trains or specially arranged trains and buses—or by taxi and private cars at their own initiative. This continued until September 13 when the Deutsche Bahn stopped the rail traffic coming from Austria, and Germany subsequently imposed border controls as well. No one was turned away at this point. Austria was well aware that if the border was sealed off it would be the first country after the "poverty line,"[33] and it would have the problem of many people applying for asylum here and so it accelerated the refugee transportation to the German border by bus.

When the German (Bavarian) government stipulated a maximum number of entrants per day, the buses didn't need to accelerate—quite the contrary—they needed to slow down the flow of people. The instructions to the bus drivers were now to drive as slowly as possible: on the one hand, to avoid causing a traffic jam on the Austrian-German border; on the other, to prevent chaos in Nickelsdorf and to give the refugees the feeling that "things are moving along." For this reason, intentional detours followed and short breaks were made just for one night in small emergency shelters far away from the actual route.[34] Initially, the passengers were brought to transit zones, such as the train station in Salzburg or directly to border crossings agreed upon with Germany. Then later they were brought intentionally to emergency shelters on the green border to Germany in the Mühlviertel part of Upper Austria, where there were hardly any obstacles—an invitation to take off on their own.

27 Mayerhofer, interview.
28 Besides Vienna West Station, refugees and migrants also arrived at Vienna Main Station. Helpers there already joined forces on September 3 under the name "Train of Hope." Subsequently, they supervised a number of emergency shelters together with other NGOs, for example in buildings of the so-called Erste (Bank) Campus, a recently completed office district near the Main Station, and the Arsenal complex, in an area used by the University of Technology. With the shift of the escape route they also transferred their activities to the border crossing at Spielfeld. At the beginning of October 2015 they founded a non-profit association, which is still today engaged in refugee aid.
29 A few days later, a local car dealer provided one of his tent halls near the town center for the collection and sorting of donations. Much later the Red Cross set up the "Basic Health Care Center." The office building of the customs office was used as the operations center and hosted the news media representatives. Gerhard Zapfl, interview.
30 Gerhard Zapfl, interview.
31 Georg Blume et al., "Grenzöffnung für Flüchtlinge: Was geschah wirklich?," *Die Zeit Online*, August 22, 2016, http://www.zeit.de/2016/35/grenzoeffnung-fluechtlinge-september-2015-wochenende-angela-merkel-ungarn-oesterreich/komplettansicht (accessed February 28, 2018).
32 The committee consisted of representatives from the Austrian Ministry for Internal Affairs, of the military, the ÖBB (Austrian Railway), and the Red Cross—deputies for all involved NGOs, from Vienna's municipal authority MA70, and representatives from the ÖBB-coach Ltd. as well as of Dr. Richard, the largest private coach enterprise in Austria. Mayerhofer, interview.
33 Nowak, Prior, and Ultsch, *Flucht*, 73.
34 Nowak, Prior, and Ultsch, 73.

But this fraught time also posed special challenges for the bus drivers—many of whom originated from the Yugoslavian successor states, and their families had personal experiences of migration and escape. In order to meet the tremendous demand for buses and drivers, statutory resting periods, for example, were officially suspended. "The burden of the many work hours was extreme for the bus drivers. Moreover, many of the refugees were full of anxiety and refused to step out of the waiting line or get out of the bus until they thought they were in a safe place—despite urgent bodily needs. As a result, the hygienic condition on the buses was out of control and nerves were on edge. Although there were rarely any breaks, the buses had to be provisionally cleaned. The bus drivers were left on their own. No police officers were on board."[35] The situation intensified even more as the refugees and migrants were predominantly young men from different ethnic backgrounds, which posed additional conflict potential."[36]

## From Bottom Up to Top Down

During these critical days the responsible government politicians in Vienna vanished from the scene. Confronted with the emergency situation and lack of instructions, the aid organizations and supervisory bodies, including those of the state, which had gathered at the border, decided to respond on their own authority. In contrast to the Hungarian government they neglected the guidelines of the Dublin II Regulation by only trying to provide for the mass of refugees, while keeping them in constant movement to prevent escalations in front of running TV cameras, rather than controlling them.[37]

Austrian "welcome culture" primarily pertained not only to their refugees but to their preferably conflict-free further transport to Germany. Buses were the best-suited means of transportation to keep the enormous stream in controlled motion and to prevent frustration among refugees (or at least keep it within limits), while those responsible in the background could still negotiate the respective destinations of the buses. In fall 2015 the reactivated border crossing was thus not a space of demobilization but one of mobilization. It revealed a state-tolerated strategy of "mobilizing away," which Austria shared with other countries along the refugee routes.[38]

During the peak phase of the refugee crisis between the beginning of September and October 15 a number of transportation companies were involved in the further transport of refugees and migrants from the border crossing in Nickelsdorf to the west in the direction of Germany and emergency shelters. The armed forces transported a total of 210,000 people with their twenty-eight buses and traveled 1.34 million kilometers. Each day during peak times there were between sixty and one hundred and sixty—on average 96—commercial buses on the road, which transported 690,000 people in 13,800 trips and traveled a total of 4.4 million kilometers. The Austrian Federal Railways transported approximately 300,000 refugees in 2015 with 674 special trains and 1,335 postal buses.[39]

On September 16 the military took over the Austria-wide coordination of the transport logistics from the border crossing to the train stations and emergency shelters. Later on, two large heatable tents were erected on the parking lot. These were never put into operation because on October 15 the refugee flow on this route came to an end. The "closing" of the border between Serbia and Hungary proclaimed by the Hungarian government and celebrated in the media now redirected the masses to another strand of the Balkan route.[40] Hence, the very same temporary structures for control and first aid were implemented at the Austrian-Slovenian border station in Spielfeld. A fence was also set up there along the border.[41]

"By October a highly efficient transit infrastructure had been established across the Balkans, reaching from the ports of Piraeus and Thessaloniki to several regional distribution centers in Germany. [...] By this time, it was no longer just a route, but rather a corridor, i.e., a narrow and highly organized mechanism to channel and facilitate the movement of people that only states seem capable of providing. [...] The EU border and migration regime did not have the capacity to stop the extraordinary movement of people across its borders, but morphing the route into a confined corridor served to re-establish some kind of control over the movements. [...] Their common affectedness and the new connection of the corridor created an ad-hoc political space, orthogonal to all previously existing spaces, such as the EU, the Schengen Area, and so on."[42]

35 Nowak, Prior, and Ultsch, 68.
36 Mayerhofer, interview.
37 "Even aid organizations wonder why there were no controls on the border crossing in Nickelsdorf. [...] The Federal Ministry of the Interior stated after the fact: Registration was not possible given the masses. [...] The head of a major aid organization said openly that Austria has the know-how in the management and documentation of larger crowds. [...] In this case it was not a question of not being able to but of not wanting to." Nowak et al., *Flucht*, 63–64.
38 Federica Benigni and Marika Pierdicca, "Keep Moving! Strategien der Wegmobilisierung als Teil des italienischen Migrationsmanagements," *TRANSIT* 10, no. 2 (2016), http://escholarship.org/uc/item/6gp1j1fn (accessed October 26, 2016).

39 Nowak et al., *Flucht*, 69.
40 The first section of the border fence between Hungary and Serbia was completed on September 14. On September 16 there was a massive police deployment with tear gas and water cannons as refugees tried to surmount the fence. On September 18 Hungary began construction work on a fence along the border to Croatia as well. From October 17 onwards, each day thousands of migrants were diverted to Slovenia instead.
41 Everyday life along the border control facilities was a topic in the documentary film *Spielfeld*. Kristina Schranz, director, *Spielfeld*, HD video, 27 min., Austria, 2017.
42 Kasparek," Routes, Corridors, and Spaces of Exception," 6–7.

## Revisiting the Re-/De-activated Border

In October 2016, upon completion of our research project and exactly a year after the influx of refugees, we repeated our bus tour to Nickelsdorf: there we found new, more solid control infrastructures built upon the large truck parking lot on the premises of the border crossing; a big facility comprised of containers with booths to check the personal data of those wanting to enter the country; another container facility for accommodating detained persons without an entry permit—a de facto custody prison; and prefabricated barrier elements that, if needed, could be assembled within a few hours into a solid fence with barbed wire topping on both sides of the border—measures, in the words of Nickelsdorf's mayor, that "will hopefully never be needed."[43]

The experience of the refugee crisis was drastic for the small border village: The events brought the previously insignificant and easily overlooked municipality into the world's press, and the concerted efforts had—according to the proud mayor—a very positive effect on the village's sense of community. Thus, the fall of 2015 will definitely play an important role in the collective memory of the village in the future. In many homes you still find one of the orange safety vests with the emblem of the village and the slogan Nickelsdorf hilft! (Nickelsdorf helps!), which the mayor had ordered during the height of the crisis to make local helpers identifiable against the visual dominance of uniformed professionals. The mayor emphasized that the temporary state of emergency caused by the mass flight of refugees was in no case unique in the history of the small border village: during the Hungarian crisis in November 1956, 180,000 refugees passed through Nickelsdorf, and in 1989, after the fall of the Iron Curtain, 40,000 exhausted GDR citizens had to be tended to. Also the escape routes that changed since October 2015 were not new: the stretch from Serbia to Croatia, through Slovenia to Austria across the Spielfeld border crossing, has been a part of mobility and migration history since the 1960s as a route for guest workers. Many of the bus drivers, who in fall 2015 transported the new refugees across Austria, had once entered the country on these very roads.

The political landscape in Austria was thoroughly shaken by the events: First—while the pro-refugee sentiment still prevailed—the careers of two managers of the crisis from the side of the Social Democrats sky-rocketed: Hans Peter Doskozil, the state police chief of Burgenland, where the border crossings are situated, became the defense minister, and Christian Kern, the CEO of the Austrian Federal Railways who endorsed the transportation and opened the railway stations as emergency contact centers, even advanced to chancellor. Following the increasingly critical sentiment toward refugees, however, the former foreign minister Sebastian Kurz from the conservative People's Party would prove to be the winner in the long term: in February/March 2016, at a conference of west Balkan countries, which was not coordinated with Brussels, he was celebrated—not completely, in truth—as the heroic initiator of closing the Balkan route, and in fall 2017 he went on to win the Austrian parliamentary elections with a new right-wing populist movement and a strict policy of exclusion.

But it is not entirely true to say that the entire Balkan route is "closed." We are only back to normality, migrants travel in smaller numbers and are less visible, but nonetheless they are using almost the same route, only the entry point into the EU has shifted to the Turkish-Bulgarian border. As was the case before the so-called crisis, wherever escape helpers have logistics and functioning networks available, sometimes including state supervisory bodies, goods and people without the right papers will cross the borders—together with countless other mobile individuals, including "research explorers" like ourselves.

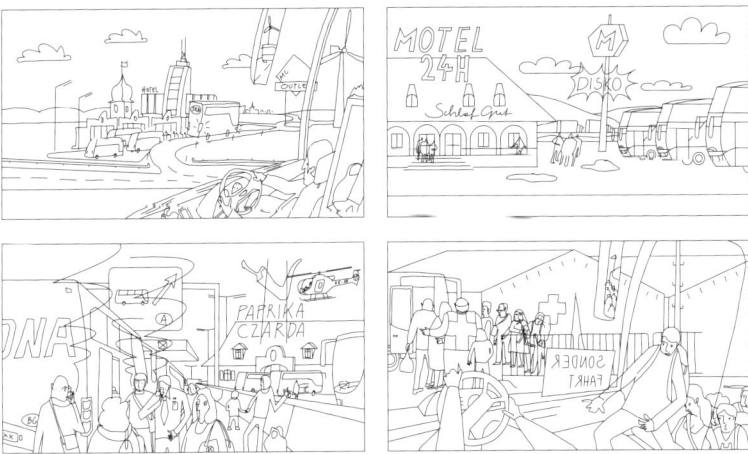

Fig. 43
Hieslmair and Zinganel, *Bus Stop Nickelsdorf*, 2016
Video stills from an animated graphic novel, 12 min., describing passengers' experiences of the Nickelsdorf border station on the Austria-Hungary border as well as fragments on the management of the enormous bottleneck of refugees in 2015 from three bus drivers' points of view: the first drove Austrian tourists across the open border station before the event, the second drove Bulgarian labor migrants to Vienna and got stuck in the reactivated border checkpoint, and the last was hired by the emergency aid organizer to drive refugees from the Hungary-Austria border to improvised accommodation units in Vienna or directly to the Austrian-German border.

43 Zapfl, interview.

## Literature

APA. "A4-Schlepperprozess: Wind blies uns Verwesungsgeruch entgegen," *Die Presse Online*, June 22, 2017, https://diepresse.com/home/ausland/welt/5273326/A4Schlepperprozess_Wind-blies-uns-Verwesungsgeruch-entgegen (accessed February 28, 2018).

ASFINAG, ed. *Das Autobahnnetz in Österreich: 30 Jahre ASFINAG*. Vienna, 2012. https://www.asfinag.at/media/1510/de_buch-30-jahre-asfinag.pdf (accessed February 28, 2018).

Bannas, Günter. "Merkel: 'Wir schaffen das.'" *FAZ Online*, August 31, 2015, http://www.faz.net/aktuell/politik/angela-merkels-sommerpressekonferenz-13778484.html (accessed February 28, 2018).

Benigni, Federica, and Marika Pierdicca. "Keep Moving! Strategien der Wegmobilisierung als Teil des italienischen Migrationsmanagements." *TRANSIT* 10 (2) (2016), http://escholarship.org/uc/item/6gp1j1fn (accessed October 26, 2016).

Blume, Georg, Marc Brost, Tina Hildebrandt, Alexej Hock, Sybille Klormann, Angela Köckritz, Matthias Krupa, Mariam Lau, Gero von Randow, Merlind Theile, Michael Thumann, and Heinrich Wefing. "Grenzöffnung für Flüchtlinge: Was geschah wirklich?" *Die Zeit Online*, August 22, 2016, http://www.zeit.de/2016/35/grenzoeffnung-fluechtlinge-september-2015-wochenende-angela-merkel-ungarn-oesterreich/komplettansicht (accessed February 28, 2018).

Bauman, Zygmunt. *Liquid Modernity*. Cambridge: Polity Press, 2000.

Haberfellner, Friedrich, head and coordinator of Vienna International Busterminal, Blaguss travel and transportation company, interview by the authors, Vienna, April 28, 2014.

Hall, Michael, and Alan M. Williams. *Tourism and Migration: New Relationships between Production and Consumption*. London: Kluwer Academic Publishing, 2002.

Kasparek, Bernd. "Routes, Corridors, and Spaces of Exception: Governing Migration and Europe." *Near Futures Online* 1, "Europe at a Crossroads," March 2016, http://nearfuturesonline.org/the-life-and-time-of-the-european-consolidation-state.html (accessed October 12, 2017).

Konstantinov, Yulian. "Patterns of Reinterpretation: Trader-Tourism in the Balkans (Bulgaria) as a Picaresque Metaphorical Enactment of Post-totalitarianism." *American Ethnologist* 23, no. 4 (1996): 762–82.

Hans-Paul Limbeck, retired railroad worker, amateur historian, and chairman of "Kulturverein Kugel," interview by the authors, Nickelsdorf, June 3, 2014.

———. retired railroad worker, amateur historian and chairman of "Kulturverein Kugel," interview by the authors, Nickelsdorf, March 18, 2016.

Maier, Ferry, and Julia Ortner. *Willkommen in Österreich: Was wir für Flüchtlinge leisten können und wo Österreich versagt hat*. Innsbruck: Verlagsanstalt Tyrolia, 2017.

Mayerhofer, Wolfgang, Logistics Command, Head of Traffic and Transport, Major at the Austrian Armed Forces, interview by the authors, Vienna, September 8, 2016.

Nowak, Rainer, Thomas Prior, and Christian Ultsch. *Flucht: Wie der Staat die Kontrolle verlor*. Vienna: Molden Verlag, 2017.

Schlögel, Karl. *Marjampole oder Europas Wiederkehr aus dem Geist der Städte*. Munich: Hanser, 2005.

Schranz, Kristina, and Carina Zech, script, Kristina Schranz, direction. *Spielfeld*. Documentation HD video, 27 min., Austria, 2017.

Simone, AbdouMaliq. "People as Infrastructure: Intersecting Fragments in Johannesburg." *Public Culture* 16, no. 3 (2004): 407–29.

Tatzgern, Gerald, head of the Central Service on Combating Alien Smuggling and Human Trafficking, Federal Ministry of the Interior, Federal Criminal Police Office, interview by the authors, Vienna, September 8, 2016.

Zapfl, Gerhard, mayor of Nickelsdorf, interview by the authors, Nickelsdorf, March 18, 2016.

———. mayor of Nickelsdorf, interview by the authors, Nickelsdorf, October 8, 2016.

# Tallinn Harbor
# Rhythms of a Road to Sea Bottleneck and the Effects on the City

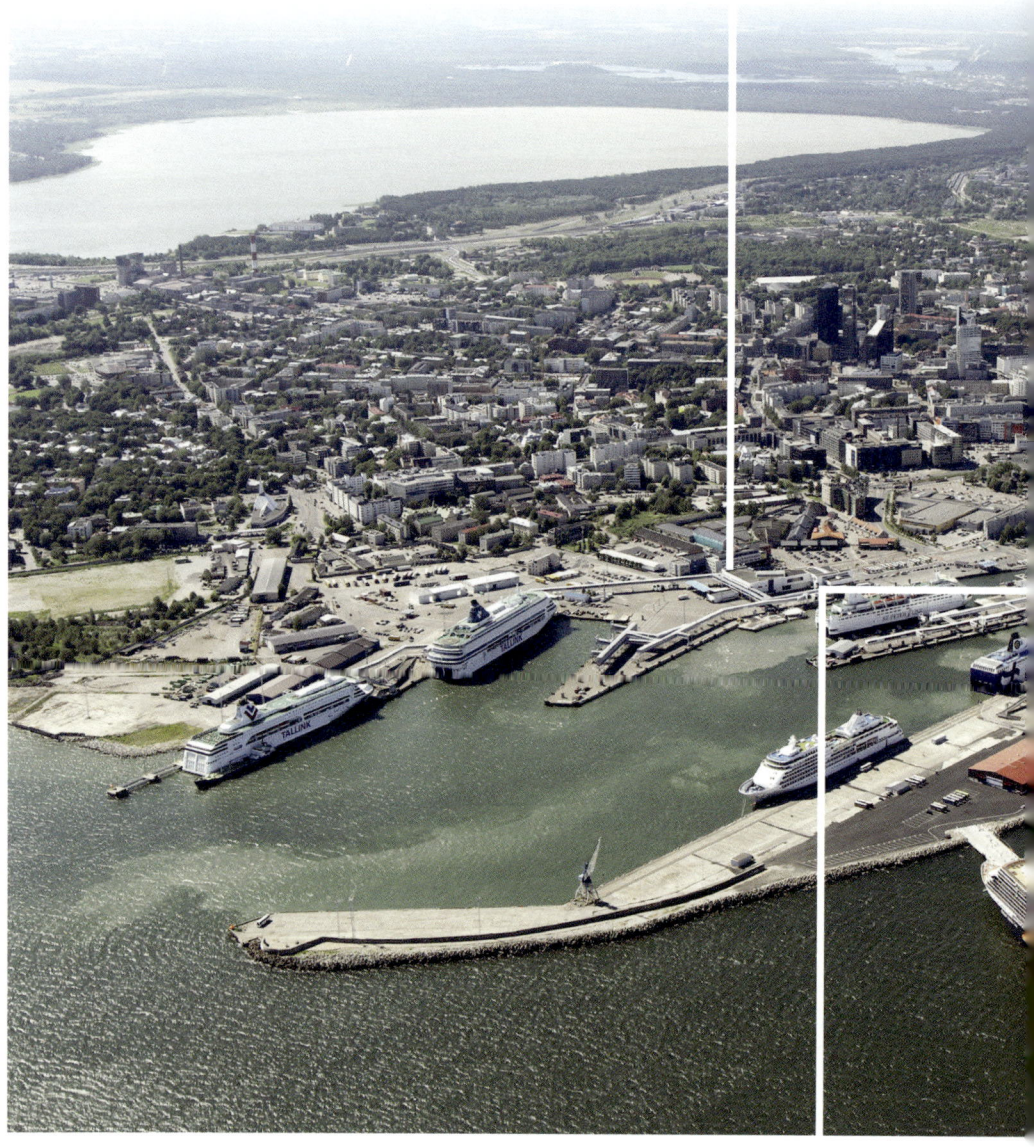

Terminal D
Tallinn — Helsinki: 7,959,700*

Terminal A + B
Tallinn — Stockholm: 955,500*
Stockholm — Tallinn — St. Petersburg: 147,000*

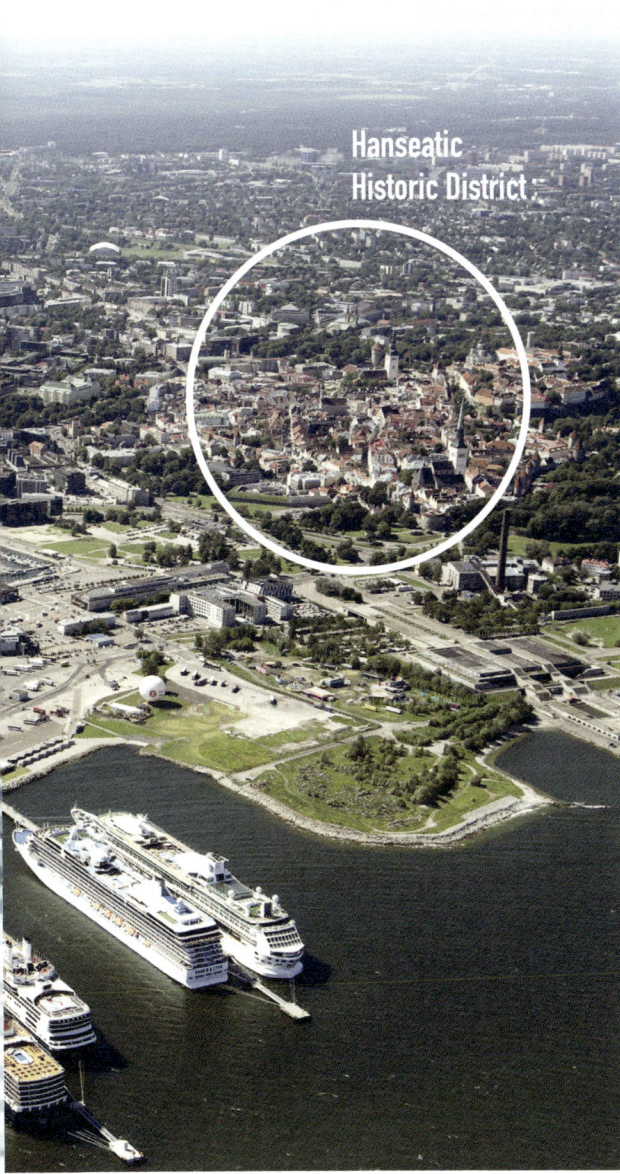

Fig. 44
Hieslmair and Zinganel, 2015
In Tallinn, a transnational road corridor comes to an end where passengers change over to a ferry link. In sharp contrast to the small Old Town a large traffic area around the harbor is developing, while the schedule of large capacity ferries (and cruise ships) is imposing its rhythm onto both the harbor and the city.

**Cruise Area**
**Baltic Sea: 486,600\***

\* Passengers per Year in 201

# A Speaking Passenger Network Diagram
## Reflections on the Applied Methodology

Michael Zinganel, Michael Hieslmair, and Tarmo Pikner

## Intervention in the Public Space

Today, between Tallinn in Estonia and Helsinki in Finland a continuation of the Pan-European road corridor(s) is in place in the form of a highly efficient regular ferry connection. Pedestrians, cars, buses, and lorries are transported across the Baltic Sea in huge ships that leave every three hours. In both cities three major highways arrive at major terminal complexes, which represent bottlenecks that narrow traffic to the limited capacities and decelerated speed of the vessels, to be delivered over to the harbor on the opposite side of the Baltic, where vehicles are redirected to the road corridors once again.

In September 2015 we employed the cultural capital of the Tallinn Architecture Biennale to convince the harbor administration of Tallinn to support our project and realize a large-scale intervention in the public space. We obtained the permission to park our trailer in front of Terminal D. With almost eight million passengers a year it is the most frequented terminal connecting Tallinn and Helsinki. Here we expected to attract a large audience to visit our intervention but also to meet a variety of people and speak about their mobility experiences.

In this context the trailer did not function as a large-scale drawing board for mapping exercises in the field like on several other occasions before.[1] Here the trailer was the supporting structure for a three-dimensional network sculpture. The yellow wooden beams represented an abstract map of the routes and paths of selected individuals who use the ferry connection—both their voyage across the sea and their landside trips from their departure point to their target destination.

Via built-in loudspeakers passersby could listen to their narrations, which introduced different motives, rhythms, rituals, and routines (here represented by the scripts of original sound files). These micro-narratives relate both to the individuals' biographies and to more general historic, political, and economic transformations of the Baltic area, thereby interrelating transnational mobility flows and place-making at very specific sites. Moreover, these stories address sociocultural/economic differences and effects that cause, amongst other things, (labor) migration and cross-border consumption. For example: an ethnic Russian teacher who works in shifts at a bar on the ferry after having lost her original job; a Russian businessman from St. Petersburg who checks his real estate investments in Estonia every other month; a Polish truck driver who passes by

1 See the chapter on mapping in Michael Zinganel and Michael Hieslmair, "Stop and Go: Nodes of Transformation and Transition," *JAR Journal of Artistic Research*, no. 14 (2017), https://www.researchcatalogue.net/view/330596/330597 (accessed January 15, 2018); and Michael Zinganel and Michael Hieslmair, "Test Run—Stop and Go: Mapping Nodes of Mobility and Migration," in "Anthropological Journal of European Cultures." Special issue, *Urban Place-making between Art, Qualitative Research and Politics*, ed. Judith Laister and Anna Lipphardt, no. 2 (2005), 117–27.

the harbor once a week; a construction worker from the south-east of Estonia who works as a labor migrant around Helsinki; a sales representative of a German company who visits clients in Scandinavia and the Baltic area; and a group of young Finns who frequently travel to Tallinn on a reduced group ticket to stroll around the bars of the Old Town of Tallinn, before returning with their shopping carts to take back as many alcoholic drinks as the carts allow—the significantly lower prices easily enable them to refinance the costs of trip.

The represented paths and narratives are based on and/or refer to thirty episodic interviews with staff and passengers of the ferry line, conducted by our Estonian research partner Tarmo Pikner either on board the boat or in the waiting areas of the terminal building. Fragments of the real experiences of many different characters were rendered anonymous and consciously merged into a reduced number of seven fictional characters, which still offer a wide range of travel biographies but did not overburden the capacities of the people passing by the installation. To enhance the degree of abstraction, each of the sound tracks was spoken by a professional radio announcer.

This installation was not only intended as a representation of the final results of our Tallinn research but also as a visually attractive trigger for collecting additional expertise from mobile actors. During the setup process, we could experience live on site how the arrival times of ferry boats dramatically increased the number of taxis, buses, and rickshaw drivers along with the presence of small-scale vendors and beggars. The seemingly oversized asphalt desert of parking lots became completely filled with vehicles for a limited period of time. Once the parking lots were empty again, the consumption zones alongside the beaten paths of tourists had become crowded: the souvenir shops and bars in the Old Town, the shopping malls along the inner ring, and the many alcohol supermarkets and hotels near the harbor.

For the installation itself the chosen site turned out to be less appropriate for our efforts: Although an enormous number of passengers passed by, they were far too busy heading for a taxi or bus or following the crowds on the path toward the city center. The only people who had time to speak with us were the staff of the terminal smoking a cigarette outdoors, passengers who had missed the boat, and people waiting to offer services to arriving passengers. For example, whenever a boat arrived several rickshaw drivers turned up and switched on certain signature tunes to catch the passengers' attention. They had time to watch us setting up the installation over the course of several days. One of them, who arrived first each day, introduced us into his precarious working life: a young, deprived ethnic Russian from far outside of Tallinn, who did not even have an apartment in town—too expensive, he said. Of course, he knew the schedule of the boats by heart, as he does with all other events in town. He works a tight schedule as long as the high summer season lasts. At night he sleeps—no more than a few hours each day—in his vehicle, parked on the waterfront or in a vacant warehouse nearby. He often takes a nap while awaiting the arrival of a ferry. The vehicle does not belong to him. He has to pay rent to a company that had taken out a monopolist license for exclusively offering these services in Tallinn and in other European cities.

Drunken Finns, who missed their ferry and had to wait for the next boat, explained the prices of alcohol to us in detail and also the best choices. They increased their virtual income by purchasing drinks in Tallinn that would cost more than double in Finland and thereby funded the costs of the trip and more. But we also learned that this specific carnivalesque ritual is not limited to lower-middle-class men: There were also whole families, each member pulling a folding trolley packed with alcoholic drinks back on board. And when buses leave the boat and pick up the passengers—mainly elderly tourists—at the big parking lot in front of the terminal, they first drive directly to one of the many supermarkets—with names like SuperAlko Store—and fill the huge boot with boxes of drinks, before they start their sightseeing trip.

On the other hand, the attempt alone to get the permission of the harbor administration to use this site for the installation opened up doors for us to inside knowledge: about the enormous revenue made from tourism and the high-risk dependency of Tallinn on low tax, low wages, cheap service, and consumer products, especially alcohol, in comparison with Scandinavian countries. Some drinks are even imported from Finland by boat to be sold much cheaper here and brought back home by the Finns. The manager also introduced us to historic details of the harbor, which was transformed from an entirely closed off cargo terminal in the communist era into an open terrain used solely by ferry and cruise ships, a promising site for real estate developments between the Old Town and the harbor front, and thus a perfect vehicle for mobilizing the flow of capital, virtually traveling parallel with the ferry lines.

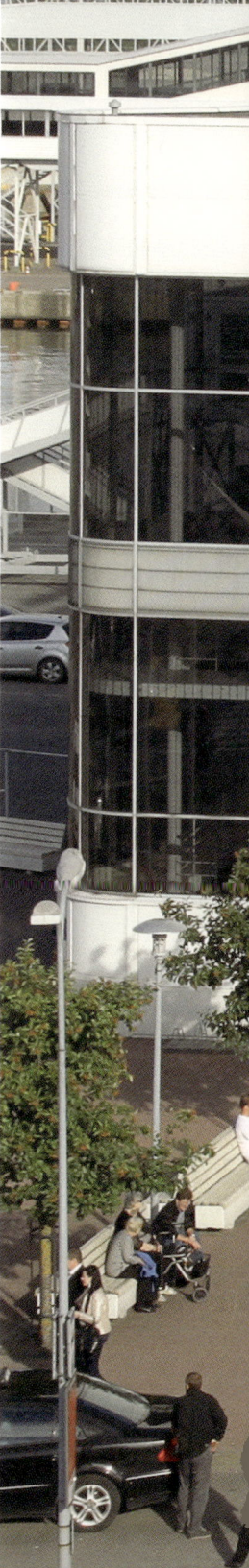

Fig. 45
Hieslmair and Zinganel with Tarmo Pikner, *A Speaking Passenger Network Diagram—Intervention in the Public Space outside Ferry Terminal D*, Tallinn Harbor, installation view, 2015
An abstracted map of routes and pathways of selected actors, who use the ferry links between Helsinki and Tallinn, with short narrations of their differing individual travel experiences, motives and rhythms, spoken by radio news announcers and broadcast via loudspeakers

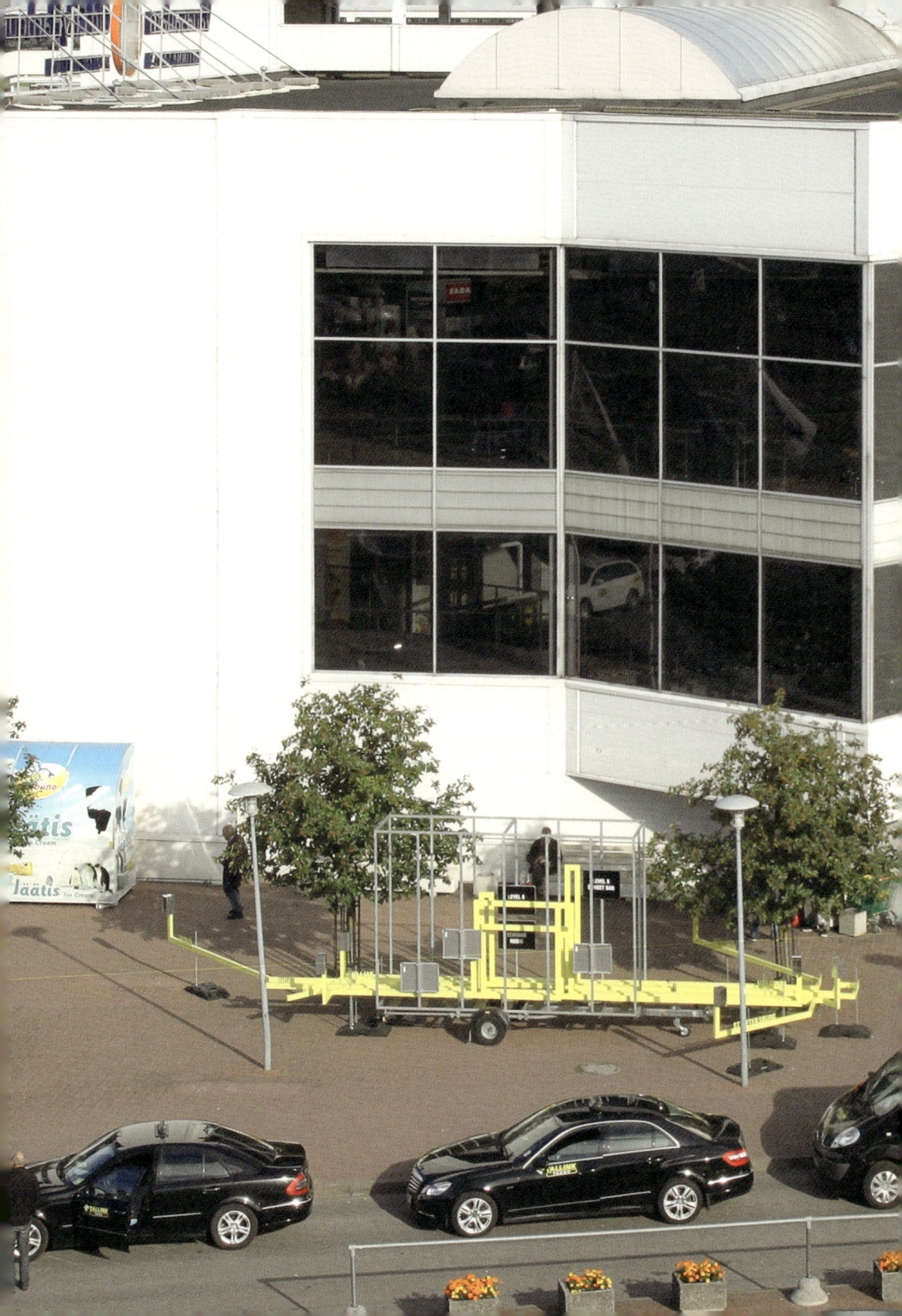

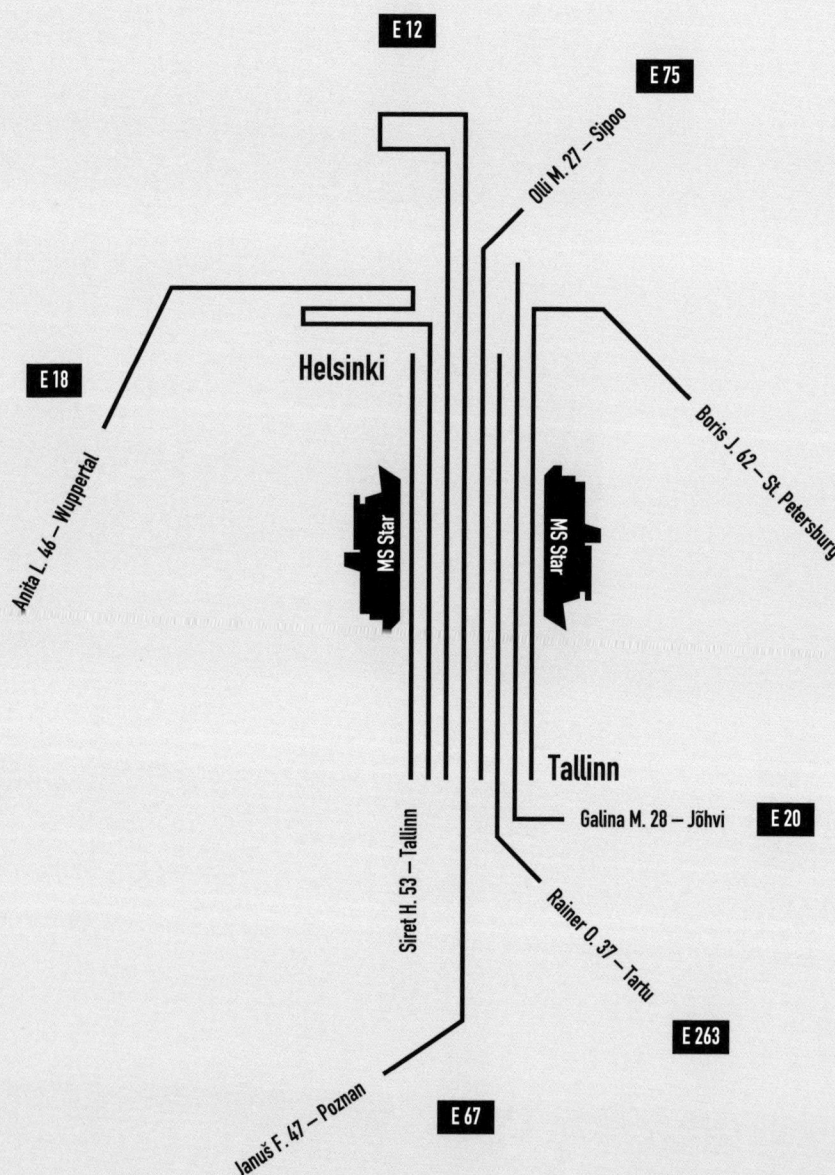

Fig. 46
Hieslmair and Zinganel with Tarmo Pikner, 2015
Scheme of the passenger network diagram, overview of actors' paths and scripts of audio tracks

## Fictionalized scripts of people's experience passing through Tallinn ferry port

**Boris J., 62,** investor and manager from St. Petersburg, Russia. He travels the 320 kilometers to Estonia four times a year. Being a child of a former *nomenklatura* family from the Soviet era he spent many holidays at the Estonian seaside—and still does today. He also deals in real estate investments in the Baltic countries, finding safe havens in the European Union for his own property and that of his friends and clients—even more intensively since the recent crisis.

The visa regime does not bother Boris J. He is privileged to have a temporary residence permit for the European Union. At 6 a.m. he leaves his apartment in the centrally situated Lermontovski street. A taxi takes him to the Finlandsky Station. At 6:40 a.m. he gets on the new Allegro high-speed train reaching Helsinki in only three hours. In Helsinki his Estonian business partners join him for a one-day meeting at a company specialized in developing high tech business parks close to harbors and airports—in both Scandinavia and Baltic countries.

The next morning, right after breakfast, Boris J. and his partners take a taxi to the ferry terminal. Immediately after checking in and boarding they enter one of the small seminar rooms for business meetings which their secretary already has booked in advance. They arrange their things and connect one of their laptops with the built-in projector.

After two hours' work, they get off in Tallinn. A driver awaits them in front of the exit of Terminal D, holding a handwritten sign with their names on it. He guides them to a black BMW X5 parked in the drop-off area in front of the terminal. They visit a logistics project at Paldiski harbor and a controversial open-sea wind energy production site near Hiiumaa Island. After another business meeting in Latvia Boris J. will take a plane back home from Riga to St. Petersburg.

Apart from work, Boris J. has also been coming here for a number of years with his family, spending the New Year in Tallinn—and then taking a short holiday in Kuressaare spa. Boris J. is not quite sure about planning holiday trips for next winter because of the increasingly difficult economic situation in Russia—he is currently short of cash having invested almost everything in real estate.

**Galina M., 28,** trained primary school teacher, currently waitress, from Jõhvi, Estonia. For three years she has been fully employed by Tallink Silja Line.

Galina M.'s parents relocated from Armenia in the 1980s because of economic and political pressures. They already had relatives living in Estonia. Due to her ethnic background, Galina M. speaks Armenian, Russian, Estonian—of course—and, having taken language lessons, also a bit of Finnish. She was originally trained as a primary school teacher and taught pupils for years in Jõhvi in the eastern part of Estonia. After losing her job because of a school system reform she was hired as a waitress with the ferry line.

Galina M. works on two of the three trips that the MS Star ferry makes daily. She usually starts 6 a.m. and ends at 7 p.m. (including breaks). She generally works and lives one week on the ship and has every other week at home. Although this schedule and rhythm seems to suit her current lifestyle, she only considers this job a temporary solution—and plans to change whenever a chance arises.

After her days off, Galina M. departs at 8:30 p.m. from her apartment in a prefab housing block in Jõhvi. The bus to Tallinn takes a minimum of two-and-a-half hours. Galina M. arrives at Terminal D before midnight and sleeps on the ferry, starting her shift the following morning. On her way to the buffet bar on Level 8 she walks by the many tax-free shops that are still closed. At 7:30 a.m., right after the MS Star has set sail, Galina M. serves the first beers to a Finnish guy and his friends.

**Januš F., 47,** truck driver, from Poznan, Poland. He is a one-man company and, for the last seven years, the owner of a second-hand Volvo FH 12, a 16.5-meter, 40-ton semitrailer that carries cargo between Poland, Finland, and Russia. Back in the mid-1990s, he started his business with an older and smaller 3.5-ton Iveco truck. Since loans from "Western" banks seemed like a good deal in 2008—before the start of the economic crisis—he invested in a truck with a maximum load capacity. Since then he goes through Tallinn's harbor terminal about five times a month.

Being an independent entrepreneur, Januš. F. enjoys freedom of choice when it comes to both his clients and his destinations in the field of logistics. In order to be able to pay back his loan, he is also happy to be frequently commissioned for jobs by larger logistics companies, like the Danish DSV or German DB-Schenker, brands that dominate the transnational markets of Northern Europe.

The truck's load can be rather diverse. This time Januš F. has transported textile and leather from Poznan to Tallinn. The trip of 1,900 kilometers started on Wednesday at 7 a.m. and took him three days and two nights sleeping in the cab. On the third day, around noon, he arrived at a big furniture company in Jüri near Tallinn. Some hours later Januš F. loaded plastic windows from a warehouse in eastern Tallinn, which he delivered to Tampere in Finland. The next morning, he picked up a load consisting of Finnish alcoholic and non-alcoholic drinks near Espoo and headed for the ferry back to Tallinn. He unloaded at the Alko supermarkets adjacent to Tallinn Harbor.

While unloading he got a phone call from the dispatcher: Because the receiving company in St. Petersburg which would have been his next point of delivery had not yet paid the prefab-parts for wooden block-houses, he can't pick up a load in Tallinn immediately. Therefore, Januš F. decides to stay in the Tallinn harbor area. He parks his truck at the TIR HGV park beside a Russian, a Lithuanian, and another Polish truck. While the other drivers continue on their journeys after a short conversation, Januš F. visits the supermarket to get food and drinks in preparation for an overnight stay—or even an unpaid long weekend.

**Rainer O., 37,** construction worker from Tartu, Estonia. For nine years he has commuted weekly, or at least every other week, between Tartu and Helsinki. For the last five years he has worked for his own small, two-man construction company operating in the Helsinki region. Acquiring sub-contracts for construction work requires a lot of effort and in periods of crisis follow-up jobs are by no means guaranteed. But still, the difference in earnings is quite remarkable.

He usually starts traveling from Tallinn to Helsinki on Sunday at 10:30 p.m. and back to Estonia on Thursday at 4:30 p.m.

On Thursday at 8:30 a.m. Rainer O. leaves the small rented apartment he shares with another worker from Estonia in the remote Kaarela district of Helsinki. He owns a Toyota pickup which he purchased at a large secondhand car market in Marijampolė in Lithuania, a car imported from Germany that very same day. Usually he would travel with public transport and use the regular bus connection between Tallinn and Tartu. But this time his van needed a service. Because this is much cheaper in Estonia than in Finland he decided to drive by car. In addition, his sister back home had ordered some specific furniture from IKEA-Vantaa in Helsinki because there is still no IKEA branch in Estonia. Therefore he passed by IKEA with his car before driving to the Helsinki ferry terminal.

After twenty-five minutes lining up in the queue of up to 150 cars he parks his pickup on board, locks it, and heads for the elevator. Going up, he is accompanied by a group of Polish truck-drivers wearing slippers and jogging pants. On Level 6 Rainer O. looks for a quiet corner. He lies down on the carpet in front of the lockers and tries to sleep for the next two hours. When he recognizes the dead sound of the ship's landing, he gets up and heads for his car. At 6:30 p.m. he passes through the exit gate of Terminal D in Tallinn.

From here he'll drive the 190 kilometers trip to Tartu, where his wife and four-year-old daughter still live. The family has already considered the option of entirely relocating to Finland. But his wife was against it—she was afraid of losing her personal contacts and her part time job.

**Anita L., 46,** export manager from Wuppertal, Germany. For over ten years now she has been traveling to Finland and Estonia about three times a year—to visit the potential clients of a German company manufacturing door panels. At the beginning of the expansion the company used to send small teams of reps but for the last five years one person has to do the job alone.

Anita L.'s current business trip started from Wuppertal. She packed her sling-bag trolley set with clothes, beauty case, laptop and high-gloss product catalogues of door and window panels. She drove thirty kilometers to Düsseldorf airport in the company's grey metallic Volkswagen Sharan and boarded the Lufthansa flight to Helsinki via Frankfurt. It took about four and a half hours.

Over the next two days Anita L. has meetings in Lahti and Turku before leaving for Tallinn. After boarding at 10:30 a.m. she does some office work on her a laptop in the comfort class zone of the ferry boat. Wi-Fi connection and drinks here are free. And guests will not feel disturbed by noisy tourists. Finishing her work, she usually goes on deck to enjoy the sunshine. Despite her long experience the crossing is still exciting for her because the sea is quite far from her current home in the middle of Germany.

Arriving in Tallinn at 12:30 p.m., Anita L. goes to pick up the rental car just across from the harbor terminal. An individual car is the most flexible means of transport to reach her geographically dispersed business partners in the region—especially with a set of trolleys, a fashionable handbag, and shopping bag with the many souvenirs she purchased during her trip.

**Olli M., 27,** car mechanic from Sipoo, Finland. Together with friends he usually takes a one- day cruise to Tallinn about three times a year—to enjoy a holiday and party.

The price of the return ferry ticket is about eighty euros—or less if purchased as a group ticket. Each person spends approx. two hundred euros on alcohol to take back to Finland. Since the price of alcohol is three times the price in Finland than it is in Estonia, the virtual revenue from that difference covers the costs of the trip.

Olli M. and his friends are on their way back to Sipoo. They have to be at the counter of the ferry-line in Terminal D by 7 p.m. for check-in at Tallinn harbor. After boarding they immediately head for the large bar on Level 6 where they order drinks.

Often on these trips, Olli M. goes around with a larger group of friends, just walking and strolling in the old city of Tallinn. (On one occasion his former military service unit, about one hundred men, met on the ferry to celebrate their tenth anniversary). Olli M. has no need for maps or information brochures because he and his friends simply follow the beaten paths of the many other tourists in town. They usually go on a pub-crawl. Today, their trip began when they left home at 6 a.m., arriving in Tallinn at 9:30 a.m. It turned out to be a bit annoying as arriving so early means no pubs were open and no slot machines were available to play on.

Every time they return to the boat in Tallinn Olli M. and his friends have folding trolleys fully loaded with boxes of long-drinks, gin, and even Finnish beer wrapped in plastic. This was purchased at Super-Alko, one of the many supermarkets near the harbor terminal that are specially tailored to tourists like him.

**Siret H., 53,** accountant from Tallinn, Estonia. Since the fall of Communism in 1989 she has made frequently trips to Helsinki. Gradually she has won customers and made friends in Finland too, most of them Estonians who emigrated to Helsinki for better job opportunities. But she is also motivated by her private obsession with flea markets, purchasing objects in Helsinki and re-selling them at Tallinn's twice-monthly Telliskivi flea market.

Usually Siret H. spends four days across the gulf in Helsinki where she tries to visit her favorite flea markets. One of them, Aino Kirpputori, is held in the old railway station of Kannelmäe located in northern part of the city. To save money she stays at a friend's place in a social housing complex in Helsinki's Malmin district.

Early in the morning Siret H. leaves the apartment to take a nine-kilometer bus ride to Aino Kirpputori flea market in Kannelmäe. When she arrives at 4 p.m. at the West Terminal to take the Tallink ship MS Star, her suitcase is full to the brim with items purchased there.

Inside the terminal building Siret H. heads straight for the Tallink Silja Line counter where she picks up her boarding pass. At Gate two she joins a long queue. One by one people pass through the barrier, swiping their tickets across the scanner. On the ship she passes the lockers where several passengers have already settled in with their luggage on the carpet. She takes the staircase to Deck 8, grabs a coffee in the self-service restaurant and takes a seat at a table where two men are already sitting.

Later Siret H. unexpectedly bumps into a former colleague who now lives in Finland permanently. They spend time talking about acquaintances they have in common. Before landing, she takes time to buy some confectionery as gifts for friends and relatives.

Early the following Saturday morning Siret H. will set up a small table at Telliskivi flea market in Tallinn. She will have time for a short chat with adjacent vendors before the first customers arrive. Many of the items in her large suitcase are already reserved for special customers who have ordered them in advance.

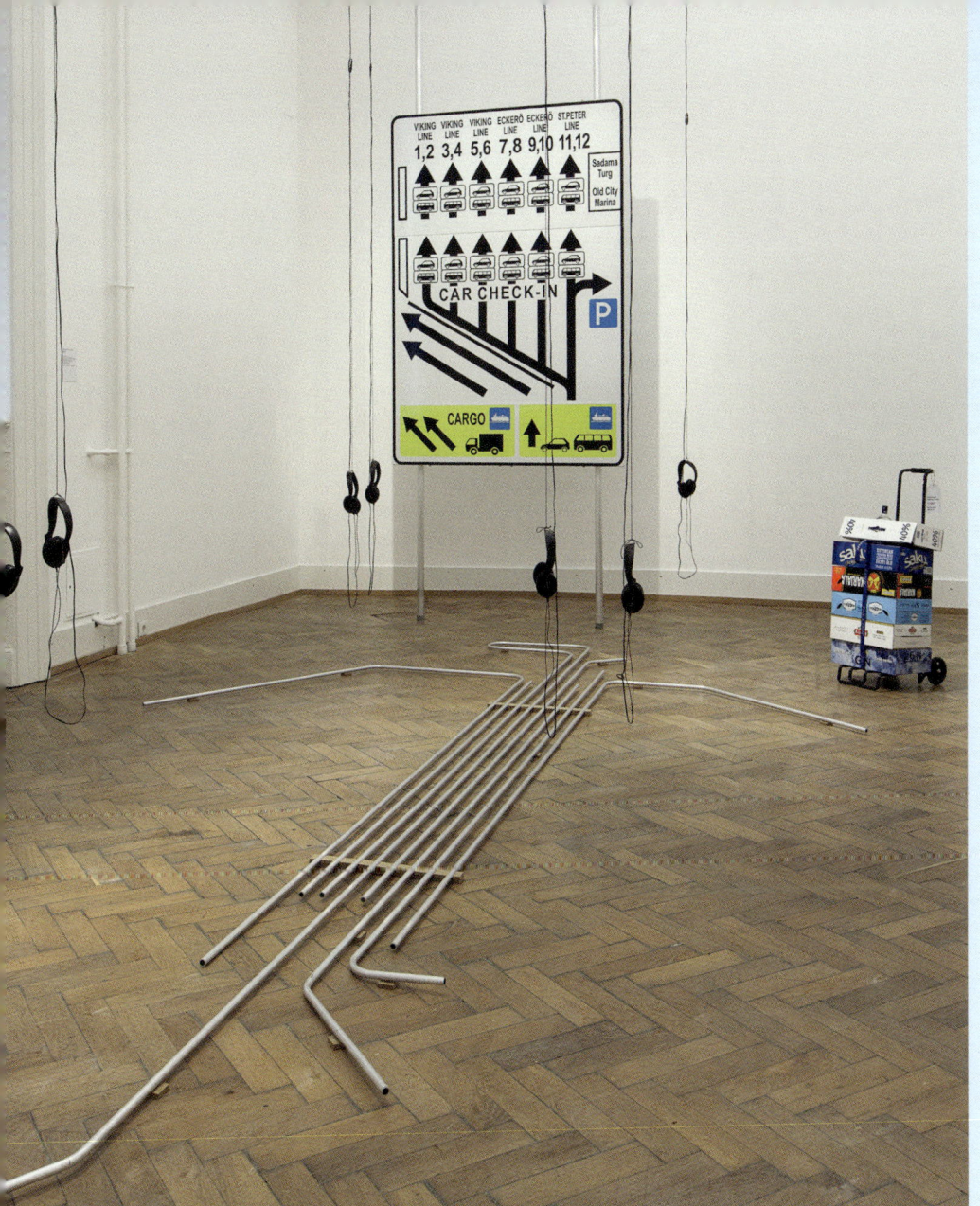

Fig. 47
Hieslmair and Zinganel, 2016
Indoor adaptation of the route network diagram, shown at the Academy of Fine Arts Vienna: The huge traffic sign at the back was reproduced by a sign maker in Tallinn and transported back to Vienna in our Ford Transit. It refers to both the heterotrophic appeal of the harbor and the potential density of traffic here. But it also reflects the universal diagrammatic visual language developed by Otto Neurath and Gerd Arntz in Vienna in the 1920s, a scientific basis for modern map-making for educational purposes. Folding trolley with six cartons of alcoholic drinks, the typical souvenir of male Finnish visitors to Tallinn

# Harbors and Practiced Lines
# Evolving Mobilities between Tallinn and Helsinki

Tarmo Pikner

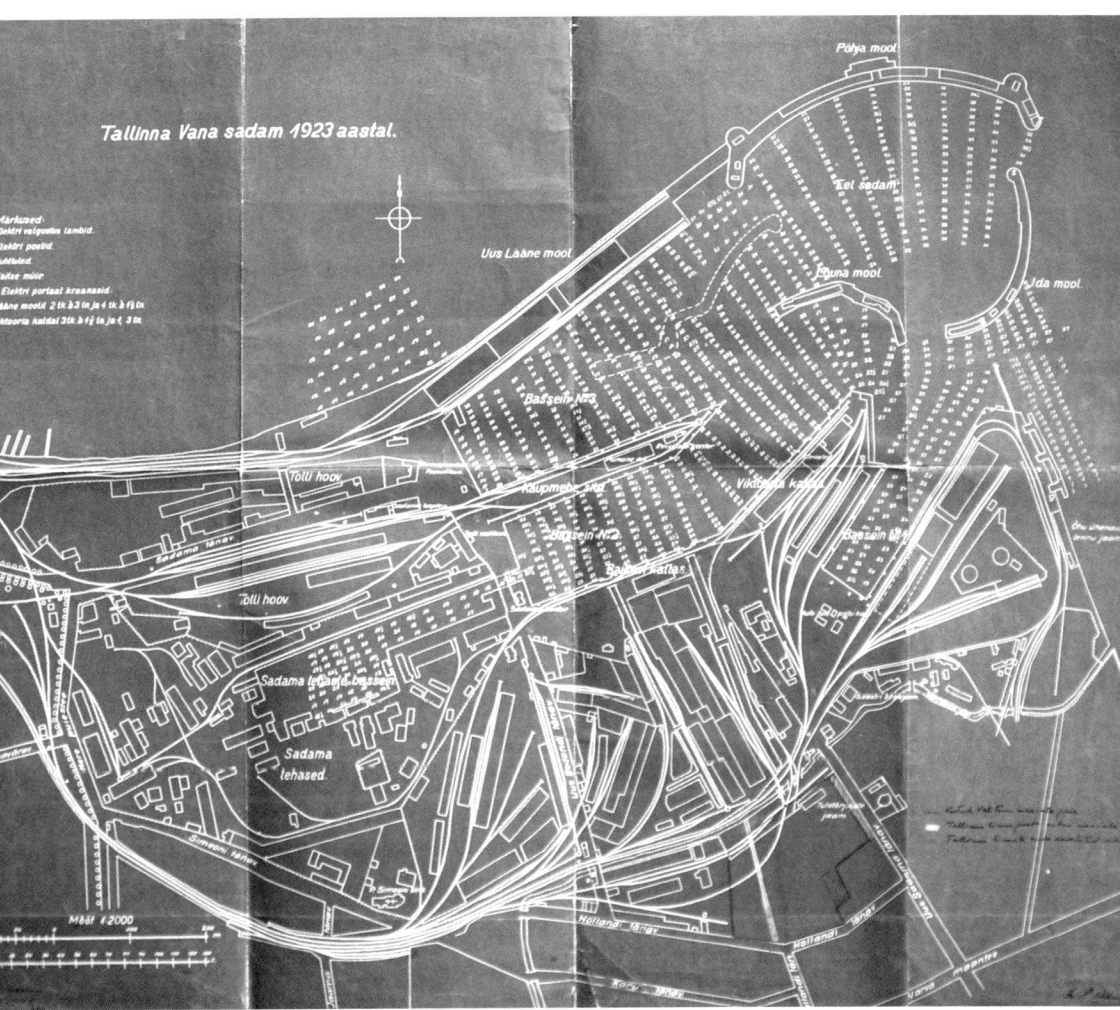

Fig. 48
The Old Harbor of Tallinn in 1923, when railroad tracks passed the inner city to the north and their routes structured the fan-folded position of limestone-built warehouses and harbor basins with loading docks

Harbors can be seen as spaces that dispersed networks of production, transportation, and consumption bring into being, and where a globalizing world is being written into the spatial formations of infrastructure.[1] This means that trajectories of movement and of change become intensified and particularly emplaced. This chapter discusses practices, experiences, and visions embedded in the harbor nodes forming diverse mobilities between Tallinn and Helsinki. My intention is to valorize dynamic harbor-related spaces, which can be understood as "the dimension of multiple trajectories, a simultaneity of stories-so-far. Space as the dimension of a multiplicity of durations."[2] Therefore, diverse stories are part of urban change, and mobility nodes order, (de-)synchronize, and affect both the urban fabric and the social encounters.

Harbors coexist with infrastructure-related moorings and circulations. Roads and streets appear on maps as lines or paths with different textures. A bird's-eye view suspends the frictions immediately activated by taking a walk or a slow drive, or by doing some other kind of embodied practice; in other words, by inscribing in one's location lines that articulate the shifting intersections of various social, spatial and affective registers.[3] The city harbors of Tallinn (population 440,000) and Helsinki (population 630,000) reveal particular aspects of mobility patterns and urban change. The old city harbor of Tallinn is the starting point of my enquiry that follows diverse lines and circuits connecting it with Helsinki (particularly the harbor in the area of Jätkasaari) across the Baltic Sea.

Like the city itself, the harbors of Tallinn and Helsinki evolved over centuries, through periods of upheaval or relative stability, as major mobility hubs. The collapse of the USSR brought about a radical shift in the broader political regimes and socioeconomic paths and forces in which the hub is embedded, and therefore also in its geographical focus. This shift includes the pattern of mobilities between Tallinn and Helsinki harbors, which assembles actual connections and projections of transmarine proximities. It is helpful to imagine the harbor as the mid-point of an hourglass (fig. 50), at which diverse fluxes intersect and mingle before individually continuing their way along disparate trajectories. Seen in this light, distinctions between motorways, city streets, transitions within terminals and situations on ferries become blurred. A dotted line or an anchor sign on a map can hardly explain the multifaceted and metamorphic mediations that a harbor effects on transnational movements and urban fabrics. Major trajectories are notable busy corridors while smaller ones may be overlooked. One may hop like a grasshopper from one metropolitan airport to the next or move along roads as intently as an ant trying to find the right direction or, perhaps, become lost. Both these different movement modes affect spatial structures and personal experience. Therefore, lines are important inasmuch as they interlink various social and spatial registers of coexistence within a particular environment.[4]

The fall of the Iron Curtain radically altered the strategic planning of international transport corridors as well as the travel-related opportunities of individual citizens. Links with Northern and Western Europe multiplied and strengthened while those with and within the former Eastern bloc, in particular with the USSR, diminished in number and importance. This radical shift left certain traces on recent initiatives bound up with transnational mobility. Tallinn's and Helsinki's harbors have been radically altered by the strategic economic interventions and tactical moves of the post–Cold War period, and therefore clearly illustrate certain trends and global-local frictions. The circulation of goods has intensified, as has the capacity of the requisite transport links, which have mostly been improved, and most spatiotemporal distances have thereby been reduced. These tendencies appear vividly when looking at the political "poetics of infrastructure" and the flows between the two harbors of Tallinn and Helsinki.[5] This acceleration of mobility, driven by multiple infrastructures, forges opportunities as well as challenges in everyday life. It seems appropriate therefore to turn the spotlight on harbor nodes as "contact zones where the over-determinations of circulations, events, conditions, technologies, and flows of power literally take place."[6]

I propose to approach these intensive contact zones in mobility nodes along both the metaphoric and embodied lines which connect Tallinn and Helsinki. As Tim Ingold argues,[7] proceeding along lines assembles walking, weaving, observing, drawing, and storytelling; and also, that life is consequently lived along paths—or "practiced lines" as he calls them— around which people construct the meaning of their respective worlds. In the context of the current chapter, walking as a particular mode of movement could be linked with ferry travel dispersing and blurring the boundaries of the experienced localities. Such paths or practices are accordingly a part of a fluid space, material flows, and sociopolitical movements, and these paths therefore contribute to our continual individual and social reconfiguration.[8] This broad framing of practiced lines poses a challenge in terms of revealing movements, situations, visions, and experiences triggering the mobilities between Tallinn and Helsinki.

1   Jana Hönke and Ivan Cuesta-Fernandez, "A Topographical Approach to Infrastructure: Political Topography, Topology and the Port of Dar es Salaam," *Environment and Planning D* 35, no. 6 (2017): 1076–95.
2   Doreen Massey, *For Space* (London: Sage, 2005), 24.
3   Tim Ingold, *Lines: A Brief History* (London: Routledge, 2007); and Kathleen Stewart, *Ordinary Affects* (Durham, NC: Duke University Press, 2007).
4   Ingold; and Tim Ingold, *Being Alive: Essays on Movement, Knowledge and Description* (London: Routledge, 2011).
5   Brian Larkin, "The Politics and Poetics of Infrastructure," *Annual Review of Anthropology*, 42 (2013): 327–43.
6   Stewart, *Ordinary Affects*.
7   Ingold, *Lines*.
8   Ingold, *Being Alive*.

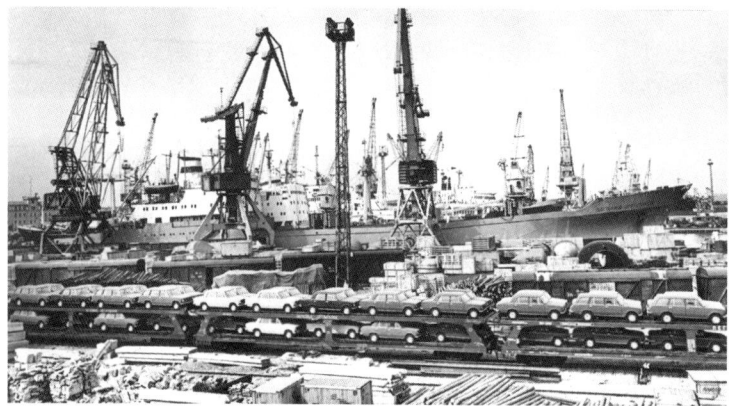

Fig. 49
Tallinn Harbor during the Soviet era: in the 1970s it was entirely fenced off and modernized to be used mainly for the transhipment of cargo.

My cross-border practiced lines bring together more-or-less tangible path(s) of coproduced situations and observations (figs. 51, 52), which also structure the stories presented in this chapter. These practiced lines are revealed by moving with and including some short conversations with diverse social actors in segments of their travel paths. Among them are people who travel rarely as well as those who are highly experienced, making preferably direct moves, due to the regularity of their journeys. This way of moving-with and perceiving-with actors and related situations makes it possible to observe what is going on, to comment on specific situations and, at certain stops, to dig into the past and reflect on the trajectories of recent urban change.[9]

## Trajectories of Urban Change Related to Helsinki's West Terminal

It is a late Friday afternoon. I start from central Finland (the town of Jyvaskylä) and drive (Saab 9-3, built in 1998) along the E75, which leads to Helsinki's main peninsula. Near the West Harbor terminal many overloaded cars appear with Estonian number plates, many trailers, heading toward Estonia (fig. 51, pos. 1). One can recognize the frequent commuters and migrant workers, as they take the most direct route to the harbor gate and line up in front of the Tallink ferryboat "MS Star." Instead of queuing up, I turn right, park my car opposite the main terminal building and get out. A short walk and observations reveal some ongoing trajectories of change (fig. 51, pos. 2).

The new West Terminal (T2) building faces the sea offering open views and presents the waterfront. Beside the Olympia Terminal, this infrastructure is the second terminal building in Helsinki, which was designed exclusively for passenger use from the very beginning. Therefore, the comfort of traveling, ferry traffic issues, and environmental aspects became more integrated. The high atriums and glass walls generate associations with a modern airport terminal, which tend to demonstrate (surrounding) velocity. For example, Yokohama International Port terminal was designed to operate "less as a gate, as a limit, and more as a field of movement,"[10] and to break the linear movement associated with a traditional pier structure. The magnetic mooring-system for ferries and additional landing bridges for vehicles accelerates ferry operations near Helsinki's Jätkasaari. However, the vehicle traffic is directed along very compact pathways in the harbor area, and people are motivated to come here on the trams that stop right by the terminal door.[11]

Since the early 1980s, the City of Helsinki has been considering ideas for converting the industrial waterfront into housing estates. This construction has required massive landfill operations and cleaning up the contaminated soil to create more than twenty kilometers of new public promenades and cycle routes. The port near the city center only serves ferries and cruise ships (South Harbor, West Terminal). The Jätkasaari area is the port for ferries from Helsinki to Tallinn; more than six million passengers travel via the terminals each year. The former industrial port and dockyards of Jätkasaari are being developed into new housing areas. The new West Terminal (T2) on Jätkasaari was opened for public use on February 27, 2017.[12]

Liven Ameel opens up diverse narrative dimensions on the shaping of Jätkasaari's future and urban planning.[13] Many apartment blocks have been built (and some are still under construction) near the harbor terminal of Jätkasaari. The public space near the new terminal mainly focuses on the transit movement pushing toward the next destination. Alongside the street toward the terminal, there stands a large IT retail outlet, a few fast-food places,

9   Here I obtained some inspiration from John Wylie, who talks about "landscape as perceiving-with" in dynamic configurations of motion and materiality. John Wylie, *Landscape* (London: Routledge, 2007), 217. And additional inspiration also derived from the writings of Tim Ingold, which are referenced in this paper.
10  Lee Stickells, "Flow Urbanism: The Heterotopia of Flows," in *Heterotopia and The City: Public Space in A Postcivil Society*, ed. Michiel DeHaene and Lieven De Cauter (London: Routledge, 2008), 248.
11  Dirk Schubert, "The Transformation of North-Western European Urban Waterfronts-Divergence and Convergence of Redevelopment Strategies," in *Waterfronts Revisited: European Ports in Historic and Global Perspectives*, ed. Heleni Porfyriou and Marciela Sepe (New York: Routledge, 2017), 191–207.
12  "Helsingin Satamaan Länsiterminaali 2 avautuu maanantaina 27.2," *Port of Helsinki*, February 24, 2017, http://www.portofhelsinki.fi/helsingin-satama/ajankohtaista/uutiset (accessed May 21, 2017).
13  Liven Ameel, "A Bildungsroman for a Waterfront Development: Literary Genre and the Planning Narratives of Jätkäsaari, Helsinki," *Journal of Urban Cultural Studies* 3, no. 2 (2016): 169–87.

a new hotel (Clarion Helsinki), apartment buildings, and old warehouses. These settings generate different patterns and rhythms of movement compared to the Tallinn harbor area, where consumption-oriented spaces are extended almost along the entire terminal entrance area.

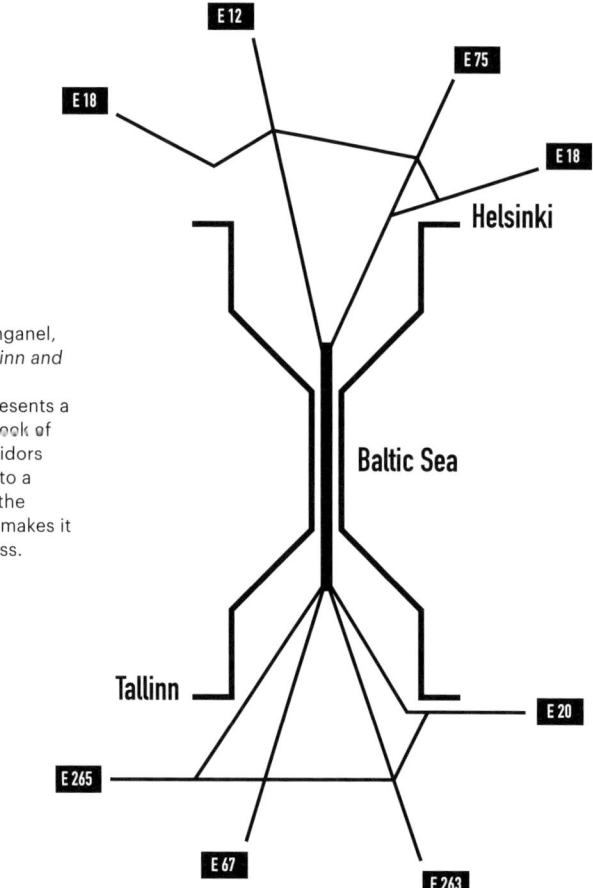

Fig. 50
Hieslmair and Zinganel,
*Twin cities of Tallinn and Helsinki*, 2016
Each harbor represents a funnel or bottleneck of several road corridors narrowing down to a single ferry line, the rhythm of which makes it a kind of hourglass.

Tarmo Pikner

## Embodied Lines between Tallinn and Helsinki: Starting from the Middle

On Friday afternoons, ferries to Tallinn depart almost every two hours from Helsinki's West Terminal. After my short walk, I get back into my car, drive a few meters to one of the twelve lanes for traffic leading to the ferry dock. I stop almost at the head of the queue, turn off the engine and wait for the ship (fig. 51, pos. 3). The ship lands and embarkation can begin; the lane next to me has trucks and coaches. Once inside the ship's belly, there is a particular machine aesthetic, which is performed. I get out of my car and walk upstairs, passing the hatchways together with all the other drivers. A walk on the car ferry reveals diverse interconnected spaces—huge parking decks for vehicles, alcohol and tax-free shops, bars, gambling zones, restaurants, exclusive VIP areas, playgrounds for children, lockers, cabins, narrow corridors, windy outdoor decks—obviously used by tourists. For them it is already an attraction when the ship casts off and they are almost the only group outside except for the smokers. Inside, in the main bar on Deck 8, I encounter groups of people, mostly men in casual outfits, absorbed in loud conversation. Throughout the ship, there are men lying on the floor in the corridors taking a nap. Many of them are probably construction workers in Finland and are now returning to Estonia for the weekend. The floor is quite comfortable since it is mostly covered with fitted carpet. They settle down in small niches underneath the main stairs, next to the lockers, in gaps between the doors on the cabin decks. There seem to be many more men than women on board this Friday afternoon.

This floating terrain is simultaneously independent and also dispersed along many places, networks and circulations, which hold the ferry together as it travels toward another port in Tallinn. Therefore, the floating ship resembles several of the characteristics of Foucault's heterotopia, as an entity or organ that has been dislocated.[14] On the other hand, the ferry can be viewed as a temporal node accommodating a wide spectrum of practiced lines, which carry and generate meanings for the traveling people. This crowded ferry between cities valorizes socioeconomic realities, and also coproduces particular trans-regional contact zones.

The fall of the Iron Curtain accelerated diverse mobilities from Estonia toward Northern and Western Europe. The importance of the Tallinn-St. Petersburg railway decreased and movements through Tallinn's port and airport increased. Today, the Estonian diaspora is considered to number 150,000 to 200,000

---

14 Christine M. Boyer, "The Many Mirrors of Foucault and Their Architectural Reflections," in *Heteroropia and the City: Public Space in a Postcivil Society*, ed. Michiel DeHaene and Lieven De Cauter (London: Routledge, 2008), 52–73.

A – South Harbour
B – Olympia Terminal
C – Merisatama Marina
D – West Harbour
E – Hietalahti Shipyard
F – Outlet/Hotel/Warehouses
G – West Terminal – T1
H – West Terminal – T2
I – Docks Cruise Ships
J – New Housing/Apartment Blocks

Figs. 51–52
Hieslmair and Zinganel, 2017
The author's path driving on and off the ferry in Helsinki and Tallinn and walking with the flow of tourists from Tallinn harbor to the city center and back, intersecting and mingling with diverse fluxes of tourists, opening up new vistas and trajectories, which evoke memories and reflections and also structure his narration on the transformation of the city

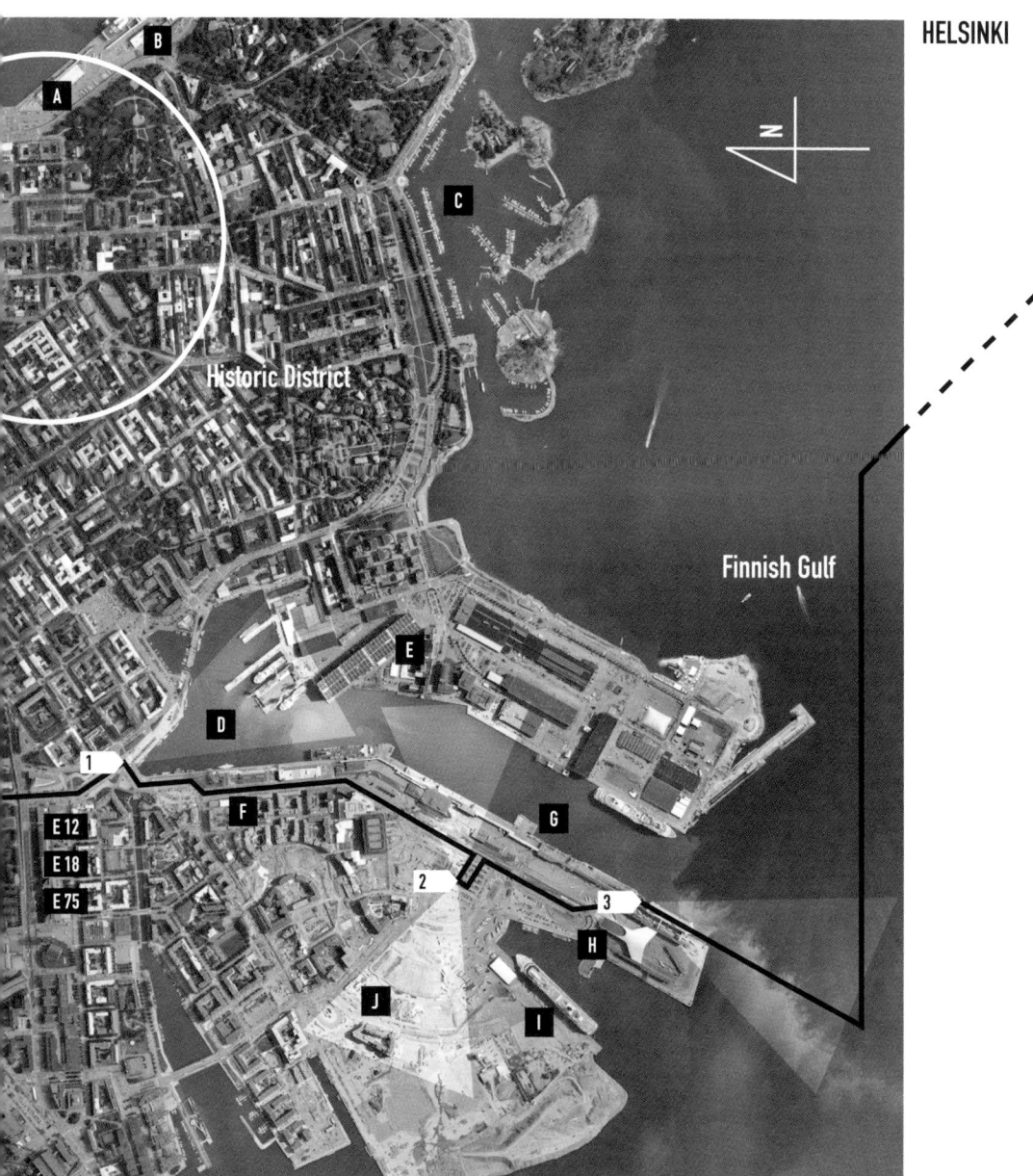

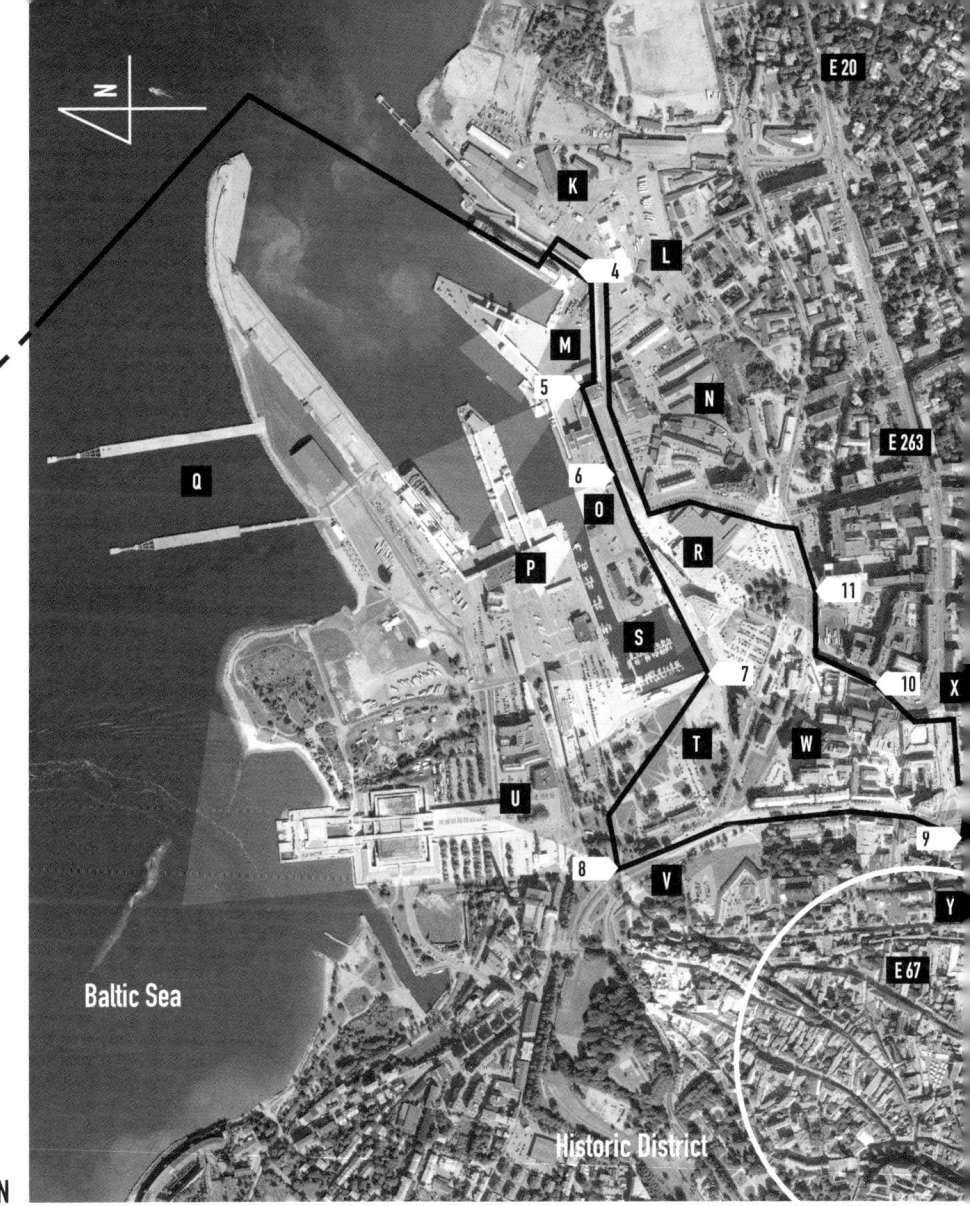

TALLINN

K – Customs Clearing
L – Truck Parking
M – Ferry Terminal D
N – Old Limestone Warehouses/Super Alko Shops and Pubs
O – Tourist Coach Parking
P – First Ferry Terminal, Tallinn – Helsinki
Q – Docks Cruise Ships
R – Nautica Rimi hyper Supermarket

S – Admiralty Basin – Marina
T – Car Parking
U – Linnahall – Multifunctional Convention Center/Concert Hall
V – Mere Boulevard – former Glacis
W – Roterman Quarter
X – Hotel Viru and Keskus Shopping Center
Y – Agglomeration of Souvenir Shops

people (depending on the statistical records); 85 percent of these people live in Western and Northern Europe.[15] Physical and cultural distances do matter in the process of the evolving migration patterns. Finnish TV, which has been reaching across the floating border since 1971, can be seen as one cultural platform that has generated affinities and (language) skills for the pragmatic labor migration between the two countries since the fall of the Iron Curtain. The documentary movie *Disco and Atomic War* vividly presents speculated ideologies of the Cold War, heroes from TV series, and everyday routines along the trans-boundary virtual channel.[16] Personal connections and institutional settings in the crossborder space take various forms; for example, almost every Estonian town has a formal twin city in Finland.

Finland is still the most popular country for Estonian emigrants. Almost half of all those who leave, travel there, and approximately 50,000 Estonian citizens live permanently in Finland.[17] There are at least another 15,000 commuters who live in Estonia permanently while working in Finland.[18] The rise of emigration to Finland has grown rapidly since the 1990s, as illustrated by the fact that there were 1,000 Estonians there in 1990 and almost 50,000 in 2015. This emigration growth trend coexists with an increase in return migration from Finland back to Estonia. Such migration tendencies are influenced by economic crises that push and pull people to find alternatives in Estonia and abroad, and particularly in Finland. The Finnish mainstream media often presents the newcomers as "convenience refugees" looking for an easy life, although empirical analysis indicates that "the majority of those that sought jobs in the Nordic countries were men in their thirties from the rural areas of Estonia, who had to find a way to support their families after being laid off."[19] A higher salary and a secure welfare system are presented as motives for those looking for jobs in Finland, and climbing the career ladder is not the most important goal for most people (fig. 53). The most common jobs when working abroad include artisan or skilled laborer; the construction business employs about 50 percent of all those who work abroad in Finland, while top-level specialists only form approximately 5 percent.[20]

For many people, traveling across the Finnish Gulf is part of a weekly commute between countries. Short distances and good ferry connections to Finland make it possible to keep a home in Estonia and become a commuter between these countries. Therefore, Estonia has become a country with one of the largest numbers of cross-commuters in Europe. About 14 percent of the working-age population of Estonia (in 2013) had experience working abroad, while the average in Europe is 9 percent.[21] Commuting practices may become part of "transnationalism" (the Estonian term *hargmaisus* indicates connections between countries/territories and less about nations), manifesting itself as "staying abroad for long periods and often" (ninety-two days and five to fifty-two trips in a year). These criteria were elaborated in order to analyze the phenomenon using mobile phone positioning methods. Based on such novel methods, Ahas and colleagues argue that "over 30,000 people from Estonia operate actively outside Estonia, while keeping their Estonian mobile phone numbers active."[22] The number of transnationals originating from Estonia is highest in Finland (about 13,000), but surprisingly low in Russia (about 1,700). This is despite the fact that the Russian community makes up approximately 25 percent of the Estonian population and there are about 75,000 without citizenship (using "gray passports") in Estonia.[23] These figures indicate intensive lines of movement between Tallinn and Helsinki, and related social networks toward Finland.

Social encounters and short conversations reveal diverse motives, rhythms, and experiences of traveling between Tallinn and Helsinki. Migration and transnational life also generate diverse stories, which become translated across cultural registers rendering particular situated experiences public. In the stories of people who have emigrated, experiences often appear about their first trip to Finland presenting relationships with the familiar and the strange.[24] These kinds of stories can be encountered in different genres. For example, the Estonian film *The Dissidents* brings together some situations from a first trip to Finland.[25] However, not all emigrants and transnational commuters feel like heroes and experiences can be rather controversial. The increased nationalism and growing number of refugees in Europe have generated negative associations with migration and migrants. The nation state is selective in presenting certain migrant groups as part of a better image of the country, and "the impact of socioeconomic changes on the changing regimes of meaning has created new inequalities, which stimulate emigration but also create and sustain inequalities between migrants."[20] These tendencies will also become visible within migration patterns between Finland and Estonia.

15 Kaja Kumer-Haukanõmm and Keiu Telve, "Estonians in the World," in *Estonia at the Age of Migration: Estonian Human Development Report 2016/2017*, ed. Tiit Tammaru (Tallinn: Cooperation Assembly Foundation, 2017), chapter 2.1.

16 Jaak Kilmi and Kiur Aarma, *Disco and Atomic War*. Documentary movie (Estonia: OÜ Eetriüksus, 2009).

17 Ene-Margit Tiit, "External Migration in Estonia in the Past 25 Years: A Statistical Estimate," in *Population Trends*, ed. Alis Tammur (Tallinn: Statistics Estonia, 2015), 56–75.

18 Siim Krusell, "Estonian Citizens Working Abroad," in *Census Snapshots*, ed. Taimi Rosenberg (Tallinn: Statistics Estonia, 2013), 129–46.

19 Kaja Kumer-Haukanõmm and Keiu Telve, "Estonians in the World," in *Estonia at the Age of Migration: Estonian Human Development Report 2016/2017*.

20 Siim Krusell, "Estonian Citizens Working Abroad."

21 Kumer-Haukanõmm and Telve, "Estonians in the World."

22 Rein Ahas, Siiri Silm and Margus Tiru, "Tracking Trans-nationalism with Mobile Telephone Data," in *Estonia at the Age of Migration. Estonian Human Development Report 2016/2017*, ed. Tiit Tammaru (Tallinn: Cooperation Assembly Foundation, 2017), chapter 2.2.

23 Statistics Estonia, 2017.

24 Pihla M. Siim, "Üle Piiride Liikuvad Pered: Mobiilsusest ja Paigal Püsimisest," in *Mäetagused* 56 (2014): 127–54.

25 Jaak Kilmi, *The Dissidents*. Fiction feature (Tallinn: Taska Film, 2017).

26 Aet Annist, "Emigration and the Changing Meaning of Estonian Rural Life," in *Estonia at the Age of Migration: Estonian Human Development Report 2016/2017*, ed. Tiit Tammaru (Tallinn: Cooperation Assembly Foundation, 2017), chapter 5.5.

Just finished my meal, but still sitting in the self-service restaurant on a bar stool at the side table attached to the window sill, next to me Finnish alcohol-tourists with some bottles of Lapin Kulta on their table. I pick up some snippets of their conversation—plans for a pub-crawl in Tallinn's Old Town. Looking through the windows I notice two of the islands the ferry passes before arriving in Tallinn. One of the islands is Naissaar. This became famous in the context of the architectural history of Estonia, triggering late modernist utopias of high-rise buildings and a free economic zone during the post-socialist transition era of the 1990s.[27] These island-based visions of a (modernist) future capture some important characteristics of the post-socialist ruptures, which articulated sharp disconnects with the previous ideological and economic system. The image of an island is associated with the free-trade zones that were presented as bright solutions for the neoliberal economic transition in the 1990s. The utopias of Naissaar remain unfinished, but several high-rise buildings between church spires become visible in the Tallinn cityscape as the ferry approaches the port terminal. Just next to the harbor area we can see terrace of Linnahall, a large dilapidated multifunctional events venue completed in 1979, which looks from a distance like a lifted plateau. Next to it two large cruise ships are moored at a dock. Beside the Tallink ferries, a number of other ferry lines also operate; for example, the St. Peter Line to St. Petersburg, the Viking Line to Finland and Sweden, and the Ekerö Line to Finland.

## Emplacement of Harbor-Related Flows

Port terminals and ships emplace passages and paths of transnational movement. These temporary emplacements are distributed along trajectories in which halts, traffic jams and forward movements are imprinted. Tallinn has a relatively large passenger and freight harbor just next to the city center. The fragmentation of Tallinn's urban space (along car-oriented roads and blocks of real estate developments) coexists with networked infrastructures, which accelerate mobile circuits and simultaneously generate splintered terrains.[28] Tallinn's harbor may often appear to be an out-of-place entity generating frictions and artificial barriers in the city. The main trajectories of the old port's growth may reveal some dimensions of mobility-related urban development.

The ship arrives—my friend volunteers to drive the car off the ferry and I decide to disembark on foot. Passengers queue up by the ferry exit door. There is also a public screen where the ferry passengers display their photos associated with the ferry trip and visiting the cities of Helsinki and Tallinn. I walk with the crowd along the elevated gangway—I look down—see the "open nose" of the ship—where vehicles disembark from the ferry (fig 52, pos. 4). A stop at a bend in the corridor offers a view over the harbor terrain and urges me to reimagine the situation before 1989, during the Soviet era, when there were very few passenger ferry connections ferry (fig. 52, pos. 5).

The city of Tallinn and its old harbor mark a point of origin and, simultaneously, the margins of international transit corridors; that is, of the motorways E20, E67, and E263 leading east (e.g., to St. Petersburg) and south (e.g., to Riga and Warsaw). Maritime ferry links ensure access to the motorways E18, E12, and E75, which run north, and to the E4, which runs via Stockholm and the Øresund Bridge to Western Europe. They therefore exist within wider logistics and mobility networks and are influenced and subsequently (re)configured in view of these dynamic trajectories.

Archival photographs and maps of Tallinn's harbor[29] document the process by which the simple pier-type structure and railway tracks (fig. 48) were superseded and partly replaced by two- and three-story terminal buildings extending onto the waterfront. The older layers of the harbor infrastructure are still marked by the limestone warehouses, which are today extensively reused by retail outlets specializing in alcohol and pubs. The passage of people and goods is transferred to elevated corridors via electrical elevators. The industrial railways and cranes as well as cargoes of timber and import cars (fig. 49) have given way to tourist-oriented ferries and coaches. About 38,000 passengers passed through the port in 1938, and by 2015 this number had risen to approximately 9.3 million people, the majority traveling to Helsinki, while the rest are either booked on cruise ships, or en route to Stockholm or St. Petersburg. Regular ferries complete the Helsinki-Tallinn route within two hours—the older and larger ships still take 3.5 hours while the hydrofoils planned for the near future will take only thirty minutes. The increasing tourist flows have generated the development of several hotels near the port terminals. But the huge expansion over the last eighty years was not linear. Soviet occupation largely disabled/blocked travel and trade connections with the Western bloc and the waterfront and harbor were reserved for industrial or military purposes. In 1956, no more than approximately two hundred foreign tourists visited Estonia. Yet by 1966, following the liberalization of the Soviet regime under Khrushchev, some 15,400 tourists had visited the city (96 percent of them from Finland). In 1983, 97,000 tourists (79 percent of them Finns) passed through the port.[30] The

27 The artist Tõnis Vint visualized these built utopias along Zen-Buddhist lines on Naissaar, as noted by Ingrid Ruudi on the thematic discussions in September 2015 and in the newspaper article "Veneetsia biennaalil näidatakse," in *Eesti Ekspress*, September 16, 2016.
28 Stephen Graham and Simon Marvin, *Splintering Urbanism: Networked Infrastructures, Technological Mobilities and the Urban Condition* (London: Routledge, 2001).
29 Andrus Helenurm et al., *Time In and Around the Port of Tallinn* (Port of Tallinn: Ajakirjade Kirjastus AS, 2005).
30 Ago Pajur et al., *Eesti ajalugu VI Vabadussõjast taasiseseisvumiseni* (Tartu: Ilmamaa, 2005).

Fig. 53
Martin Eelma (Tuumik Stuudio O.),
*Statistics Diagrams*, 2016

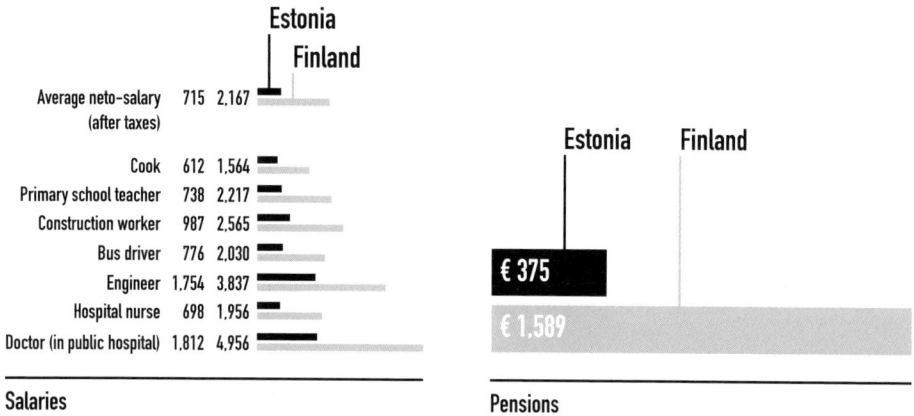

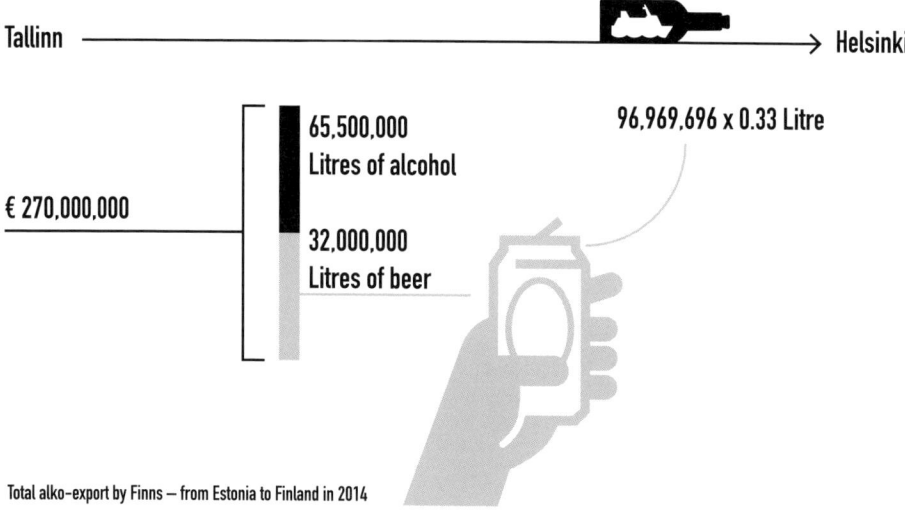

symbolic reopening of the maritime frontiers and the Tallinn-Helsinki ferry link took place on June 7, 1965. In 1980, the passenger terminal (like other elements of infrastructure in Tallinn) was extended because the city was to host the sailing regattas of the Moscow Summer Olympics. A new terminal was designed to cope with half a million passengers annually and plans for opening up the city's waterfront were likewise made and implemented in time for the international event (fig. 52, pos. 6).

The expansion of passenger terminals in Tallinn's Old Town harbor kept pace with the gradual lifting of international visa and trade restrictions after the fall of the Iron Curtain. The former state-owned passenger and freight line ESCO (Estonian Shipping Company) was restructured and privatized under the name Tallink. The company proved successful, underwent several mergers and then, in 2006, acquired the rival Silja Line company Sea Containers Ltd.[31] Additional moorings were acquired and new harbor terminals built to accommodate this increase in traffic. According to architect Irina Raud, harbor terminals are generally experienced along situated directions of mobility, depending on whether people are arriving in or leaving the city.[32] The design of Tallinn's harbor terminals accentuates the contrast between the iron ships and the warm tactile surfaces and effects in the passenger terminals (e.g., wooden floors, lighting). Besides facilitating consumption and access, port terminals are spaces for the control of state borders and their design must accommodate all such functions. However, visa restrictions were increasingly removed after 1989, so several checkpoints have since given way to small boutiques.

## Streetscapes and Trajectories of Urban Change connecting Tallinn's Port and the City

Hundreds of cars and thousands of people disembarking from the ship are fed through the harbor terminal node before dispersing in the urban fabric of Tallinn. Traffic signs and GPS navigation devices direct trucks to circumvent the city center. Tourist coaches make a short stop in front of the terminal to gather up their faithful groups. Bearings are an issue if people exit the terminal and start to walk toward the Old Town center. Church spires and shiny high-rise buildings give the impression that the distance is modest. Hesitation can be minimized by following others on well-trodden paths (fig. 52).

31 Tallink, "History."

32 Irina Raud, architect and architecture scholar, interview by the author, Tallinn, June 14, 2015.

Terminal D, the busiest with eight million passengers per year, is presently able to handle a flow of 4,000 passengers per hour but plans are in place to increase its capacity to 6,000 travelers per hour. Instead of the many currently dispersed (alcohol) outlets, the harbor operators hope to create a more mall-style shopping experience in the port area. For this, Amsterdam Airport Schiphol serves as a model. Since its entrance hall is designed as a city plaza, a space where all kinds of movements can take place and a quasi-tolerance or disinterest is enhanced.[33] The circulation of alcohol is a remarkable feature of Tallinn-Helsinki ferry trips, because beverages in Estonia cost about a third of what they do in Finland (fig. 53). Actually, some of the cheap alcohol sold in the terminal is imported in bulk from Finland then shipped back across the Gulf by individuals. People load their trolleys (brought with them or purchased in Estonia) and vehicles full of alcohol or even have pre-ordered boxes delivered to the terminal departure gate. Many of the large tourist coaches drive to the 'Super Alko' shops to load up with boxes of drink. But the transmarine consumption flows related to cheap booze might shift toward Latvia, since Estonia raised excise-taxes for light alcoholic drinks by about 20 percent in the period 2016–17.[34] Each Tallink ferry can accommodate up to 2,000 passengers and hundreds of (cargo) vehicles. The integration of two transport modes optimizes profit yet simultaneously keeps the cost of passenger tickets relatively low. Cruise ship–related tourism is largely seasonal, occurring from May until mid-October. More than 8,000 cruise tourists may then visit the city of Tallinn daily. However, the total passenger flow of cruise ships accounts for only 0.5 percent of the annual travel flows in the old port terminals. But the number of tourists spilled out by a single cruise ship in Tallinn Harbor is significantly higher than that of a ferry, and therefore many more people come to explore the picturesque historic Old Town in a rather dense period of time.

In Tallinn, no single street or boulevard connects the port with the town's center directly. People find their way along several paths, and these paths are partly forming in response to different periods of urban development. Here I will articulate just one of these possible lines of walking connecting the harbor settings within the wider urban spaces of the city that is frequently used (fig. 52). After leaving the exit door of Terminal D, the most frequented terminal for ferries, tourists on foot often encounter trishaw and semi-legal taxi drivers, who propose a faster trip. People get by without maps, simply by reading the cityscape, following the crowd, and watching what others do. Chartered tourist coaches line up before setting off on package holidays or excursions, possibly to Estonian seaside resorts or national parks. White stripes on the asphalt encourage people to head for the "Nautica" supermarket (fig. 52, pos. 7). Many people walk even further, to the docks dotted with port facilities. On the other side of the road, on the ground floor of a narrow apartment building, there are small boutiques. Then seawater comes into view again, next to another hotel. The Admiralty Basin, a former shipyard, has already been turned into a marina, representing the future centerpiece of a new, up-market district still under development. A short conversation reveals that almost every day, two elderly women sit on the corner of the Basin, holding a small plastic box in their hands and hoping for donations from generous tourists. They have agreed to stick to a certain timetable so each of them can have an equal share of this site for potential additional income and social interaction. The women choose to wait in this pedestrian zone because many tourists pass by and because they feel safe under the persistent gaze of the harbor surveillance cameras.

I mingle with the crowd of people, which find their way among the hoardings and new office buildings. Between the harbor and the city center, lie some large parking lots, which indicate the interim use of privatized land in the process of change in the city. The intersection of a three-plus-three lane road interrupts an otherwise smooth path to the supermarket (fig. 52, pos. 8). The once Hanseatic city center of Tallinn was surrounded by a wall and glacis.[35] After the 1860s, this fortification wall lost its military function and the area became a park and the ring road—in this section named Mere Boulevard—and tourist paths now partly also follow this ring trajectory. Although Mere Boulevard might not have any significance for most of today's tourists, for me it conjures up memories of an outstandingly ambitious urban design project. In a master plan in the 1980s, Mere Boulevard was intended to mark a rather monumental main axis linking the modern part of the city of Tallinn and the waterfront. Linnahall, built as a theater, concert hall, and conference venue on the occasion of the sailing contest for the Moscow Olympic Games in 1980, was meant to draw people down the boulevard to the seafront.[36] The remarkable size of this almost windowless limestone construction typical of the bunker style can easily be dismissed at street level and only becomes more tangible on an aerial photograph or map. The roof of Linnahall forms a multi-level walkable and stadium-like terrace and accommodates a helicopter landing pad and the dock for seasonal fast ferries to Finland. The concert hall at Linnahall has been listed as an architectural monument since 1992, and poses questions about the coexistence of a bygone socialist era and the new era in the same structure.[37] This hall is vacant

33 Tim Cresswell, *On the Move: Mobility in the Modern Western World* (London: Routledge, 2006).

34 This tax increased the price of a bottle of beer by about forty cents. The aim of this state alcohol policy is to make Estonian people consume less alcohol. However, many people are already purchasing cheaper alcohol from Latvia and tourist flows have decreased in Tallinn. This tendency will affect the newly established stores in Tallinn's harbor area as well as the hotels there too.

35 Four cities in Estonia, incl. Tallinn, were part of the Hanseatic League between the fourteenth and sixteenth centuries (see Zetterberg, *Viron historia*).

36 Dimitri Bruns, *Tallinna peaarhitekti mälestusi ja artikleid* (Tallinn: Museum of Estonian Architecture, 2007).

37 Andres Kurg, "The After-History of the Linnahall Concert Hall," in *How Long Is the Life of a Building: Estonian National Exhibition at the XIII International Architecture Exhibition – la Biennale di Venezia*, ed. Tüüne-Kristin Vaikla (Tallinn: Estonian Centre of Architecture, 2012) 189–94.

today and urgently requires renovation, but people still like to climb the stairs to enjoy the sea views from the roof area, and occasionally partake in the cultural events and guided tours that are organized here. The winners of an international architecture competition held in 1988–89 designated Mere Boulevard and its environs a post-industrial quarter for commercial services, and tram and pedestrian use only.[38] Cars still run on Mere Boulevard, although car-free solutions have been tested during some festival events. Today's walkers turning here toward the city center can get a glimpse of the flickering facade of the international-style, high-rise Hotel Viru.

I walk along Mere Boulevard where in high season tourist coaches struggle to find parking. I stop at the corner of Viru Street, near the ancient gate to the Old Town (fig. 52, pos. 9). It is a very busy location, where people and vehicles rush in different directions—tourists, vendors, and the inhabitants of Tallinn encounter each other. From here onwards an agglomeration of souvenir shops surrounds one of the most beaten paths to the main attraction—the picturesque Old Town—which has been almost entirely transformed into a shopping precinct, a kind of large outdoor entertainment center interlinked with the harbor and tourism flows.

Nearby is Viru Square, Tallinn's busiest traffic junction and currently a quasi roundabout for cars and trams. For the moment the passionate tourist has to make a U-turn to reach Hotel Viru. This important node is emblematic of the connections between harbor-related influxes and the rest of the city, and how they are embedded in socioeconomic regimes. The rise in the numbers of foreign (mainly Finnish) tourists, which started in the 1960s, prompted the construction of this modern twenty-two-story hotel between 1969 and 1972. Several hundred Finnish construction engineers were hired for this project and generated particular flows of know-how, trade and evolving (family) affinities. The architecture and luxury interior design of the hotel has been considered an important element of Westernization. Beforehand, a group of Estonian designers had been part of study visits to Finland to learn the latest design trends, skills, and materials.[39] In the documentary film *Viru: The Embassy of Freedom* the hotel is described as an oasis in the USSR, since it offered limited access to exceptionally high standards of food and entertainment.[40] For Finns, the hotel was synonymous with a trip to Estonia. In the Finnish language the word *Viru* stands for Estonia. It had been the only international hotel in Tallinn until the completion of the Olümpia in 1980. The Soviet Committee for State Security (KGB) benefited enormously from the concentration of foreigners in the city. This part of the hotel's history remains visible in the KGB museum on its top floor as well as in its Hard Currency Bar (Valuutabaar). From a contemporary perspective, Hotel Viru did not only provide particular settings in the border zone, which "not only represented this paradoxical Westernization, but also played a significant part in how this period of late-Soviet contradictions and boundary crossings opened out."[41]

The hotel's commodified history stands alongside the modern Viru Keskus shopping center, constructed on a former car park and minibus station and opened in 1995, and subsequently extended in 2004 to establish its present form. It includes a car park combined with an underground public coach terminal for urban connections across greater Tallinn. This shopping center is part of the total retail surface available in the country of 988,000 square meters for its 1.3 million inhabitants.[42] Some simple arithmetic suffices to show that each citizen of Tallinn has 1.85 square meters of shopping terrain at his or her disposal, considerably more than their counterparts in other Baltic countries and elsewhere in Europe. The influx of tourists via the harbor is certainly a main driver of the development of major shopping malls in the city. In addition, three large hotels with many hundreds of beds are located close to Viru Square. The intensive influx of tourists has strikingly altered the streetscape of the historic city center, spawning amber jewelry shops, themed Hanseatic-era restaurants, and pubs screening football matches as its most visible signs. However, urban terrain devoted to everyday practices and social encounters still exists in parallel.

## Acceleration of Spaces near the Harbor

Here we have described a kind of transmarine circle of movement between the cities: my trip back to Finland happens to be on a late Sunday afternoon. It is rush hour when Finnish tourists and Estonian migrant workers head back to Finland for another week. I get off a tram in the city center and walk toward the harbor along Hobujaama Street (fig. 52, pos. 10). Many other people are on this street—families with children, tourists with boxes of alcohol and shopping bags, elderly couples, a small group of youngsters—all moving toward the harbor terminals. Rickshaws pass me several times carrying tourists heading for a ferry. Currently, this rather narrow street is loaded with cars and coaches, but according to the spatial planning projections will become one of the connecting pedestrian-friendly paths between Viru Square and the old harbor area.[43] The smooth walk to the harbor terminal becomes slightly disturbed by busy car traffic, temporary walls of construction sites, and billboards blocking sightlines. But the short distances help everyone find the right direction.

38 Ingrid Ruudi, "Visions for a New Society," in *Unbuilt. Visions for a New Society 1986–1994*, ed. Ingrid, Ruudi (Tallinn: Museum of Estonian Architecture, 2015), 20–32.
39 Andres Kurg, "Modernist in Form, Late-Socialist in Content: The Viru Hotel in Tallinn," in *Hotel Lobbies and Lounges: The Architecture of Professional Hospitality* (London: Routledge, 2013), 178–85.
40 Margit Kilumets, *Viru: The Embassy of Freedom*, documentary film (Tallinn: EstDoc, 2013).
41 Kurg, "Modernist in Form."
42 Kaja Koovit et al., "Baltimaade kaubanduspindade võrdlus. Eesti teeb ilma, aga kaotused terendavad," *Delfi Ärileht*, February 9, 2016.
43 Estonian Centre of Architecture, "Peatänav."

Although most of the tourists stay just for one day in Tallinn and then travel back or onwards, the hotels are largely clustered around Viru Square, around the passenger harbor terminals and in the Old Town. But the entire harbor area will change radically in the near future: in September 2017, Zaha Hadid Architects won a design competition on urban visions for Tallinn's Old Harbor area. According to the competition jury,[44] the famous architecture bureau managed to find the best balance between the demand for public urban space and steps for real estate development, integrating the harbor area and the city center, by introducing several lively streetscapes encouraging people to walk from the Old Town to the harbor terminals. This attractive trajectory of urban change co-exists with the initiative to redirect the main traffic flow of cargo vehicles coming from the ferries to the new road (to be completed in 2019) (fig. 52, pos. 11). However, this new road infrastructure directing cars from the harbor toward the eastern waterfront sparked public debate because the busy road would run over a popular green area near the seashore. Pressure groups demanded a more modest scale for the planned road. According to their arguments and public declarations, changes were made to the project—one traffic-lane was dedicated to pedestrians and greenery near the waterfront. This tension reveals the nexuses between the place-based values of residents, cargo flows, and particular planning rationalities, nature protection, and future projections of the harbor area.

I approach Ferry Terminal D: taxis bring additional passengers, cars, and coaches drive through the ticket check and immediately begin to embark, masses of people enter into the harbor terminal building. The impact of the ferry departure and arrival times is plain to see around the port terminals. These kinds of rhythmic intensities of the urban fabric become affected by the timetables of the ferries. Some traffic jams occur if ferries arrive and direct all vehicles into the city during the evening rush hour. However, the harbor logistics usually operate like clockwork and the vehicles and people suddenly disappear into the ferries. My walk along the elevated corridors in the port terminal takes a while before reaching the ferry. I look down: port staff equipped with hi-vis vests and signaling discs guide the queuing vehicles—it looks like highly practiced choreography. I take a seat on Deck 9 in the small cafeteria area. The departure of the Tallink ferry "MS MegaStar" causes me to reflect on the future of the trans-regional metropolitan area and potential mobility changes within large-scale infrastructure projects.

## Tunnel Dreams

These intensive practiced lines of travel over the Finnish Gulf have triggered diverse visions of infrastructural connectivity, which would allow faster movements and trans-regional commuting. The idea of connecting Tallinn and Helsinki has a long history. Finnish geologists already presented a construction engineering analysis of a hypothetical Tallinn-Helsinki tunnel a year after the collapse of Soviet Union in 1992.[45] In Estonia, the idea of a tunnel link was not taken seriously in the 1990s, but a remarkable upturn in (public) concerns and related analysis has taken place in the last decade. This has been triggered by the project of establishing the fast Rail Baltic connection from Tallinn to Poland and Germany.[46] It is evident that Finland is greatly interested in participating in a project that connects their product flow via a tunnel and the Rail Baltic line to Central Europe. The realization of the fast-train link was decided at government level in the Baltic states in January 2017, although this project sparked a great deal of public debate in Estonia. According to preliminary estimations, the rail infrastructure works on Estonian territory will cost 1.3 billion euros, and 85 percent of this can be covered by EU funds.[47] According to study forecasts, marine traffic between the two cities will not disappear after the tunnel has been built, but it is estimated that 11 million trips will be made annually via the tunnel by 2042, with 25,000 people passing through it daily.[48] This trajectory of becoming a twin-city can be compared with what took place after the bridge/fast-train link was established between Copenhagen and Malmö. These infrastructural tendencies indicate "engineering and imagineering"[49] in the bridge-building project and an artificial island, which re-shaped the transnational Øresund Region.

The future projections of the Tallinn-Helsinki region coexist with current mobilities and city plans. The key question is how the emergent nodes of Rail Baltic and of a possible transmarine tunnel will reconfigure urbanities. Some trajectories of potential change became visible with the publication of these architectural visions. For example, the vision of the Architectural Design Office

---

44 Peeter Pere, "Vau-faktorit Vanasadama arhitektuurivõistlusel ei hinnatud," *Sirp*, September 15, 2017.

45 Aet Ader, "Urban Space at the End of the Tunnel," *Maja* 3 (2017): 73–75.

46 The quality of train connections in Estonia has improved over the last five years. But internationally there exist two incompatible systems of railway infrastructure—Russian (and former areas of the Soviet Union) and European. The plans of a fast Rail Baltic link challenge these infrastructure gaps, change geopolitical settings and envision increasing flows of cargo and of passengers. However, this large railway infrastructure has generated significant tensions and public opposition in Estonia.

47 Rail Baltic, "Balti riikide peaministrid kirjutasid Rail Balticu leppele alla," January 31, 2017, http://railbaltic.info/et/10-ee-sisu/446-balti-riikide-peaministrid-kirjutasid-rail-balticu-leppele-alla (accessed March 15, 2017).

48 Ader, "Urban Space at the End of the Tunnel."

49 Orvar Löfgren, "Island Magic and the Making of Transnational Region," *Geographical Review* 97 (2007): 244–59.

PLUSS and Futuredesign (2015) positions the entrances of the transmarine rail-tunnel in the very heart of both cities, and the entrances appear as gates leading people to an underground mobility infrastructure. The rail-tunnel is projected to accommodate passenger and cargo flows. But the transmarine mobility of cars and trucks would still require ferry-related terminals somewhere. This means that the floating spaces of ferries may become only partly replaced by the accelerated forms of movement via fast trains connecting the centers of Tallinn and Helsinki within only fifteen minutes.

Research conducted for this chapter was also supported by the Estonian Research Agency grant IUT3-2: Culturescapes in Transition.

Literature

Ader Aet. "Urban Space at the End of the Tunnel." *Maja* 3 (2017): 73–75.

Ahas, Rein, Siiri Silm, and Margus Tiru. "Tracking Trans-nationalism with Mobile Telephone Data." In *Estonia in the Age of Migration: Estonian Human Development Report 2016/2017*, edited by Tiit Tammaru, chapter 2.2. Tallinn: Cooperation Assembly Foundation, 2017.

Ameel, Liven. "A *Bildungsroman* for a Waterfront Development: Literary Genre and the Planning Narratives of Jätkäsaari, Helsinki." *Journal of Urban Cultural Studies* 3, no. 2 (2016): 169–87.

Annist, Aet. "Emigration and the Changing Meaning of Estonian Rural Life." In *Estonia in the Age of Migration: Estonian Human Development Report 2016/2017*, edited by Tiit Tammaru, chapter 5.5. Tallinn: Cooperation Assembly Foundation, 2017.

Boyer, Christine M. "The Many Mirrors of Foucault and Their Architectural Reflections." In *Heterotopia and the City: Public Space in a Postcivil Society*, edited by Michiel DeHaene and Lieven De Cauter, 52–73. London: Routledge, 2008.

Bruns, Dimitri. *Tallinna peaarhitekti mälestusi ja artikleid*. Tallinn: Eesti Arhitektuurimuuseum, 2007.

Cresswell, Tim. *On the Move: Mobility in the Modern Western World*. London: Routledge, 2006.

Estonian Centre of Architecture, "Peatänav," 2018, http://www.peatanav.ee/en (accessed February 12, 2018).

Graham, Stephen, and Simon Marvin. *Splintering Urbanism: Networked Infrastructures, Technological Mobilities and the Urban Condition*. London: Routledge, 2001.

Helenurm, Andrus. *Time in and around the Port of Tallinn*. Tallinn: Port of Tallinn, Ajakirjade Kirjastus AS, 2005.

Hönke, Jana, and Ivan Cuesta-Fernandez. "A Topographical Approach to Infrastructure: Political Topography, Topology and the Port of Dar es Salaam." *Environment and Planning D* 35, no. 6 (2017): 1076–95.

Ingold, Tim. *Lines: A Brief History*. London: Routledge, 2007.

———. *Being Alive: Essays on Movement, Knowledge and Description*. London: Routledge, 2011.

Kilmi, Jaak. *The Dissidents*. Fiction feature. Estonia: Taska Film, 2017.

Kilmi, Jaak, and Kiur Aarma. *Disco and Atomic War*. Documentary movie. Estonia: OÜ Eetriüksus, 2009.

Kilumets, Margit. *Viru: The Embassy of Freedom*. Documentary movie. Estonia: EstDoc, 2013.

Kumer-Haukanõmm, Kaja, and Keiu Telve. "Estonians in the World." In *Estonia in the Age of Migration: Estonian Human Development Report 2016/2017*, edited by Tiit Tammaru (Tallinn, Cooperation Assembly Foundation, 2017), chapter 2.1. Tallinn: Cooperation Assembly Foundation, 2017.

Koovit, Kaja. "Baltimaade kaubanduspindade võrdlus: Eesti teeb ilma, aga kaotused terendavad." *Delfi Ärileht*, February 9, 2016.

Kurg, Andres. "Modernist in Form, Late-Socialist in Content: The Viru Hotel in Tallinn." In *Hotel Lobbies and Lounges: The Architecture of Professional Hospitality*, edited by Anne Massey and Tom Avermaete, 178–85. London: Routledge, 2013.

———. "The After-History of the Linnahall Concert Hall." In *How Long Is the Life of a Building: Estonian National Exhibition at the XIII International Architecture Exhibition—la Biennale di Venezia*, edited by Tüüne-Kristin Vaikla, 189–94. Tallinn: Center for Estonian Architecture, 2012.

Krusell, Siim. "Estonian Citizen Working Abroad." In *Census Snapshots*, edited by Taimi Rosenberg, 129–46. Tallinn: Statistics Estonia, 2013.

Larkin, Brian. "The Politics and Poetics of Infrastructure." *Annual Review of Anthropology* 42 (2013): 327–43.

Löfgren, Orvar. "Island Magic and the Making of Transnational Region." *Geographical Review* 97 (2007): 244–59.

Massey, Doreen. *For Space*. London: Sage, 2005.

Pajur, Ago. *Eesti ajalugu VI: Vabadussõjast Taasiseseisvumiseni*. Tartu: Ilmamaa, 2005.

Pere, Peeter, "Vau-faktorit Vanasadama arhitektuurivõistlusel ei hinnatud." *Sirp*, September 15, 2017.

Rail Baltic, "Balti riikide peaministrid kirjutasid Rail Balticu leppele alla," January 31, 2017, http://railbaltic.info/et/10-ee-sisu/446-balti-riikide-peaministrid-kirjutasid-rail-balticu-leppele-alla (accessed March 15, 2017).

Raud, Irina. Architect and scholar of architecture. Interview by the author, Tallinn, June 14, 2015.

Ruudi, Ingrid. "Visions for a New Society." In *Unbuilt: Visions for a New Society 1986–1994*, edited by Ingrid Ruudi, 20–32. Tallinn: Estonian Architecture Museum, 2015.

Schubert, Dirk. "The Transformation of North-Western European Urban Waterfronts-Divergence and Convergence of Redevelopment Strategies." In *Waterfronts Revisited: European Ports in Historic and Global Perspective*, edited by Heleni Porfyriou and Marciela Sepe, 191–207. New York: Routledge, 2017.

Siim, Pihla M. "Üle Piiride Liikuvad Pered: Mobiilsusest ja Paigal Püsimisest." *Mäetagused* 56 (2014): 127–54.

Statistics Estonia. "Rahvaarv rahvuse järgi 1.01.2017," https://www.stat.ee/34267 (accessed June 17, 2017).

Stewart, Kathleen. *Ordinary Affects*. Durham, NC: Duke University Press, 2007.

Stickells, Lee. "Flow Urbanism: The Heterotopia of Flows." In *Heterotopia and The City: Public Space in a Postcivil Society*, edited by Michiel DeHaene and Lieven De Cauter, 247–58. London: Routledge, 2008.

Tallink. "History." 2018, https://www.tallink.ee/firmast#tabs-content-2 (accessed May 11, 2018).

Tiit, Ene-Margit. "External Migration in Estonia in the Past 25 Years: A Statistical Estimate." In *Population Trends*, edited by Alis Tammur, 56–75. Tallinn: Statistics Estonia, 2015.

Wylie, John. *Landscape*. London: Routledge, 2007.

Zetterberg, Seppo. *Viron historia*. Helsinki: Suomen Kirjallisuuden Seura, 2007.

# Corridors Rerouted and the Choice of Vehicles

# Secondhand Car Markets and Mobilization in Eastern Europe

Michael Zinganel

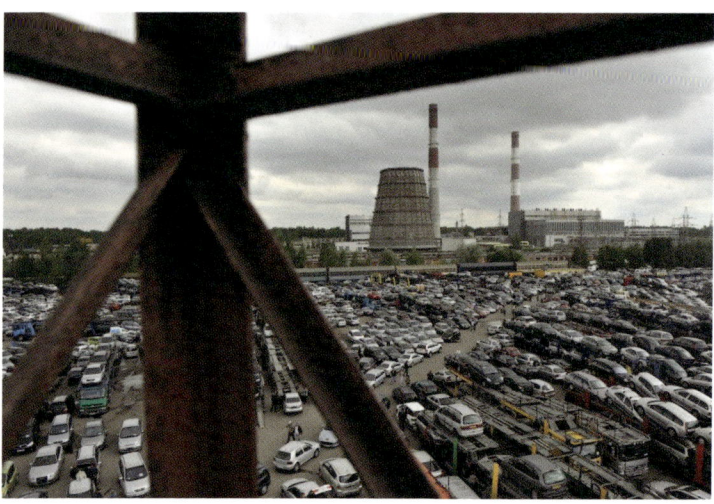

Fig. 54
Mindaugas Kavaliauskas, *Secondhand car markets in the Baltic region*, 2008
Kaunas secondhand car market back in 2008, photographed by the Lithuanian artist, who devoted most of his career documenting the Baltic populations' obsession with cars

Purchasing a secondhand car for our research trips to Estonia and Bulgaria turned out to be a difficult task. In the entire metropolitan area of Vienna all secondhand cars suited for fitters and vendors had already been sold to, or reserved for, car dealers from Eastern Europe. They have established a network of scouts who drive around the Western countries and purchase almost every suitable car, which is either still drivable or usable as a source of spare parts. The scouts usually pay cash on site and take the certificate of approval with them. Later their buddies pass by with car trailers to pick up the cars and export them to markets in their former homelands. Also we were considered to be car dealers, who are not interested much in details but in the prize. And, obviously, we always arrived far too late to each of the vendors. Even when we expanded our search radius to more than one hundred and fifty kilometers we failed. Coincidentally, we passed by a rural gas station, where several Ford vans were parked. The owner, a motocross racing driver, had spent the time in hospital after a bad accident. His wife told us he urgently needed to sell one of his vans to refinance spare parts for his bike. We took our chances! When we returned a few days later to pick up the van, we learned that several Serbian car vendors had already asked for it.

Purchasing a car is far from being a rational act. A car is expected to be a reliable companion in good and bad times—a business partner and family member. And—at least for men—each type of car inevitably evokes different kinds of memories: in Britain a mighty Ford Transit van, like ours, had been a minor national institution, the by far best-selling transporter van and minibus, so beloved by tradesmen and small-business owners—but also by sports clubs officials, fire and policemen, campers and many more. It had been a rather sad day for many when in June 2013 the last of seven million Transit vans rolled off the company's Southampton production line, bringing forty years of automotive history to an end. In continental Europe the Ford Transit is also strongly associated with the many families of Turkish guest workers who would pass in huge convoys through Germany, Austria, former Yugoslavia, and Bulgaria, driving an average of four thousand kilometers from their German place of work to their Turkish home region during school and factory holidays in the 1970s and '80s. Therefore, we were pretty happy with this make of car, whose name, Transit, fitted so perfectly to the topic of our research.

But later during our research trips we soon learned that the connotations of a specific type of car are read differently in distinct geographic, social and ethnic milieus: a Ford Transit can also be considered a less reliable British car produced in Turkey today and driven mainly by Turks on the Balkan routes. And Turks are not very popular due to the contested history here. The first choice for vendors in Slavic countries is clearly a German Mercedes Sprinter, a car considered to be indestructible, no matter how old it is. On the other hand, the bad reputation of our car turned out to be lucky turn of fate for us: a Ford Transit would not be stolen that often, Slavic experts told us.

Having learned that we would get significantly more money selling a secondhand car in Eastern Europe than in the West we shifted our interest to a specific kind of market. We hoped to recoup the significant private investment one day in the future: our plan was to resell the vehicle at the end of the project and export and offer it for sale at one of the many secondhand car markets along our routes, thereby also reintegrating it into the economic cycles of our research destinations.[1]

But there had been other less personal arguments for our interest: Used cars were the most important means of individual mobilization in Eastern Europe during the period of transition: "A shortage of new family cars that had gripped the country due to waiting periods, often surpassing ten years and prices of 2.5 average annual salaries, quickly created a demand for cheap secondhand, and even stolen cars, immediately after the political changes of 1989. The newly created class of nouveaux riches and their growing conspicuous consumption increased the demand, particularly for luxury vehicles."[2] Furthermore, transporter vans like ours became a basic prerequisite for supplying (gray) markets with all kinds of goods needed and expanding the suitcase trade of the early days into a small- and medium-scale capitalist business.

Demand for used cars had grown so large that an enormous gray market for secondhand cars was soon established. Before the EU accession of Hungary, the Czech Republic, Slovakia, and Poland in 2004, and the Baltic states, Romania and Bulgaria in 2007, these gray markets had been far closer to black than to white: the Council of the European Union then considered intensified car theft in the West and car trafficking to non-EU member states as a pivot point for many other forms of crime, such as drugs, firearms, and trafficking in human beings.[3] But according to Europol and leading criminologists in Southeast Europe, trafficking of stolen cars is still a serious problem, strongly associated with organized crime.[4]

There seems to be a significant interest by (male) Western artists in Eastern Europeans' obsession for large cars and car markets,[5] and from 2001 until today the Lithuanian photographer Mindaugas Kavaliauskas has devoted almost all his career to this issue (fig. 54).[6] But surprisingly, the transnational trade in used cars has received limited geographical and anthropological attention. And if so, it had been focusing merely on Africa.[7] In contrast to the many studies about informal economy and open-air markets in Eastern Europe, there has so far been almost no research on transport routes to and markets for used cars in Eastern Europe.[8]

Although the secondhand car trade had normalized since EU accession of the new Eastern European member states, some of the major collecting sites and distribution hubs of the heydays are still operating, albeit with less intensity than before: one of the most famous sources for purchasing used cars in the West was Autokino Automarkt Essen, located at a drive-in cinema parking lot in heart of German Ruhrgebiet, still offering up to 900 vehicles each Saturday from 6 a.m. to 5 p.m. Another huge car market is located in Marijampolė, in Lithuania, famously introduced by Karl Schlögel in support of his thesis of an European East-West integration starting from below: Forget about Brussels and Strasbourg, Schlögel argued, some of the true heroes of a new Europe are to be found here once a week, when this provincial Lithuanian town is transformed into Europe's largest used car market and the East of the continent picks up cars from the West.[9] These people—"ant vendors" as Karl Schlögel named them[10]—would never be capable of establishing any expensive infrastructure themselves, but they use an existing one, and by importing secondhand cars via the highways and bridges of Pan-European road infrastructure they enable others to use these infrastructures as well, contributing to an increase in individual mobilization, in trade, and European integration.

When approaching Lithuania during our very first trip in summer 2014 we were already very curious to verify Schlögel's arguments by visiting this secondhand car market in Marijampolė, a town is located very close to the Polish border at an intersection of the freeway E 67 Via Baltica connecting Warsaw with Helsinki

1  Moreover, tracing the future mobility career of our Ford Transit would also be a nice follow-up project to our research.
2  Philip Gounev and Tihomir Bezlov, "From the Economy of Deficit to the Black-Market: Car Theft and Trafficking in Bulgaria," *Trends in Organized Crime* 11, no. 4 (2008): 410–29, 414.
3  Council of the European Union, "Comments on the Decision on Tackling Vehicle Crime with Cross-border Implications," document 5216/04, January 13, 2004, 1.
4  See https://www.europol.europa.eu/crime-areas-and-trends/crime-areas/trafficking-in-stolen-vehicles (accessed November 12, 2018); see also: Atanas Rusev, ed., "D9.3 Four Case Study Reports: Corruption and Trafficking in Women. The Case of Bulgaria," in *Anti-corruption Policies Revisited: Global Trends and European Responses to the Challenge of Corruption* (Sofia: Center for the Study of Democracy, 2016).
5  E.g., Markus Krottendorfer, *Automarket Tbilisi*, Fotohof edition, vol. 117 (2008); Matthias Aschauer, *Stars of Albania*, Fotohof edition, vol. 166 (2012).
6  See his contribution to exhibitions in the framework of this project: Michael Zinganel and Michael Hieslmair, *Road*Registers: Logbook of Mobile Worlds*, exhibition catalogue (Vienna: Academy of Fine Arts, 2017).
7  E.g., Andrew Brooks, "Networks of Power and Corruption: The Trade of Japanese Used Cars to Mozambique," *Geographical Journal* 178, no. 1 (March 2012), 80–92; Joost Beuving, "Cotonou's Klondike: African Traders and Second-hand Car Markets in Benin," *The Journal of Modern African Studies* 42, no. 4 (2004): 511–37; Jojada Verrips and Birgit Meyer, "Kwaku's Car: The Struggles and Stories of a Ghanaian Long-Distance Taxi Driver," in *Car Cultures*, ed. Daniel Miller (Oxford: Berg, 2001), 153–84.
8  E.g., expanding beyond Eastern Europe: Wladimir Sgibnev and Andrey Vozyanov, "Assemblages of Mobility: the Marshrutkas of Central Asia," in *Urban Spaces and Lifestyles in Central Asia and Beyond*, ed. Philipp Schröder (London: Routledge, 2017).
9  Karl Schlögel, *Marjampole oder Europas Wiederkehr aus dem Geist der Städte* (Munich: Hanser, 2005), 9ff.
10  Karl Schlögel, "Die Ameisenhändler vom Bahnhof Zoo: Geschichte im Abseits und vergessene Europäer," *Osteuropa* 11 (2009): 53–60.

and the freeway E 28 connecting Kaliningrad with Minsk and leading further to Moscow, a perfect geographic location to establish a distribution hub.

Starting immediately after the fall of the Iron Curtain, secondhand cars purchased and sometimes stolen in Western Europe, especially in Germany, were brought to a huge parking lot in front of an empty factory. Some were sold directly from big trailers to the end users on site, others to vendors who transported them to post-Soviet states reaching from Kaliningrad and the Baltic to the Caspian Sea and even to Central Asia, also using Russia's wider gauge railway starting here to forward vehicles in large numbers, up to one hundred cars, by train.[11] Originally, this market happened only one weekend a month. It then expanded to every weekend and finally became a permanent marketplace, managed by a private company which sublet parcels of land to other companies or even individual vendors. During our second visit a year later, the parking lot was almost empty of cars. Karl Schlögel's favorite market was forced to declare bankruptcy. But another new market was due to open soon, located at a much more visible site, directly at the highway bypass to the north of the city. One of the last vendors recommended we visit another market, specialized in transporter vans, like ours, many of them to be converted later into *marshrutkas*, semi-legal minibuses for passengers, which are part of a very popular gray market business in Eastern Europe and Asia (fig. 55).

Here we met an overqualified guard, a computer programmer, he told us, who spoke excellent English and who was happy to explain to us the current rules of the game and how changing of laws, exhaust emission regulations, and taxes had affected the demand for specific types of car. Big cars with huge cylinder capacity and fuel consumption, once so prestigious in Eastern Europe, had been literally driven out of the market, gradually displaced further to the East, first to Russia, then to Central Asia, while the demand for new economical cars with minimal exhaust values increased.[12]

Being intrigued by this experience and the many cars with trailers we passed, we got curious comparing markets in the northeast and southeast of Europe with each other. Therefore, we kept an eye out for similar kinds of markets, and found an interesting example in Dimitrovgrad, Bulgaria, among others.

## "Informal" Markets and the Planned Economy in an Ideal Communist Model Town

Dimitrovgrad was famous for being the first planned town after the Communist Party gained power in Bulgaria: this entirely newly built city based on a typical Stalinist urban design scheme with neoclassical architecture alongside generous

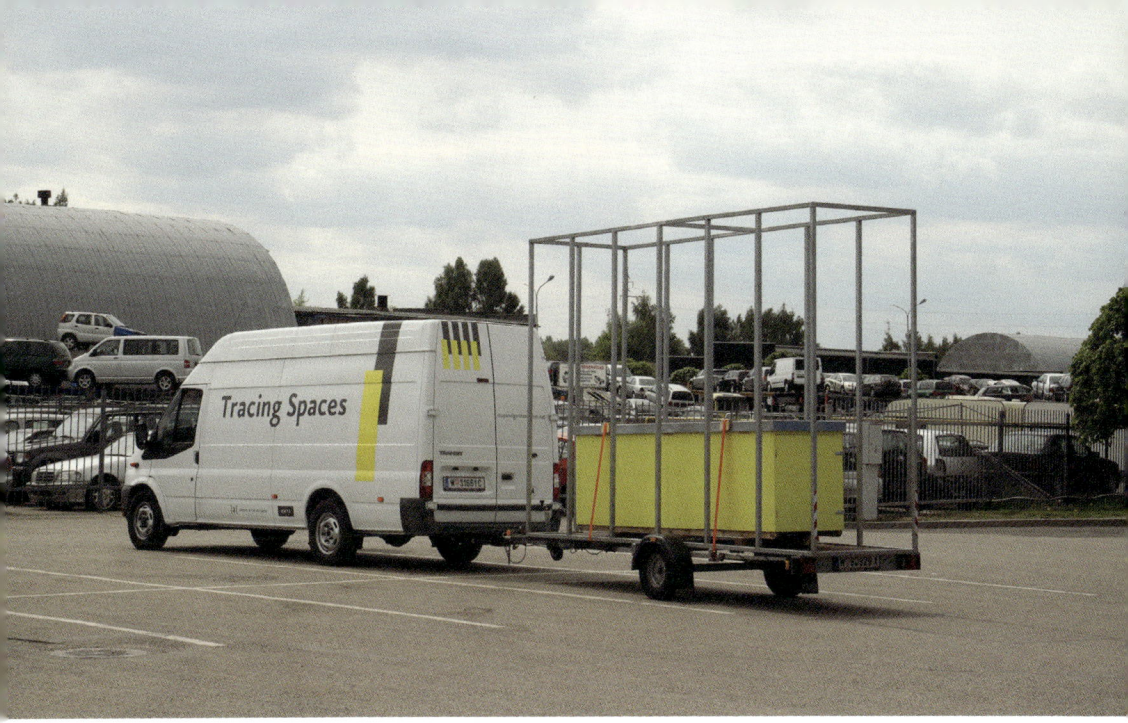

Fig. 55
Hieslmair and Zinganel, 2016
Marijampolė car market that we visited in 2016, with cars "collected" in Western Europe and sold to end consumers or dealers—who then transport them further to other post-Soviet regions using the Russian railway with its wider track gauge that also starts from here

boulevards and squares, was not only to symbolize the victory of socialism but also contribute to its triumph, functioning as an educational institution for creating nothing less than a new socialist man.[13] Ironically, this ideological model for an ideal communist town also hosted the first and biggest informal open-air market during the communist era in Bulgaria, tolerated to compensate for the failures of the system.[14] Its geographic location at, or at least close to, several major rail and road corridors and the relative proximity to the Black Sea port of Burgas (200 km) and the Turkish border (100 km) made it a hotspot at the time.

11  Sgibnev and Vozyanov, "Assemblages of Mobility."
12  N. N., interview by the authors, Marijampolė, May 18, 2015.
13  Ulf Brunnbauer, "Dimitrovgrad: Eine sozialistische Stadt in Bulgarien," in *Urbanisierung und Stadtentwicklung in Südosteuropa vom 19. bis zum 21. Jahrhundert*, ed. Marie-Janine Calic and Thomas Bohn (Munich: Kubon and Sagner, 2010), 199.
14  Endre Sik and Claire Wallace, "The Development of Open-Air Markets in East-Central Europe," *International Journal of Urban and Regional Research* 23, no. 4 (1999): 697–714.

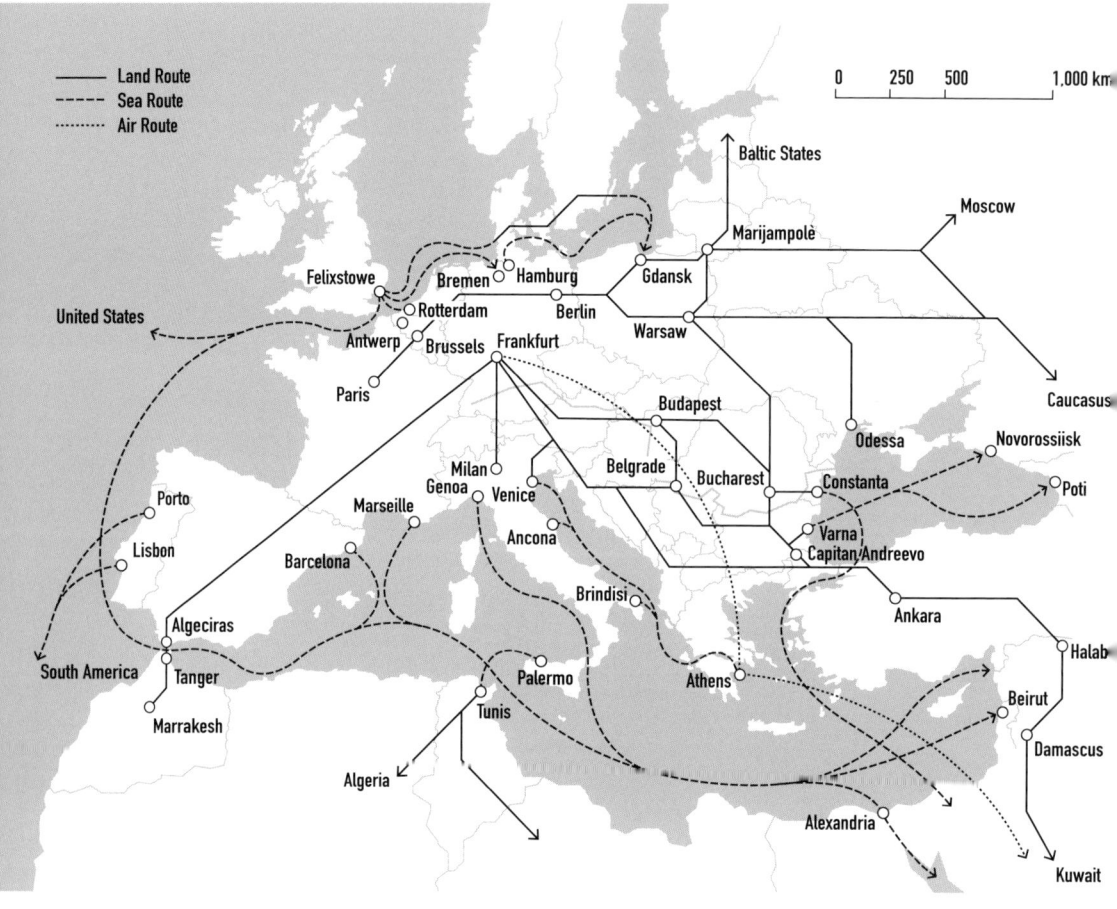

Fig. 56
Hieslmair and Zinganel, *International routes for the trafficking of stolen cars around 2000*, 2016

During the years of endless transition after 1989, this market took on even greater significance: Designed as a center of heavy industry, Dimitrovgrad suffered badly during the post-socialist transition. And those who already had experience with smuggling before the fall of Communism, who did not trust the state any longer with good reason, and especially those who could count on trans-border kinship relations, in particular, were the ones to take their chances first.

After suffering from state violence, "economic violence," intense discrimination, loss of jobs, and even outright physical attacks during the nationalist Zhivkov government in communist Bulgaria, 360,000 Turkish Bulgarians and Roma had (forcibly) left Bulgaria for Turkey within one month in 1989. This expulsion/emigration was euphemistically known as the "Great Excursion."[15] But many of them returned later and facilitated the tense cross-border relations they had involuntarily established with Turkey, to become the pioneers of the suitcase trade first, also teaching Slavic Bulgarians lessons in how to start a (gray) capitalist market economy the bottom up.[16] Other traders were Vietnamese and Chinese, who had established wholesale markets in Eastern Europe since the 1990s and Slavic Bulgarians, Serbs, and the famous "Russian traders," to mean Russian but also Ukraine and Polish traders, who privately "liberated" goods for warehouses and sold them all over Europe.[17]

In the meantime, the market in Dimitrovgrad assumed enormous importance as a driver of local light industry: textile products manufactured in small workshops in Dimitrovgrad and the surroundings were offered for sale, and new business networks with distributors and resellers were established here. The market opened at a site with easy access for both vendors and visitors, in the immediate vicinity of the central bus station, where the first suitcase vendors had arrived by their preferred means of transport: which were used to smuggle goods purchased at the market in Istanbul.[18] The infrastructure of a big indoor sport stadium proved the perfect site: in order to guarantee evacuation routes and fire brigade access but also to enhance the monumental qualities of the building, the modernist stadium stands alone on a large square, functioning as a landmark, which no one could miss. The paved parking lots and the public square around the stadium were appropriated for market purposes, which soon also expanded to part of the parks, green land, and even into the

15   John Pickles, "There Are No Turks in Bulgaria: Violence, Ethnicity, and Economic Practice in the Border Regions and Muslim Communities of Post-socialist Bulgaria," *Working Paper 25* (Halle/Saale: Max Planck Institute for Social Anthropology, 2001).
16   Yulian Konstantinov, "Patterns of Reinterpretation: Trader-Tourism in the Balkans (Bulgaria) as a Picaresque Metaphorical Enactment of Post-totalitarianism," *American Ethnologist* 23, no. 4 (1996): 762–82; Yulian Konstantinov, Gideon M. Kressel, and Thuen Trond, "Outclassed by Former Outcasts: Petty Trading in Varna," *American Ethnologist* 25, no. 4 (1988): 729–45.
17   Sik and Wallace, "The Development of Open-Air Markets in East-Central Europe."
18   Konstantinov, "Patterns of Reinterpretation."

yards of the surrounding housing blocks accommodating, among others, the remaining Vietnamese guest workers, who had played a significant role in the informal trading boom.[19] Today, this market is institutionalized and highly regulated by the municipality.[20] The products offered for sale are limited to clothes and shoes and all kinds of textile products. The entire area is also physically and visually separated from the city side by a row of solid prefab kiosks with their entirely closed rear facing the main street, preventing a direct gaze into the less formal parts of the market.

When the import of cars from Western Europe to Bulgaria significantly increased a second market was established by the municipality of Dimitrovgrad at walking distance from the first, but at a site that could easily accommodate many more cars: the car market (avtopazar) offering 550 parking lots for cars to be sold and even more space for spare parts, is located at the western margin of the beautiful Maritsa park,[21] in front of a large outdoor sports stadium named Minyor in honor of the hard-working coal miners, who once upon a time produced the basic resources for communist modernization (fig. 57). The appropriation of sports infrastructure to accommodate "informal markets" follows many international examples, epitomized most famously by Jarmark Europa at the abandoned tenth anniversary stadium in Warsaw, a communist showpiece built in 1955 capable of housing 100,000 spectators.[22] In Dimtrovgrad the stadium itself is not appropriated for market purposes. Although the stadium looks rather derelict and abandoned and suffers from lack of investment, it is still in use for popular events and sports matches of all kind, for instance, the local football team Minyor 1947 currently playing in the third Bulgarian league.

## Factors Driving the Import of Secondhand Cars in Bulgaria

Like in other socialist countries, there was a delay in individual motorization and therefore an increasing demand for cars (there was only a short period of passenger car production in communist Bulgaria[23]). But the economic crisis during transition, followed by high unemployment rates and hyperinflation, made new cars a luxury good, affordable only to a small minority. Hence, the early 1990s were characterized by a booming business of illegal import of both new and secondhand cars—many of them stolen in Western Europe—to Eastern Europe. Furthermore, one of the main corridors for trafficking stolen cars to the Middle East (and vice versa one of the main corridors for trafficking drugs toward the West) passed and passes through Bulgaria (fig. 56).[24]

The very loose control of import and resale, almost free of customs duties and VAT (when sales prices are estimated close to zero), not only encouraged organized crime in Bulgaria, many individuals and small newly founded companies also began importing secondhand vehicles themselves. According to

Eurostat, in the year 2000 secondhand cars accounted for the largest share in Bulgarian imports in value terms.[25] Today, Bulgaria is characterized by a relatively high rate of passenger car ownership, compared to the nation's GPD. Nevertheless, due to the generally low incomes the vehicle population in Bulgaria is quite old and the age of vehicles significantly exceeds EU averages.[26] You still can see some old Renault, FIAT, and Moskvitch on the streets, especially in rural areas. Switching from a vehicle of more than twenty years to a car of only eight years (!) is still considered a big upgrade there.

After Bulgaria joined the EU in 2007, the import of secondhand cars became even easier, while the economic crisis of 2009 suddenly ended the abundance of financing opportunities, and the number of new vehicles sold dropped to half the levels posted the year before. Today, a Bulgarian citizen can purchase a secondhand car from a professional vendor or a private individual—then it is even free of VAT—in any EU member state, simply drive it to Bulgaria and resell it on an open-air market, paying a tax of only 2.5 percent of the specified value of the vehicle. Only if the transaction sum exceeds BLN 15,000 (7,500 euros) does the payment have to be made via bank transfer. This limit can be easily maintained when dealing with secondhand cars. So this policy invites more and more people to deal in this semi-legal market in which only cash is circulating. Although Bulgaria is a desirable destination to outsource the production of car components to for many manufacturers in the automotive industries, there has yet to be a relevant car producer operating in Bulgaria who would lobby against the lack of import barriers.

19  Velislava Petrova, "Take the Market Out of Sight!" *Seminar_BG [En ligne], Issues, New Media, New Cultures, Old Cities*—Selected Papers from 2009/2010, updated: 5/2/2012. http://revues.mshparisnord.org/seminarbg/index.php?id=104 (accessed September 12, 2017).
20  There exists a comprehensive web page in Bulgarian: http://www.dgpazar.eu and even a very short one in English: http://dgrpazar.weebly.com/sunday-market.html (accessed September 12, 2017).
21  Dimitrovgrad market, https://www.pazardimitrovgrad.bg.
22  Joanna Warsza, *Stadium X: A Place That Never Was: A Reader* (Warsaw: Bęc Zmiana Foundation, 2009); Gertrud Hüwelmeir, "From 'Jarmark Europa' to 'Commodity City': New Marketplaces, Post-socialist Migrations, and Cultural Diversity in Central and Eastern Europe," *Central and Eastern European Migration Review (CEEMR)* 4, no. 1 (2015): 27–39.
23  From 1967 to 1990 Balkan in Lovech assembled 304,297 Moskvitch from knock-down kits imported from the Soviet Union. The same factory also produced less than 800 Fiat 850 and Fiat 124 between 1967 and 1971, unofficially called "Pirin-FIAT." The factory of Bulgarrenault in the city of Plovdiv assembled about 4,000 Renault 8 and Renault 10 in the years between 1966 and 1970. The factory also produced a few examples of the famous sports automobile Bulgaralpine.
24  Boiko Todorov, Ognian Shentov, and Aleksandur Stoianov, eds., *Corruption and Illegal Trafficking: Monitoring and Prevention*, CSD report 9 (Sofia: Center for the Study of Democracy, 2000), 29–30.
25  Todorov, Shentov, and Stoianov, 29–30.
26  "Bulgarians Are Driving the Oldest Cars in Europe," *novitne.com*, October 13, 2017, https://www.novinite.com/articles/184252/Bulgarians+are+Driving+the+Oldest+Cars+in+Europe (accessed August 10, 2018).

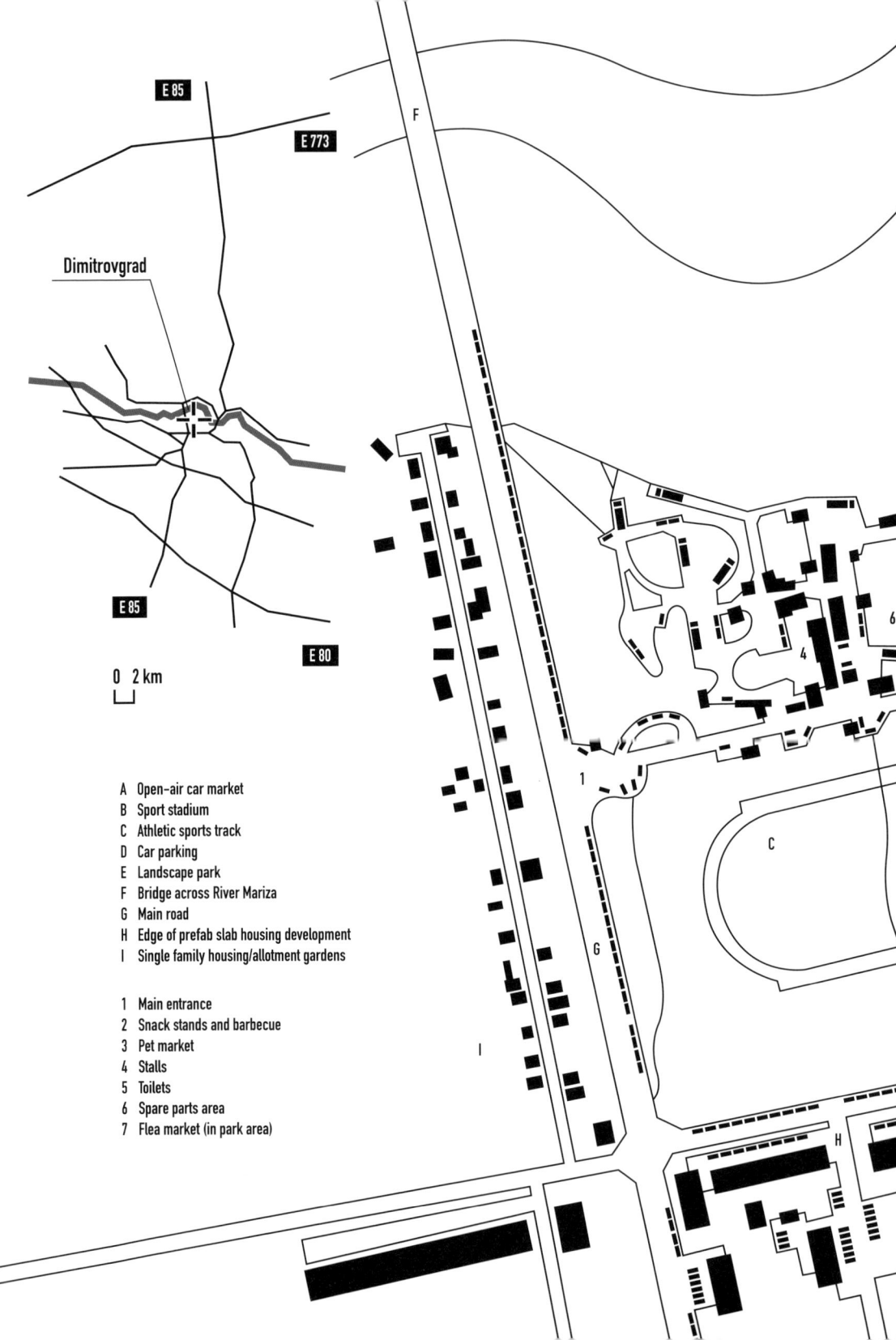

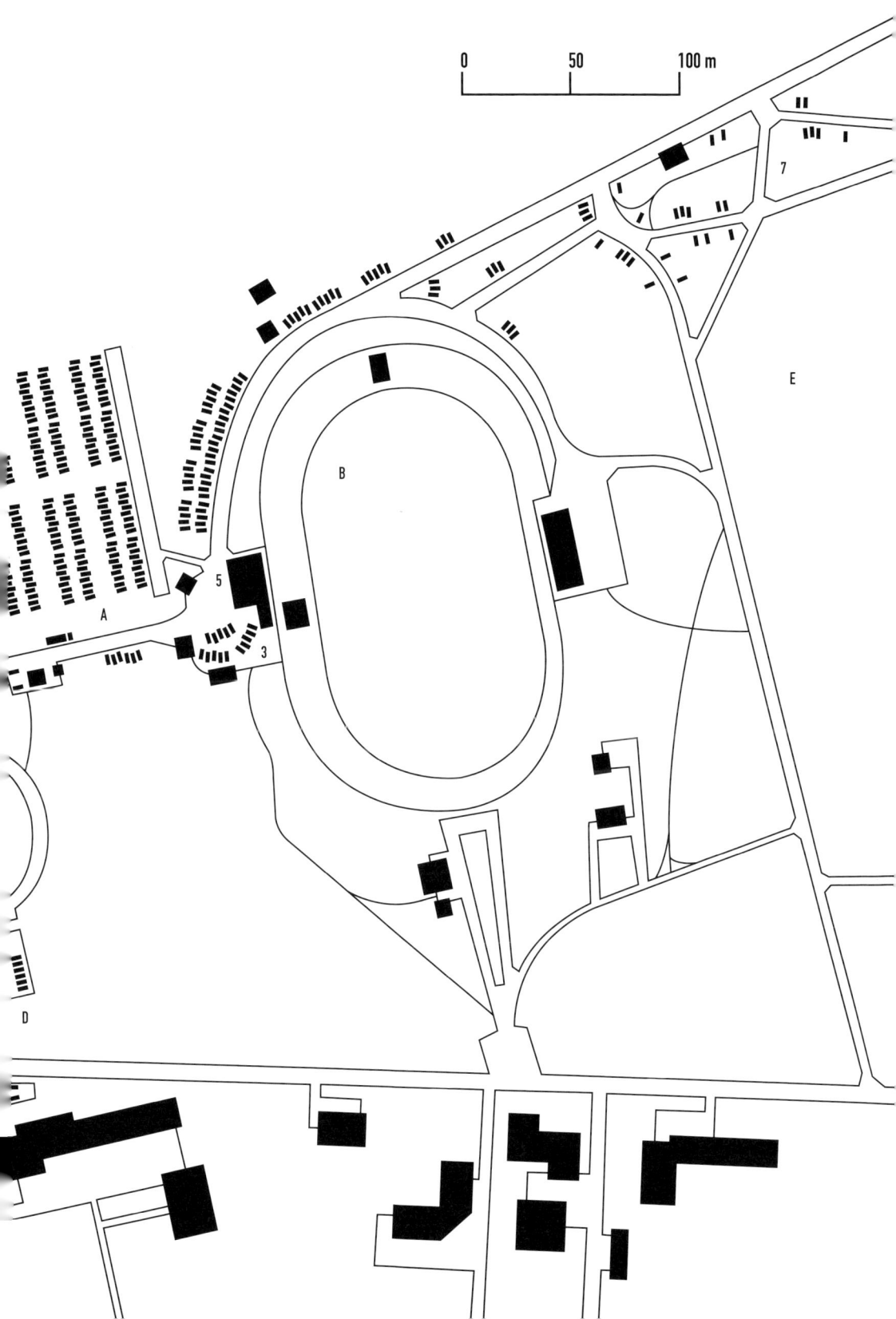

Fig. 57
Hieslmair and Zinganel, 2018
Temporary adaptation of stadium facilities for the semi-informal trading node for used cars and spare parts held once a month at the edge of the modernist, planned town of Dimitrovgrad, Bulgaria

## Back on the Ground

And indeed, we observed the effects of the secondhand car markets when driving the Pan-European corridors from the former West to the former East—both north and south! Starting in Vienna we tested all the different arms of the bundle of streets named Balkan corridors today. No matter whether we drove to Bulgaria via Hungary, Serbia, or Romania, we followed trucks and trailers of all sizes bringing secondhand cars from Germany and Austria, but even from France and England, to their target destinations. And when we drove back, we met many empty trailers. We met Serbs and Bulgarians living and working in Germany and Austria today, who take a secondhand car whenever they drive back home. Not all of them depend economically on exporting cars, but they feel obliged to do a favor for their friends and relatives, who expect them to bring prestigious goods from the West, which also includes secondhand cars of specific brands. But others, of course, do depend on this practice. If they do not have access to a trailer, they just drive down the car directly to the market and use a cheap bus connection to get back up north. And if they fail to sell their car at the first market, they try at another one or leave the car with professional vendors.[27]

## From Compensation for Missing Supply to Pure Enjoyment of the Special Market Atmosphere

One might suppose that the booming years of a "wild" secondhand car trade must be over at some point. That there might be some modest saturation one day and many of the former informal traders would have professionalized, resulting in endless clusters of secondhand car parks along all entrance roads to the bigger cities. If so, then the Dimitrovgrad market already responded to this tendency: Here, there are not only cars for sale. There are diversified zones characterized by the different goods offered, each with a rather different atmosphere, different social ranking, and a different degree of formalization.

Vendors already arrive during the night before or very early in the morning. During the opening hours on Sundays from 6 a.m. to 2 p.m., crowds of people walk in both directions along the main street, which connects the clothes market and the car market. Many vendors leave the market when they have successfully sold their goods. The access from the main road to the stadium also marks the entrance to the market (fig. 57). There is no fence or gate, only a security guard is there to regulate traffic arriving and departing to and from the market. And there are no fixed stalls at all. The market starts immediately at the entrance, following a tree-lined road to the parking lot in front of the stadium, and wrapping around its terraces into the public park. Alongside the access road are several solid kiosks that offer drinks and food—especially grilled meat—in the shade of the trees. The old stadium opens its many toilets to the vendors and visitors. The best spots are located between the entrance and the stadium, and obviously the most professional vendors can be found there. They use a stall system built up in front of their parked van. The deeper visitors enter into the area, the smaller the items are for sale. The grassland behind the alley close to the entrance is offered to those who need more space, for example, to park a transporter loaded with secondhand cars, a larger van with a trailer, or to display larger-scale spare parts for cars (fig. 58). There is an entire section specialized in spare parts for TIR trucks only and another for tires, which are arranged in a rather artistic manner. Where space is limited the cars and the goods for sale become smaller. Most cars are used to transport, store, and display other goods as well: trunks are open to offer views like into a showcase; hoods are covered with goods of all kinds, mainly technical gadgets, from microwave ovens, vacuum cleaners, sewing machines to consumer electronics, records, audio cassettes, and CDs, while larger objects like washing machines or fridges are placed beside the car (fig. 59). At the deepest point, in the park, the market takes on the look of a traditional flea market where you can find all kinds of small-scale items, offered by non-motorized vendors mainly Roma people, laying their goods on the ground. Although there are many children's toys offered in front of the stadium, and there is even a section offering pets, mainly dogs, birds, and fish for sale, our Bulgarian research partner Emiliya Karaboeva noted that this market seems to primarily attract men, while the clothes market primarily attracts women. If that is true, then both are successfully complementing each other. From our perspective, a Western European male intellectual's romantic gaze, the Dimitrovgrad car market was far more attractive than the clothes market (and the car market in Marijampolė) because it had kept its "informal" appeal and a more exotic "flea market" atmosphere, with masses of people strolling around in the beautiful park with a strange mix of all kinds of technical gadgets on display, while vendors of

27 N. N., Serbian car dealer, interview by the authors, Serbia-Hungary border station at Röszke, August 13, 2014.

different ethnic backgrounds shouted and the smoke of grilled meat wafted in the air. Another interesting feature is the rhythm this market imposes on the place: by opening just once per month early on Sunday morning and closing down soon after noon. This lack of continuation, of time to look around at the offered wares, digest, and eventually purchase goods, increases both the curiosity and the demand of visitors. It prevents the vendors from investing into solid stalls and transforms the market into a sort of event, a festival—or at least a sort of Sunday ritual—which people obviously enjoy very much.

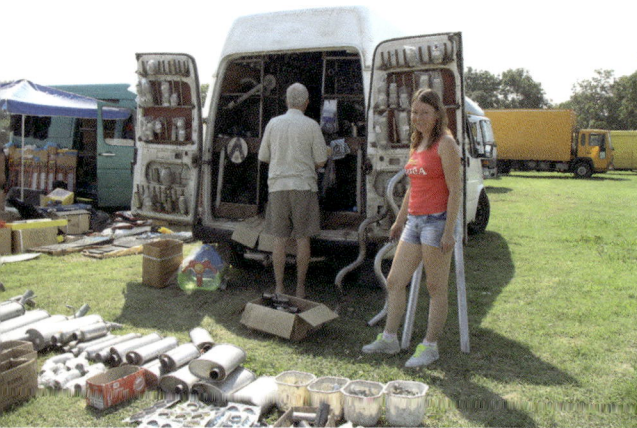

Figs. 58–59
Hieslmair and Zinganel, 2018
Dimitrovgrad secondhand car market with vendors selling spare parts directly from vans—which serve as transportation, but also as storage, market stalls, and sometimes even as accommodation

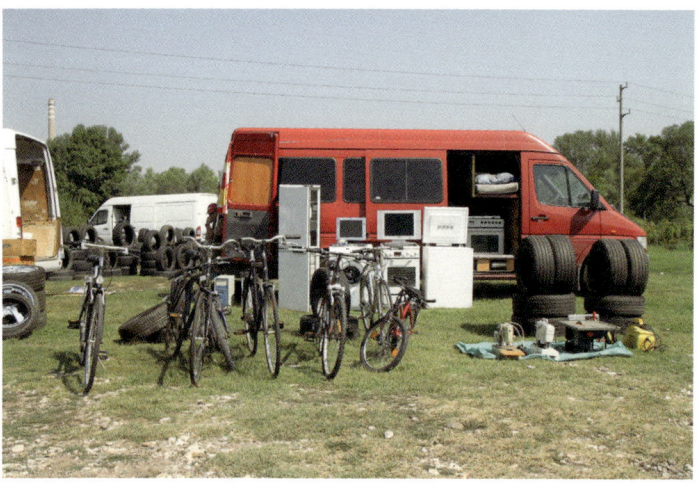

## Literature

Aschauer, Matthias. *Stars of Albania*. Fotohof edition, vol. 166 (2012).

Beuving, Joost. "Cotonou's Klondike: African Traders and Second-hand Car Markets in Benin." *Journal of Modern African Studies* 42, no. 4 (2004): 511–37.

Brooks, Andrew. "Networks of Power and Corruption: The Trade of Japanese Used Cars to Mozambique." *Geographical Journal* 178, no. 1 (March 2012): 80–92.

Brunnbauer, Ulf. "Dimitrovgrad. Eine sozialistische Stadt in Bulgarien." In *Urbanisierung und Stadtentwicklung in Südosteuropa vom 19. bis zum 21. Jahrhundert*, edited by Marie-Janine Calic and Thomas Bohn, 197–219. Munich: Kubon & Sagner, 2010.

Council of the European Union. "Comments on the Desicion on the Tackling Vehicle Crime with Cross-border Implications." *document 5216/04*, January 13, 2004, 1.

Gounev, Philip, and Tihomir Bezlov. "From the Economy of Deficit to the Black-Market: Car Theft and Trafficking in Bulgaria." *Trends in Organized Crime* 11, no. 4 (2008): 410–29.

Hüwelmeir, Gertrud. "From 'Jarmark Europa' to 'Commodity City': New Marketplaces, Post-socialist Migrations, and Cultural Diversity in Central and Eastern Europe." *Central and Eastern European Migration Review (CEEMR)* 4, no. 1 (2015): 27–39.

Konstantinov, Yulian. "Patterns of Reinterpretation: Trader-Tourism in the Balkans (Bulgaria) as a Picaresque Metaphorical Enactment of Post-totalitarianism." *American Ethnologist* 23, no. 4 (1996): 762–82.

Konstantinov, Yulian, Gideon M. Kressel, and Thuen Trond. "Outclassed by Former Outcasts: Petty Trading in Varna." *American Ethnologist* 25, no. 4 (1988): 729–45.

Krottendorfer, Markus. *Automarket Tbilisi*. Fotohof edition, vol. 117 (2008).

Petrova, Velislava. "Take the Market Out of Sight!" *Seminar_BG [En ligne]*, Issues, New Media, New Cultures, Old Cities—selected papers from 2009/10, updated: May 24, 2012, http://revues.mshparisnord.org/seminarbg/index.php?id=104 (accessed September 12, 2017).

Rusev, Atanas, ed. "D9.3 Four Case Study Reports: Corruption and Trafficking in Women. The Case of Bulgaria." *Anti-corruption Policies Revisited: Global Trends and European Responses to the Challenge of Corruption*. Sofia: Center for the Study of Democracy, 2016.

Schlögel, Karl. *Marjampole oder Europas Wiederkehr aus dem Geist der Städte*. Munich: Hanser, 2005.

———. "Die Ameisenhändler vom Bahnhof Zoo: Geschichte im Abseits und vergessene Europäer," *Osteuropa* 11 (2009): 53–60.

Sgibnev, Wladimir, and Andrey Vozyanov. "Assemblages of Mobility: The Marshrutkas of Central Asia." *Central Asian Survey* 35, no. 2 (2016): 276–91.

Sik, Endre, and Claire Wallace. "The Development of Open-Air Markets in East-Central Europe." *International Journal of Urban and Regional Research* 23, no. 4 (1999): 697–714.

Todorov, Boiko, Ognian Shentov, and Aleksandur Stoianov, eds. *Corruption and Illegal Trafficking: Monitoring and Prevention*. CSD report 9. Sofia: Center of the Study of Democracy, 2000.

Verrips, Jojada, and Birgit Meyer. "Kwaku's Car: The Struggles and Stories of a Ghanaian Long-Distance Taxi Driver." In *Car Cultures*, edited by Daniel Miller, 153–84. Oxford: Berg 2001.

Warsza, Joanna. *Stadium X: A Place That Never Was: A Reader*. Warsaw: Bęc Zmiana Foundation, 2009.

Zinganel, Michael, and Michael Hieslmair. *Road*Registers: Logbook of Mobile Worlds*. Exhibition catalogue. Vienna: Academy of Fine Arts, 2017.

# From Guangdong to Wólka Kosowska
## Migrants' Transnational Trade

Katarzyna Osiecka and Tatjana Vukosavljević

Beginning in the late 1980s, a network of wholesale markets operated by different migrant groups developed gradually in post-communist Eastern Europe providing local markets with affordable Asian goods. This network expanded from assemblages of informal structures, bazaars—Jarmark Europa—to a commercial complex, Wólka Kosowska, with an annual turnover of several millions of euros. Today Wólka Kosowska, located on the southern outskirts of Warsaw is one of the biggest Asian wholesale and retail markets in Central and Eastern European Countries (CEEC).[1] Over nearly thirty years, the market, partly thanks to the resourcefulness of the entrepreneurs who sold and supplied there, and partly through significant infrastructure spending, grew from a single distribution hub to a multi-ethnic village structure. We will argue that together with the other Asian trading clusters Wólka Kosowska can be seen as a foundation for increased economic integration between CEECs and China: "New Silk Road" project. Wólka Kosowska can be regarded as a dynamic hub, part of a larger social and economic network.

## Jarmark Europa: Prehistory of One of the Most Significant Post-socialist Trading Nodes

When discussing the trading cluster of Wólka Kosowska it is crucial to explore its origins and its predecessor: Jarmark Europa (Europe's Fair), a huge bazaar located near the city center of Warsaw, was one of the biggest informal markets in Central and Eastern Europe. The market was born in 1989 on the site of *Stadion Dziesięciolecia* (10th-Anniversary Stadium)—one of the main landmarks of socialist Warsaw.[2] The 10th-Anniversary Stadium was built between 1953 and 1955 from the rubble of the destroyed city.[3] In 1983 the stadium was abandoned due to technical problems and began being used as a flea market. It was known as the "Russian market." In the early days, customers came largely from the Eastern European countries and the former Soviet Union. After 1989, the government sports agency (Centralny Ośrodek Sportu) leased

---

1  Albania, Bulgaria, Croatia, the Czech Republic, Hungary, Poland, Romania, the Slovak Republic, Slovenia, and the three Baltic states: Estonia, Latvia, and Lithuania. *The Organization for Economic Co-operation and Development (OECD)*. https://stats.oecd.org/glossary/detail.asp?ID=303 (accessed March 11, 2018).

2  *Stadion Dziesięciolecia* (10th Anniversary Stadium) was built to commemorate the 10th Anniversary of the establishment of the People's Republic of Poland in 1945. It was one of the largest stadiums in Poland and constituted the principal venue for Party and state festivities.

3  Grzegorz Piątek, "Palimpsest wpisany w Elipsę," in *Stadion X: Miejsce, którego nie było*, ed. Joanna Warsza, (Kraków, Warszawa: Bęc Zmiana Foundation and Ha!art, 2008), 20–25.

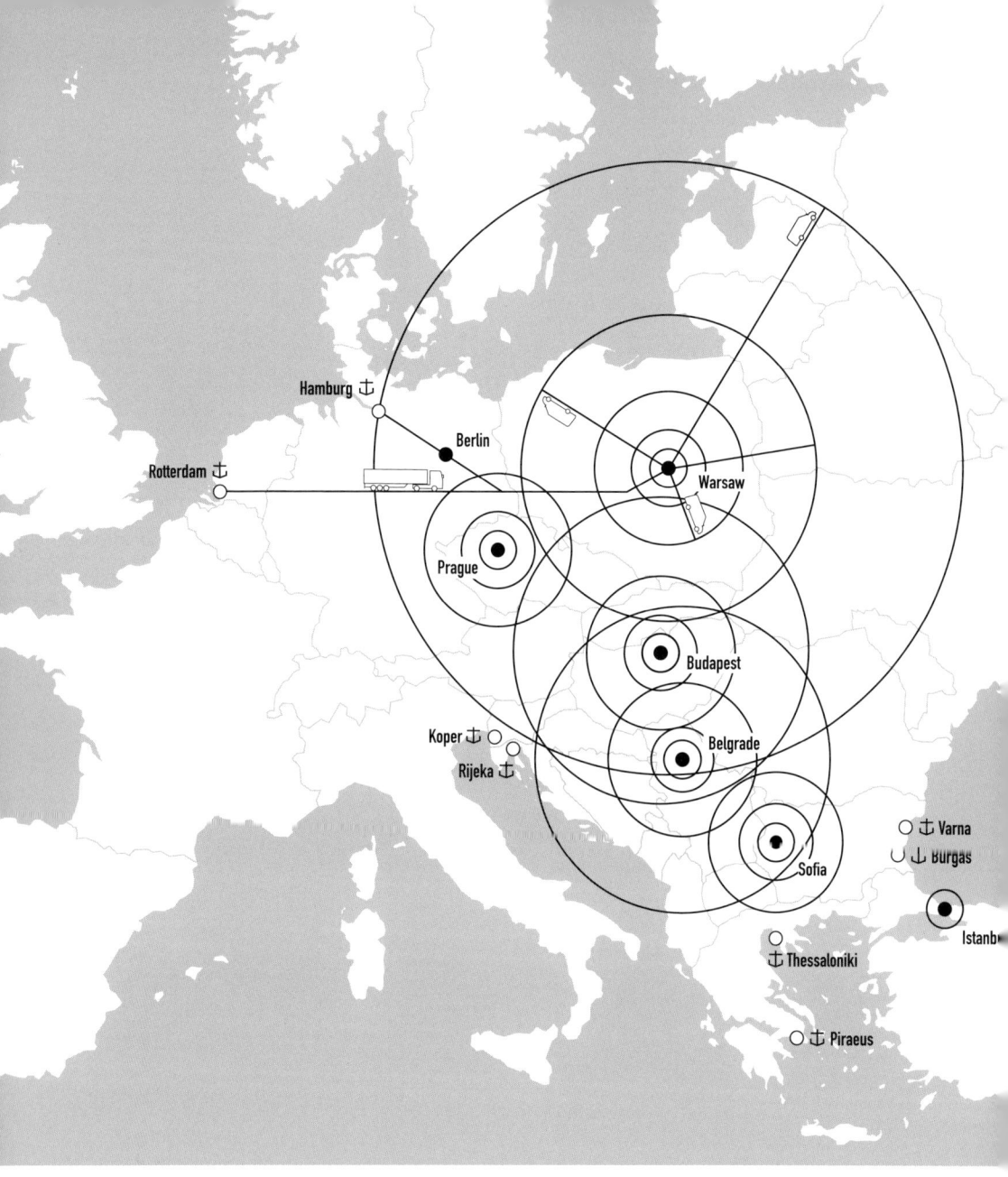

Fig. 60
Katarzyna Osiecka and Tatjana Vukosavljević,
*Network of Asian wholesale markets in Eastern Europe and the flow of goods using the example of Wólka Kosowska south of Warsaw*, 2016

the area to *Damis*,[4] a private operator that turned it into an outdoor market—Jarmark Europa—visited by up to one hundred thousand people a day.[5] The transformation of the former sports venue into a trading ground represented a form of "vernacular cosmopolitanism"[6] or "globalization from below" that was slowly changing the city's make-up.[7] The dilapidated and empty space was revitalized by traders inspired by the new entrepreneurial spirit of the free market. They altered the space of the once glorious sporting arena to pursue the opportunities of the new economy.[8] The traders at this enormous sprawling bazaar were predominately migrants—Vietnamese, Turkish, Russian, and citizens of former Soviet republics as well as tradesmen from Pakistan, India, and Africa. The overall impression of this multi-ethnic site was colorful, picturesque, and informal. The multilevel construction of the stadium's complex was transformed into a labyrinth of retail spaces: tents and stalls. "On a micro-level, the space of Jarmark Europa was created and organized around cardboard boxes originally utilized for packing goods, which got 'recycled' and reused in various other ways, for instance, as building material for stalls, tables, shelters, etc."[9] The Stadium-Bazaar was a place where people were able to buy goods such as pirate computer games, software programs, or denim garments at affordable prices for most, during the time of the changing economy. It operated as a retail and wholesale hub for Central and Eastern Europe as well as beyond the region. Although the official name of the bazaar was *Europa*, most of the traders working there were from outside of continental Europe.[10] According to rough estimates, every fifth stall had been rented by a trader from Vietnam.[11] The market used to serve not only as a workplace, but also as a community hub where businesses and services for the large Vietnamese population were concentrated, such as eateries, ethnic grocers, barbers, beauty salons, bookshops, newsagents, and video stores. The market

4  Established in 1989 by Bogdan Tomaszewski, Damis was one of the biggest private companies in Poland at that time. After the closing of the market, Damis had the idea to build a new Jarmark Europa in attempt to continue the tradition of the famous bazaar. The location for the investment was chosen in the district of Praga-Północ, on the site of the former FSO (Fabryka Samochodów Osobowych) car factory. See http://www.damis.pl/aboutus.html (accessed January 15, 2018).
5  Roch Sulima, "The Laboratory of Polish Postmodernity: An Ethnographic Report from the Stadium Bazaar," in *Chasing Warsaw: Socio-Material Dynamics of Urban Change since 1990*, ed. Monika Grubbauer and Joanna Kusiak (Frankfurt am Main: Campus Verlag, 2012), 241–68.
6  Homi Bhabha, "Unsatisfied: Notes on Vernacular Cosmopolitanism," in *Text and Nation*, ed. Laura Garcia-Morena and Peter C. Pfeifer (London: Camden House, 2001), 191–207.
7  David Crowley, *Warsaw* (London: Reaktion Books, 2003), 40.
8  Sulima, "Laboratory of Polish Postmodernity."
9  Sulima.
10  Magdalena Góralska, Helena Patzer, and Małgorzata Winkowska, "The Stadium as a Witness: A Story of a Changing Monument," *Journal of Latin American Cultural Studies*, no. 9 (2016): 1–36.
11  Aleksandra Grzymała-Kozłowska, "Migration and Socio-demographic Processes in Central and Eastern Europe: Characteristics, Specificity and Internal Differences," *Central and Eastern European Migration Review* 2, no. 1 (2013): 5–11.

area also hosted a Vietnamese association and a Buddhist temple.[12] It represented an urban, social and aesthetic phenomenon interesting to scholars and artists.[13] Places such as Jarmark Europa contributed to the proliferation of transitory spaces[14] in which cultures engage in a variety of encounters despite the often homogenizing forces of globalization. In doing so, these places have become a vital source for architects, artists, and theorists to study the potential of accelerated spatial appropriation and self-organization.[15]

## A Legacy of the Planned Economy

The countries of Central and Eastern Europe underwent a socioeconomic transformation in the 1990s and made the shift from state-planned to free-market economy. As a direct consequence of this phenomenon, numerous large-scale informal markets run by migrants have emerged (Hüwelmeier on a bazaar in East Berlin; Korać on Blok 70 in Belgrade; Nagy on the Red Dragon Market in Bucharest; Nyírí on Chinese bazaars in Budapest; Marcińczak and van der Velde on bazaars in Poland).[16] At the beginning of the transformation process, many bazaars constituted a basic source of goods otherwise unavailable in socialist Central and Eastern European Countries (CEEC).[17] Further into the transition process these sites were tolerated by the governmental institutions and became a main source of consumer goods. In that sense the emerging bazaars were spatial manifestations of basic and untamed forms of capitalism. For millions of people in post-socialist Europe different kinds of migration for the purposes of trade and work have become the major "occupation" or "profession."[18] It not only applies to the Polish "pioneers," the short-term commuter laborers and suitcase traders operating since the 1980s but also to other migrants from Eastern Europe to Polish or Czech informal labor markets.[19] These mobility patterns had been historically rooted in the COMECON space before 1989.[20] Migrants used their experience in circumventing the system during the communist period when traveling and consuming was a way of overcoming the uniformity, inadequacies, and shortages of state-regulated supply.[21] At that time, a pair of jeans and a denim jacket were highly desired and valued goods in the Eastern bloc. Many Eastern Europeans, as well as Poles, saw a good business opportunity and started smuggling textile products from Turkey gaining small fortunes from that trade. The grand bazaar of Istanbul was the most important spot for doing business of this kind and where adventurous traders came to purchase stock. A number of Turkish traders saw their opportunity and followed the Poles and other suitcase merchants back to their home countries.[22] As a result of these migrations, an active trade in textiles between Poland and Turkey was established. Furthermore, Turks became important players in the textile market and production in Poland in the late 1980s and were a significant migrant group working at the Stadium-Bazaar.[23] However, the Vietnamese constituted and still constitute one of the largest and most established foreign communities in Warsaw. Their roots can be traced back to the first wave of migration from communist North Vietnam in the 1960s and 1970s as part of a general intra-socialist bloc student exchange program,[24] which offered grants in several socialist countries in Eastern Europe including, for instance, Bulgaria, the GDR and Poland. In the 1990s, some of these Polish-educated Vietnamese returned as founding members of a larger

12 Aneta Piekut, "Visible and Invisible Ethnic Others in Warsaw: Spaces of Encounter and Places of Exclusion," in *Chasing Warsaw Socio-material Dynamics of Urban Change since 1990*, ed. Monika Grubbauer and Joanna Kusiak (Frankfurt am Main: Campus Verlag, 2012): 189–212.

13 The initiatives were summed up in the event *Stadion X-lecia: Finisz*. See Związki Muzeum web profile: www.msl.org.pl/wydarzeniams/archiwum/finisz-stadion,428.html (accessed January 15, 2018). There is also the documentary film *Jarmark Europa* by Minze Tummescheit capturing the last days of the Stadium-Bazaar.

14 Martina Löw, "The Constitution of Space: The Structuration of Spaces through the Simultaneity of Effect and Perception," *European Journal of Social Theory* 11, no. 1 (2008): 25–49.

15 Peter Mörtenböck and Helge Mooshammer, "Spaces of Encounter: Informal Markets in Europe," *Architectural Research Quarterly* 12, nos. 3–4 (2008): 347–57.

16 Gertrud Hüwelmeier, "From 'Jarmark Europa' to 'Commodity City': New Marketplaces, Post-socialist Migrations, and Cultural Diversity in Central and Eastern Europe," *Central and Eastern European Migration Review*, vol. 4, no. 1 (2015): 27–39; Szymon Marcińczak and Martin van der Velde, "Drifting in a Global Space of Textile Flows: Apparel Bazaars in Poland's Łódź Region," *European Planning Studies* 16, no. 7 (2008): 911–23; Gertrud Hüwelmeier, "Postsocialist Bazaars: Diversity, Solidarity, and Conflict in the Marketplace," *Laboratorium: Russian Review of Social Research* 1 (2013), http://www.soclabo.org/index.php/laboratorium/article/view/62/956 (accessed January 15, 2016); Maja Korać, "Transnational Pathways to Integration: Chinese Traders in Serbia," http://www.doiserbia.nb.rs/img/doi/0038-0318/2013/0038-03181302245K.pdf (accessed January 5, 2018.); Dorottya Nagy, "Fiery Dragons: Chinese Communities in Central and Eastern Europe: With Special Focus on Hungary and Romania," *Religions & Christianity in Today's China* I, no. 1 (2011): 71–86.

17 Piekut, "Visible and Invisible Ethnic Others in Warsaw."

18 Krystyna Iglicka, "The Economics of Petty Trade on the Eastern Polish Border" in *The Challenge of East-West Migration for Poland*, ed. Krystyna Iglicka and Keith Sword (London: Macmillan, 1999): 120–44.

19 Ewa Morawska, "Transnational Migrations in the Enlarged European Union: A Perspective from East Central Europe," in *Europe Unbound: Enlarging and Reshaping the Boundaries of the European Union*, ed. Jan Zielonka (London: Routledge, 2002); Keith Sword, "Cross-border 'Suitcase Trade' and the Role fo Foreigners in Polish Informal Markets," in *The Challenge of East-West Migration for Poland*, ed. Krystyna Iglicka and Keith Sword (London: Macmillan, 1999): 145–67.

20 Michael C. Kaser, *Comecon: Integration Problems of the Planned Economies* (Oxford: Oxford University Press, 1967).

21 Anna Wessely, "Menschen, Objekte und Ideen auf der Reise," in *Das Phantom Sucht Seinen Mörder*, ed. Justin Hoffmann and Marion von Osten (Berlin: b-books, 1999): 211–15; Małgorzata Irek, *Der Schmugglerzug: Warschau-Berlin-Warschau; Materialien einer Feldforschung* (Berlin: Das Arabische Buch, 1998).

22 *Shuttle Trade*, report of the eleventh meeting of the IMF Committee on Balance of Payments Statistics (Washington, DC, October 21–23, 1998): 6; Aydin Kenan, Oztig Lacin Idil and Bulut Emrah, "The Economic Impact of the Suitcase Trade on Foreign Trade: A Regional Analysis of the Laleli Market," *International Business Research* 9, no. 3 (Canadian Center of Science and Education, 2016): 14.

23 Marcińczak and Van der Velde, "Drifting in a Global Space of Textile Flows."

24 Hüwelmeier, "From 'Jarmark Europa' to 'Commodity City.'"

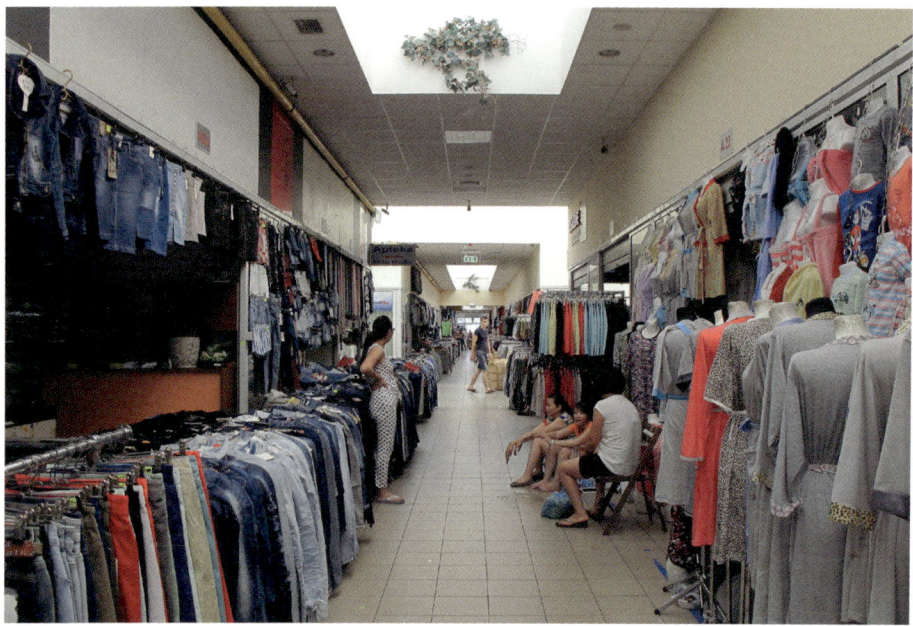

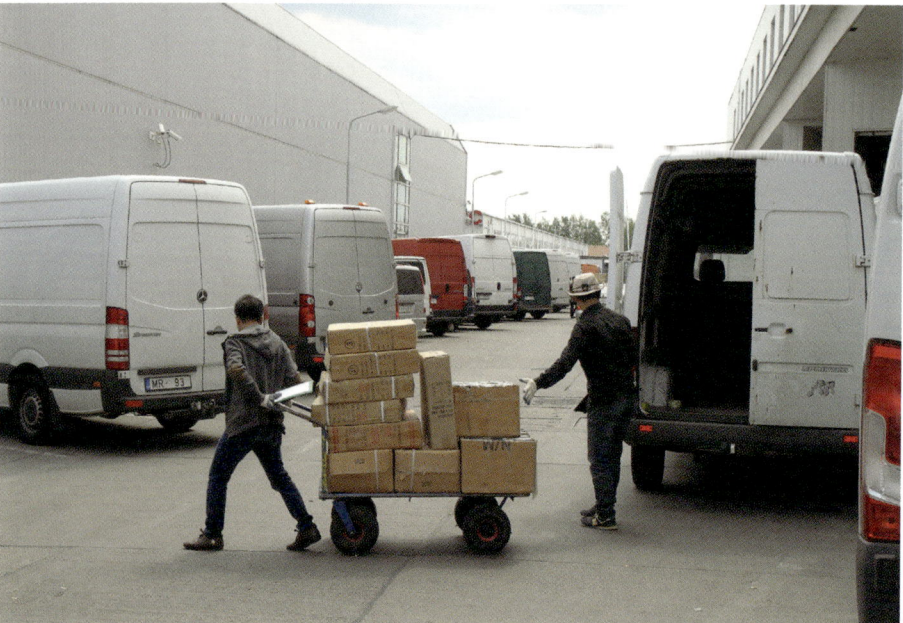

Figs. 61–64
Katarzyna Osiecka, Michael Hieslmair, and Michael Zinganel, *Everyday routine in the endless aisles inside the market halls at Wólka Kosowska*, 2016

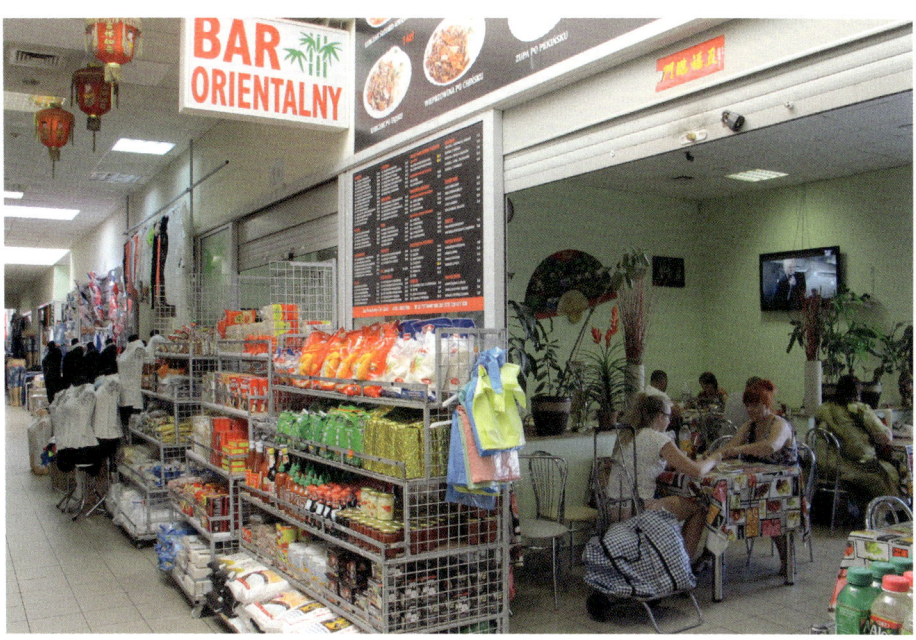

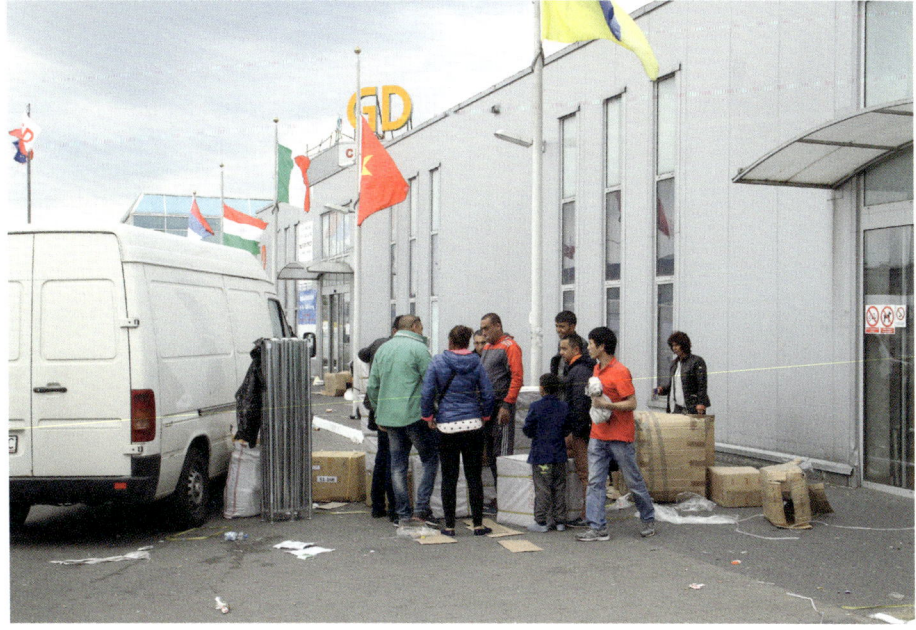

and more complex migration network of subsequent immigration from Vietnam to Central and Eastern Europe.[25] Moreover, economic migrants appeared in Polish cities as street vendors, and traders in the open-air markets (OAM) that flourished all over Central and Eastern Europe.[26]

After 1990, thousands of Vietnamese came to Poland as legal and illegal migrants. The Vietnamese played a crucial role in establishing Jarmark Europa and contributing to its economic success. Most textile imports and sales were managed by Vietnamese traders who imported hundreds of cardboard boxes of clothing every day from Asia, mostly from China. In the years of the economic transition, the market provided employment for more than 6,500 people—about 3,000 of them were considered to be foreigners.[27] Moreover, about 60,000 people found work linked to the bazaar activities, such as in factories producing goods for trading.[28] Given the prehistory of the market, and its unplanned, bottom-up, entrepreneur-driven character, we argue together with Hüwelmeier, that the establishment of Jarmark Europa in Warsaw is directly linked to the fall of Communism and the increasing complexity of global migration.[29]

## Translocation of the Market

As the free-market economy evolved in Poland, Jarmark Europa slowly lost its special role as a substitute economy and no longer attracted as many customers as in its heyday at the end of the 1990s. People were able to find the necessary goods in other places as shops became better supplied and equipped, Western brands gained access to the Polish market, and the first shopping malls in Warsaw opened.[30] With these new developments and changes, consumer habits and behaviors gradually evolved.[31] The success or failure of bazaars like Jarmark Europa depended on traders, as well as customers, coming from abroad, especially from Eastern countries. The tightening of the borders in the run-up to Polish Schengen membership, which started in 1997,[32] and the introduction of visas for non-EU citizens, but also the financial crisis in Russia from 1998 onwards, caused the decline in profits and put additional pressure on the stall-holders.[33] The estimated number of traders at the *Jarmark* fell from 7,000 in 1997 to 5,000 in 1998. Sales fell from 450 million euros in 1997 to two hundred million euros in 1998 to 160 million euros in 2000.[34]

Starting from 2002, the informal and multiethnic bazaar gradually closed down and was finally dismantled when the construction of the National Stadium,[35] built to host the 2012 European Football Championships, began. With the closing of the bazaar in the heart of Warsaw in 2007, Vietnamese and Turkish,[36] but also Polish traders, agreed to relocate their businesses to other centers or the peripheries.[37] Many of the traders from Jarmark Europa decided to move to the Wólka Kosowska trading area in the municipality of Lesznowola, thirty kilometers south of the center of the Polish capital. Wólka Kosowska is directly connected and located in the immediate vicinity of the European route E77, an important transit way between Southeastern Europe and the Baltic states. At the same time, it is close to the motorway ring road around Warsaw, and so connected to the transit corridors of Belarus, Ukraine, Russia, and Western Europe.

## The Rise of Wólka Kosowska

The first facility of the trading cluster in Wólka Kosowska was built by the Chinese company GD Poland Investment on farmland and berry fields as a result of a bilateral agreement between Poland and China. After the cornerstone ceremony in 1992, an official Polish-Chinese delegation opened the first free-standing, two-story market hall in 1994 (fig. 65).[38] The name GD Poland Investment indicates the origins of the company. The two capital letters GD stand for the Chinese province of Guangdong, the biggest exporting region of China known

25 Teresa Halik, "New Patterns in Vietnamese Migration: The Case of Vietnamese Migration to Poland in the 1990s," in *Challenges of Cultural Diversity in Europe*, ed. Janina Wiktoria Dacyl (Stockholm: CEIFO, 2001): 189–213.
26 Piekut, "Visible and Invisible Ethnic Others in Warsaw"; and Marcińczak and Van der Velde, "Drifting in a Global Space of Textile Flows."
27 Krystyna Iglicka, "Shuttling from the Former Soviet Union to Poland: From 'Primitive Mobility' to Migration," *Journal of Ethnic and Migration Studies* 27, no. 3 (2001): 505–18.
28 Marek Okólski, "Regional Dimension of International Migration in Central and Eastern Europe," *Genus* 54, nos. 1/2 (1998): 11–36.
29 Hüwelmeier, "From 'Jarmark Europa' to 'Commodity City.'"
30 Karina Kreja, "Changes in Spatial Patterns of Urban Consumption in Post-Socialist Cities: New Large-Scale Retail Development in Warsaw" (paper presented at the Conference *Winds of Societal Change: Remaking Post-Communist Cities* at the University of Illinois, June 18–19, 2004).
31 Góralska, Patzer, and Wińkowska, "Stadium as a Witness."
32 Poland joined the EU in 2004.
33 Martin van der Velde and Szymon Marcińczak, "From Iron Curtain to Paper Wall: The Influence of Border Regimes on Local and Regional Economies—The Life, Death, and Resurrection of Bazaars in the Łódź Region," in *Borderlands: Comparing Border Security in North America and Europe*, ed. Emmanuel Brunet-Jailly (Ottawa: University of Ottawa Press, 2007), 165–96.
34 Szymon Marcińczak and Martin Van der Velde, "Drifting in a Global Space of Textile Flows: Apparel Bazaars in Poland's Łódź Region," *European Planning Studies* 16, no. 7 (2008): 916.
35 Its current official name is PGE Narodowy.
36 Michał Wiśniewski, "W poszukiwaniu polskiego Las Vegas," in *Polskie Las Vegas i szwagier z Corelem. Architektura, moda I projektowanie wobec transformacji systemowej w Polsce*, ed. Lidia Klein (Warsaw: Fundacja Kultura Miejsca, 2017), 112–41.
37 The traders from Jarmark Europa also moved their businesses to the following new trading centers: Marywilska 44, CH Land and Maximus.
38 Stanisław Fiuk-Cisowski, Plewa, S. and Christow, S. dir., "Chiny blisko." *Polska Kronika Filmowa*, no. 38 (September 21, 1994), https://www.youtube.com/watch?v=gOZaSQHevjM&index=38&list=PLyMy-ROJMB95likz13pjK4IlkURkqOXgq (accessed December 15, 2018).

for numerous special economic zones[39] and the city of Shenzhen—the important financial and economic center, which borders Hong Kong to the south. The original intention was to open an exhibition center where Asian (Chinese) goods would be sold to retail outlets from all over Europe.
They chose Poland as a location due to its geographical position, where two markets meet: the developed and already existing Western market and the emerging markets of the East.[40] Eventually the Chinese exhibition center redefined its business idea and developed itself as a wholesale market. Initially Wólka supplied Jarmark Europa as well as other markets, but Wólka's rapid growth began after 2007/08 when Jarmark Europa was closed. Chinese infrastructure and investment were crucial for Wólka's establishment but it also was supported by immigration. Chinese migrants were hardly present in Poland until the early 2000s. According to a study into Chinese investment and migration by Kaczmarczyk, Szulecka, and Tyrowicz in 2013: "The growth of the number of Chinese migrants to Poland has shifted China to being in 2011 the most important sending country [...]. In 2011 the inflow from China was over twice as high as the inflow of workers from Vietnam."[41]

According to its profile website, today the different trading centers at Wólka Kosowska form the biggest Asian wholesale hub in all of Europe.[42] It still offers Polish and Turkish goods, but now the majority are Chinese.

## Planned (North) and Organic (South): A Trading Cluster at the Center of a Global Network

A connecting road (ul. Nadrzeczna) divides the trading cluster in two parts: the Chinese part in the north and the Vietnamese-Turkish-Polish part in the south. In the northern part of the cluster, the Chinese trade center seems to be planned and managed top-down: identical warehouses and halls are organized in an orthogonal grid. Supply and pickup zones are clearly separated. The asphalted lanes between the buildings are spacious. The office buildings facing Nadrzeczna Road have a blue mirror glass facade with a row of tall poles with European and Asian flags. The interiors of the front building have stone flooring and, though only two stories high, they are equipped with elevators. There is one uniform and clear corporate identity and an overall navigation system to find your way in the rather vast complex. By contrast, the southern part of the Wólka Kosowska trading cluster is characterized by a more spontaneous expansion: the different buildings of the Vietnamese-Turkish-Polish center are more heterogeneous, distinct in material and style and not as large-scale as the ones on the Chinese side. It is a combination of bigger halls with top-lit corridors and smaller retail buildings or sometimes even sheds. The facades are chaotically adorned with a variety of company adverts as well as LED signs creating a bustling cluster of signs. There are, in fact, not just one or two major players involved but a number of independent companies that had bought the land, developed it and rented the space for retail and service to smaller entities.[43]

At the present moment, there are officially a total of some 800 individual trading companies registered in Wólka Kosowska and, according to the research conducted by Klorek and Szulecka, there are about 2,000 single stores.[44] The assumption is that some of the trading activities in Wólka Kosowska represent a *gray zone*,[45] nevertheless the center contributes to the municipal budget and enhances the local labor market. The local government initially saw the Chinese investment as a means to develop the mostly rural, *Lesznowola* municipality with a population of 20,000, and offered their full support toward facilitating the undertaking—a position that has not changed to this day. With the support of the local authorities, agricultural land was transformed into a suburban logistics and housing landscape. This new development includes all the aspects of life, not only commercial activities, but also dwellings with official hotels and apartments or single rooms (beds in dormitories) for rent, Asian supermarkets, restaurants, and even a Buddhist temple. This mix of services and living spaces make Wólka Kosowska a self-sufficient entity for

39 "In the late-1970s, China's experiment with the zone as a free market tool was so successful that it generated its own global trading networks, which in turn accelerated zone growth worldwide." Keller Easterling, *Extrastatecraft: The Power of Infrastructure Space* (Verso Books, 2016), 26.
40 Wade Shepard, "A Look at Wolka Kosowska, Europe's 'First One Belt, One Road Place,'" *Forbes*, 2016, https://www.forbes.com/sites/wadeshepard/2016/07/11/a-look-at-wolka-kosowska-europes-first-one-belt-one-road-place/#791aa9587c1c (accessed January 10, 2017).
41 Paweł Kaczmarczyk, Monika Szulecka, and Joanna Tyrowicz, "Chinese Investment Strategies and Migration—Does Diaspora Matter? Poland—Case Study," *MPC Research Reports*, 2013/10 ed. Robert Schuman Center for Advanced Studies (San Domenico di Fiesole: European University Institute, 2013), http://www.migrationpolicycenter.eu/docs/MPC-RR-2013-10.pdf (accessed February 15, 2018).
42 See company profile: http://www.wolka-centrum.eu/ (accessed March 10, 2018).
43 This includes following companies: ASEANEU Vietnamese board, area of over three hectares, three buildings, opened in 2008, about 160 stores; ASEANPL Sp. z o.o. (operating the Polish Trade Center, Vietnamese board, two trading centers, opened in 2006, about 450 stores); ASG-PL Sp. z o.o. (Vietnamese board, three buildings, opened in 2002, about one hundred companies); EACC Investments Sp. z o.o. (Vietnamese-Turkish board, covering four hectares, four buildings, opened in 2003, over 250 companies); GD Poland Investments Sp. z o.o. (Chinese board, covering over fifteen hectares, six buildings, opened in 1994, about 1,000 stores). See Natalia Klorek and Monika Szulecka, "Migrant Economic Institutions and their Environmental Influence: A Case Study of Trade Centers Located in Wólka Kosowska," *Analyses, Reports, Expertises*, no. 3 (2013).
44 Klorek and Szulecka, "Migrant Economic Institutions and Their Environmental Influence."
45 In 2017 Polish authorities conducted a series of raids on the trading center in Wólka Kosowska closing illegal gambling halls and confiscating counterfeit consumer goods. Radio broadcast OFF Czarek (December 13, 2017): *Spóźnione państwo interweniuje w Wólce Kosowskiej*, Warsaw: Grupa Radiowa Agory.

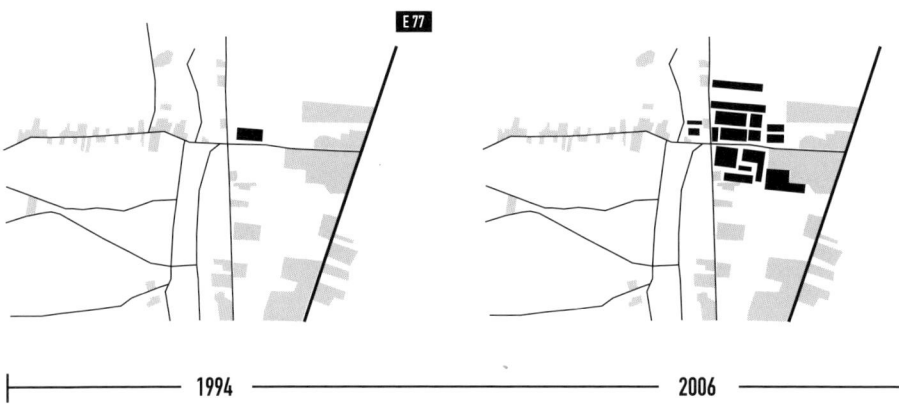

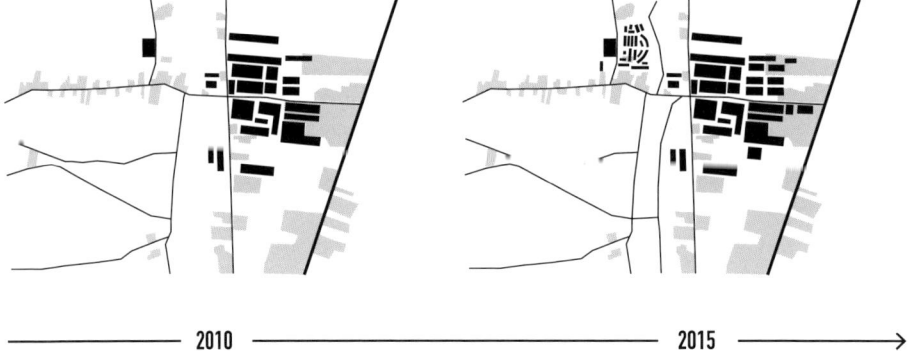

Fig. 65
Katarzyna Osiecka and Tatjana Vukosavljević, *Development of Wólka Kosowska*, 2016
Located on the northern part of the access road are storage and sales sheds of Chinese entrepreneurs newly immigrated since the mid-1990s, also including a gated community that is home to Chinese traders. To the south you find storage and sales sheds of Vietnamese and Turkish entrepreneurs relocating here from the old market at the big football stadium (the Vietnamese had emigrated from the former GDR and had been collaborating with Turks at Polish markets already since the late 1980s).

the traders and their families, replacing the need to travel to larger cities, including Warsaw.[46]

The Asian investors developed an international trading hub offering a wide range of consumer goods shipped from Asia to Europe in containers. The products on offer are mainly textiles and shoes, but also furniture, retail displays, shelving or mannequins, toys, and other everyday items. The channel of distribution follows a simple pattern. According to the Deputy CEO of GD Poland Investments Felix-Qi Wang, goods are transported in forty-foot shipping containers and arrive at the European cargo ports of Hamburg and Rotterdam. These containers are further transported by lorry to Warsaw and unloaded in Wólka Kosowska, at the rear of the trading center halls. The unloading process is hardly visible to the random visitor. From the warehouses the goods are redistributed within the complex of the trading cluster by traders or their employees using small trolleys. In this way every single stall is supplied with new stock. Each stall is equipped with a shutter and can be closed off from the main alley if a trader takes a break or needs to run some errands. On the other side of Nadrzeczna Road there are large lots where hundreds of small retailers park their pickup vans and vehicles to upload goods purchased at the center. These cars are mostly white secondhand vans without corporate branding, often rather old and overloaded. It is important to emphasize that in Wólka Kosowska products can be purchased in very large quantities—but also as single items. This dual trading (wholesale and retail) is a legacy of Jarmark Europa where at dawn wholesale deals were struck, and during the day individuals could buy a single T-shirt or a pair of shoes. The content of one shipping container will fill up to twenty pickup vans. The merchandise is delivered by these vans to their final destination, indoor shops or open-air markets, where it is sold, sometimes directly from the vehicle's trunk. Both the traders on site and the mobile traders with their vans have created a system of low capital investment and large potential profit to their businesses. Furthermore, they have in aggregate established a globally connected trading infrastructure. The fact that the trade center in Wólka Kosowska is a suburban cluster and a European form of Ethnoburb,[47] and not merely a workplace, means that it meets the social and economic needs of the migrant community.

46 The development plans were intentionally prepared by the local authorities to attract investors: "The plans are interactive, available online, so when someone from New York suddenly decides to start a business near Warsaw and would like to purchase some land, they may have a look at the plans online." Klorek and Szulecka, "Migrant Economic Institutions and their Environmental Influence."

47 Li Wei, *Ethnoburb: The New Ethnic Community in Urban America* (Honolulu: University of Hawai'i Press, 2009).

The trading cluster in Wólka Kosowska grew from one market hall in 1994 to an area of over forty hectares with fifteen market halls and 2,000 stalls.[48] Though very pragmatically focused on matching supply and demand, the Wólka Kosowska trading cluster does not give the impression of a homogeneous structure. It was built gradually over more than a decade. The Asian traders reacted to the changing social and economic conditions in Poland and market opportunities in the neighboring countries: the Baltic states, the Czech Republic, Germany, and Russia. They bought up new plots of land in order to enlarge the trading cluster as demand grew and their businesses expanded. Because of this organic growth the built physical entity resembles a patchwork more than a homogeneous, master-planned project of a conventional shopping mall or a distribution center.

The spatial expansion also reflected the needs of users and owners providing them with a range of services and amenities. Furthermore, recreational institutions and facilities like tennis courts and golf clubs were built focusing on wealthier Vietnamese and Chinese entrepreneurs. Around 2007, a gated community, a housing estate following the typical US model, was constructed nearby. It is a walled-off area with limited access, controlled by a private security guard. It consists of semi-detached, two-story houses with front and back gardens. The street layout follows a semi-circular pattern and is reminiscent of a master-planned community (suburbia).[49]

## The Micro Level: "The Market and Its Makeup"

The density and the atmosphere of Wólka Kosowska depend on the day of the week and the time of the day: The market can be empty and rather quiet—but also extremely busy and loud. When visiting Wólka Kosowska at midday during the week Nadrzeczna Road is full of people of different ethnic backgrounds and the parking lots are full of vans entering and leaving, while people gather around cars to collect and load up goods. On the parking lot and inside the warehouses, vendors and customers pull large trolleys with delivery goods packed into cardboard boxes or sheets of cloth. People driving engine-less scooters frequently pass by as they transport smaller items from one end of the huge complex to the other. They carry handy cardboard boxes with goods, but also drinks and food purchased from the many kiosks and restaurants located in and around the warehouses. Sometimes it is even money in cash just picked up at the ATM or ready to be deposited at the bank. While the traders go about their businesses, their children often play in the side alleys or in the seemingly endless aisles of the trading halls. Among the crowds of traders there are sometimes also visitors who come especially from Warsaw to try out the Vietnamese Phô soup or shop at the Asian grocery store. At times, the densely packed trading cluster also attracts others, who offer their goods and services: Polish farmers from the neighborhood tend to sell their products along the side streets. Some of them even put up small handwritten signs in Chinese with the product's name and price. They offer fresh eggs, fruits and vegetables. The owners of the trade center rent spaces to traders who individually operate their businesses and decide on the product range they offer. Most of the employees are Asian but there are also Poles and Ukrainians, mainly engaged in jobs as sellers or security personnel.

Henri Lefebvre perceived these Asian markets as a mechanism that transforms urban spaces creating new types of social relations, which are influencing social behaviors.[50] Edward Soja argues that "social and the spatial relationships are dialectically interactive, interdependent; the social relations of production are both space-forming and space-contingent."[51] According to Yeung, "economic actors are [...] embedded in social discourses and practices [...]. [T]he behavior of corporate firm and economic actors is by no means governed by a singular logic of profit maximization. Rather, these actors are subject to multiple discursive practices governed by power relations and influenced by the actors' gender, ethnicity, and culture."[52] Or as Martina Löw argues: "Spatial structures, like temporal structures, are forms of societal structures. [...] Interaction between different societal structures forms societal structure."[53]

## The Macro Level: "A Global Hub"

Wólka Kosowska constitutes a node within a bigger trading network of institutional and private actors operating on a local and global scale (fig. 60). The supplied area includes Poland and its neighboring countries to the north, east, south and west. Even street vendors from as far as Tallinn, the Estonian capital some 1,000 kilometers away from Warsaw, are regular and frequent customers. It is a trading microcosm embedded in the Central and Eastern European context while also tightly connected to Asia. Like Jarmark Europa, Wólka Kosowska is not a stable structure in social or spatial terms. Both local and

48 By comparison the largest shopping center in the United States of America, the Mall of America in Bloomington, Minnesota, occupies 38.85 hectares. The Mall of America was built in the early 1990s. It has over 520 shops and includes hotels, an amusement park, and an aquarium. This all-encompassing mega center attracts forty-two million visitors annually. See the company's website: https://www.mallofamerica.com/ (accessed February 8, 2018).
49 The gated community was developed by Agat Nusret Sancak, Tran Quoc Quan Spółka Komandytowa, a company established in 2006. See http://www.parkagat.pl/o-deweloperze.html (accessed February 17, 2018).
50 Henri Lefebvre, *The Production of Space* (Oxford: Wiley-Blackwell, 1991).
51 Edward Soja, "The Socio-spatial Dialects," *Annals of the Association of American Geographers* 70, no. 2 (1980): 211.
52 Henry Wai-chung Yeung, "Practicing New Economic Geographies: A Methodological Examination," *Annals of the Association of American Geographers* 93, no. 2 (2003): 445.
53 Löw, "Constitution of Space."

global changes result in its development. In this sense, Wólka Kosowska can be seen as a more sophisticated form of Jarmark Europa. Though there are both Turkish and Vietnamese traders present in Wólka Kosowska, the Chinese presence is likely to grow in importance. If we look at Wólka Kosowska as part of the New Silk Road one can argue that this new Chinese trading initiative was founded on the experiences gathered in places like the old socialist stadium in Warsaw.

Asian migrants came to the periphery of Warsaw as investors and entrepreneurs. They transformed the village of Wólka Kosowska with its originally 400 inhabitants into a trading cluster and major supply hub for small retailers from Poland as well as the neighboring countries. In spite of its peripheral location, Wólka Kosowska grew into a lively (sub-)urban structure, a node that enables the commercial as well as the everyday practices of a dynamic new community. Despite the fact that bazaars and OAMs have been relocated to the periphery of the city's economic and social life, the entrepreneurs found new successful forms for their business activity.[54] "The 'Asian' markets have become access points to transnational networks and flow nodes."[55] Furthermore, we could argue that these peripheral nodes are part of a system of several interdependent market places—a larger network.[56] Similar trading places exist in Belgrade (Block 70), Berlin (Dong Xuan Center), Bucharest (Dragonul Rosu), Budapest (Monori Center and Józsefvárosi Piac), Prague (Sapa), and Sofia (Iliyanski Market). This indicates that in Central and Eastern Europe there is a widespread market network that offers affordable mass consumer goods from Asia. This trading network operates on the macro level through large-scale import in cargo container ships[57] as well as government-led infrastructure projects like *Wólka* and comes down to informal suitcase trading at its micro level.

## China: A Networked State

The entry of China as a strong player in the global economy has been assisted by the activities of Chinese migrants. Budapest, Belgrade, Bucharest, Prague, Berlin, Sofia, and Warsaw were hub nodes from which migration business began to spread across Central and Eastern Europe. These nodes are indeed transnationally interconnected; managers, businessmen and traders working there, meet on a regular basis and at the same time maintain economic and political ties to their home country. These nodes are transnational trading points, linking cities, areas and people. Being nodes of imported goods distribution, Asian markets turn out to be the points of intersection of numerous relations between actors (suppliers, traders, intermediaries, visitors, farmers, etc.) and vital access points to the system of cross-boundary interactions for the city.[58]

The New Silk Road initiative aims to strengthen China's economic position through a vast program of infrastructure building,[59] representing the largest development plan in modern history. It incorporates advanced infrastructure projects (high speed trains, highways, ports, etc.) in order to connect East Asia with Western Europe. This is apparent in a number of investments on the edges of the European Union: Among others, Greece's Port of Piraeus, which is considered to be a European gateway for Chinese goods and a southern entrance / gate to Europe. Furthermore, this points also to the modernization of the railway link from the Port of Piraeus, through the Balkans (Belgrade) to Hungary (Budapest) that is currently underway. This will connect already existing nodes and Asian markets (Belgrade, Budapest, and others), further strengthening connections in the existing Asian market network.[60]

According to the Chinese, the New Silk Road cannot be fully realized, specifically the land route, without the node in Poland, due to its geographical location and the preponderance of transport and logistics connections.[61] Poland and the Wólka Kosowska trading cluster can potentially work as distribution centers to transfer products from countries along the Silk Road Economic Belt onwards to many other European destinations.[62]

54 Viktor Dyatlov, "'Chinese' Market 'Shanghai' in Irkutsk: Its Role in the Urban Community Life," *Bulletin Of Irkutsk State University* 10 (2014): 331.
55 Konstantin Grigorichev. "The Bazaar and the City: 'Chinese' Market as the Assemblage Point of the City," in *Ethnic Markets in Russia: Space of Bargaining and Place of Meeting*, ed. Viktor Dyatlov and Konstantin Grigorichev (Irkutsk State University, 2015): 330–31.
56 Manuel Castells, "The Rise of the Network Society," in *The Information Age: Economy, Society and Culture* 1 (Oxford: Blackwell, 1996), 323.
57 Pál Nyíri, "Chinese Migration to Eastern Europe," *International Migration* 41 (2003): 239–65.
58 Caroline Humphrey and Vera Skvirskaia, "Trading Places: Post-socialist Container Markets and the City," in *Focaal: European Journal of Anthropology* 55 (2009): 61–73; Gertrud Hüwelmeier, "Postsocialist Bazaars." http://www.soclabo.org/index.php/laboratorium/article/view/62/956 (accessed January 15, 2016).
59 China's Belt and Road Initiative, also known as One Belt, One Road (OBOR) initiative.
60 China Ocean Shipping Company (COSCO) leased two terminals at the Port of Piraeus in 2008 and acquired a majority stake in the port in August 2016; A few months later the Chinese had entered into an agreement for the purchase of a 35 percent stake in the Euromax container terminal at Rotterdam (subject to regulatory approval). See Zhang Yumei, "Land and Sea Route to Open New Channel between China and Europe," *Guoji shangbao*, February 20, 2017, http://finance.jrj.com.cn/2017/02/20114022079091.shtml (accessed January 5, 2018); Yao Ling, "A New Chapter in Economic and Trade Cooperation between China and Greece," in Dragan Pavlicevic, "China Docks at Southern Europe's Ports." *China Analyses. China and the Mediterranean: Open for Business?* ECFR/219 (June 21, 2017): 2–4.
61 Bogdan Góralczyk, "The Chinese Are Coming to Poland," *Central European Financial Observer*, March 2, 2017, http://www.financialobserver.eu/poland/the-chinese-are-coming-to-poland/ (accessed February 28, 2018).
62 Yao Le, "China and Poland: Economic Cooperation Under the 16+1 Formula," in *Nouvelle Europe*, January 2, 2017, http://www.nouvelle-europe.eu/en/china-and-poland-economic-cooperation-under-161-formula (accessed February 26, 2018).

## Conclusion

These findings suggest that once facilities—bazaars, trading centers or trading clusters—are established they become node access points of transnational trade, later creating a network of service hubs at local/regional level. Once these trading facilities are organized into networks on a regional scale, their importance for the local and national economy—is recognized and business relations are formalized. In the case of Wólka Kosowska, both China and Poland supported the market's development, promoting trade-related infrastructure, trade facilitation, and effective state-business relations.

Furthermore, this did not happen by chance but was built on the experience and the legacy of less formal structures—of bazaars and OAMs, operated by different migrant groups and developing organically in post-socialist Eastern Europe. We could ponder whether the New Silk Road results from the legacy of the Old Silk Road or whether the new initiative recasts, or even reproduces, an old trading route in order to suit modern needs.[63] Whatever the case, the established network of Asian trading centers in CEEC is part of a global supply network—a New Silk Road, which might continue to expand with further investment. The crucial consideration is whether the network of Asian trading centers gives meaning and value to the New Silk Road or, perhaps, whether the opposite is the case.

The Wólka Kosowska trading cluster is built on the legacy of the informal bazaar Jarmark Europa and is a factor in the economic integration of Poland into the global economy and links Europe and China as part of a global production network—the New Silk Road.

---

63 "The Silk Road, a trans-Eurasian network of trade routes connecting East and Southeast Asia to Central Asia, India, Southwest Asia, the Mediterranean, and northern Europe, which flourished from roughly 100 BCE to around 1450." Alfred J. Andrea, "The Silk Road in World History: A Review Essay," in *Asian Review of World Histories* 2, no. 1 (January 2014): 105–27.

Literature

Andrea, Alfred J. "The Silk Road in World History: A Review Essay." *Asian Review of World Histories* 2, no. 1 (January 2014): 105–27.

Aydin, Kenan, Lacin Idil Oztig, and Emrah Bulut. "The Economic Impact of the Suitcase Trade on Foreign Trade: A Regional Analysis of the Laleli Market." *International Business Research* 9, no. 3 (2016): 14–24.

Bhabha, Homi. "Unsatisfied: Notes on Vernacular Cosmopolitanism." In *Text and Nation*, edited by Laura Garcia-Morena and Peter C. Pfeifer, 191–207. London: Camden House, 2001.

Castells, Manuel. "The Rise of the Network Society." *The Information Age: Economy, Society and Culture*, vol. 1. Oxford: Blackwell, 1996.

Crowley, David. *Warsaw*. London: Reaktion Books, 2003.

Dyatlov, Viktor. "'Chinese' Market 'Shanghai' in Irkutsk: Its Role in the Urban Community Life." *Bulletin of Irkutsk State University* 10, (2014): 331.

Easterling, Keller. *Extrastatecraft: The Power of Infrastructure Space*. New York: Verso Books, 2016.

Góralczyk, Bogdan. "The Chinese Are Coming to Poland." *Central European Financial Observer*, February 3, 2017, https://financialobserver.eu/poland/the-chinese-are-coming-to-poland/ (accessed February 28, 2018).

Grigorichev, Konstantin. "The Bazaar and the City: 'Chinese' Market as the Assemblage Point of the City." In *Ethnic Markets in Russia: Space of Bargaining and Place of Meeting*, edited Victor Dyatlov and Konstantin Grigorichev, 330–31. Irkutsk: IGU, 2015.

Grubbauer, Monika, and Joanna Kusiak, eds. *Chasing Warsaw: Socio-material Dynamics of Urban Change since 1990*. Frankfurt am Main and New York: Campus Verlag, 2012.

Grzymała-Kozłowska, Aleksandra. "Migration and Socio-demographic Processes in Central and Eastern Europe: Characteristics, Specificity and Internal Differences." *Central and Eastern European Migration Review* (CEEMR) 2, no. 1 (2013): 5–11.

Góralska, Magdalena, Helena Patzer, and Małgorzata Wińkowska. "The Stadium as a Witness: A Story of a Changing Monument." *Widok: Teorie i praktyki kultury wizualnej* 9 (2015), http://pismowidok.org/index.php/one/article/view/271/542 (accessed February 2, 2018).

Halik, Teresa. "New Patterns in Vietnamese Migration: The Case of Vietnamese Migration to Poland in the 1990s." In *Challenges of Cultural Diversity in Europe*, edited by Janina Wiktoria Dacyl, 189–213. Stockholm: CEIFO, 2001.

Humphrey, Caroline, and Vera Skvirskaia. "Trading Places: Post-socialist Container Markets and the City." *Focaal: European Journal of Anthropology* 55 (2009): 61–73.

Hüwelmeier, Gertrud. "From 'Jarmark Europa' to 'Commodity City'. New Marketplaces, Post-socialist Migrations, and Cultural Diversity in Central and Eastern Europe." *Central and Eastern European Migration Review* (CEEMR) 4, no. 1 (2015): 27–39.

———. "Postsocialist Bazaars: Diversity, Solidarity, and Conflict in the Marketplace." In *Laboratorium: Russian Review of Social Research* 1 (2013), http://www.soclabo.org/index.php/laboratorium/article/view/62/956 (accessed January 15, 2016).

Iglicka, Krystyna. "Shuttling from the Former Soviet Union to Poland: From 'Primitive Mobility' to Migration." *Journal of Ethnic and Migration Studies* 27, no. 3 (2001): 505–18.

———. "The Economics of Petty Trade on the Eastern Polish Border." In *The Challenge of East-West Migration for Poland*, edited by Krystyna Iglicka and Keith Sword, 120–144. London: Palgrave Macmillan, 1999.

Irek, Małgorzata. *Der Schmugglerzug: Warschau-Berlin-Warschau; Materialien einer Feldforschung* (Berlin: Das Arabische Buch, 1998).

Kaser, Michael C. *Comecon: Integration Problems of the Planned Economies.* Oxford: Oxford University Press, 1967.

Kaczmarczyk, Paweł, Monika Szulecka, and Joanna Tyrowicz. "Chinese Investment Strategies and Migration—Does Diaspora Matter? Poland—Case Study." In *MPC Research Reports*, 2013/10, edited by Robert Schuman Center for Advanced Studies. San Domenico di Fiesole: European University Institute, 2013. http://cadmus.eui.eu/handle/1814/29931 (accessed February 15, 2018).

Korać, Maja. "Transnational Pathways to Integration: Chinese Traders in Serbia." http://www.doiserbia.nb.rs/img/doi/0038-0318/2013/0038-03181302245K.pdf (accessed January 5, 2018).

Kreja, Karina. "Changes in Spatial Patterns of Urban Consumption in Post-socialist Cities: New Large-Scale Retail Development in Warsaw." Paper presented at the Conference: "Winds of Societal Change: Remaking Post-Communist Cities," University of Illinois, June 18–19, 2004.

Klorek, Natalia, and Monika Szulecka. "Migrant Economic Institutions and Their Environmental Influence: A Case Study of Trade Centers Located in Wólka Kosowska." *Analyses, Reports, Expertises*, edited by Association for Legal Intervention Warsaw, no. 3 (2013).

Le, Yao. "China and Poland: Economic Cooperation Under the 16+1 Formula." *Nouvelle Europe* (January 2, 2017), http://www.nouvelle-europe.eu/en/china-and-poland-economic-cooperation-under-161-formula (accessed February 26, 2018).

Lefebvre, Henri. *The Production of Space.* Oxford and Cambridge: Wiley-Blackwell, 1991.

Li, Wei, "Ethnoburb versus Chinatown: Two Types of Urban Ethnic Communities in Los Angeles." *Cybergeo: European Journal of Geography*, document 70, October 12, 1998, http://journals.openedition.org/cybergeo/1018 (accessed February 28, 2018).

———. *Ethnoburb: The New Ethnic Community in Urban America.* Honolulu: University of Hawai'i Press, 2009.

Yao Ling. "A New Chapter in Economic and Trade Cooperation between China and Greece." In Dragan Pavlicevic. "China Docks at Southern Europe's Ports." *China Analyses: China and the Mediterranean: Open for Business?* ECRF 219 (June 21, 2017): 2–4. https://www.ecfr.eu/page/-/China_Analysis_June_2017.pdf.

Löw, Martina. "The Constitution of Space: The Structuration of Spaces through the Simultaneity of Effect and Perception." *European Journal of Social Theory* 11, no. 1 (2008): 25–49.

Marcińczak, Szymon, and Martin van der Velde. "Drifting in a Global Space of Textile Flows. Apparel Bazaars in Poland's Łodz Region." *European Planning Studies* 16, no. 7 (2008): 911–23.

Morawska, Ewa. "Transnational Migrations in the Enlarged European Union: A Perspective from East Central Europe." *EUI Working Paper RSC* 2000/19.

Mörtenböck, Peter, and Helge Mooshammer. *Networked Cultures: Parallel Architectures and the Politics of Space.* Rotterdam: NAi Publishers, 2008.

Nagy, Dorottya. "Fiery Dragons: Chinese Communities in Central and Eastern Europe: With Special Focus on Hungary and Romania." *Religions & Christianity in Today's China* I, no. 1 (2011): 71–86.

Nyíri, Pal. "Chinese Migration to Eastern Europe." *International Migration* 41, no. 3 (2003): 239–65.

Okólski, Marek. "Regional Dimension of International Migration in Central and Eastern Europe," *Genus* 54, nos. 1/2 (1998): 11–36.

OECD Directorate, ed. "Glossary of Statistical Terms—Central and Eastern European Countries (CEECs) Definition," November 2, 2001, https://stats.oecd.org/glossary/detail.asp?ID=303 (accessed February 2, 2018).

Patzer, Helena, Magdalena Góralska, and Wińkowska, Małgorzata. "The Stadium as a Witness: A Story of a Changing Monument." *Widok. Teorie i praktyki kultury wizualnej* 9 (2015), http://pismowidok.org/index.php/one/article/view/271/542 (accessed February 2, 2018).

Piątek, Grzegorz. "Palimpsest wpisany w Elipsę." In *Stadion X: Miejsce, którego nie było*, edited by Joanna Warsza, 20–25. Kraków, Warszawa: Bęc Zmiana Foundation and Ha!art, 2008.

Piekut, Aneta. "Visible and Invisible Ethnic Others in Warsaw: Spaces of Encounter and Places of Exclusion." In *Chasing Warsaw Socio-material Dynamics of Urban Change since 1990*, edited by Monika Grubbauer and Joanna Kusiak, 189–212. Frankfurt am Main: Campus Verlag, 2012.

Portiakov, Vladimir. "Russian-Chinese Trade and Chinese Migration into Russia." In *The People's Republic of China: Economic Policy of the 1990s*, edited by Vladimir Portiakov. Moscow: Progress Publishing Group, 1999.

Shepard, Wade. "A Look at Wólka Kosowska, Europe's 'First One Belt, One Road Place.'" *Forbes, Asia, Economy* (2016). https://www.forbes.com/sites/wadeshepard/2016/07/11/a-look-at-wolka-kosowska-europes-first-one-belt-one-road-place/#791aa9587c1c (accessed January 10, 2017).

Soja, Edward. "The Socio-spatial Dialects." *Annals of the Association of American Geographers* 70, no. 2 (1980): 207–25.

Sulima, Roch. "The Laboratory of Polish Postmodernity: An Ethnographic Report from the Stadium Bazaar." In *Chasing Warsaw: Socio-material Dynamics of Urban Change since 1990*, edited by Monika Grubbauer and Joanna Kusiak, 241–68. Frankfurt am Main: Campus Verlag, 2010.

Van der Velde, Martin, and Szymon Marcińczak. "From Iron Curtain to Paper Wall: The Influence of Border Regimes on Local and Regional Economies—The Life, Death, and Resurrection of Bazaars in the Łódź Region." In *Borderlands: Comparing Border Security in North America and Europe*, edited by Emmanuel Brunet-Jailly, 165–96. Ottawa: University of Ottawa Press, 2007.

Wai-chung Yeung, Henry. "Practicing New Economic Geographies: A Methodological Examination." *Annals of the Association of American Geographers* 93, no. 2 (2003): 445.

Warsza, Joanna, ed. *Stadion X: Miejsce, którego nie było*. Kraków, Warszawa Korporacja Ha!art, 2008.

Wiśniewski, Michał. "W poszukiwaniu polskiego Las Vegas." In *Polskie Las Vegas i szwagier z Corelem: Architektura, moda I projektowanie wobec transformacji systemowej w Polsce*, edited by Lidia Klein, 112–41. Warsaw: Fundacja Kultura Miejsca, 2017.

Yumei, Zhang "Land and Sea Route to Open New Channel between China and Europe." *Guoji shangbao*, February 20, 2017, http: http://finance.jrj.com.cn/2017/02/20114022079091.shtml (accessed January 5, 2018).

Films

Fiuk-Cisowski, Stanisław, Plewa, S. and Christow, S. dir., "Chiny blisko." Polska Kronika Filmowa, no. 38, September 21, 1994, https://www.youtube.com/watch?v=gOZaSQHevjM&index=38&list=PLyMy-R0JMB95likz13pjK4lIkURkqOXgq (accessed December 15, 2018).

Tummescheit, Minze, dir.: *Jarmark Europa*. Berlin: Cinéma Copains, 2004.

Radio Broadcast

Radio TOKFM. OFF Czarek, December 13, 2017, *Spóźnione państwo interweniuje w Wólce Kosowskiej*. Warsaw: Grupa Radiowa Agory.

# The Last European
## A Romanian Driver Navigates the Soul of the EU

Juan Moreno

For the past decade, Viktor Talic has been driving a van across Europe, delivering people and goods. His fifty-hour, nearly sleepless journey offers a disquieting, yet inspiring, glimpse into the continent's soul. The hero of this story looks older than his thirty-four years. He has powerful upper arms, a gentle demeanor—and he knows what many people think when they hear "Romania."

There are countries in Europe with a bad reputation, there are those with a very bad reputation, and then there is Romania. It's a country with anti-corruption department heads forced to step down amid accusations of corruption, and a prime minister who stands accused of money laundering. It ranks lowest for toothpaste consumption in the European Union, and high for alcohol consumption. Our man knows all about these things, because he is well traveled in Europe. In political speak, one could say that he is always on the go, driving the deepening of the European Union.

In 1992, Romania still had twenty-three million inhabitants. Today there are four million fewer. Those who emigrated profit from the fact that Europe has an undeclared division of labor that goes something like this: Wherever uneducated, rather than educated, workers are needed, employers look for Romanians. Even the Germans.

If it weren't for Romanians, slaughterhouse owners would be chest-deep in pig halves. Without them, real estate developers could forget about Germany's glorious construction boom. The same goes for asparagus and potato harvests. In their view, anything is better than staying in Romania. As a result, leaving home is about the most Romanian thing a person can do—and that's not difficult at all.

All it takes is climbing into a minibus and rattling westward. There are hundreds of these buses in every Romanian city. A one-way ticket to Germany costs seventy euros (seventy-seven US dollars); to the Netherlands, eighty euros; Belgium, eighty euros, France, Italy, Portual, 120 euros. A massive armada of small Romanian buses has been traversing Europe for years.

## A European Hero

This is where our hero comes in, a hero for freedom, a hero for the market economy—somehow, in his own way, a hero for Europe. He prefers to be called Viktor Talic. His real name, he claims, would be unwise to use—it would put him in danger of being persecuted, as heroes so often are.

Talic is on his way to Portugal. He's more than just a bus driver, he's also a shipper, money courier, messenger, and smuggler rolled into one. With eight of his compatriots in his Mercedes Sprinter, he moves people and goods from

Point A (Romania) to Point B (Portugal), a route many Romanians have taken. Several of his customers are trying their luck outside their home country for the first time, others are leaving for a short while to harvest asparagus, work on construction sites or in frozen-food plants, or do whatever else. Others were back in Romania only briefly because they needed to take care of paperwork in Bucharest. When they head to Portugal, they aren't leaving home, they're going home.

Talic's trunk is always filled with packages. Most are presents for relatives living abroad, items that are self-slaughtered, self-knitted and, especially, self-distilled. Everything he transports, whether package or person, is brought door-to-door regardless of the final destination in Portugal. There are no receipts and no paperwork, but nor are there any problems, not even when Talic is asked to deliver half of someone's yearly salary to his or her family.

It's mid-May and Talic is standing in the town center of Satu Mare, his hometown in northwestern Romania, with his bus. His customers are all punctual, showered, somewhat melancholic, and all have more than the agreed-upon single suitcase with them. There are seven of them, each with their own dreams of the West. There is a young married couple and an older one, a heavyset woman who will not utter a single word during the entire fifty-hour drive and a haggard, thin man, the kind frequently cast as a terrorist sleeper agent in Hollywood. There is also a beautiful girl in a white, shiny, sequined outfit that is actually a sweat suit.

Of all the drivers in Satu Mare, Talic offers the toughest journey. From here to Portugal, his route spans about 4,000 kilometers (2,500 miles). His way may not be the most direct, but it is one he has optimized in the ten years that he has been in business.

He avoids Italy even though it would be shorter. In the past the Carabinieri have confiscated Romanian cars for the slightest of irregularities. Drivers have supposedly received notes saying their car had been confiscated and that they needed to wait for a court hearing. But wait? For a court hearing in Italy? Talic would rather go 500 kilometers out of his way to avoid the country.

The final stop is always Portimao, on the south-western tip of Europe, where Talic's mother has now moved. It's almost impossible to go any further west in Europe. The drive takes fifty hours, and the first Romanian word one learns during the journey is *cinci*, meaning five. That's exactly how many minutes Talic takes as a break after filling up with gas. The second word is *cincisprezece*, or fifteen, which is the length of the meal breaks. As far as sleep breaks go, only three hours are allotted for the day after tomorrow somewhere in northern Spain. The rest of the time, Talic stays awake.

"Crazy, right?" Talic asks.

Juan Moreno

## Feeding a Family at Fourteen

Fifty hours to travel 4,000 kilometers through Europe in an old green Mercedes Sprinter van with 1.2 million kilometers on the clock. The seats are rock-hard and worn, the biaxial trailer in tow filled to the brim. And then there's the Romanian disco-pop playing at full blast and in an endless loop, so that Talic doesn't fall asleep before he reaches northern Spain.

In France, he avoids the highways—they're too expensive—which means that Europe's largest country by area is crossed via country roads. A ten-hour break in Portugal is all Talic allows himself before turning around and heading home. That makes for 8,000 kilometers of driving, one hundred hours at the wheel in a bit over five days. Is this crazy, suicidal or just business as usual?

Talic is a pleasant man who has not been put off by the million kilometers he has spent behind the wheel. He understands people's criticisms of his lifestyle, and explains that he wasn't always a bus driver.

He says he was a decent student who was good at math. But one day, when his father was sawing a tree, an oak branch fell on the back of his head, knocking both of his eyes out of their sockets. He toppled forward onto his still-running chainsaw, a red, Soviet-made Drujba that cut his heart into shreds. Talic was fourteen years old at the time. He left school a week after his father died in the forest, using the heavy Drujba to feed his family for four years. After that, he went to Portugal and worked in construction.

Talic tells the story warmly. He isn't one to exaggerate, and his mother, with tears in her eyes, confirms the entire story fifty hours later at the southwestern tip of Europe. For someone who, as a child, used a chainsaw to feed his family, 4,000-kilometer journeys through Europe don't seem so crazy. In fact, it's a rather pleasant job.

Talic starts the bus. The overloaded Mercedes creaks and jerks, but it drives. "The water in the back, in the cargo space," says Talic. "I don't think that's normal." Stowed under a dozen packages there are fifty bottles of Romanian mineral water. Some guy in Lisbon orders them every month. The man doesn't drink Portuguese water, Talic says, he has the Romanian water brought to him. "Every kilogram that I transport costs two euros. That's pretty expensive water."

We soon reach Hungary.

## Special Cover Charge for Romanians

Nothing moves at the border. A dozen Mercedes Sprinters are lined up behind one another, most of them with trailers—Romanian import-export businesses. It's a hot day and the Hungarian border guards are sweating in their blue uniforms and demonstrating how slowly a person can leaf through a passport. Talic's boss, the owner of the Mercedes van, is one car ahead in the line, waiting in a VW Passat. He always comes along to the border, because he knows the customs people best. He and Talic had words as they were leaving, the boss complaining about the ever-present extra luggage. "Three fucking suitcases per person," he bickered.

Instead of asking for money in exchange for the extra weight, Talic pressed two cartons of cigarettes into each passenger's hands, as many as a person can carry customs-free in the EU. Now they are, so to speak, legally smuggling cigarettes. In Romania, a pack costs two euros, in the Ukraine where his boss bought them, they cost a bit over one euro. Somewhere in southern France, Talic will give them to a man at a highway rest stop—the sixteen legal cartons being carried by him and his passengers, as well as the approximately twenty illegal ones hidden somewhere in the cargo space. In France, a pack of cigarettes costs between six and seven euros, a nice by-catch.

When Talic doesn't get any further at the Hungarian tollgate, his boss gets out in front and greets one of the customs officials. They hug. They know each other. A short chat, a quick look in the passport. There is something between its pages, which the official takes with practiced fingers. Two minutes later Talic can leave the line, and as he drives by, the Hungarian in the uniform cheerfully wishes the Romanians in the Mercedes a good trip.

How much was that? "A bit more than we need to give the one here," says Talic. The next highwayman is about one kilometer after the border. This time it's a fat traffic cop in a red safety vest. He stands at the edge of the road and reaches out his hand. Every small bus loaded up with Romanians needs to stop here in order to pass. The drivers roll down their windows and press some money into the hand of the man in the police uniform. Nobody speaks, the communication occurs wordlessly. It's a kind of cover charge that only Romanians pay.

And what if you don't pay? "Packages are opened and placed on the road," says Talic. "The interior lining is stripped and the engine space is examined. Three hours at least." Talic turns toward the back. "Which one of you has Palinka?" Palinka is the name of the self-distilled fruit schnapps. Everyone knows it is illegal to bring it along. All of them raise their arms. "Then ten thousand forint it is." Ten thousand forint, equivalent to thirty euros, is what the police officer pocketed.

Figs. 66–68
Thomas Grabka,
*Across Europe in a Mini-Van (The Last Europeans)*, 2015

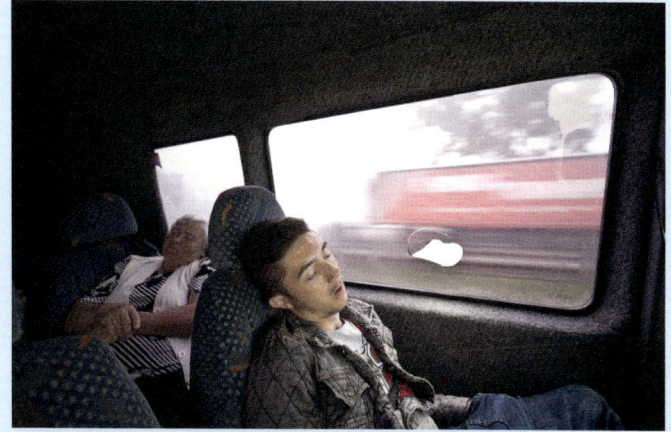

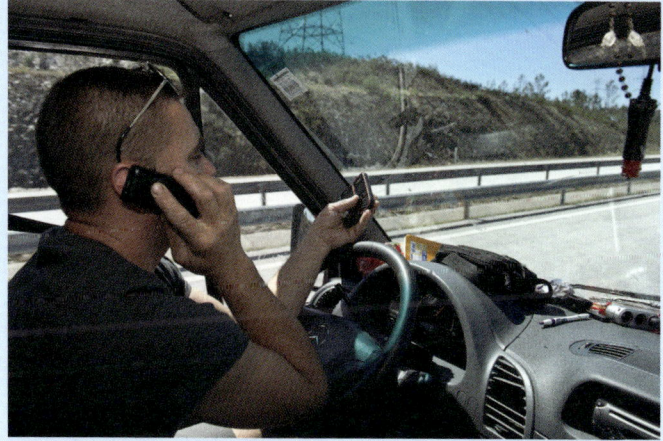

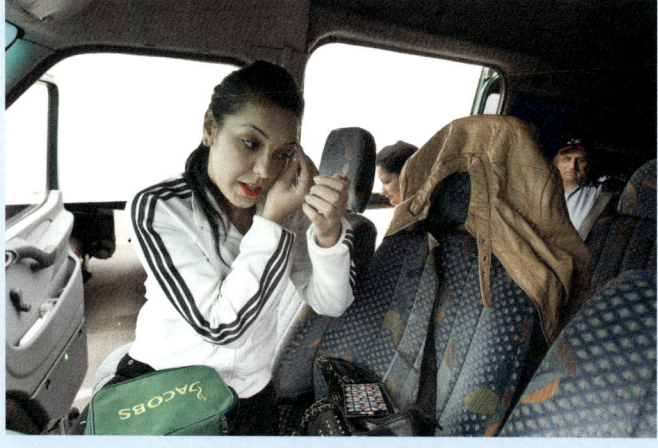

Talic bends forward and turns up the music. He's attached a USB stick with hundreds of hours of Romanian folk-pop to the radio. To Western ears, they are hundreds of hours of the exact same song. Talic seems to like it, the others stare contentedly at the monotonous Hungarian Pannonian steppe. It's a calm journey. A Hungarian police car stops the bus shortly before Budapest, and once again demands two hundred euros, but Talic doesn't want to get worked up about it. He actually likes Hungary. He knows that most people here can't stand Romanians, but at least they're up front about it.

## The German Dream

And then we enter Austria.

The older married couple has dozed off, the younger couple is holding hands, the gaunt man is trying to start a conversation with one of the passengers. Talic is racking up the kilometers.

The beats from the radio blend with the wind that is streaming through the open window. The passengers' back muscles long ago gave up their resistance to the much-too-hard seats.

Talic's cellphones are on the dashboard, eight of them: two Romanian ones, one German one, one French one, one Spanish one and three Portuguese ones. If a customer would like to have a package dropped off in Portugal, he or she calls Talic. The same applies if Talic is already on his way. Then he takes a small detour. The conversations are never brief. Romanians like to chat, possibly even more than the Italians do.

For many Romanians, Talic is one of the few connections they still have with home. Sure, there's Facebook, WhatsApp, and flat-rate plans for mobile phones, but they don't eliminate the homesickness—they simply exacerbate it. Among Talic's customers are migrant laborers who might work in a field in Alentejo, Portugal, for fifteen hours a day, seven days a week. Sometimes they give him packages to deliver just to be able to speak Romanian with him for a bit and feel a tie to their home country.

After Austria comes Germany.

"Why does everybody actually start their drive on Fridays?" the girl wonders out loud. It's her third journey. She has already worked in Germany, in the south, in a cannery. She can say exactly four words in German, the ones for pickle, red beet, and business license.

Back then, the young woman made eight-fifty euros per hour on the production line, and was not officially on the staff. But she had to spend four hundred euros of her wages on a tiny room in a residential trailer next to the factory. She always had to share her ten-square-meter room with another Romanian. She learned that an eight-fifty euros minimum wage doesn't mean that you earn eight-fifty euros. It just means that some companies make more hassle, and still only pay you six euros.

The Romanian small-bus armada prepares for Germany, or more specifically, its police officers. Unlike in Hungary, the Germans can't be bribed. Of course, there are fines, fifty euros, rarely more. The problem is the upstanding officials. Only in Germany does a police officer go to the effort of stopping a transporter van filled with Romanians on the highway to check if the car or the trailer is overloaded. In hardly any country will the police officer want to see latex gloves in a Romanian first aid box designed to protect against HIV infections.

Talic doesn't think the Germans are particularly mean. Or that they want to cause trouble. They are simply, he says, correct. Correct and annoying. The French, Spanish, and Portuguese are, for the most part, simply happy when they don't have anything to do with the Romanians and don't have to do any work because of them. For them, every small bus is a mountain of paperwork, because of course something always isn't quite right. Too many cigarettes, too little tread on the tires, illegal spirits, no road-worthiness certification for the vehicle.

## Their Land, Their Rules

That explains the Friday thing, the calculation is simple: a driver needs about ten hours to drive the 900 kilometers from the Hungarian border to Passau. If you leave Romania early on a Friday afternoon, you reach Germany just after the sun sets. A Romanian license plate is harder to recognize at night, and the German officials are partly on their weekend, the beautiful German highway is empty, the likelihood of not being stopped is high. And by Saturday morning, before the sun goes up, the Romanians have passed. If all goes well, no person has noticed that they've gone through Germany in the night.

Talic thinks it's right, what the Germans are doing, even if he himself is breaking all of their rules. His bus turns into a rolling deadly weapon by sun-up on Saturday mornings—despite the pounding pop music, he is extremely tired. It doesn't change things that the Germans are right, Talic says, in principle. But he needs to break those laws in order to make things halfway worth it.

Their land, their rules, he says about the Germans, nothing wrong with that, but he counters: "my life, my risks." He sees it as a sport. He would like his daughter in Romania to grow up well, so that she can go to college later and live in a nice house. If he obeyed the German rules that wouldn't be possible. So he does what he must. And Germany does what it must. And Europe too. It's actually very simple.

One will, so to speak, meet few people who are as passionate Europeans as Viktor Talic. For him, the European Union is not a monster that lives in Brussels, it is a sea of possibilities. Nothing is given, he says, of course not, but if you make an effort, you are rewarded.

Many people who have ridden with him might come back to Romania a couple of years later with a big car and move into a big house that they never would have been able to afford if they had not left the country. They may have lots of back pain, and ruptured disks, and scratched-up fingers, but the car, the house, nobody can take that away. So who says that the European dream doesn't work?

Talic says he doesn't understand what is currently going on in Europe, not at all. This hostility, this Greece problem, the discussions about austerity policies or not, about national debts, are all beside the point, he argues. For him, Europe means that a person can work and make an okay living from it. So where is the problem?

## An Impossible Life in Romania

Of course, he says there are differences but they don't have anything to do with injustice. Germany, for example, is a great country. In Germany, Talic says, nobody needs to work hard. Working is enough, and that is the main difference between Romania and Germany. In Romania, working isn't enough, not even working hard. The actual minimum wage per month is 217.50 euros. Doctors work for 450 euros. And where do most of the foreign doctors in Germany come from? Romania, of course.

It's not true that everything is considerably cheaper in Romania—groceries or rents. So how does a person support a family with only one wage?

"Not at all," says Talic.

The van rolls into France.

The radio unit comes on. A truck driver is offering Talic a tank of diesel. In the past, Talic took these kinds of offers more frequently. Truck drivers earn some extra money by selling diesel on their way to Romania. But these days, this is more closely monitored by the shipping companies. And Talic just filled up with cheap gas near Montlucon, in the Auvergne region. Instead of showering, he went into the drugstore department of a supermarket and sprayed perfume onto his upper arms. Unfortunately, the other passengers did the same. Now the bus smells like a perfume outlet store at the height of summer.

Talic has never had problems in France. If he has believably reassured the police officers that he is only traveling through and will be in Spain in a few hours, they let him pass. He has only had difficulties once. "That was with the pigs."

Word had spread about the kinds of things that Talic transports. Two euros per kilogram, that was the only rule. Last year, around this time, he received a phone call from a Romanian working in a slaughter business near Lisbon. The boss there was refusing to pay the wages of the Romanian workers and saying they should take him to court. The Romanians had another idea—they decided to steal his pigs.

They built a very large wooden crate, put fourteen live pigs in, and gave everything to Talic, who lashed the stolen goods to the trailer. Since all the people involved decided that the 4,000 kilometers from Portugal to Romania were pretty far for the pigs to travel, they decided to send the pigs to an acquaintance in Paris.

Talic and the pigs were caught up in a police inspection. A gendarme stopped them and asked for veterinary documents. Talic, who had understood him, showed him the vehicle license and explained that the delivery was going to Paris. Who knows what the police officer was thinking, perhaps he didn't like Paris, or maybe he didn't want to wait for the department veterinarian. He shook his head and allowed Talic to keep driving with his pigs. "They all survived," says Talic. At least the trip. "Don't ask me what they did with them. They lived in a high-rise, in the city."

And thus we enter Spain.

## Arrival in Portugal

After the thirty-fifth hour, time goes by in thick clumps. Bilbao, Valladolid, Salamanca, the cities pass by. At least now the bus is driving on the highway again. Nobody looks at the time, nobody seems to care if the drive will ever end. The flat land in northwestern Madrid, formerly Castalia, is made up of spacious steppe, which doesn't make things easier. Talic slept for exactly three hours near Burgos, and afterwards he looked more tired than before. He says that he's feeling well, but the right hand tires frequently rumble over the road markings, and the sound of the grooves scares everyone every few minutes. Talic says that he can only actually remember one accident. A friend of his, who was driving a Sprinter to France, drifted out of his lane near Rastatt and ran into a truck. One passenger died immediately. Ten minutes after the accident, a helicopter landed on the A5, and now the friend has a plate-sized piece of metal in his head, and works near Milan. Talic says, the man would have been dead in any other country. Since that story, German police officers can ask about the AIDS gloves as often as they want. Talic won't say anything bad about them, about Germany.

Spain is the worst part of the journey. The passengers lay on their seats as if sedated. Conversation topics ran out by Basel if not before. It's the moment when people ask themselves why they would subject themselves to this for 120 euros. A flight would have cost only double that. But presumably a person has to earn two to four euros per hour to be able to answer that question. Never has it felt nicer to arrive in Portugal. The madness begins.

From this point onwards, none of Talic's eight cellphones stay quiet. Everybody knows that he arrives in Portugal on Sunday afternoon. Everybody wants to discuss when their package, their relative, their boyfriend will arrive. At moments, Talic speaks with three people simultaneously on the phone. If he doesn't answer, people get worried and call even more frequently.

After he has dropped off the older married couple and the gaunt man in a village near Lisbon, Talic drives into the Portuguese capital. There, at a traffic circle, several of his customers are waiting with their cars to pick up packages. Thirty or forty Romanians besiege Talic's Mercedes. He distributes package after package and picks up new ones. To passersby it looks like one big fight, but Talic claims it is all in order.

## Romanian Is a Job

The fatigue is gone. The phone is ringing every minute. Talic drives to small villages, collects packages, jumps out briefly somewhere with an envelope filled with money, drops off the rest of the passengers at their front door. The last hours pass quickly.

Early on Sunday evening, the drive ends at Portimao, a tourist spot near the Algarve, which the Portuguese construction boom has gifted with a pair of very ugly high-rise buildings. Talic's mother lives in one of them. His sister and step-brother live below her.

The mother cleans a hotel for five euros per hour. The new construction in which she lives isn't finished yet, but she doesn't want to return to Romania no matter what, she is that happy here.

Talic sits next to her at her kitchen table and is too tired to talk. Tomorrow at eight he goes back to Romania. He says that he just remembered something. To the question, what it's like to be a Romanian in Europe. He has the answer. Being Romanian in Europe is no nationality at all. Being Romanian is a job.

# Retraveling and Reknotting Ideas and Interim Findings of Our Project
## Summary

Michael Zinganel

Michael Zinganel

This project is based on prolonged (in time) and extended (in space) research at nodes and knots alongside major Pan-European road corridors connecting the former East and West in a geographic triangle between Vienna, Tallinn, and the Bulgarian–Turkish border, investigating how people are "doing with space" and what the transformation of road networks and road infrastructures are doing with/to people.

The transition of the eastern frontier of the former West of Europe—or the western frontier of the former East, a place of becoming, with borders changing and new roads implemented, is a blurred, unstable space marked by mobility and informal activities, which can only be traced and investigated with the means of mobile strategies—such as nomadic ethnography, whose field works are the nodes where this hidden world becomes temporarily tangible. By exploring interconnections between the personal and the geopolitical, this project demonstrates the spatial and historical complexities of European networks, and it has become particularly timely with regard to migration management, the threat of new/old borders brought about by the restrictive policies of European nations from East to West, and Brexit, the prospective withdrawal of the United Kingdom from the European Union.

Escape as a travel motive was far from being the research focus of our project. We viewed it as one of many motives and modes in a continuum of mobilities,[1] which is characterized, above all, by the daily transport of goods and people along these corridors, although it also includes the transport of legal and illegal goods as well as persons with or without papers, whose motives range from tourist interests and trade and business travel to migration and escape.[2]

In 2013, when we submitted our research project, refugees from Syria were not yet a sensational theme for the mass media—even though, by that point if not before, thousands were already on their way. Instead, populist politicians and media in Austria were still spreading doomsday scenarios of a migrant invasion from Bulgaria and Romania, which had been full EU members since 2007, even though their citizens could only work legally in Germany or Austria from 2014, after the end of the seven-year transition phase. The route of this imagined invasion corresponded with the so-called Balkan route or, more precisely, the network of roads traversing Southeast Europe. In our project we did not intend to support this thesis of an invasion—quite the contrary— the aim was to document the normality of a multi-local existence, the continuous experience of being on the road and becoming accustomed to a life in

1  Michael Hall and Alan M. Williams, *Tourism and Migration: New Relationships between Production and Consumption* (London: Kluwer Academic Publishing, 2002).

2  Zygmunt Bauman, *Liquid Modernity* (Cambridge: Polity Press, 2000).

transit. In this light, especially for those who do not own their own vehicle, minivans and transnational bus services are the preferred means of transport, which also provide capacities to transport substantial amounts of goods.

After the wave of refugees in fall 2015, we refocused on migration management and border logistics, also learning that customs offices had been the main employers in all the border areas we passed through during our trips and that it had been the bureaucratic obstacles and the severity of border controls that increased the value of the expertise about how to successfully pass them—whether legally or illegally. The economic interests of these local networks will keep these borders much more permeable than politicians might wish they were.[3]

## Effects of the Embodied Research Design

Our toolkit of methods comprised the strategy of embedded and embodied research, which involved transgressing the boundaries and limited capacities of a stationary lab and driving these routes ourselves in a mobile lab, doing interviews and live-mapping exercises at relevant sites alongside our paths, realizing artistic interventions in public spaces, academic workshops and exhibitions in Tallinn, Sofia, and Vienna, and trying to make both objects and subjects "speak." This led to a continual rhythm of research, dissemination, and reevaluation taking place almost simultaneously. The aesthetic quality of the large-scale mappings and exhibited objects readily attracted people of different qualifications and backgrounds, and the universal readability of the visual languages we applied enabled them to easily join the project and bring in their own individual mobility expertise.

Both the performative practice as well as its visual results, mimetically applying to the visual language of road maps and other navigation tools so characteristic for driving the roads, can be perceived as a kind of counter-mapping, attributing respect to people, places, and networks otherwise ignored or misrepresented. In this way we attempted to escape the dilemma of privileging a selective (macro-political) overview by augmenting abstract diagrams with comic-like depictions and audio tracks in order to reflect the different scales, levels, and experiential forms of everyday mobility and to provide micro-political narratives with a more intimate space. By applying methodologies familiar both to social scientists and artists, by combining and superimposing several paths of different mobile people, and by showing the results both at the nodes and knots of our field of research, and in institutions of humanities and art, the research practice literally becomes a practice of knotting.[4]

The informal nature of our mobility and of our creative practice allowed us to get close to the people and infrastructures that use and facilitate a range of mobilities, including shipping, working, trade, and migration. The size of our vehicle and trailer automatically predetermined the places where we parked or stayed overnight, at parking lots for lorries and TIR stops, protected areas for international truck drivers, where we were literally embedded and embodied in the social field of our research. But often we were identified as non-professionals or even absolute beginners, having a car not as heavily loaded as all the others, not knowing a thing about how to fill in papers and bribe border control staff or police officers. For us, being stopped in a check for illegal or criminal activity (by real or fake police officers), which would otherwise be an embarrassing interruption of a trip, became an exciting subfield of research. And even the seemingly endless time spent driving the Pan-European corridors was not considered "dead time" in our minds but rather a productive period for rediscussing and reevaluating interim research findings and for improving and preparing methods for conversation and elicitation to be applied at the next stop.

While we investigated how other people are "doing with space" at these nodes and what these spaces are doing with them, we became aware of how we ourselves are "doing with space," what it does to us in return and to the people we invited to join us: whether while driving, selecting the nodes where to stop, setting up the mobile display at specific places, performing while drawing, or dramaturgically arranging the relations of objects and people in workshop spaces, for interventions in the public space, and also for exhibitions—at social condensers in the field of research and at the Academy of Fine Arts.

Our own multidisciplinary backgrounds, and the car that enabled us to drive the roads and nodes, encouraged us to radically expand the geographic scope of research, the number of case studies, the material considered worthy of inclusion (deriving from the field of research, from other scholars, as well as from journalists, and artists), and the mix of methods far beyond the usually tolerated limits of an average academic research project. This is the "artistic" freedom we empowered ourselves to choose, namely, not to focus on one node only, one route from A to B, but to capture as much of the shades of

---

3  As brilliantly shown in the video-documentary *Corridor #8* by Boris Despodov from 2008, who interviewed people living in border regions alongside a projected new highway intended to connect the Bulgarian Black Sea ports and the Mediterranean Sea ports of Albania.

4  Sarah Green, "Anthropological Knots," *Hau: Journal of Ethnographic Theory* 4, no. 3 (2014): 1–21; and Tim Ingold, *The Life of Lines* (New York: Routledge, 2015).

gray (spaces, economies, politics, and aesthetics)[5] at the nodes alongside our routes, thereby comparatively freely referring to mobilities studies, anthropology of infrastructures, network-theories and—albeit not too much—also on art-based research itself. We were aware of the risk that the vast variety of materials collected during this project would expand the capacities of a single academic book only.

## Nodes, Roads, Vehicles, People, and Their Networks Networked

Expanding the arguments of actor-network theory (ANT), John Law famously introduced the different levels of scale of a network (or of interrelated networks), taking a historic Portuguese vessel as an example: "Hull, spars, sails, stays, stores, rudder, crew, water, winds, all of these (and many others) have to hold in place *functionally* if we are to be able to point to an object and call it a (properly working) ship. All these bits and pieces have to do their jobs. All have (as ANT sometimes puts it) to be enrolled and stay enrolled. So a properly working ship has to borrow the force of the wind, the flow of the current, the position of the stars, the energy of the members of the crew, it has to borrow all these and include them (so to speak) within itself."[6] And on a larger scale, according to Law, the Portuguese imperial system as a whole, with its ports, vessels, military dispositions, markets, and merchants can also be thought of in the same terms.[7]

Then a distribution center, for instance, is perceived as not a single place, or at least not a place confined to a single building, but as a place-as-network, a distributed place, existing over miles of rails and roads;[8] also the nodes and knots, we found, are networks, interconnected by the polyrhythmic flows of different kinds of mobile actors. Furthermore, the ferries, the trucks, buses, and transporter vans driving on route-networks from node to node, based on and interconnecting political and social networks of a different kind, represent such multilevel and multi-scale networks, contributing to the social production of space and publics—as our own stationary and mobile research labs had done that enabled us to achieve the current status of our research project of these polyrhythmic ensembles.

## The Notion of Public Spaces in Transition

With regard to the issues in the call of the funding program "Public Spaces in Transition," the key method of our project—driving along the Pan-European road corridors with our own vehicle—enabled us to recognize a wide variety of qualities of "publics" and "places" as well as the quite different ways of appropriation and the effects of urban transformation. This variety is also exemplary in the three central case studies:

The network of the former state monopolist company SOMAT for transnational cargo transport in socialist Bulgaria was, of course, based on state-run facilities and infrastructure, which had also been used for the private side-businesses of the truck drivers. In the first period of transformation and privatization, a range of privately operated service stations and kiosks popped up along the main roads, which were appropriated for all kinds of business and social interaction. But with expansion of the EU and large-scale infrastructure programs these smaller semi-formal nodes of interaction are being repressed by a new set of regulations.

Vienna International Busterminal has suffered a series of dislocations over time as it was increasingly shunned by public authorities because of its reputation as a harbor for labor migrants since 1960s and, more recently, for shopping migrants from southeastern European countries since 1989. Managed by a private company, it is located today beneath a highway bridge on a piece of land owned by a 100 percent state-owned subsidiary. The buses and bus lines are owned by a variety of private companies, mainly from Eastern European destination countries, and again are considered by the passengers to be public lines. In contrast to the general fear of the impact of privatization of public spaces, this terminal, although privately run, is accessible day and night.

The area of the Port of Tallinn was entirely closed off during the socialist period. After the fall of the Iron Curtain, the port—formerly used for cargo of all sorts—was transformed into a passenger terminal for ferries and later also for cruise ships. The harbor is located on public ground and managed by the state. But because they represent a transnational border and are a high-risk target for terror attacks the terminal buildings are highly controlled, like international airports. Although the ferry lines are run privately, they are seen as a means of public transport serving tourists and commuters.

5   Martin Demant Frederiksen and Ida Harboe Knudsen, "Introduction: What Is a Grey Zone and Why Is Eastern Europe One," in *Ethnographies of Grey Zones in Eastern Europe: Relations, Borders, and Invisibilities*, ed. Ida Harboe Knudsen and Martin Demant Frederiksen (London: Anthem Press, 2015), 1–22.

6   John Law, "Objects and Spaces," *Theory, Culture and Society*, 19 (2002): 95.
7   Law, 93.
8   Julie Cidell, "Distribution Centers as Distributed Places: Mobility, Infrastructure and Truck Traffic," in *Cargomobilities*, ed. Thomas Birtchnell, Satya Savitzky, and John Urry (London: Routledge, 2015), 17–34.

When expanding our analyses also applying different points of views and scales of perception to the many other nodes we have visited and investigated during our round trips, the variety and multilayered character of public places and their appropriation by mobile actors increased radically. But the people we spoke to during our research trips were not at all concerned about ownership issues of the nodes they encountered, no matter if they were large in size or small, formal or informal, if harbors, bus stations, borders, highway service stations, or markets, as long as they had access to do their jobs and were able to shelter there in case of need. What they did care about, however, was safety and security, gathering with people of similar language or ethnic background, and the appeal of Wi-Fi access to contact their peer group at home or elsewhere. They were all willing to pay a reasonable fee for it. Referring to property issues or the romantic perception of public space as the site of a democratic political discourse, or as a space for the development of a public-minded rational consensus (re-imagining the Greek agora), where publics are constituted as a political whole did not seem appropriate here at all. Therefore, like Collier, Mizes and von Schnitzler,[9] we also propose to follow the suggestions of the American philosopher John Dewey, who argued in the 1920s that in a period of intense migration flows and rapid industrialization people in the USA were not joined together because they had "voluntarily chosen to be united" through some original act of will. Rather, they had been and are linked by "vast currents" of circulation and interconnection.[10] Instead, Dewey was interested in the way that publics were "called into being" by problems and events, that people share (for instance, while driving, or gathering at one of the nodes), or how publics were "called into being" by (for example, road and road side) infrastructure.[11] Indeed, infrastructures themselves can mobilize publics around their capacities, flows, and durability.[12] But with infrastructures repeatedly modernized, flows redirected to new roads, and nodes and knots of transnational mobilities visited in different rhythms by different people, we suggest that these publics are rather unstable. At these polyrhythmic ensembles they are constantly undone and remade.

---

9   Stephen J. Collier, James Christopher Mizes, and Antina von Schnitzler, eds., "Public Infrastructures/Infrastructural Publics," *LIMN* 7 (2017): 4.
10  John Dewey, *The Public and Its Problems* (Athens, Ohio: Ohio University Press, 1927).
11  Noortje Marres, "Issues Spark a Public into Being: A Key but Often Forgotten Point of the Lippmann-Dewey Debate," in *Making Things Public*, ed. Bruno Latour and Peter Weibel (Cambridge, MA: MIT Press, 2005), 208–17.
12  Antina von Schnitzler, "Traveling Technologies: Infrastructure, Ethical Regimes, and the Materiality of Politics in South Africa," *Cultural Anthropology* 28, no. 4 (2013): 670–93.

Literature

Bauman, Zygmunt. *Liquid Modernity*. Cambridge: Polity Press, 2000.

Cidell, Julie. "Distribution Centers as Distributed Places: Mobility, Infrastructure and Truck Traffic." In *Cargomobilities*, edited by Thomas Birtchnell, Satya Savitzky, and John Urry, 17–34. London: Routledge, 2015.

Collier, Stephen J., James Christopher Mizes, and Antina von Schnitzler, eds. "Public Infrastructures/Infrastructural Publics." *Limn* 7 (2017).

Demant Frederiksen, Martin, and Ida Harboe Knudsen. "Introduction: What Is a Grey Zone and Why Is Eastern Europe One." In *Ethnographies of Grey Zones in Eastern Europe: Relations, Borders, and Invisibilities*, edited by Ida Harboe Knudsen and Martin Demant Frederiksen, 1–22. London and New York: Anthem Press 2015.

Dewey, John. *The Public and Its Problems*. Athens, Ohio: Ohio University Press, 1927.

Green, Sarah. "Anthropological Knots." *Hau: Journal of Ethnographic Theory* 4, no. 3 (2014): 1–21.

Hall, Michael, and Alan M. Williams. *Tourism and Migration: New Relationships between Production and Consumption*. London: Kluwer Academic Publishing, 2002.

Ingold, Tim. *The Life of Lines*. New York: Routledge, 2015.

Konstantinov, Yulian. "Patterns of Reinterpretation: Trader-Tourism in the Balkans (Bulgaria) as a Picaresque Metaphorical Enactment of Post-Totalitarianism." *American Ethnologist* 23, no. 4 (1996): 762–82.

Konstantinov, Yulian, Gideon M. Kressel, and Thuen Trond. "Outclassed by Former Outcasts: Petty Trading in Varna." *American Ethnologist* 25, no. 4 (1988): 729–45.

Law, John. "Objects and Spaces." *Theory, Culture and Society*, 19 (2002): 91–105.

Marres, Noortje. "Issues Spark a Public into Being: A Key but Often Forgotten Point of the Lippmann-Dewey Debate." In *Making Things Public*, edited by Bruno Latour and Peter Weibel, 208–17. Cambridge, MA: MIT Press, 2005.

Pickles, John. "There Are No Turks in Bulgaria: Violence, Ethnicity, and Economic Practice in the Border Regions and Muslim Communities of Post-socialist Bulgaria." *Working Paper 25*, Halle/Saale: Max Planck Institute for Social Anthropology, 2001.

Von Schnitzler, Antina. "Traveling Technologies: Infrastructure, Ethical Regimes, and the Materiality of Politics in South Africa." *Cultural Anthropology* 28, no. 4 (2013): 670–93.

# Modernize or Die!
# Artist Insert

Johanna Kandl

Johanna Kandl offers a basically descriptive "travelogue," reflecting upon her own travel experiences to Eastern Europe. In her paintings she critically juxtaposes banal handwritten text lines and often emphatic, neo-liberal slogans with the everyday life at nodes of transnational transit in locations that have undergone post-socialist transformation but remained of unspectacular appearance: for instance gas stations, bus stops, and open-air (car) markets. The final image focuses on a filling station just across the Austrian border in the Czech Republic. The statue of the knight advertises a shopping experience in an outlet ambience—Excalibur City—a mock medieval theme park in the no-man's-land between borders, which is even linked to Vienna by shuttle bus. In the paintings selected for this "travelogue," she also introduces the types of vehicles that are key "actants" driving these corridors and thereby interconnecting the very nodes and knots with different velocities and rhythms.
(Michael Hieslmair and Michael Zinganel)

Fig. 69
Johanna Kandl, *The Bus leaves*, 1999
Fig. 70
Johanna Kandl, *Untitled (... change comes)*, 2014
Fig. 71
Johanna Kandl, *Modernize or Die!*, 2002

Johanna Kandl

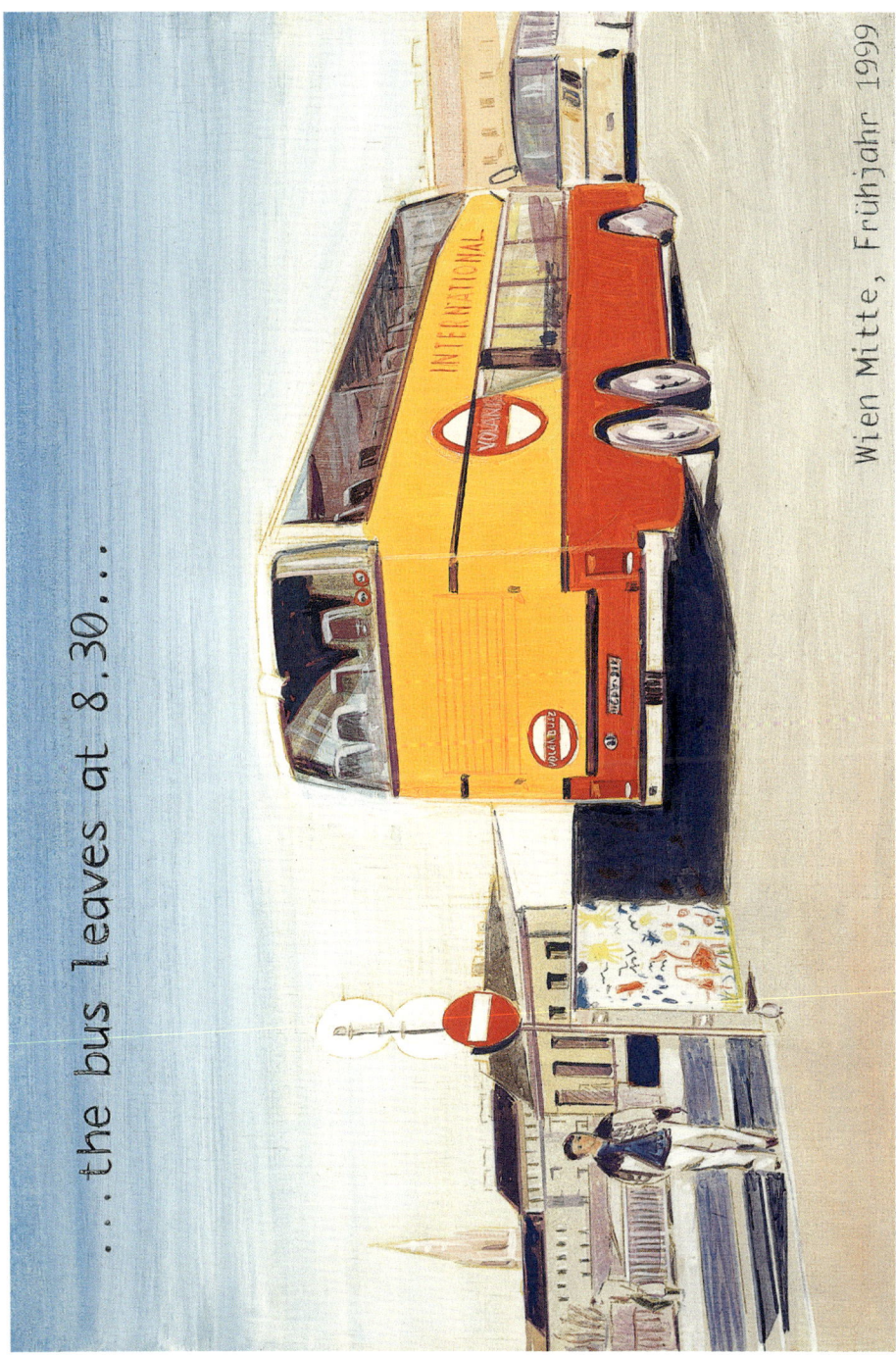

...the bus leaves at 8.30....
Wien Mitte, Frühjahr 1999

246    Modernize or Die! Artist Insert

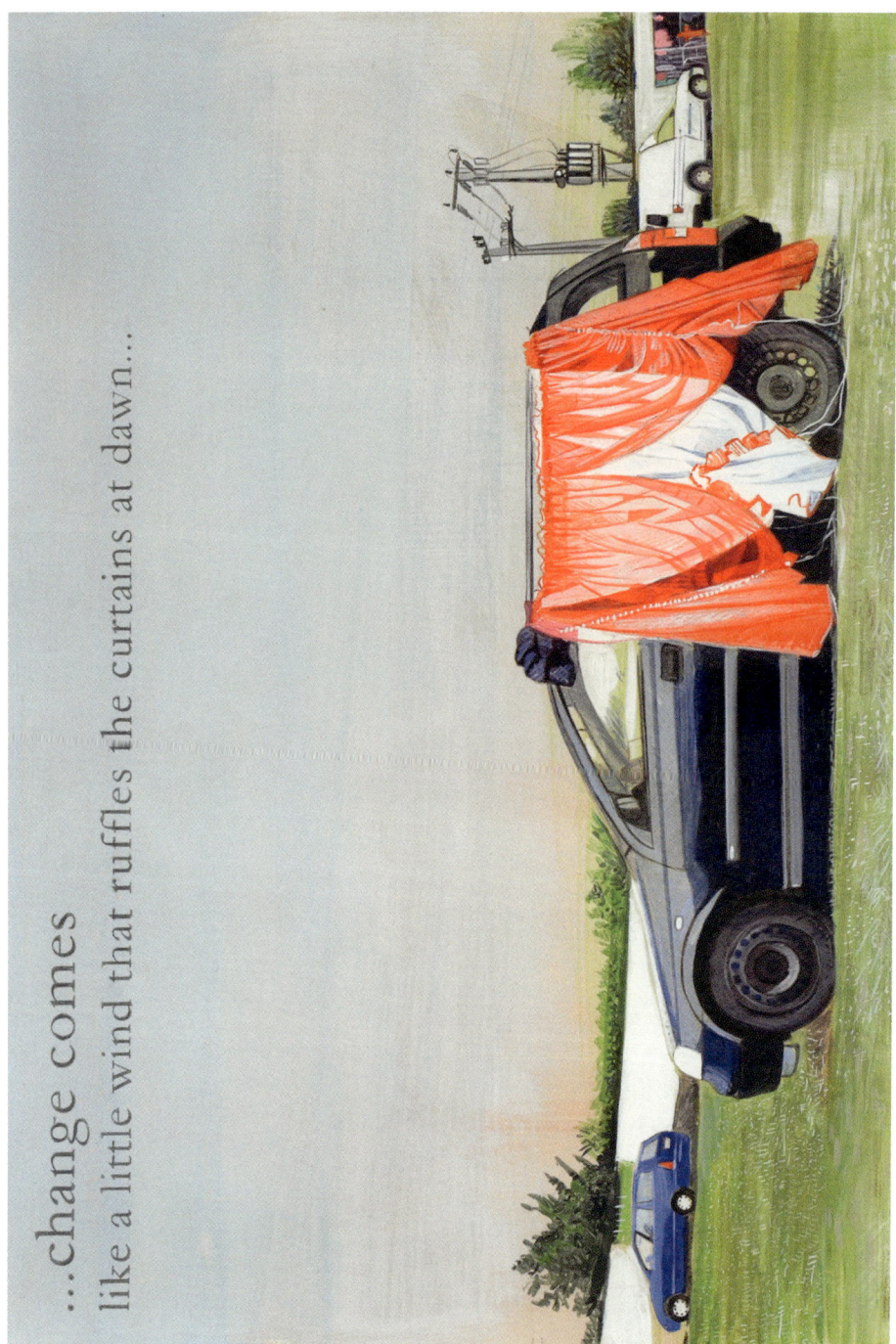

...change comes
like a little wind that ruffles the curtains at dawn....

# Johanna Kandl

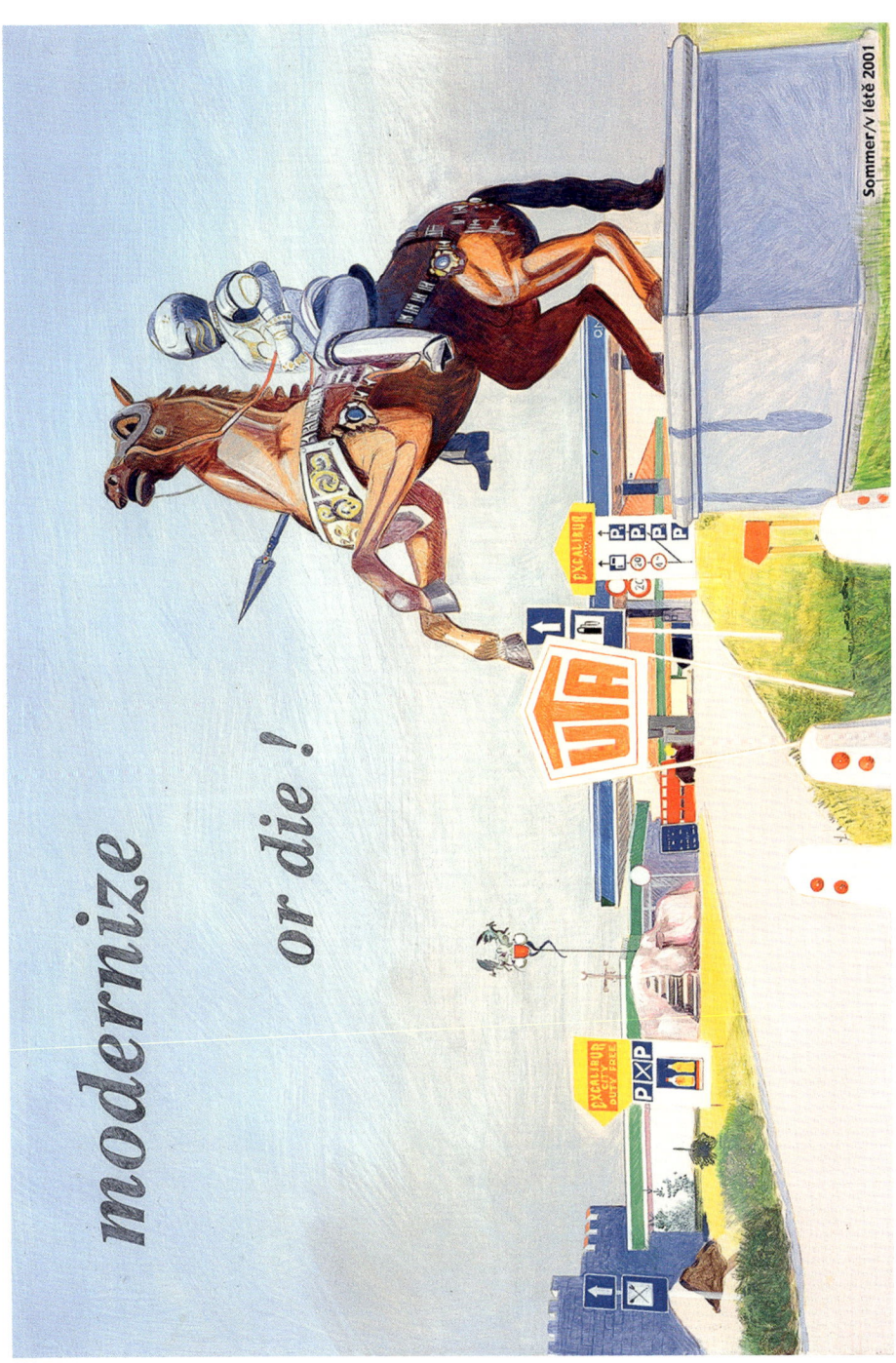

Image Credits

# Image Credits

**Placeholder/Substitution**
Sonia Leimer
Figs. 1–3
Sonia Leimer, *Untitled*, 2015–16. Place markers, steel, plastic, asphalt. Courtesy of Galerie nächst St. Stephan, Rosemarie Schwarzwälder, Vienna.

**Road Map of Research: Introduction**
Michael Zinganel
Fig. 4
Map of Pan-European corridors, 2018. © Drawing: Hieslmair and Zinganel.
Fig. 5
Photo of Mobile Lab, 2014. © Photo: Hieslmair and Zinganel.
Figs. 6–14
The many shades of gray at highway service stations, 2014. © Photos: Hieslmair and Zinganel.

**Networking Eurasia: Bulgarian International Truck Drivers and SOMAT in the Cold War Era**
Emiliya Karaboeva
Fig. 15
Poster of SOMAT, 1984. © SOMAT Archive.
Fig. 16
Water towers of Bagdad, 1984. © Photo: SOMAT Archive.
Fig. 17
Transnational network of SOMAT (around 1980), 2016. Map, reproduced on the basis of an undated original found in the SOMAT archive. © Drawing: Hieslmair and Zinganel.

**Memoryscapes and the Legacy of SOMAT Networks and Nodes Today**
Michael Zinganel, Michael Hieslmair, and Emiliya Karaboeva
Fig. 18
Former SOMAT lorry wash station at in Pazardzhik, 2015. © Photos: Hieslmair and Zinganel.
Figs. 19–20
Vacant SOMAT service station with hotel, canteen, gas station, workshop, and lorry wash station located close to the Bulgarian-Turkish border, 2015. © Photos: Hieslmair and Zinganel.
Fig. 21
Plan of SOMAT's former headquarters in Sofia-Gorublyane, as used in 1984 [and in 2014], 2018. © Graphic: Hieslmair and Zinganel.
Fig. 22
Exhibition in the canteen of SOMAT's former headquarters in Sofia-Gorublyane, 2016. © Photos: Hieslmair and Zinganel.
Figs. 23–30
The life and times of the world of SOMAT, 1984. © Photos: SOMAT Archive.
Fig. 31
Sign addressing Bulgarian truck drivers at a border station before leaving Bulgaria, 1984. © Photo: SOMAT Archive.

**Gates to the City: Transformations and Encounters at Vienna's International Coach Terminals**
Michael Hieslmair
Fig. 32
Gastarbeiter (guest workers), 1990. © Photo: Holzer.
Fig. 33
Ostbusparkplatz (East Bus Terminal) at Handelskai, 1990. © Photo: Kolarik.
Fig. 34
Bus terminal in Vienna's Landstrasse district, 1990. © Photo: Schraml. Courtesy VGA—Verein der Geschichte der Arbeiterbewegung.
Fig. 35
Vienna International Busterminal today, 2014. © Martin Grabner.
Fig. 36
Archipelagos and locations of Vienna's International Coach Terminals, 2017. © Graphic: Hieslmair and Zinganel.
Fig. 37
Vienna at the center of a network of international bus connections, 2016. © Graphic: Hieslmair and Zinganel.
Fig. 38
Cross-sectional diagram of a tour coach, 2016. © Graphic: Hieslmair and Zinganel.
Fig. 39
Location and surroundings of Vienna International Busterminal, 2018. © Graphic: Hieslmair and Zinganel.

**Check Point Nickelsdorf, 2015: Reactivation of a Border for the Mobilization of Forced Migration**
Michael Zinganel and Michael Hieslmair
Figs. 40–41
Vestiges of once-booming border economies at the border checkpoint of Nickelsdorf-Hegyeschalom, 2018. © Hieslmair and Zinganel.

Fig. 42
Isometric drawing of the reactivation of border infrastructure, 2016.
© Graphic: Hieslmair and Zinganel.
Fig. 43
Bus Stop Nickelsdorf, video stills from an animated graphic novel, 2016.
© Animation: Hieslmair and Zinganel.

**A Speaking Passenger Network Diagram: Reflections on the Applied Methodology**
Michael Zinganel, Michael Hieslmair, and Tarmo Pikner
Fig. 44
Aerial view photograph of Tallinn, 2015.
© Photo and Data: Port of Tallinn Ltd., Graphic: Hieslmair and Zinganel.
Fig. 45
A Speaking Passenger Network Diagram—Intervention in the Public Space outside Ferry Terminal D, Tallinn Harbor, 2015. Installation by Hieslmair and Zinganel with Tarmo Pikner, © Photo: Hieslmair and Zinganel.
Fig. 46
Scheme of the passenger network diagram, overview of actors' paths and scripts of audio tracks, 2015. © Drawing and audio tracks: Hieslmair and Zinganel with Tarmo Pikner.
Fig. 47
Indoor exhibition view at the Academy of Fine Arts Vienna, 2016. Installation: Hieslmair and Zinganel. © Photo: Lisa Rastl.

**Harbors and Practiced Lines: Evolving Mobilities between Tallinn and Helsinki**
Tarmo Pikner
Fig. 48
Blueprint of the Old Harbor of Tallinn in 1923. © Port of Tallinn collection.
Fig. 49
Port of Tallinn during the Soviet era.
© Photo: Dmitri Prans, Marine Museum of Estonia, first published in *Morjak Estonii* 48 (1976): 4.
Fig. 50
Diagram: Twin cities of Tallinn and Helsinki, 2016. © Graphic: Hieslmair and Zinganel.
Figs. 51–52
Diagrams of combined aerial views of Tallinn and Helsinki with the author's path, 2017. © Orthophoto by Estonian Land Board, 2014, Orthophoto by City survey services Helsinki, 2018, Graphic: Hieslmair and Zinganel.

Fig. 53
Statistic diagrams, 2016. © Graphic: Martin Eelma (Tuumik Stuudio OÜ) adapted by Michael Hieslmair. Sources: "Statistics related to average saleries," Estonian Statistics (2015); Anu Jögi, "Soomlased viisid Eestist 65 miljonit liitrit alkoholi," Äripaev (02.02.2015); Siim Krusell, "Eesti elanike töötamine välismaal: Pitte rahvaloendusest" ["Estonian Citizen Working Abroad"], Census Snapshots, edited by Taimi Rosenberg, 129–46; Tallinn: Statistics Estonia, 2013.

**Secondhand Car Markets and Mobilization in Eastern Europe**
Michael Zinganel
Fig. 54
Kaunas secondhand car market, 2008.
© Photo: Mindaugas Kavaliauskas.
Fig. 55
Marijampolė car market, 2016.
© Photo: Hieslmair and Zinganel.
Fig. 56
Map of trafficking cars, 2016. Redrawn after diagrams from the Center for the Study of Democracy report 9 (2000): 29, 30. © Graphic: Hieslmair and Zinganel.
Fig. 57
Map of Dimitrovgrad road network and car market, 2018. © Graphics: Hieslmair and Zinganel.
Figs. 58–59
Dimitrovgrad secondhand car market with vendors selling spare parts directly from vans, 2018. © Photos: Hieslmair and Zinganel.

**From Guangdong to Wólka Kosowska: Migrants' Transnational Trade**
Katarzyna Osiecka and Tatjana Vukosavljević
Fig. 60
Network of Asian wholesale markets in Eastern Europe, 2016. © Illustration: Katarzyna Osiecka and Tatjana Vukosavljević.
Figs. 61–62, 64
Everyday routine in the endless aisles inside the market halls at Wólka Kosowska, 2016. © Photos: Hieslmair and Zinganel.
Fig. 63
Everyday routine in the endless aisles inside the market halls at Wólka Kosowska, 2016. © Photo: Katarzyna Osiecka.

# Image Credits

Fig. 65
Development of Wólka Kosowska, 2016.
© Illustration: Katarzyna Osiecka and Tatjana Vukosavljević.

**The Last European: A Romanian Driver Navigates the Soul of the EU**
**Juan Moreno**
Figs. 66–68
*Across Europe in a Mini-Van (The Last Europeans)*, 2015. © Photos: Thomas Grabka, Courtesy of Der Spiegel.

**Modernize or Die!**
**Johanna Kandl**
Fig. 69
Johanna Kandl, *The Bus leaves*, 1999. Painting, egg tempera on wood. Courtesy of the artist and collection of Kulturabteilung der Stadt Wien—MUSA.
Fig. 70
Johanna Kandl, *Untitled (… change comes)*, 2014. Painting, egg tempera on wood. Courtesy of the artist and collection of Kulturabteilung der Stadt Wien—MUSA.
Fig. 71
Johanna Kandl, *Modernize or Die!*, 2002. Painting, egg tempera on wood. Courtesy of the artist and collection of Kulturabteilung der Stadt Wien—MUSA.

# Biographies

# Biographies

Michael Hieslmair studied Architecture at the Graz University of Technology and Delft University of Technology. He was fellow at Künstlerhaus Büchsenhausen Innsbruck and architect in residence at the MAK Center for Art and Architecture Los Angeles and taught at various universities such as University for Art and Design Burg Giebichenstein Halle an der Saale, Innsbruck University, Graz and Vienna Technical Universities. He collaborated on the research project "Crossing Munich, Places, Representations and Debates on Migration in Munich" (with Sabine Hess) which culminated in an exhibition at the Rathausgalerie. In 2012 he co-founded the independent research institute Tracing Spaces, also producing and curating the art in public space project City on the Move—a Farewell to a Logistic Area (with Michael Zinganel). From 2014–16 he was research associate at the Academy of Fine Arts Vienna and co-head of research of "Stop and Go: Nodes of Transformation and Transition" investigating the production of space along Pan-European Traffic Corridors in East Europe.

Johanna Kandl lives in Vienna and Berlin. For years she has been a critical observer of the economic and social situation of our time. In her artistic works she often combines concrete persons, places, and events with quotations and slogans from the economic world. In connection with her artistic and curatorial projects, she traveled to many regions in transition, such as Georgia, Azerbaijan, Ukraine, Russia, Poland, Romania, Lithuania, former Yugoslavia, and the Czech Republic. Since 1997 she has regularly realized research and participatory projects with her husband, Helmut Kandl.

Emiliya Karaboeva is a historian and received her PhD (Candidate of Ethics) for a dissertation on Gender Social Research at Sofia University. She is currently studying for her second PhD in anthropology and history of technology at Eindhoven and Plovdiv Universities, and conducting research into the topic of "Mediating East-West: International Bulgarian Truck Drivers during the Cold War Era." She is a professor at the National College of Ancient Languages and Cultures and part-time lecturer in the Faculty of Cultural Studies at Sofia University.

Sonia Leimer lives and works in Vienna. She studied architecture at the Technical University in Vienna and the Academy of Fine Arts, where she taught from 2012 to 2016 under Martin Guttmann. From 2007 to 2012 she ran the radio program *Image and the City*. Her installations examine the individual historical and media-influenced patterns of perception and experience as a result of the transformation of spaces and objects. These have been exhibited at international galleries and museums, most recently at the Leopold Museum and the Galerie nächst St. Stephan in Vienna, at the Ludwig Forum for International Art in Aachen, and the Barbara Gross Gallery in Munich.

Juan Moreno was born in Spain and lives in Berlin. He studied economics in Constance, Florence and Cologne. After his studies he attended the German School of Journalism in Munich. He worked as a talk show editor for ARD and as a radio presenter for WDR. Until 2010 he was author and columnist for the newspaper *Süddeutsche Zeitung*. Since then he has been writing reports for the German weekly magazine *Der Spiegel*.

Katarzyna Osiecka is an architect and researcher. She graduated from the Faculty of Architecture at RWTH Aachen. In 2011/12 she was a scholar at the Bauhaus Foundation in Dessau focusing on the mechanisms of global suburbia. She is currently a doctoral student at the Chair of Theory of Architecture at RWTH Aachen. Her doctoral thesis examines the "blind spots" in the late-twentieth-century Polish housing catalogues. She lives and works in Cologne.

Tarmo Pikner holds doctoral degree in human geography from the University of Oulu. His thesis focused on cross-border urban networks in the Baltic Sea area. He currently works as a senior researcher at the Center for Landscape and Culture at Tallinn University. His research topics include environmental legacies, sociality of infrastructures, and effects of late modernity. Pikner has published in several peer-reviewed journals and edited books. He also holds lectures on the MA program of Urban Governance at Tallinn University. His current research is part of the ERDF-financed project "SustainBaltic" and the Estonian Research Agency grant IUT 3-2 "Culturescapes in transformation."

Tatjana Vukosavljević graduated from the Faculty of Applied Arts in Belgrade, Department of Interior Design. In 2011/12 she was a scholar at the Bauhaus Dessau Foundation and received her specialization in the field of urban studies. She is an interdisciplinary artist, exploring and developing specific concepts at the intersection of urbanism, architecture, art, and culture. In her work she promotes new approaches in the field of public open space interventions through interdisciplinary collaboration and participatory co-design. Currently she works as project coordinator at Belgrade International Week of Architecture (BINA).

Michael Zinganel graduated from the Faculty of Architecture at Graz University of Technology and obtained a PhD in contemporary history from the University of Vienna. He was a research fellow at the IFK (International Center for Cultural Studies) in Vienna, taught at various universities and academies, such as the postgraduate academy of Bauhaus Dessau Foundation, AAU Klagenfurt, and TU Graz and Vienna. In 2012 he cofounded the independent research institute Tracing Spaces, also producing and coediting *Holiday after the Fall—Seaside Architecture and Urbanism in Bulgaria and Croatia* (with Elke Beyer and Anke Hagemann) (Berlin: Jovis Verlag, 2013). From 2014 to 2016 he was research associate at the Academy of Fine Arts Vienna and head of research for "Stop and Go: Nodes of Transformation and Transition" investigating the production of space along Pan-European traffic corridors in East Europe.

]a[ academy of fine arts vienna     WWTF     Sternberg Press